gratitude

gratitude

AN INTELLECTUAL HISTORY

Peter J. Leithart

BAYLOR UNIVERSITY PRESS

Cover Design by Jeff Miller, Faceout Studio
Book Design by Diane Smith

Library of Congress Cataloging-in-Publication Data

Leithart, Peter J.
  Gratitude : an intellectual history / Peter Leithart.
  350 pages cm
  Includes bibliographical references and index.
  ISBN 978-1-60258-449-5 (hardback : alk. paper)
  1. Gratitude. I. Title.
  BJ1533.G8L45 2014
  179'.9--dc23

                                2013016354

Printed in the United States of America on acid-free paper with a minimum of 30% post-consumer waste recycled content.

To Pastor Douglas Wilson,
with thanks,
for his example of giving thanks for all things

Contents

Acknowledgments

I received assistance from many people on this project. Donny Linnemeyer was an indispensable assistant in researching the crucial thinkers of the early modern period and the Enlightenment. Ryan Handerman provided me with a translation of the entry on *gratitudo* from Johannes de Bromyard's *Summa Praedicantium*. Gary Glenn shared his work on Locke, Joan Tronto provided me with a copy of her indispensable unpublished paper on Hobbes and gratitude, and Andrew Galloway gave me direction for medieval conceptions of gratitude. John Barclay was most generous in giving me an advance look at his forthcoming volume on Paul and the gift, a book I await with great anticipation. Early in my research, I was honored to speak on the topic at Union University, Jackson, Tennessee, and I learned much from the faculty's questions and feedback. I also benefited by presenting this material at the Biblical Horizons Summer Conference in 2011. The graduate students in my "Gift and Gratitude" seminar were splendid interlocutors during the middle stages of my research and writing. As always, members of my family were swept up in my research. My son, Woelke, provided innumerable articles and other sources, my daughter, Emma, informed me of the ways gratitude worked in Herodotus, and my wife, Noel, and other members of my family listened gamely as my ideas gradually took (more or less) coherent form.

As I move on to new ventures in a new/old location, I dedicate *Gratitude: An Intellectual History* to Pastor Douglas Wilson, with whom I have worked for the past fifteen years in Moscow, Idaho. I am grateful for the many productive and happy years my family and I have spent in the Moscow community. For reasons that will be clear in the book, I do not offer thanks *to* Doug, but I do thank God *for* him, not least for the many things he has taught me, by word and example, about what it means to live in and out of gratitude.

Of Circles, Lines, and Soup Tureens

So far as I can reconstruct it, this book originated in frustrations with indexes, Google, and Amazon.com. For a decade or more, I have been intrigued by the way the concept of "the gift" has spread from cultural anthropology into philosophy and theology. I share the enthusiasm for this category, which helps us reconceive issues in theological ontology, ethics, and politics in fruitful ways.[1] Twice I have taught courses on "Gift and Gratitude," and have found that mulling over the ins and outs of gift giving is a delightful and illuminating way to get some serious business done.

At the same time I have been frustrated by what seems to me a fairly obvious gap in the literature on gift. If gift is everywhere, if gift is *everything*, then one would think that responses to gifts would also be quite important. One would think there might be equal attention to gratitude. As I searched index after index for substantive discussions of gratitude, however, I largely came up empty. The most recent translation of Marcel Mauss' *The Gift* does not list "gratitude" in its index. I came across Heidegger's dictum *denken ist danken* ("to think is to thank," one of those happy puns that works in both German and English!), but Richard Polt's superb *Heidegger: An Introduction* has no entry for "gratitude." Postmodern thought is obsessed with gifts, but there is no entry for "gratitude" in John Caputo and Michael Scanlan's collection of essays *God, the Gift, and Postmodernism* or in Caputo's *The Prayers and Tears of Jacques Derrida*. (Derrida's *The Gift of Death* does not even have an index, which raises frustrations of a different sort.) Theologian John Milbank has many illuminating things to say about gratitude, but the publishers of his *Being Reconciled* could not find it in themselves to make

1

an entry for it in the index. Amazon.com searches were similarly fruitless. There are many, many books about gratitude on today's market. Most would be found on either the "Self Help" or the "New Age" shelf at bookstores.[2] There are devotional books and popular treatments of the theme from biblical or theological viewpoints. Yet there are very few intellectually or academically weighty treatments of the subject.

The inattention to gratitude did not make much sense. Gifts, one would have thought, are given only when there are recipients to receive them. How, I wondered, could scholars devote such obsessive attention to the gift, and presumably to givers, and so little to receivers? Where are the philosophical, theological, political, or anthropological works on *gratitude*?

I also found it odd that our intellectuals give so little attention to gratitude at a *theoretical* level in a culture that clearly puts a premium on gratitude. "Thank you" is one of the first disciplines we teach our children, and English speakers especially say "Thank you" incessantly, whether they feel the smallest twinge of gratitude or not.[3] To listen to our political rhetoric, you would think gratitude was still a critical public virtue. We express gratitude to the troops in Afghanistan and to those who fought in wars before our lifetime, gratitude for the abundance we enjoy, gratitude for our freedoms. But that sort of popular political expression does not seem to be part of political theory. Gratitude is *de rigueur* for academics themselves: No academic book is complete without acknowledgments that fairly drip with gratitude (not, of course, to say flattery or obsequiousness). But the academics who express gratitude do not seem much interested in analyzing it.

It was not always so. I had read just enough to learn that for centuries gratitude had been an important theme in philosophy, ethics, and even political theory, not to mention drama and poetry. It no longer enjoyed such stature. When had gratitude fallen out of the great conversation? And *why*? Here if anywhere there is a chasm between the intellectuals and the rest.

As I searched, I realized that the landscape was not as bleak as I had initially thought. Early on, I stumbled across the "positive psychology" movement, whose branch of "gratitude studies" is well represented by Robert Emmons and Michael McCullough's groundbreaking *The Psychology of Gratitude*. The incomparable Margaret Visser came out with *The Gift of Thanks: The Roots and Rituals of Gratitude* in 2009, and prior to that was Terrance McConnell's *Gratitude*, along with a spate of articles on gratitude in philosophy journals during the 1980s and 1990s. Academic political theorists had been exploring the question of whether gratitude was the foundation of the obligation of political obedience and loyalty, and William Buckley Jr. had published his patriotic *Gratitude* as recently as 1990. Not *as* bleak, but still bleak. An Amazon.com search for "gratitude, politics" yields only one title that is genuinely on subject—Mark T. Mitchell's 2012 *The Politics of Gratitude*.

Gratitude: An Intellectual History is my meager effort to provide the book I searched for and could not find, and to find at least an initial answer to gratitude's absence from serious discussions.

Intellectual History

The subtitle of this volume is *An Intellectual History*. It is a grand subtitle, and my first order of business is to deflate it. I do not offer a global intellectual history of the concept of gratitude. Because of the limits of my knowledge, energy, and time, I have limited the scope to the history of the concept of gratitude in *Western*, and specifically in *European*, intellectual life. There is a volume of at least equal size waiting to be written about gratitude in American intellectual history, in Islam or Hinduism or Buddhism, in the intellectual history of China or Japan.[4] There are large but more narrowly tailored books to be written on the concept and practice of gratitude in different periods of history, gratitude in different nations, gratitude in epic, drama, poetry, fiction, film. There are studies to be made about the rituals as well as the concepts of gratitude. When all that is done, someone might have the resources to write a global history of the concept of gratitude, and to correct what I am sure are the many infelicities of this volume. I could have waited for all that detailed work to be done, but I will be long in the grave when it is. Besides, there is a heuristic value in trying to tell a big story *before* all the details are in place.

The subtitle contains that contested phrase "intellectual history," and I should give some indication of what I mean. I do *not* believe that ideas operate in a realm separate from passions and commitments or separable from the personal, social, and political circumstances of the thinker. I have done my best to keep this history from being a loose chain of book summaries and quotations (though there are plenty of both), as if books give birth to books, ideas beget ideas. It is not strictly true that *ideas* have consequences. Yet, on the other hand, I also do *not* mean to reduce ideas to epiphenomena on the edges of social life. My assumption, unsuccessfully realized as it certainly is, is that intellectual history is a history of *persons* responding to social and political circumstances with the intellectual resources at their disposal. *People* have consequences, as they have ideas, articulate ideas, and write and publish ideas, and as those articulated ideas affect choices and actions. Of course, those ideas depend in large part on the resources available to the men and women having them. When Thomas Aquinas wanted to discuss gratitude, it was natural for him to turn to Seneca's *De beneficiis*, but Aquinas used Seneca to articulate a conception of gratitude that responded to the philosophical, theological, and political concerns of the thirteenth rather than of the first century. On still another hand (I am up to three or four hands by this time), people do have *original* ideas, and those original ideas forge new avenues of action and new forms of political community. I argue that Paul's "Give thanks in all circumstances" and "Owe no one anything except to love" were new and revolutionary ideas that have marked Western intellectual and cultural history to the present.

The title above the subtitle also needs clarification. Contrary to what you might have heard from anthropologists and their groupies, there is no such thing as "*the* gift." "Gift" is a concept with a history. That history is neither a story about an unchanging something moving through changing circumstances, nor a story that moves slowly but inevitably toward the perfection of the concept. The history of concept*s* (note the plural!) of the gift is naturally also a history about the appropriate and expected response to gifts—that is, a history of gratitude, broadly construed.

When I say "broadly," I mean "*very* broadly." One of the risks of all intellectual history is the danger that historians predefine the concept to be investigated from their own tradition and outlook, and then test other conceptions by their own. On this basis, anthropologists have sometimes argued that primitive peoples have no concept of gratitude, and at least one classicist said the same about ancient Greeks. That is true only if one defines "gratitude" in a peculiar way that excludes other conceptions from meriting the name. (The classicist I have in mind defines "gratitude" in a specifically modern way, and then, to his surprise [a *surprising* surprise], finds that no ancients agree with him.) To avoid that problem, I use the word "gratitude" and its opposite "ingratitude" very flexibly throughout this book. Gratitude is the label for a favorable response to a gift or favor, while ingratitude labels an unfavorable response to a gift or favor. What constitutes a "favorable response" changes over time and across cultures; that is precisely the history I recount here. In ancient Rome, gratitude would typically take the form of a return gift or favor; in contemporary America or Europe, gratitude is more typically understood as a sentiment expressed verbally ("Thanks"). Using this broad and flexible notion of gratitude enables me to demonstrate that gratitude, like gift, is a concept with a history. This is not a bow to relativism. There are better and worse ways to describe what constitutes a proper response to a gift. I happen to believe that there is a "theology" of gratitude, and I admit readily that this theological model has guided my assessment of the history. But I have tried to avoid turning the history of Western ideas about gratitude into a Whiggish or Hegelian movement toward that concept or into a pessimistic story of a decline from a golden age of gratitude.

Even with all these limitations and qualifications, it is still rather a grand project. Simpleminded as I am, I have been able to make sense of it by thinking of different conceptions of gratitude in geometric terms. I can make sense of this complicated history only if I can draw it with crayons. The story I have to tell is a story of circles and lines.

Circles and Lines

The arrangement of the book is largely, though not altogether, chronological. There are times when it has seemed clearer to treat writers and ideas topically rather than chronologically. Chapters 1 and 2 move from Greece to Rome, but then I backtrack to take account of the biblical tradition through the New Testament. Chapters 4 through 6 are again basically chronological, but to keep the issues clear I artificially separate "political theory" (chapter 6) from "philosophy" (chapter 7). The final chapters (8–10) return to a chronological arrangement, leading to a more thematic wrap-up in the conclusion. Three moments of disruption give shape to the story: the disruption of early Christianity, the disruption of the Reformation, and the disruption of the Enlightenment.

Ancient societies, and the tribal societies studied by anthropologists, think of gift giving and gratitude in circular terms. A donor gives a gift or does a favor for a "donee" or a beneficiary, and the donee is expected to return a gift or favor at some future time to the donor. To put it "algebraically," A gives B to C, and A expects C to give D back. The second clause of the sentence summarizes what is meant by "gratitude" in ancient societies.[5] Over the course of history, the circles of reciprocity have been of different sizes. Greeks and Romans saw their relations with the gods in reciprocal terms, which scholars often summarize (somewhat misleadingly) with the Latin phrase *do ut des*, "I give that you may give (to me!)." In social and political life, Greek warriors expected their superiors to give them an equitable share of the plunder they helped to win: military service should be rewarded with honorable gifts, and continuing military service was in part a grateful response to those gifts. Roman patrons expected their clients to return faithful service and to express enthusiastic gratitude. Circles of gift and gratitude bound together the aristocracy of Republican Rome, and in Imperial Rome, circles of gift and response bound officials and the Roman people to the generous emperor, cities to their provincial governors, provinces to the capital. For Cicero, the Roman practices were both right and useful. Seneca was more skeptical, and offered an idealized portrait of givers as generous as the gods and recipients grateful to the point of embarrassment.

Close personal bonds of obligation could be suffocating, and the classical world produced another model that promised liberation from constricting circles. For a century and a half (462–322 B.C.), Athens experimented with a political system that detached the cycles of giving and gratitude from institutions of power. On the assumption that human beings are most fulfilled when they are independent, self-sufficient, and autonomous, Athenians loosened the ties of personal patronage in the name of democratic freedom and equality. Athens attempted to institutionalize *non*circular political authority, an unprecedented experiment in detaching political power from the dynamics of gratitude. Those who held power were not expected to win votes by gifts to powerful allies, and they were expected to resist the influence of benefactors. They were to use their authority for the common good of the city, rather than for the particular good of their circle of friends. If there was a circle at all, it was the circle of Plato's *Crito*, which binds not friend to friend but city to citizens. Gratitude took the form of civic patriotism, rather than loyalty to kin, clan, or clique. Though relatively short-lived, the Athenian political experiment fired the political imagination of the West all the way to the present.

Some imagined a more linear conception of giving, in which a gift is given without expectation of a return. For Aristotle's self-sufficient magnanimous man, giving is still part of a circular relationship, but the magnanimous man closes the circle as quickly as possible so as to remain free of the dependency and obligations that come from receiving favors. He remembers favors given, not favors received. The Roman Stoic Seneca also flattened the circle of reciprocity by encouraging good men to give like the gods, even to the ungrateful, in the hope that gifts will induce the ungrateful to turn grateful. The Jewish and Christian tradition introduces something more radical. Jesus tells his disciples to give without thinking of a return, and to imitate the heavenly Father in giving to the ungrateful and even to enemies. In Paul, the proper reception of gifts includes the giving of thanks to God, but he accents making good use of the gift. Giving appears to be a linear selfless sacrifice, and gratitude does not curve back to the giver but branches out as the gift disseminates forever. Romans naturally regarded early Christians as antisocial ingrates. Christians broke the circle, and began to unravel the fabric of Roman society and politics.

In an important sense, the Romans were right. By every common standard of ancient social practice, Christianity introduced a corrosive ingratitude. Jesus denounced the traditions of the elders, and taught his disciples to put loyalty to him even above grateful honor to parents. Jesus proclaimed a kingdom where debts are all forgiven, including debts of gratitude, and Paul followed Jesus in teaching that Christians owe no one anything. As in democratic Athens, Christianity freed people from onerous personal bonds by defining gratitude as *right use* of the gift rather than gratitude as *return*. Christianity planted in Western civilization a permanent impulse of "ingratitude," a recurring power to disrupt circles and embark on a new line of cultural and political development.

The New Testament, following the Torah, does include a certain kind of circularity. With Jesus and Paul, the line of the unrequited gift, and the branching line of grateful dissemination, is circumscribed by a circle with an infinite diameter. Gifts flow on and on, but the generous, cheerful giver *can* hope for a return. The circle is infinite because God is the source of *every* gift, even gifts mediated through human beings. Thanks is due, but it is due to the ultimate Giver, the Father. Human givers give, but recipients owe thanks and grateful service not to the giver but to God. The circle is infinite also because the promised return does not necessarily happen in time; it may be requited at the final judgment.

According to Jesus and Paul, the infinite circle of Christianity liberates. Because givers can expect a return from the Father, they can give generously without anxiety about depleting their resources. The Father, after all, has infinite resources. On the other hand, because givers do not expect return from the recipient, givers give without imposing debts of obligation on their beneficiaries. There are no permanent "clients" in the community of believers. The infinite circle of Christian reciprocity opened up a space of freedom for both givers and recipients, for givers to give without strings but yet with hope of return, for recipients to receive without incurring obligations to repay. Paul is quite strict: to live as a Christian is to live without debts, including *especially* without debts of gratitude. Christian givers impose no debts; Christian recipients acknowledge no debts, except to love.

Jesus gave priority to gifts to those who could not repay—hospitality to the homeless, alms for the poorest, generosity to those without resources to return. This was consistent with the instructions of the Torah, but it was revolutionary in the Greco-Roman world, where it was common sense to give to those who had the capacity to repay. Even here Jesus envisioned a circle, because the Father who sees in secret rewards those who give alms without fanfare and those who give to the poor who cannot repay can expect a reward at the resurrection of the just. Almsgivers are liberated to give without counting their pennies, confident the Father will provide all they need. The recipients of alms do not become clients or slaves of their benefactors, but are brothers with their benefactors and, like those benefactors, slaves of God. Recipients complete the infinite circle of gift and gratitude by giving thanks to God. Following the teaching of Jesus, early Christians were convinced that certain kinds of gifts—gifts to the poorest—broke through the barrier that separated heaven and earth. Their gifts evoked returns not from earth but from heaven, not in time but in eternity.

The rest of the story I tell in this book involves clashes, alliances, and peace treaties between the circles of Greco-Roman giving and gratitude and the infinite circle of Christianity. More specifically, the remainder of my story is primarily about the fortunes of the infinite circle of the New Testament since later Western conceptions of gratitude are mostly disconnected fragments of the New Testament, crumbs from the table of Jesus and Paul.

The medieval world that took form on the ruins of the Roman Empire was deeply marked by the New Testament's infinite circle. Much of ancient Roman reciprocity remained. Medieval politics was patterned by the narrow circles of lords and "vassals," scholastic theologians like Aquinas restated Senecan themes in their discussions of *gratitudo*, and especially in the later medieval period popular devotion became infected with a quid pro quo, *do ut des* mentality that seemed to put God in debt to his worshipers. Yet aspects of the biblical conception of giving and gratitude took form in new institutional arrangements. Hospitals (as we know them) were unknown to the ancient world, but expressed the "linearity" of Christian giving. The New Testament's accent on alms took some unexpected turns. By the early sixth century, monks had become identified as "God's poor," and donations to monasteries were viewed as alms. Some of the gifts to monasteries made their way to the poor, and others were used to maintain the monastic community. Wherever they ended up, the donors viewed their gifts as means for storing up treasure in heaven. Ancient forms of patronage invaded Christian charity. Gifts to monasteries were seen as gifts to the patron saint of the monastery, a means to befriend and win the support of the saint, who, being a close associate of God, could serve as the donor's broker. Paul's exhortation to "give thanks in all circumstances" left its mark on theologians like Anselm and especially among mystics like Meister Eckhardt, for whom gratitude is the Christian's fundamental stance in a world envisioned as sheer gift.

During the fourteenth and fifteenth centuries, the religious practices of the Catholic Church took on a more narrowly circular shape. In the eyes of the Protestant Reformers, indulgences were a commerce in holy things and the Catholic Mass had inverted the proper order of gift and gratitude. For Luther and Calvin the Mass was a *gift* from God, given out of God's goodness and not for the merits of the recipients, but the Catholic Church had turned it into a religious performance that attempted to win favors from God. What was intended to be a thanksgiving *to* God for His gifts had become a work that tried to win thanks *from* God. The Reformers attempted to restore the Bible's infinite circle of gift and gratitude, but their polemical emphasis on the gratuity of grace made it difficult for them to appreciate fully the circularity of the New Testament's teaching about gifts. Protestants worked to incorporate New Testament passages about rewards and reciprocity into their theology, but the pressure of their commitment to *sola gratia* pushed toward a linear view of gifts offered without any expectation of reward. By institutionalizing almsgiving, the medieval world had picked up one fragment of the New Testament's infinite circle. The Reformers picked up different fragments—Jesus' insistence that Christians must give without expecting return and Paul's condemnation of notions of human merit. But they did not capture the entirety of the Bible's infinite circle, and thus the Reformers and their heirs prepared the way for the linear altruistic gifts of the modern era.

The politics of gift and gratitude were shifting during the Reformation era as well. Already in the late medieval period, some European cities had resurrected the Athenian dream of curing politics of the virus of favors and return favors. The image of the incorruptible public official, devoted to selfless service in splendid detachment from powerful and wealthy interests, began to occupy the Western political imagination. Even if everyone else wanted returns for their service, bureaucrats were expected to serve without hope of return. With changes in military technology and economic life, kings began to pay soldiers rather than using retainers to whom they were personally tied with bonds of gift and gratitude. Money replaced gifts as the bond of service. The breakdown of the medieval order that had cohered practically and theoretically through ties of benefit and gratitude led to a widespread sense of crisis. What could hold society together if not gifts and gratitude? In England Seneca was translated, printed, and reprinted in an attempt to shore up an older system of gift and gratitude. Shakespeare expressed the anxieties of his time in tragedies of ingratitude like *King Lear* and *Coriolanus*.

The chaos of post-Reformation Europe inspired political thinkers to abandon the theological principles that had dominated medieval political thought and practice. To prevent war, some argued, it was necessary to purge the state of debatable religious commitments, which can lead only to violence, and to found the state on the basis of universal, self-evident truths. At the same time, political writers tried to imagine states where obligations of gratitude no longer played a foundational role. Personal bonds of loyalty were damaging to the common good of nations and kingdoms, and thus political life should be founded on, and run off of, different principles than families and networks of friends. Power should not be beholden to favors or those who can bestow them; no one should be able to dangle a debt of gratitude over the head of a ruler. What this required in practice was the destruction of medieval aristocracies, whose power was all but entirely dependent on gift alliances.

This new vision of politics took some time to take shape among political theorists. Realist as he was, Machiavelli thought it essential for political leaders to manipulate the dynamics of favors and gratitude to their advantage. Hobbes viewed gratitude as one of the laws of nature that was impotent to promote peace until a sovereign power to quell the war of all against all. From the perspective of gratitude, Locke was the great innovator of modern political theory. From Locke on, liberal political theory is founded on the deliberate uncoupling of relationships of benefit and gratitude from the laws, procedures, and practice of politics. Civil order was founded on consent, and had to run according to regular rules and processes, free from the disruptions of gifts. Locke's theory did not "privatize" gratitude, which would imply that there was a preexisting private space into which gratitude was confined. Rather, Locke's theory *constituted* the private sphere as a "space" where circles of favor, thanks, and return favors operated as they did before, but without touching public order. Locke allowed that social life would continue to run in circles, but wanted public life to be linear.

A fervent if somewhat eccentric Christian, Locke produced a theory that was unthinkable without the impact of Christianity. Like medieval thinkers and the Reformers, Locke collected a few fragments of the New Testament in constructing his theory. Locke's theory justified resistance to tyranny, which was impossible on a tightly circular theory of gratitude. If the king gives you benefits, and if you owe a debt of gratitude for those benefits, and if gratitude entails obedience, then resistance is impossible. Locke constructed a theory that would enable a nation to break with its own political tradition to start fresh, and the heritage of early Christian "ingratitude" made this possible. Yet Locke used only a few arcs borrowed from the Christian circle. Instead of working from the premise of the infinite circle of Christian reciprocity, Locke effectively excluded God altogether from the political realm. Locke's politics, and liberalism since, was built on a mirage. Even theoretically, Locke could not ensure that politics would be a gratitude-free zone, and in practice liberal politics is full of cronyism as any other political order. Locke's theory did not even match his *own* experience: Locke's political clout depended entirely on the patronage of powerful friends. Locke's hope for a politics freed from circles of gift and gratitude was an unrealized dream. Ever since Locke, liberal theory is fabulous.

What Locke did for political theory, Adam Smith accomplished for economic theory. Gratitude plays no role in *Wealth of Nations*; it has virtually no place in the exchanges of the market. Yet in social, domestic, or private life, gratitude plays a large role, and Smith devotes many pages to considering gratitude in his *Theory of Moral Sentiments*. For Smith and other political and economic thinkers of the Enlightenment, the modern system of capitalist economic and democratic polity opened up a newly freed zone for private friendship. Exchanges are inherently self-interested; everyone seeks his own advantage. But in the modern era such self-interested exchanges have been safely confined to the hard masculine public world, the world of politics, commerce, and industry. Happily, this leaves a private, feminine world of sentiment and friendship to operate on a completely altruistic basis. Circles, sometimes narrow and vicious, are the stuff of economic life, but the social world has become a world of straight lines. In such a setting, gratitude becomes a soft virtue reserved to drawing rooms, dance halls, romances, and novels of manners. Gratitude becomes a sentiment, rather than a Senecan return gift. It moves from the realm of ethics to the realm of etiquette. It no longer has a place in the hard public world; it is no longer worthy of serious study. It can be safely left to the Jane Austens or Henry Fieldings of the world. Like Locke's theory, Smith's is illusory. Gifts are big business, and favors and gratitude have a significant role in the upward mobility of the upwardly mobile. There never has been a "modern" economy bereft of gift and gratitude. Such an economy exists only in the dreams of economists.

As a philosophical movement, the Enlightenment posed a fundamental challenge to the Western tradition of gratitude. Descartes purified his mind of all he had learned from teachers and books in order to reconstruct thought itself on the basis of the undeniable truth of his own existence and of other clear and distinct ideas that could be inferred from that indubitable truth. Kant exhorted Germans to grow up and shed their childish dependence on tradition. The Enlightenment was premised on what might be called systematic ingratitude, and according to Edmund Burke this ingratitude took political form in the French Revolution's demolition of the ancien régime. Yet the Enlightenment program, like Locke's political theory, was a secularization of an originally Christian instinct. Christianity began as an "ungrateful" renunciation of the tradition of the Jewish elders, and penetrated the Roman Empire as an community of "ingrates" who renounced Rome's gods and traditions and refused to acknowledge debts of gratitude. Like the early Christians, like the Reformers, the Enlightenment refused to receive an engrained and decadent Christianity of the ancien régime. Unlike the early Christians, they stated their renunciation not in the name of the Messiah but in the name of Reason.

Both Descartes and Kant wrote very traditional things about gratitude and ingratitude in their ethical writings, but what they passed to the future was their renunciation of the authority, especially the authority of tradition, in favor of the sovereignty of critical reason. Highly sensitive to the artificiality of the social dance of gratitude and the burdens of gift debt, Rousseau claimed to see through it. More than any thinker before him, he grasped the radicalism of the Western impulse toward ingratitude. Kant was a staid Pietist by comparison. His ethical theory was complex and developed over time, but the theme that left the deepest impact was his insistence that one must do good purely out of duty, without any thought for the good that might come to oneself or even to others. His ethical theory again picked one shard of the New Testament emphasis—the commandment to give without thought of return—but rejected as subethical the other half—the promise that the Father rewards. Kantian ethics was a purely linear ethics. By the nineteenth century, then, ethics had become identified as altruism (a term coined by Auguste Comte), doing good for the sake of others. In theology, linear agapic love was seen to be superior to the circularity of erotic love, the love that longs for return love and union with the beloved. Economics was self-interested; interest had no place in private lives. The classics that encouraged the circularity of ancient giving and gratitude fell out of favor. No century had less interest in Cicero than the nineteenth. Circles were out; lines were in.

In this intellectual culture, the publication of Marcel Mauss' *The Gift* came as a detonation. Mauss drew on the work of nineteenth-century economists and legal scholars, and many of his conclusions were already well known to specialists. By detailing gift practices in exotic places like Polynesia and Melanesia, and among the Indians of the Pacific Northwest, Mauss seemed to open a window to a world the West had never known, perhaps a window to the West's own exotic past. For some post-Kantian European intellectuals, *The Gift* revealed the astonishing news that there is no free gift, that all gifts are "contaminated" by returns of gratitude. For others, Mauss' book seemed to offer an alternative to the self-interest of modern capitalist economies. Mauss was no utopian, but gave some encouragement to utopian readings of his text by noting "survivals" of gift culture in the modern West and suggesting new ways to incorporate primitive gift practices into modern societies. Gratitude as "countergift" returned. The circle had made a comeback. For some, this was a circle almost untouched by the disruptive force of Christian and Enlightenment "ingratitude."

Around the same time, some philosophers were rediscovering gratitude. Kierkegaard drew on biblical sources to revive a view of gratitude as expansive as that of the medieval mystics. Gratitude was a chosen stance toward the world, rooted in an unproven belief in the reality of God's love. Nietzsche's view of gratitude was as expansive as Kierkegaard's, but anti-Christian. Gratitude for Nietzsche is the defiant response of a strong pagan to the threats and dangers of the world around him, the manly revenge against a world that tries to harm us but cannot. Event and gratitude form a circle, but it is a circle of negative reciprocity. In the twentieth century, Heidegger's emphasis on the embeddedness of human knowledge and the "ready-to-handedness" of the objects of this world made gratitude an appropriate accompaniment of philosophical reflection. In his late work *What Is Called Thinking?* Heidegger developed the Pietist slogan *denken ist danken* to argue that thought itself is grateful receptiveness to the givingness of being.

Postmodern reflections on gift and gratitude combine Maussian reflections on gift exchange with post-Heideggerian ontological concerns. In Jacques Derrida's work, there is also a powerful, if somewhat residual, linear Kantianism and an equally powerful, if even more residual, Platonism. Derrida denies that gifts exist. Gifts must be entirely free, entirely purged of self-interest (this is Derrida the Kantian). Every gift that aims for or gains a response of any kind becomes, by virtue of that response, economic. Even the slightest inflection of gratitude, even the self-con*gratul*ation of feeling good about your generosity, contaminates the purity of the gift. Yet gratitude such as this is virtually impossible to eradicate. Gifts must be pure to be gifts at all; pure gifts are impossible; therefore, there is no gift. Yet the ideal of the pure gift, like the ideal of justice or the ideal of complete hospitality, hovers at the horizon, beckoning us to keep giving the gifts we know we cannot give (Derrida the Platonist). In his philosophical work, the phenomenologist Jean-Luc Marion concedes Derrida's distinction between gift and economy, but attempts to recover "givability" by a phenomenological "reduction" of the gift. In his theological work, Marion falls back into a Kantian linearity uncomfortable with the reciprocities of the New Testament. For Marion, gratitude is sheer dissemination of the received gift. Viewed at a somewhat greater distance, the postmodern project appears to be a new phase of Enlightenment, applying the systematic ingratitude of the Enlightenment to the Enlightenment itself. Kant and Descartes are the first masters of ungrateful suspicion, and Derrida stands on their shoulders. Once again, behind all these are the original masters, Jesus and Paul.

Even from this relatively brief summary, it is evident that my story is a complicated one. It touches on many of the major problems and episodes of Western intellectual (not to mention social and political) history. By using gratitude as a "stethoscope,"[6] I try to catch the heartbeat of Western intellectual life, both its regularities and its arrhythmias. Viewing Western history from the viewpoint of gratitude offers (what I hope is) fresh insight into the differences between archaic and political Greece, and the character of the Athenian experiment in democracy; the differences between Greek and Roman civilizations; the social and ethical ideals of Stoicism in relation to Roman social practices, and the Stoic anticipation of certain Christian themes; the intellectual and social disruptiveness of the Christian gospel; the central importance of alms in Christian intellectual and social history; the degree and form of the Christianization of Europe during the Middle Ages; the sources and shape of the Protestant Reformation; the social and intellectual dynamics behind the rise of the modern state and modern economies; the novelty of liberal political theory, and its debt to Christianity; the character of the Enlightenment, and *its* debt to Christianity; the impact of cultural anthropology in a post-Enlightenment intellectual world; the continuities and discontinuities between the Enlightenment and the cluster of movements and thinkers bundled under the umbrella of "postmodern."

Gratitude takes us to the heart of modernity, and certain theoretical questions about modern civilization become more and more insistent as the book proceeds:

- Personal ties of gift and gratitude obligate and can enslave. Modern structures are designed to give room for maneuvering, but they do so at the cost of personal connection. Is it possible to retain the gains of modern freedom while restoring the goods of personal ties of gratitude? Is it possible to reconcile personalism and freedom? Can we renew personalism in social, economic, and political life without reimposing unbearable burdens of debt from which modernity freed us?
- The market economy is a unique order of human interaction "founded on the immediate and permanent liquidation of debt." Each exchange "is clear and complete," each is "punctual."[7] An order purged of debts of gratitude unburdens us, but appears to leave us wandering alone in a void. Can we sustain the freedom of the market without becoming isolated individuals? Does the freedom of the market *necessarily* corrode social bonds?
- More philosophically, we are constituted by our relationships, relationships forged and sustained by exchanges of gift and gratitude.

If that is so, how can I hope to be made new? Will I not forever be bound to my past? If, on the other hand, I am *not* what I am in relationship—if I am most deeply an individual above and outside the exchanges of gift and gratitude—I can make myself anything I want, but what exactly *am* I? Is there a way to extricate myself from the nexus of exchange and remain a being-in-relationship? Is there any way to extricate myself without deleting myself? Is the modern effort to dissolve bonds of gratitude inevitably nihilistic?

- Modern science depends on a willingness to probe and manipulate nature, but this can come at the cost of gratitude for good of nature as it comes to us. Can we preserve the advances of science while trying to restore a sense of grateful wonder at the natural world?

- The modern separation of private and public life aimed in part to purge government of personal ambition and interest. Can gratitude function as a political virtue without justifying corruption and cronyism?[8]

In the final chapter, I throw off my mask of historical objectivity (which never quite fit my face to begin with and wears thinner and thinner as the book progresses) to show my true face, the face of a theologian. In that guise, I argue that only the infinite Christian circle is capable of preserving the political, scientific, economic, and social advances of modernity, while restoring a personal and human world. Modernity's gains can be preserved only within the Christian circle, the bits and pieces of which gave rise to modernity in the first place.

Conclusion
Grandma's Soup Tureen

In teaching on gift and gratitude, I have found it useful to describe the magic of gifts with the following illustration: Imagine that your beloved grandmother gave you a rather ugly soup tureen as a wedding gift. Seeing as you have no use for the tureen, how ought you respond? You would, of course, write an appropriately deceptive note of thanks, but what then? Would you box the tureen away and never use it? Would you use it to feed the cat? What if Grandma were coming for dinner? Would you let her see you using her gift to feed the cat? Most of my students (though, surprisingly, not all) have had the sensitivity to refrain from using the tureen for the cat. Nearly all have had the good sense to say they would not let Grandma *know* that her tureen was serving the cat.[9] Change the scenario: What if *you* had bought the ugly soup tureen? Would you have any qualms about using the tureen to feed the cat? What if the Walmart checkout girl were coming to dinner—would you have qualms about letting her see the cat eating from the soup tureen she had rung up for you? Nearly all my students agree they have no obligations to treat the tureen in a way that respected the wishes of the checkout girl.

Variations on the hypothetical can be spun out further (what would you do if you had *bought* the tureen from Grandma?), but the point is clear enough. Gifts, especially gifts from a respected giver, carry something of the giver with them. We do not have to believe Mauss' theory about the "hau" of the gift (see chapter 8) to see that gratitude involves treating the thing given with honor, *at the very least* in the presence of the giver. Obligations attach to gifts that do not attach to purchases. We take possession of gifts and purchases, but the form of possession is importantly different. Grandma's soup tureen returns in the book's final chapter, but if you want to keep score as you read, ask yourself these questions at the end of each chapter: What would this philosopher, chronicler, poet, theologian, dramatist, political theorist, sociologist, or anthropologist advise you to do about the tureen? How would he tell you to show gratitude?

To my knowledge, no one has attempted a history of Western gratitude before, and that makes my venture into this territory riskier than most. I know of many gaps in my knowledge and research, and I am certain the unknown gaps and traps outnumber the known. I do not pretend to have told the whole story, or even to have told the story I do tell with complete accuracy. I suspect there is a subterranean Western tradition of reflection on gratitude that I have largely missed by concentrating my attention on heavy hitters like Seneca, Jesus, Paul, Aquinas, Luther, Calvin, Descartes, Hobbes, Locke, Rousseau, Kant, Nietzsche, Heidegger, Mauss, Marion, and Milbank. I am not a specialist in most of the areas I touch upon, and I am sure that my efforts as an uninformed outsider will have to be corrected at many points.

What I *do* know is that gratitude is a big and important and *untold* story, and I will consider my effort a success if my telling is just beautiful enough—or just ugly enough—to launch a thousand monographs from readers who say, "No, that's not it at all." I will be content if I am proven wrong in every particular (well, *most* particulars), so long as my book helps put gratitude back into the indexes, search engines, and syllabi.

Peniel Hall
Fourth day of Christmas, 2012

PART I

~

Circles

ONE

Circles of Honor

Reciprocity was written into the language of archaic Greece. Ancient Greeks had no specific word for "thanks" or "gratitude," and the word "grace" (*charis*, pl. *charites*) did double duty, naming both a gift and response. *Charis* means "pleasure" or "favor" and then, also, anything that brought pleasure or favor. Gods bestowed charis when they delivered a favorite from harm's way, filled a man's mouth with gracious, persuasive words, or lent some of their glistening beauty to make a man glitter like a god.[1] Human charis was favor, an expression of favor, and brought pleasure to others through the bestowal of favors. A gift expressed the giver's favor/charis to the recipient, and the recipient experienced pleasure/charis in receiving the gift.[2] That experience of pleasure in receiving a gift remained in the memory of the beneficiary, and provoked a response in turn, a response that took a form similar to that of the original gift. Verbal thanks was thus expressed using the same word, in phrases translated literally as "I know grace" (*oida charis*) or more commonly "I have grace" (*echo charis*), both of which mean "I give thanks." In later Greek, the word *eucharistia* become the standard word for thanks, but that too included the original root: for charis one ought to return *eucharistia*. A charis was not merely a sentiment of favor or a verbal expression of friendship but a concrete object or service, so too the response normally took objective form. Gifts given evoked gifts given in return. From archaic Homeric times through classical Greece and beyond, it was common sense that charis would beget charis.[3] That meant "favor begets favor," "pleasure begets pleasure," and also "gift begets gift." Not

19

only the generous giver but also the grateful recipient was grace-full, and gifts flowed from grace to grace.[4]

The same was true in Latin, which in its classical and early Christian vocabularies lacked the word *gratitudo* that is the root of our English "gratitude." Instead, both gifts or favors and the response of thanks were forms of *gratia*. Gratia originally had a religious significance, and in that context often referred to acts and gifts from or to the gods, not merely sentiments of favor or goodwill.[5] A Roman, like a Greek, could express verbal thanks with "I have grace" (*habeo gratias*).[6] Also like in ancient Greece, the appropriate response to a gift was expressed not only verbally but also in concrete actions and return gifts. To give thanks was to *reddere grates* or *referre grates*—that is, "to return grace"—and in religious contexts this took the concrete form of sacrifice, expressed by *agere grates*, "to do grace."[7] In nonreligious contexts, the return gratia was also to be more than a mere feeling of gratification or a passing "thank you." For the recipient of a favor, gratia means memory of the favor received and a desire to repay,[8] a desire that was to be fulfilled in the bestowal of a return benefit as a marker of favor. That mark of favor was itself gratia.[9] A failure to return favor showed that one was *ingratus*, not only "ungrateful" but also "lacking grace," and for Romans the someone who was ingratus lacked all the ethical, aesthetic, and social qualities associated with gratia.[10]

Across the centuries from Homer to Seneca that we survey in this chapter and the next, gratitude was understood as the closing curve of a circle that began with a gracious gift, and it was common sense that the circle would be closed by an in-kind gift in response to a favor or a gift. Ancient society was constituted by multiple circles of reciprocity, the first of which is the circle formed by gifts and gratitude between gods and human beings.

Reciprocal Religion

In Greco-Roman religion, reciprocity of gift and gratitude exists among the gods.[11] When one god does service for another, the recipient is obligated to remember and repay. Early in the *Iliad*, Achilles appeals to his divine mother, Thetis, to approach Zeus and plead for him. Achilles suggests that she remind the king of the gods:

> How you and you alone of all the immortals
> rescued Zeus, the lord of the dark storm cloud,
> from ignominious, stark defeat.
> That day the Olympians tried to chain him down,
> Hera, Poseidon lord of the sea, and Pallas Athena—
> you rushed to Zeus, dear Goddess, broke those chains,

quickly ordered the hundred-hander to steep Olympus,
that monster whom the immortals call Briareus
but every mortal calls the Sea-god's son, Aegaeon,
though he's stronger than his father. Down he sat,
flanking Cronus' son, gargantuan in the glory of it all,
and the blessed gods were struck with terror then,
they stopped shackling Zeus. Remind him of that. . . .
So all can reap the benefits of their king—
so even mighty Atrides can see how mad he was
to disgrace Achilles, the best of the Achaeans![12]

Thetis approaches Zeus as a suppliant (*hikateia*), clasps his knees, and prays as Achilles suggests. Zeus acquiesces: "I will see to this. I will bring it all to pass. / Look, I will bow my head if that will satisfy you."[13] Gratitude to Thetis weighs even more heavily with Zeus than his immortal fear of Hera's wrath. Supplication is a reminder of past favors that express the hope for continuing favors. Divine favors beget divine favors.

Most often, the religious circle of reciprocity joins immortals and mortals. Gods were benefactors, showing favor to individuals, peoples, or cities by bestowing favors upon them. Human beings responded with gratitude, grace for grace, expressed in sacrificial gifts. The reciprocal dynamic of Greco-Roman religion is often expressed in the Latin formula *do ut des*, "I give that you may give." Insofar as it expresses the expectations of the religious world, it is accurate enough, and, so far as we know, might have summed up the religious beliefs of many ancient people. Many might have believed that they could, like Thetis, put the gods in their debt and imposed an obligation on the gods through their regular acts of devotion and sacrifice. In many ancient depictions of worship, human beings bear an offering for the gods in their hands or on a tray looking for something from the god in return, and the Roman Lucian was evidently satirizing a recognizable religious outlook when he portrayed sacrifice as a purchase of favor from the gods.[14] *Do ut des* is an accurate summary of Greco-Roman religion insofar as charis/gratia existed on both sides of the divine-human transaction. Mortals brought the gods pleasing things, so that the gods might "rejoice in" the offerings, and they hoped to gain charis/gratia in return.[15]

Still, the transactions of Greek and Roman religion were *not* trade. A sacrifice may look like a payment or even a bribe, but a sacrifice was often a response to prior gifts as much as an effort to induce the gods to show favor. For sophisticated literate elites, and perhaps for many worshipers, the relationship with the gods was reciprocal without being crassly commercial.[16] Gods expected favors from men in return for favors, and human beings could appeal to the gods for further favors on the basis of favors performed, but this pattern of gift and return gift was part of an ongoing relationship with the gods. Friends too were expected to exchange favors with one another, but only the ethically blind thought friendship was simply identical with commerce.

Having made all the necessary qualifications, and recognizing variation over time, it is undeniable that the standard pattern of Greco-Roman religion for many centuries was a reciprocal one. Archaic Greeks regarded Zeus as both king and father, as well as the savior who rescued one from war, sickness, natural disasters, who protected the community, and benefited his favored human friends. Gods made the rain, gave food, protected from the dark chthonic powers, made women and animals and the land fruitful. Across many centuries, writers described the gods as benefactors (*euergetes*). Diodorus of Sicily claims that Uranus "gathered human beings within the shelter of a walls city and caused his subjects to cease lawless ways and bestial manners of living." He led them to discover "the uses of cultivated fruits, how to store them up" and also "subdued the larger part of the inhabited earth." In deference to the common people "he introduced the year on the basis of the movement of the sun and the months on that of the moon."[17] According to Dio Chrysostom, Zeus, of many names, is called "king" because of power, "father" because of gentleness, "protector" because he upholds the law and the city, "protector of suppliants" because he hears prayer, "god of hospitality" because he remembers strangers, "god of increase" because all the teeming fruitfulness of the world comes from him.[18] Seneca pithily summed up the common belief that "any name you choose will be properly applied to god," so long as it implies a force that "operates in the domain of heaven," for the names of god are "as countless as are his benefits."[19]

Sacrifice and prayer were the chief means of inducing the gods to respond favorably with services and benefits. Near the beginning of the *Iliad*, Agamemnon and Menelaus offer a "fat five-year-old bull" to Saturn with the request that the god give the Greeks victory over Hector.[20] Saturn refuses to answer, but later Agamemnon offers sacrifice to Zeus, with a memorial prayer reminding Zeus of Agamemnon's faithful worship: "Not once, I swear, did I pass a handsome altar of yours, / sailing my oar-swept ship on our fatal voyage here, / but on each I burned the fat and thigh bones of oxen, / longing to raze Troy's sturdy walls to the roots."[21] There is a competition for the favor of the gods, and sacrifice is the coinage of the competition. When Agamemnon refuses to return Chryseis to her father Chryses at the beginning of the *Iliad*, he reminds Apollo how often he "dressed your temple with wreaths when it lacked them before," how often he has "burned in your honour all those thighs of bulls and goats upon your altar." "If ever" (*ei pote*) he has done this, then Apollo should respond.[22]

Similar sentiments are expressed regularly over the whole sweep of Greco-Roman history. Xenophon offers instructions for prayer to the Greeks of the classical age: "I start cultivating the good will of the gods. And I try to behave so that it might be right for me when I pray, to acquire good health, physical strength, distinction in the city, good will among friends, survival with honour in war, and wealth that has been increased by honest means."[23] A hymn of Isidorus from the first century A.D. reiterates that worshipers look to the gods for all good things, and can expect the gods to respond to their petitions. The writer praises Isis-Hermouthis for giving life and cereal food, who assists traders in their commerce. If anyone prays, he is relieved from the grip of death; the barren pray and become fruitful. All these gifts of Isis encourage people to "set aside for you one tenth of these blessings (*charitas*) / rejoicing each year at the time of your Panegyrie."[24] The emperor Hadrian's prayer to Aphrodite is more explicit about his hope that his actions will induce a response from the goddess. "Grant me your favours," he says, adding, "What Hadrian offers you, receive it as the first fruits of a she-bear which he has killed in striking it from the top of his horse." He asks favors "in return" (*anti*), specifically the favor that she would "breathe to him the *charin* of Aphrodite Ourania."[25] Charis descends from gods in the form of specific benefits, which elicits prayers for more charites, prayers that are accompanied by gifts to the god. James Harrison vividly describes the process as a "tide": grace "flows from the gods over the human shoreline, and then slowly ebbs back toward them."[26]

In many settings—in inscriptions, private correspondence, and literary works—the proper performance of ritual sacrifice is essential to the success of one's appeal. If the performance were done correctly, the worshiper could expect a response, though not necessarily immediate, not necessarily of the same value as the sacrificed gift. But the gods could be expected to respond gift for gift, and some texts even claim that the gods themselves are grateful for the benefits given by worshipers: "Zeus is justly grateful to us," says the Chorus in Euripides' *Heracleidae*.[27] Worshipers often complain that the gods have ignored their offerings. In his retelling of the prayer of the Trojan priest Chryses, Lucian captures the tone of complaint: "You neglect me when I am in such straits and take no account of your benefactor (*euergeten*)."[28] Though not stated so baldly in Homer's account, the import is there. If Apollo refuses to hear Chryses after all he has done, the god opens himself to a charge of ingratitude.

Greek philosophers and their Roman heirs probed and purified the practices of ancient religion, but in the main they continued to think of religious life as a circle of gift and gratitude, with gift and gratitude on both sides of the exchange. Plato claims that the gods feel not only good will but also gratitude (*charin*) toward generous worshipers,[29] and argues that the gods are gratified (*kechairismenon*, linked to the root *chair-*, meaning "joy") by holiness expressed in prayer and sacrifice.[30] Gratitude has a particularly prominent role in the writings of Xenophon.[31] He tells his Greek readers that the Persians took ingratitude so seriously that they subjected it to civil punishments, and at the end of his *Cyropaedeia* he transcribes Cyrus' remarkable prayer of thanks:

> O ancestral Zeus and Helius and all the gods, accept these offerings as tokens of gratitude for help in achieving many glorious enterprises; for in omens in the sacrifice, in signs from heaven, in the flight of birds, and in ominous words, ye ever showed me what I ought to do and what I ought not to do. And I render heartfelt thanks to you that I have never failed to recognize your fostering care and never in my successes entertained proud thoughts transcending human bounds. And I beseech of you that ye will now also grant prosperity and happiness to my children, my wife, my friends, and my country, and to me myself an end befitting the life that ye have given me.[32]

Plutarch claims that the gods are gratified (κεχαιρισμένον) when children are grateful for parental favors.[33] Even Lucian, who satirized commercialized sacrificial worship, acknowledges that the gods accepted sacrifice if it was offered by worshipers in their own land.[34] Apart from the Epicureans, who believed that the gods were blissfully indifferent to human life anyway, ancient philosophers shared the assumption that religious life involved exchange.

Of course, philosophers question some of the questionable assumptions built into popular Greek religion. In his dialog with Euthyphro, Socrates asks whether the gods need what worshipers give them in worship. Euthyphro denies the gods have any need, but emphasizes that worshipers offer "honor and recognition and *charis*."[35] One of Xenophon's characters concludes that he has no way of "repaying the benefits of the gods by adequate returns of favour."[36] Some writers turned attention from the procedures of sacrifice toward the uprightness and intentions of the sacrificer. Theophrastus offers a Greek version of the biblical "I desire mercy not sacrifice" in his discourse on piety (*Peri eusebias*): Sacrifice is done to bestow honor (*time*), out of lack, or out of gratitude (*charin*) for favors done. Destroying an animal for the honor of a god is nonsensical; it is an act of injustice to kill an animal who has done no injustice. Nor should anyone destroy an animal "when we return a favor (*charin apodidontas*) to the gods for their kindness." What the gods expect is kindness, good works (*euergesias*) rather than sacrifice.[37] The Stoic Epictetus warned against seeking benefits from the gods that will do nothing but enhance honors. If one's desires are fixed on health, or offices or honors of friends, they will come to nothing. Rather, desire is to be focused on "Zeus and the other gods," and the pious are to give (*charisai*) to them.[38] In the first century A.D., Musonius criticized the practice of bestowing temples and other buildings on the city rather than spending money on men: "What would one gain from a large and beautiful house comparable to what he would gain by conferring the benefits of his wealth upon the city and his fellow citizens."[39] Faith in the existence of the gods, Plutarch insisted, is more likely to find favor with the gods than any sacrifice.[40] The gods are above bribery. Reciprocity remains in place, but in the hands of the philosophers the exchange was moralized. It became an ethical rather than a ceremonial transaction.

Heroic Reciprocity

In Athens stood a temple to the *Charites*, the "Graces," three beautiful and utterly naked goddesses believed to be the dispensers of charis in all its senses. Originally fertility goddesses, they were later honored for their contributions to civic and social life. Youth, marriage, health, and other social benefits were under their bailiwick.[41] Aristotle expresses the opinion that worship of Charites was important to the health of the city. "We set up a shrine of the Graces in a public place," he suggests, "to remind men to return a kindness," because "that is a special characteristic of grace (*charis*), since it is a duty not only to repay a service done, but another time to take the initiative in doing a service oneself."[42] Centuries after, Seneca describes the Roman equivalents, the *Gratiae*, which he traces all the way back to Hesiod. Some, he admits, see the three women as representations of "those who confer benefits, those who return them, and those who accept benefits and return them at the same time." Others allegorize their joyful expressions (gods love cheerful givers), their youth (remembrance of benefits do not grow old), their nakedness (benefits are bestowed openly). Seneca finds these mythologies contradictory and nonsensical, and leaves the myths to the poets.[43] For Aristotle, though, the Graces provide a link between divine reciprocity and human. It was a tenuous link. For the most part, the social gift-gratitude nexus among men formed a circle separate from the liturgical circle of sacrifice. It was one of the revolutionary contributions of Christianity to break through the barrier of heaven to imagine interhuman gifts as treasures in heaven.[44]

With or without clear divine sanctions, gifts and obligatory grateful returns constituted the circle of social and political life in the Greco-Roman world.[45] Gifts might be genuine acts of altruistic kindness. They might be intended as instruments of power and control. Whatever the intention, a gift imposed a debt on the recipient that could be cashed in later. A giver expected a "grateful" response. The earliest Greek literature reflects this cultural assumption. During the Iron Age, Hesiod predicts, "Men will dishonor their parents as they grow quickly old, and will carp at them, chiding them with bitter words, hard-hearted they, not knowing the fear of the gods. They will not repay their aged parents the cost of their nurture, for might shall be their right: and one man will sack another's city,"[46] and he advises elsewhere, "take fair measure from your neighbor and pay him back fairly (*apodounai auto to metro*) with the same measure, or better, if you can."[47] Pindar establishes links among thankfulness, reciprocity, and memory that remained a constant of Western thought for many centuries. Ancient charis sleeps, he writes, "and mortals are forgetful (*amnamones de brotoi*) of whatever does not reach the highest bloom of skillful song."[48]

Homer's epics evidence similar concerns. The *Iliad* is a tragedy of failed reciprocity, of gifts given and taken back, of failures of charis and broken obligations of return charis, of gifts refused. The war began when the goddess Eris (Strife) tossed the poisoned gift, a golden apple labeled "for the fairest," into the wedding party of Peleus and Thetis, the parents of Achilles. The apple is claimed by three goddesses—Hera, Athena, and Aphrodite—and each offers a bribe to the judge, the Trojan Paris. Paris accepts Aphrodite's gift, Helen, the most beautiful woman in the world, and takes possession of her in violation of the hospitality shown to Paris by her husband Menelaus. The epic itself focuses on the last years of the war, and there too the action is dominated by problems of reciprocity and its failures.

We can fully grasp the significance of reciprocity in the *Iliad*, however, only by linking it to the heroic temperament.[49] *Philotimia*, love of honor, was the central value of the Greek hero.[50] "Ah, my friend," said Sarpedon to Glaucus on the windy plains of Troy, "if you and I could escape this fray / and live forever, ever a trace of age, immortal, / I would never fight on the front lines again / or command you to the field where men win fame." Sarpedon's is a fragile wish: "as it is, the fates of death await us, / thousands poised to strike, and not a man alive / can flee them or escape—so in we go for attack! / Give our enemy glory or win it for ourselves!"[51] The old horseman Peleus gave the heroic advice to his son Achilles: "always be the best, my boy, the bravest."[52] Honor was achieved through birth, because of the contagious honor of a family reputation, or through one's own achievements.

Men won honor through displays of excellence (*arete*) in verbal combat in the assembly or in sexual conquests. Above all, though, warriors displayed their *arete* on the battlefield, with displays of physical prowess and power. By the excellence of his achievements, the hero sought to achieve *kleos*, repute or fame, among his fellow warriors and aspired especially to gain sufficient fame to be commemorated eternally in epic poetry.[53] Greek heroes also aimed for *time*, a word often translated as "honor" but etymologically related to "compensation" or even "price." *Time* is achieved by the performance of a hero on the battlefield. By his acts, a warrior proves his worth, and that price is paid in the respect shown him by his fellow warriors. Acts of prowess impose on other warriors a debt of respect and gratitude. Given the commercial connotations of the term, it is not surprising that *time* is signified by material goods—oxen taken from raids, tripods and other metal items, women—the hero's plunder, his *geras*.[54] A warrior is expected to be generous with his fellows, especially with those who fight under his command. Just distribution of plunder proves a hero's worth as much as killing enemies does. His honor rises not only by collecting geras but also by giving it. Generosity displays his charis, the sparkle of his glory, and simultaneously binds the recipients to him. Warriors who benefit from the generosity of a chief are expected to repay with faithful service in the future.

In the heroic world, gifts are integral to the relations between one clan or kingdom and another. Alliances are forged by guest gifts and hospitality, by respect for the rights of strangers, *xeneia*. Exchanges of women are particularly important in forming bonds between households (*oikoi*) and nobles (*aristoi*) or kings (*basileus*). The host is obliged to receive guests, to give them a bath and food, and the guest receives this hospitality by taking on certain obligations. A guest commonly offered a guest gift when leaving. Such "friendships" might evoke strong feelings, but they were interested, utilitarian, and reciprocal. A friend was someone with whom you were involved in an ongoing circle of mutual service. The strange scene between Glaucus and Diomedes on the battlefield on the windy plains of Troy shows how longlasting guest friendship could be. As the two heroes prepare to fight, they discover that their fathers had once entered into a host-guest relationship. The alliance is intergenerational, and the sons bear the obligations of their fathers. Gifts were exchanged by the fathers, and so the sons renew the hospitality relationship by exchanging gifts again. They never fight, though Diomedes seizes mastery by getting a more valuable gift than Glaucus.[55]

The *Iliad* as a whole turns on the rage of Achilles.[56] Achilles is enraged because Agamemnon has taken away his war bride, his geras, Briseis. Agamemnon takes her from Achilles because he has been forced to give up his own war bride, Chryseis, daughter of Chryses, priest of Apollo. When Chryses offers gifts for the return of Chryseis, Agamemnon initially refuses and then gives in because Apollo attacks the Greeks in retribution for Agamemnon's snub to Chryses. Agamemnon looks to compensate his loss, which is not just a loss of plunder but also a loss of honor: "Fetch me another prize, and straight off too, / else I alone of the Argives go without my honor (*geras*). / That would be a disgrace. . . . [M]y prize is snatched away."[57] He seizes Briseis in petty revenge for Achilles' opposition to him.

Achilles acknowledges that Agamemnon has the authority to share the spoils, and Achilles acquiesces to Agamemnon's power to take back his gift. But if Agamemnon can force Achilles to give up his bride, he cannot force him to fight.[58] Achilles charges that Agamemnon is greedy and shamelessly profit-minded because he takes back booty that he had distributed.[59] To Achilles, Agamemnon's demand manifests a deeply ungenerous character. The real disgrace is not a loss of geras but the seizure of another man's prizes.[60] Dashing his gold-studded scepter to the ground with an oath that he will not fight, Achilles charges that Agamemnon has failed to pay Achilles his proper *time*. When Agamemnon's men die on the battlefield before "man-killing Hector," the Greeks will learn Achilles' worth: "then you will tear your heart out, desperate, raging / that you disgraced the best of the Achaeans."[61]

Agamemnon eventually concedes to send a delegation to Achilles laden with gifts to win him back: "Seven tripods never touched by fire, ten bars of gold, / twenty burnished cauldrons, a dozen massive stallions, / racers who earned me trophies with their speed." Agamemnon even promises to return Briseis, accompanied by an oath that he has not touched her.[62] Achilles again zeroes in on the issue of gift, compensation, and gratitude: "there was no *charis* given for fighting incessantly forever against your enemies."[63] Achilles has promised to use all his skill to fight Troy, and Agamemnon's compensation is too late and too little. "This is the thanks I get," is Achilles' response. Achilles also recognizes that the offered gifts are a power play to subordinate Achilles. Agamemnon's overwhelming gifts impose a burden Achilles will never be able to pay back. Agamemnon even offers to make Achilles his son-in-law, an apparently generous act that in fact makes Agamemnon's superiority permanent. Homer's characters know that gifts can be acts of domination, imposing impossible obligations on the recipients. Though his companions criticize Achilles for refusing the gifts, he knows what he is doing. Agamemnon is the one who loses face in having his gifts rejected.[64] In the *agon* of gifts and gratitude that dominate the epic, Achilles wins another round.

Achilles eventually returns to the battlefield after the death of Patroclus, to take revenge ("negative reciprocity") on Hector, who killed his friend. Agamemnon tries again to bring peace with gifts.[65] It is an abortive effort, as Achilles brushes Agamemnon aside: "produce the gifts if you like, as you see fit / or keep them back, it's up to you." Achilles is too eager to return to the field to stop for ritual expressions of friendship with Agamemnon.[66] He even rejects Agamemnon's suggestion that they share a sacrificial meal to "seal our binding oaths in blood": "You talk of food? / I have no taste for food—what I really crave / is slaughter and blood and the choking groans of men!"[67] Odysseus brings the treasure anyway and prepares the meal, but Achilles will have none of it. He returns to the battle fed instead on nectar and ambrosia brought by Athena.

Agamemnon's failures as the lead chief of the Achaeans are evident in the hard-handed way he distributes and seizes the geras that signals the distribution of worth, *time*, among the warriors in his retinue. He demands immediate compensation for a loss; he retracts a gift already given; when he finally gets around to compensating Achilles, it is such an excessive gift that Achilles must refuse; the reconciliation he finally achieves is a faux reconciliation. The contrast between the disarray in the Greek camp and the tight-knit community within the walls of Troy is striking. Most of the examples of successful reciprocity in the epic are from the Trojan rather than the Greek side. It is no accident that the two camps are so spatially distinctive. Trojans remain within the circle of their walls, continuing their circular obligations of gift giving as they defend their city. Meanwhile, the Greeks are arranged in a line along the shore, broken up into self-contained tribal units.[68] The Greek circle has been undone. Only near the end of the epic do the Greeks restore a proper circulation of gifts and compensation. During the funeral games for Patroclus, Achilles, his wrath appeased, displays his superiority as a ruler. He distributes gifts with magnanimity,[69] and none is more dramatic than the climactic prize he awards to Agamemnon for spear throwing.[70] Roles are reversed. Agamemnon offers no more inept gifts. Achilles achieves peace by an act of generosity that puts Agamemnon in *his* debt.[71]

The circle of the *Iliad* is not yet closed. The Greek versus Greek quarrel has been resolved by Achilles' gift giving at the games, but the Greeks are still at odds with the Trojans, especially over the body of Hector. Exhibiting a ring construction, the epic begins and ends with scenes of supplication and gift exchange.[72] At the outset, a father, Chryses, comes to Agamemnon with gifts and a plea for the ransom of his daughter, Chryseis. Agamemnon's foolish rejection of his suit is the beginning of a downward spiral for the Greek forces. At the end of the poem, another mourning father appears, Priam, the king of Troy, bearing a great ransom to recover the body of his son from his son's killer, Achilles. In the chest are "twelve robes, handsome, rich brocades, / twelve cloaks, unlined and light, as many blankets, / as many big white capes and shirts to go with them . . . / ten full bars of gold / . . . two hundred burnished tripods, four fine cauldrons / and last a magnificent cup the Thracians gave him once."[73] Though the gifts are excessive, the king comes into the Greek camp dressed in a simple robe and riding an ox cart. He adopts the position of suppliant.[74] Unlike Agamemnon and his excessive gift, Priam does not claim superiority but humbles himself before his son's slayer. Achilles receives the gift and welcomes the giver as a *xenos*, a stranger who becomes a guest friend. In the morning, they part with mutual tears. Achilles grieves for his father, Priam for his son:

> Overpowered by memory
> both men gave way to grief. Priam wept freely
> for man-killing Hector, throbbing, crouching
> before Achilles' feet as Achilles wept himself,
> now for his father, now for Patroclus once again,
> and their sobbing rose and fell throughout the house.[75]

For a brief moment, in a scene of reconciliation that haunts the Western imagination up to the present, Greek and Trojan join in a community of grief and gift. Death unites. Hope for peace is invested in the power of the gift, joined with the tragic power of mutual loss.

Democratic Reciprocities

Archaic Greek society was structured by a double circle: There were reciprocal relationships between mortals and immortals, and there were intrahuman circles of grace for grace. The pattern of gift and response remained circular, both socially and theoretically, as Greek society was transformed from the archaic patchwork of "kingdoms" into a sleek patchwork of city-states (*poleis*). Yet, political Greece had a different structure than heroic Greece. In place of the circulation of gifts between princes and warriors and warriors and warriors, the city-state witnessed a proliferation of circles: aristocrats formed bonds of mutual service as they had always done, both within each Greek city and among elites between cities. But the city itself was imagined as a benefactor to which the citizens owed debts of loyalty and service. Individual citizens became benefactors of the city by performing the liturgies (*leitourgia*) of civic donations, and within the city "private" friendships were formed by exchanges of favors. Each of these circles turned round and round in the same pattern we have already described: benefactors gave benefits, and could expect their beneficiaries to repay them with service and often with goods; recipients felt the burden of obligation and looked for chances to repay their debts of gratitude with return services or goods. None of this "commerce" was regulated by explicit contract or enforced by law, but it was the heartbeat of Greek society.

Sparta brought much of the older heroic model into its own civic practice. Spartans often charged that the Athenians were ungrateful, which provided a pretext for attack. Herodotus identifies two reasons for Spartan anger against Athens: the Athenians had driven Peisistratids, the Spartans' "guest-friends," into exile, and Athens had not returned favors for Spartan services to Athens. The Spartans claimed, "[W]e do acknowledge that we have done wrongly; for . . . we drove from their native land men who were our guest-friends and promised to make Athens dependent upon us, and having done this we delivered the city of Athens into the hands of an ungrateful people."[76] Spartan complaints notwithstanding, in Athens too, ancient techniques and principles remained in place. Sophocles could still endorse the traditional notion that "one favor always begets another," and the Athenian elites maintained their bonds of reciprocity with elites from other cities. Athenians saw the world through a series of oppositions—Greek/barbarian, slave/free, friend/enemy. Yet the opposition of friend and enemy was not permanent and fixed. Enemies, including enemy cities, could be brought into the circle of friends (*philoi*) through gifts and favors. Brought into the circle of Athenian society, they were expected to live virtuously, as virtue was articulated by Xenophon—doing good to friends, doing harm to enemies.[77] Out of gratitude for being favored by Athens, newly befriended cities and rulers would support and benefit Athens in turn.[78] According to Thucydides, Athenian policy differed from earlier patterns because Athens aspired to be a benefactor more than a recipient of benefits:

> [I]n the matter of generosity we are the opposite of most people: that is, we acquire our friends not by receiving but by conferring favours. If someone confers a favour out of good will he is in a better position to preserve the recipient's feeling of gratitude as owed in the same spirit of good will; by contrast, if a person who owes a favour that his generosity will be recognized not as a favour but as a repayment of debt, then he is less keen to remain grateful. Thus, we are the only people who help others not out of calculation of any profit or loss, but out of confidence in generosity, without fear of consequence.[79]

High-minded Athenian foreign policy was not always successful. Favors were not reciprocated. When Athens offered citizenship to Thracian rulers, the Thracians turned the situation to their own advantage. Thrace was more important to Athens than the Athenian alliance was to Thrace. Thus, instead of imposing a debt on the Thracians, Athens was put in the position of a suppliant, courting the favor of their putative ally and leaving themselves vulnerable to Thracian treachery. Athenians remained loyal to Thrace even when it was not in their interests to do so. Philip of Macedon mocked the Athenians for their naïveté. When Cotys of Thrace was assassinated, Athens befriended his murderer, the new ruler of Thrace, and even promised to ally with Thrace against Philip. Philip commented sardonically, "You did this in the full knowledge that none of those who receive such gifts pay any attention to your laws."[80]

For a century and a half, Athens attempted something dramatically different.[81] From the democratic revolution in 462 B.C. until the end of democracy in 322 B.C., Athens attempted to form a polity without debt, where power was freed from obligations of reciprocity, benefits, services, and grateful returns. Earlier Athenian leaders had won mastery by traditional methods of gifts, largesse, and patronage. In the world outside Athens, and in Athens before 462, exchanges of gifts and imposition of debts of gratitude were normal practice. They were the way power was exercised and the way that elites maintained their superiority above the common citizens. Cimon became a big man by opening his fields and his house to the poor, who became his clients, if not his slaves. In 461 Cimon was ostracized, and the following year the Athenians erected a polity intended to prevent any future Cimons from gaining dominance in the city.[82] If not entirely in reality, at least in the rhetoric of democracy's advocates, the old system of gift and gratitude was nothing more than a system of gift and graft, which aristocrats used for their personal enrichment or at least to maintain the power. In Athens a new civic ideal emerged, in which the people ruled.

At the heart of the Athenian experiment was a shift in the dynamics of gift and gratitude. Democracy was an unprecedented effort to detach the distribution of political power from obligations of gift and gratitude,[83] and it brought with it a new set of political values and practices. Officials were chosen by lot and paid from the public treasury, which broke the power of networks of gift friends.[84] Instead of personal loyalty expressed in gift exchange, the nine archons of Athens swore "not to accept *dora* on account of their office."[85] Thucydides praised Perikles as *adoratatos*, incorruptible, which meant "beyond the reach of gifts and bribes."[86] When Perikles suspected that the Spartan king might spare Perikles' land during raids on Attika because of personal favor and guest friendship, Perikles hurried to explain his position by announcing "to the Athenians in their assembly that while

Archidamos was indeed a guest-friend of his, this relationship had certainly not been entered upon for the detriment of the state."[87] Centuries later, Plutarch was still singing the praises of Perikles, and for the same reasons: "He was to be seen travelling on one street only in the city, the one which led to the agora and the council chamber. He declined invitations to dinner, and all such activities of social and familiar character, so that during the long period of his political involvement, he did not attend a single friend's house to dine, except that of his kinsman Euryptolemos at his wedding feast; there, he stayed until the libations were made, and then immediately departed."[88] When Lykidas laid a request for civic friendship before the town council of Salamis, which was part of the Athenian orbit, the unfortunate Lykidas was stoned because he was suspected of pursuing personal interest.[89] Demosthenes insisted that supporting the "policy of the many" was essential, more important than maintaining connections with others of one's class. People commit crimes when they "fancy themselves important enough to be called *xenoi* and *philoi* of Philip." The charge against Alkibiades was that he had maintained loyalties to noble friends abroad rather than loving his city, including the inferiors.[90] Democracy thus was a victory of the community over the hero.[91]

The effect of Athenian democracy on the political imagination of the West, and of the world, is inestimable. Prior to 462 corruption and bribery were not deviations from some pure norm of disinterested political behavior. Corruption *was* the system. Corruption was not even identifiable as corruption. Bribery was an "invention" of classical Athens.[92] Corruption became identifiable *as* corruption only when the reforms of Kleisthenes broke the dominance of the elite families and subjected the politics of Athens to the *demos*, the people. The crime of being a traitor was also invented by classical Athens. Traitors could be identified as such only after the common good of the whole city became the standard by which policies would be tested and judged.[93]

The Athenian example fired the imaginations of thinkers in the early modern period, and more systematically than the Athenians others were able to formulate political theories in which power was detached from the "corruptions" of gratitude. As for Athens itself, democracy did not involve a complete "privatization" of reciprocity. Few followed Thucydides' proto-Hobbesian notion that human beings are motivated by fear and the instinct for self-preservation.[94] Most continued to believe that political order rested on reciprocal relations and mutual gifts, but they believed that democracy relocated the circle of reciprocity to political leaders and the people. From the side of the rulers, the results were not always an improvement. Perikles "began to fawn upon the many," in the hope that they would help secure his political power.[95] With democracy came the potential for demagoguery. For citizens, dynamics of gift and gratitude remained but were translated into state-citizen relations. Plato's Socrates reflects the change in the center of gratitude. Instead of personal bonds of loyalty established by direct gifts, Socrates feels obligations to the state that gave him life. Without using the terminology of gratitude, Socrates describes the debt he owes to the city for the gifts that the city and its *nomoi* (law, custom) have bestowed on him. He is beholden not to any person but to the mother city itself. The laws brought Socrates into existence because it was under their auspices that Socrates' father and mother were married. The laws demanded that Socrates be trained in music and gymnastics. As a result of this nurture and education, Socrates belongs to the state as "child and slave." He has no more right to strike against the state or revile it than he would his own father or mother. In all his philosophical investigations, Socrates tells Crito, he has surely discovered that "our country is more to be valued and higher and holier far than mother or father or any ancestor, and more to be regarded in the eyes of the gods and of men of understanding." Wherever she sends, even "if she leads us to wounds or death in battle, thither we follow as is right. . . . [W]hether in battle or in a court of law, or in any other place, he must do what his city and his country order him, or he must change their view of what is just."[96]

Xenophon's Socrates, in contrast to Plato's, explicitly uses gratitude as a political category. He claims that the state penalizes filial ingratitude, and explains that the ungrateful are not entrusted with civic office because it would be an evil for such a man to offer sacrifices for the state:

> Don't you know that even the state ignores all other forms of ingratitude (*acharistias*) and pronounces no judgment on them, caring nothing if the recipient of a favour neglects to thank his benefactor, but inflicts penalties on the man who is discourteous to his parents and rejects him as unworthy of office, holding that it would be a sin for him to offer sacrifices on behalf of the state and that he is unlikely to do anything else honourably and rightly? Aye, and if one fail to honour his parents' graves, the state inquires into that too, when it examines the candidates for office.[97]

The charites given by Athens had to be repaid with the grateful obedience. In place of a circle of gifts and gratitude binding rulers to one another, democracy involved a gift-and-gratitude circle between the rulers and people.

Other circles of reciprocation are evident within democratic society. Prominent and wealthy citizens were expected to offer gifts and services to the city, in the form of "liturgies," public service. Court speeches from the democratic age indicate that such contributions to the polis counted as evidence of good character and could be part of a man's legal defense. Isaios defends two brothers by reminding the jury that their father "has before now performed liturgies and made contributions, and generally been a keen citizen." In fact, "the brothers themselves have never gone away, unless they were sent by you; and, while staying here, they are not unhelpful (*akhresoi*) to the polis: they serve in the army, they make contributions of tax . . . and—as everyone knows—they behave in an orderly way."[98] Another orator, Antiphon, presents a speaker defending himself by calling attention to the services he had performed for the city: "I have made many substantial *eisphora* payments, I have many times served as a trierarch, and I have furnished a brilliant chorus. . . . If my character is such as thus, you must not deem me guilty of anything sinful or shameful."[99]

For some Greek philosophers, the detachment of gratitude from power afforded an opportunity for "private" friendships among equals. Epicurus and his followers took the opportunity to explore the emotional dimension of gratitude and ingratitude. Epicurus' views on the emotions of anger and gratitude are known only in fragments, and most have to do directly with Epicurus' denial that the gods experience anger or gratitude. A later Epicurean, Philodemus, discussed gratitude directly in his treatise *On Anger*. Apparently following Epicurus, Philodemus claims that anger and gratitude are opposites. A man feels anger toward those who harm him, and gratitude toward those who do favors for him. Gratitude and anger are responses to voluntary acts, Philodemus says. It is silly to be angry at inanimate objects, or to be grateful even to animate ones that benefit us unintentionally.[100]

The Hero in the City

The most important treatment from ancient Athens, though, comes from Aristotle, who raises civic "liturgical" donations to an ethical status in his *Nicomachean Ethics*, where he analyzes the virtue of liberality and gives ethical advice on the right ways to give and receive gifts.[101] Aristotle's was fundamentally an ethic of independence, an ethic for citizen heroes in a democratic polis.[102] A free man, Aristotle writes in the *Rhetoric*, is one who is not dependent on any other man,[103] and he argues elsewhere that any man whose life circled around another is little better than a slave.[104] Freedom means doing what you like, and that means keeping some distance from the benefits that others might bestow. Aristotle's reflections on liberality, reception, and friendship are always checked by the dominant drive for a heroic autonomy.[105] It is not surprising that he has no place in his list of virtues for "gratitude."[106]

For Aristotle, excellence is always a mean between two extremes. There is always an extreme of excess—too much—and an extreme of defect—too little. With regard to the use of wealth, the excess is "prodigality" (*asotia*), the vice of "wasting substance," which often becomes a "sort of ruining of oneself, life being held to depend on possession of substance." The defect of meanness (*aneleutheria*) has two dimensions, deficiency in giving and excess in taking, though in practice only one of these usually appears in a mean man—he either gives too little or takes too much, and either way he ends up hoarding. The mean man is known "by such names a niggardly, close-fisted, and stingy all fall short in giving."[107] Stinginess is a vice worse than prodigality, and more common. Liberality (*eleutheriotetos*) is balanced on both ends of the reciprocity spectrum. The liberal man does not give away too much or to the wrong people, and he is careful to make sure that his giving is to noble ends. He is careful to take only from noble sources, and he does not give to all and everyone, or take from just anyone.

"Magnificence" (*megaloprepeia*) is not identical to liberality because magnificence characterizes not all the exchanges of the virtuous man but only those that involve "largeness of scale" (*megethos*). In contrast to the defect of paltriness and the excess of vulgarity, the magnificent man is "an artist in expenditure," who knows how to spend great sums with good taste. The magnificent man will spend as is fitting for his wealth and station. It is relative to his own standing and net worth.[108] He is a big man who shows his bigness in the way he spends his wealth. He is able "at an equal expense [to] produce a more magnificent result" than a rival.[109] Magnificent expenditures are often expenditures on behalf of the city, religious gifts like "votive offerings, buildings, and sacrifices," or donations that reflect civic-minded ambition.[110] A magnificent man will also spend great sums on certain private occasions, weddings, receptions for foreign visitors, furnishings for his house, a tomb. The magnificent man does not spend on himself, and his gifts to private causes are a sort of "votive offering" that have public consequence.[111]

Aristotle subsumes these virtues of liberality and magnificence under the crowning virtue of his ethical system, the virtue of "pride" or "great-souledness" (*megalopsychia*). The great-souled man is one who knows his worth, and acts according to that worth, who has a high but appropriate self-image. This virtue is also reflected in the way that the great-souled man uses his wealth: "[H]e is the sort of man to confer benefits, but he is ashamed of receiving them; for the one is the mark of a superior, the other of an inferior. And he is apt to confer greater benefits in return; for thus the original bene-factor besides being paid will incur a debt to him, and will be the gainer by the transaction."[112] He goes on to say that men of great soul do not "seem to remember any service they have done, but not those they have received (for he who receives a service is inferior to him who has done it, but the proud man wishes to be superior), and to hear of the former with pleasure, of the latter with displeasure; this, it seems, is why Thetis did not mention to Zeus the services she had done him, and why the Spartans did not recount their services to the Athenians, but those they had received."[113]

A magnanimous man aims for independence, and reception of gifts, Aristotle knows, imposes dependence. Thus, "it is a mark of the magnanimous man also to ask for nothing or scarcely anything, but to give help readily."[114] He should not waste his time with the common run of projects and aims, but should instead "be sluggish and to hold back except where great honour or a great work is at stake." If his deeds be few, let them be at least "great and notable ones." He is not easily impressed, and he quickly forgets wrongs done to him. He would rather overlook wrongs than hold them in memory. He does not care to be praised, and he rarely gives praise.[115] Here especially Aristotle makes a tight connection between virtue and independence. Giving is an act of superiority, and therefore the virtuous man gives much; reception means humility, inferiority, and dependence, and the virtuous man avoids reception as much as possible. The virtuous man tries to pull apart the circle of gift and gratitude, and turn it into a line of unilateral, dominating gift giving.

Aristotle does envision circles of reciprocity, but only among equals, among friends (*philoi*). In Athenian democracy, bonds of friendship were no longer supposed to play a prominent political role, but Aristotle did not think this eliminated the value of friendship. Anticipating the arguments of Adam Smith and others, he instead saw that the detachment of friendship from favors and obligations opened up room for friendships in which the friend was the end rather than a means. *Philia* always depends on a response of philia from the other (*antiphilesis*), which is why Aristotle thinks it is mistaken to speak of philia for wine. Friendship takes many forms, among them the friendship between parents and children. This is, of course, an unequal friendship, since the parents' benefits to their children always surpass any return benefit a child might offer. Children have, after all, received their very lives from their parents, and are to respond with honor and service, and an affection that is like the affection of men for the gods.[116] Outside the family, friendships may be based on pleasure or on goods (*agatha*), but both are ultimately selfish, since such friendships aim only to fulfill needs.[117] Neither of these reaches the heights of friendship. For Aristotle, the highest form of philia is *philia kat' areten* (friendship according to virtue). In contrast to other forms of friendship, the virtuous friend values the friend for what he is, rather than for some accidental good that he can provide. For Aristotle, friendship according to virtue depends on mutual good will, recognition that good will is returned, and the desire for the good of the other for his own sake.[118] Friendships are reciprocal and circular, but each friends aims not to elicit favors but to do favors. They are circular relations but not calculating, interested relationships.

Aristotle's treatment of friendship is undermined by his commitment to the virtue of independence. Aristotle's magnanimous man aspires to remain independent of gifts, since they place him in a position of dependence and inferiority. A magnanimous man does many favors, and will remember them; but he will receive few and forget them as quickly as they are performed. Self-sufficiency is the aim of the virtuous life. Few can attain this, but once a man achieves the ability to engage in philosophical *theoria* he can become entirely self-sufficient: "the quality which is called self-sufficiency would exist most in relation to the theoretic life," because when his basic necessities are taken care of "the wise man can indulge in *theoria* even by himself." The just man needs others on which to practice justice; the philosopher needs none.[119] But the aspiration to philosophical autonomy undermines Aristotle's endorsement of philoi as an essential component of virtue. After all, a friendship is a circle of mutual favor, at its best an exchange of wisdom that enables both parties to achieve virtue. By eschewing dependence and receptivity, Aristotle allows that arete floats off from philia and the good man. The truly good man needs no friends to attain virtue.[120] The life of virtue is no longer a life of gift and gratitude but an isolated and self-sufficient life of theoretic contemplation. This is a detachment from reciprocity far more radical than anything achieved by Athenian political order, and it, of course, implies a fairly complete break with politics. Throughout Western intellectual history, there is tension between two paths to virtue: friendship (necessarily involving gift and gratitude) and isolation, conversation, and philosophical or mystical ascent.

Conclusion

Democratic hopes for a community of equals are consistently dogged by some of the tangles that we find in Aristotle. Relationships of benefit and gratitude do not disappear in a democracy. Perikles may stay away from tempting dinners all he wants, but Athens was still filled with friends doing services for one another, and a group of friends can always serve as a power base. It is not so easy to cleanse politics of gratitude's obligations. Besides, the equality of democracy depends on a relocation of the circle of reciprocity between the state and the citizen, and in Athens (and perhaps everywhere) that required redistribution of resources from the wealthy to the poorer. Patronage is not eliminated, but the state becomes the universal patron. Nonplussed as Socrates may seem as he reminds Crito of his debts to Athens and its laws, it is well to remember that he offers his reflections while on death row.[121] Once focused on a motherly state, political gratitude can turn totalitarian.

The Roman solution is to reject the aspiration for independence, to accept and celebrate the asymmetries of reciprocal relations, of benefit and gratitude. From its beginnings, Roman order was founded on a premise of interpersonal *dependence* instead of autarchic Aristotelian freedom. That alternative circle, of course, comes with its own set of tangles, which we explore in the next chapter.

TWO

Benefits and Good Offices

Romans were unique in antiquity. In no other society were the ruling classes so thoroughly bound together by *beneficia* and *gratia*, by gifts and reciprocal gratitude. In no other society did the unequal relationships between benefactors and their beneficiaries, patrons and their clients, play such a prominent role.[1] Benefits hold society together, Seneca says, reflecting the Roman notion that humans are fundamentally dependent beings.[2] Whether those involved "patronage" in the strictest sense or merely "benefactions," they were everywhere. Most social relationships in Rome outside of family relations were molded by gifts, reception, and return gifts.

It was a principle that Athenians, with their bias in favor of independence, autonomy, and freedom, would have barely understood.[3] Romans were closer to Xenophon's Persians who imposed civic sanctions on the ungrateful. Suetonius and Tacitus both refer to prosecutions against ungrateful clients and children.[4] It is no surprise that Rome produced some of the most important writings on gratitude, writings that profoundly affected Western ethics, philosophy, political theory, and literature for nearly two millennia.

"Patronage" refers to asymmetrical, permanent relationships between high-status patrons and lower-status clients, whose relationship is established and maintained by exchanges of services or objects. Being wealthier and better connected, patrons were able to meet the needs of their clients. Clients could not offer anything that patrons needed, but strove to satisfy their desires. Romans of lower classes sought necessities in the marketplace, but to obtain anything beyond necessaries required connection to someone with access to goods that were not available to most Romans. A patron owed his clients protection, advocacy in court, and sometimes gifts of money, and, just as importantly, these services and benefits from patron to client placed a debt of gratitude on the client, who was obligated to repay the patron with services of his own. Gratitude was not merely warm feeling toward the benefactor, but reciprocal service and benefaction. Benefits imposed a debt on the recipient that had to be discharged through a return of service or benefit.

Patronage relationships could take many forms. Landlords were patrons to tenants, patricians to plebeians, and Rome itself stood in a relationship of patronage to its allies and territories. Patron relationships were founded on mutual trust, *fides*, and on reciprocal service, *officia*. Such relationships were often described as relations of friendship (*amicitia*), a term that in Rome covered not only intimate relations between equals but also a wide range of asymmetrical relations based on obligations of reciprocity. Patrons considered their clients to be their *amici*, and vice versa.

According to the *Roman Antiquities* of Dionysius of Halicarnassus, patronage was as old as Rome itself. Romulus divided the original Roman community between aristocrats and the plebs (*eupatridas* and *demotikoi*). The former were charged with the management of religious and political life while the plebs gave themselves to farming and trade. By giving particular tasks to the plebs, Romulus aimed "to prevent them from engaging in seditions, as happens in other cities when either the magistrates mistreat the lowly, or the common people and the needy envy those in authority."[5] To describe these classes by titles of authority seemed too domineering. To promote affection among different classes, he described the relationship with kin terminology. Aristocrats were not despots but father figures. Through the institution of *patroneia* that assigned "friendly offices to both parties," Romulus ensured that "the connection between them [was] a bond of kindness befitting fellow citizens."[6]

For Dionysius, it was not a one-sided system. Both patrons and clients had responsibilities toward one another. Clients assisted patrons in raising dowries for their daughters, ransomed patrons if they were taken prisoner in war, helped pay fines when patrons were liable, and shared the costs of magistracies that were won by their patrons. Patrons for their turn were responsible to explain the law to their clients, to care for them as fathers for children in financial and contractual matters, to defend them in court, and to "secure for them both in private and in public affairs all that tranquility of which they particularly stood in need."[7]

The patronage system never existed in the form that Dionysius describes. He claims that patron-client relations and obligations were enforced by law, which was never the case. Dionysius, writing shortly after the ascent of Augustus, outlines a highly sanitized portrait of patronage in the early Principate.[8] Patronage was not as blissful as Dionysius makes it sound. In practice, patronage secured the power of patrons over clients, gave extralegal support for the advantages of the oldest families in Rome, and limited the access that clients had to goods that, as citizens, they theoretically enjoyed directly.[9] Dionysius is also idealistic in highlighting only the cohesive function and power of patronage relations. Of course, a generous benefactor won the loyalty of his clients, and faithful clients maintained the patronage of their patrons. Because gifting went in both directions, it bound both patrons and clients, and often bound them tightly and enduringly. Patronage relations often extended, like the guest-friend relations of the Homeric period, across generations. The patronage system helped unify the spreading empire. Emperors displayed their generosity toward conquered territories by building temples and coliseums and by sponsoring games. Such acts of "euergetism" erected monumental reminders of Roman power throughout the empire, but were also intended to win the loyalty and gratitude of provinces. Provincial officials, generals, and local authorities also deployed the techniques of euergetism and patronage to establish bonds with conquered cities and territories, including the provincial elites. Within the patronage network, the bonds were strong, but each patronage network also had a boundary, an outside, and it was not unusual for one patronage network to vie for power with another. One of the factors behind Caesar's assassination was a clash of alliances. A general who could call in debts of gratitude not only from subordinate commanders in the Roman military but also from powerful provincial leaders was a potential threat to Rome. Thus Caesar joins with his adopted son Octavian and Mark Antony in opposition to Cassius and his network of clients. As Shakespeare understood, the tragic choice has to be made by Brutus rather than Caesar, who abandons his "friend" with an "unkind" (i.e., ungrateful) cut in order to pursue his ideal of Republican revival. Rivalries between "families" of political patronage revived in Italy during the Renaissance, much to Dante's horror.

As in Homeric Greece and in Athens, the benefit-gratitude system in Rome was interwoven with the pursuit of honor. A patron expected his clients to form an entourage to blow trumpets and shout his praises as the patron passed through the streets of Rome. Acts of euergetism had a similar aim. Like Aristotle's magnanimous man, a euergetes sponsored the building of an aqueduct, hippodrome, or temple in a city, sponsored poetry and athletic contests, and fulfilled a religious or administrative function in the city. Like the private gratitude of a client, the public gratitude for benefactors was more than mass enthusiasm. It took external, ritualized forms. In return for his public favors, the benefactor received the honor (*time*) of the masses, often in the public form of an honorific inscription in a public place, a bronze statue in the forum or a park, special seats at games, crowns, and positions at feasts and in temples. This grateful honor was especially necessary when the burdens of public works were considered onerous. Nobles had to be induced to make voluntary gifts to the public, and since the gift brought no financial rewards and the failure to give was not punished by any legal sanctions, they had to be induced with ego-stroking promises of gratitude.

The circle of benefit for honor did not stop with one round. An inscription or a statue not only was repayment for a benefit given but also won the benefactor a reputation for generosity, a reputation that he would have to live up to or suffer—also entire cities among his clients.[11] Since generals were mostly of the senatorial class, the patrician network that gave shape and consistency to the society of the capital extended its power throughout the empire. A public honor was simultaneously an appeal from the people for further benefits. Public benefits could be paid out for more immediate political benefits as well. Roman emperors commonly distributed grain to the Roman populace during shortages. The purpose was rarely humanitarian or charitable. Too little was distributed to save many lives, and many were excluded from the distribution. But the distribution enhanced the benefactor's reputation and bolstered his political authority, especially at the expense of other less generous patricians.[12]

Good Offices

Roman moralists castigated the system, especially as it exhibited an unseemly love for honor and public glory. According to Dio Chrysostom, even those who disdain greed and gluttony commend those who "crave distinction and reputation." The modest who try to hide their incontinence in other areas are happy to carry on their pursuit of honor in public. The rewards are lousy, impressive only to "simpletons"—rewards like "crowns and front seats and public proclamations."[13] Plutarch recommended unexpected and sudden donations, given without any calculation of possible benefits.[14] Such gifts were more purely gifts than more calculated benefits.

Like Aristotle, Cicero attempted to bring patronage into conformity with an ethical ideal, but, though influenced by Aristotle at various points, he assumed that relations of dependence were unavoidable in any society. He composed his *De officiis*, one of the most extended Roman meditations on gratitude obligations, in the aftermath of the plot against Caesar and the outbreak of the civil war between Mark Antony and Octavian.[15] Caesar is named as a negative example at various points in the treatise, and though Antony is unnamed, he is likewise an example of a man who failed in his obligations. Addressed to his military son, Cicero's treatise provides an overview of the Platonic virtues of wisdom, justice, courage, and temperance, first explaining what is honorable in each area and then describing the "useful." Utility refers particularly to usefulness in advancing one's interests; the *utile* is what advances a political career in service to the state. One of Cicero's dominant theses is that the honorable and the useful are perfectly harmonious. Virtue is its own reward, but nature has cunningly designed the world so that virtue brings other rewards as well.

Originating a long tradition that ends only in the early modern era, Cicero treats beneficence and the obligation of gratitude under the heading of justice. Justice is twofold. On the negative side, justice means that no one should suffer wrong from another; on the positive side, justice is promotion of the common good. In the latter sense, justice is concerned with how "communal property should serve communal interests, and private property private interests."[16] Generosity obviously fits the second category. For Cicero, "nothing more accords with human nature" than munificence. Because generosity is supposed to promote the common good, it should not be indulged indiscriminately; "it has many pitfalls."[17] Resources are not costless, and therefore giving to one person means *not* giving to another. The wrong kind of benefit given to a person can harm the recipient, and kindness paid to the wrong person may harm the public good. Cicero lays out three rules: benevolence must not damage the recipient so that it seems to be a harm to him or to others, it should not deplete our own resources or steal our goods from those who are nearest to us (our family especially),[18] and it should be given to the recipient "according to his worth." Generosity is a form of justice because both negative and positive justice deals out what is deserved to each. The last is particularly important. A good recipient is "notably endowed with the milder virtues of moderation, self-control, and justice."[19] A benefactor has to judge the character of the recipient by his affection, the degree of association he has with us, and whether he has proven reliable in the past. If these character qualities are lacking, a benefit is not genuinely beneficial. The first rule of benevolence is to do no harm, either to the recipient or to yourself.

Cicero distinguishes between benefits paid in money and those paid in service, and considers the latter far superior. Giving money is easier, but "active help" is "nobler, more impressive, and worthier of a courageous and eminent man."[20] An eminent man like Cicero himself: he often uses his own experiences in Roman law courts as a model for his son. Most of the benefits he commends have to do with legal assistance. A patron represents his client in court, helps him write a will or a contract, and dislodges legal logjams. Gifts of money are legitimate in certain circumstances, but, following Aristotle, Cicero argues that proper generosity avoids the extreme of extravagant. It is excessive to distribute money on feasts, gladiatorial shows, public games, and chases, but generous to pay to release a friend from pirates, pay off a friend's debt, supply a daughter's dowry, or give money toward the purchase of property. Like other moralists, Cicero is keenly aware of the abuses of generosity to promote reputation and personal honor, and he is skeptical concerning euergetism. "Many people are not so much open-handed by nature as motivated by a sense of vainglory, to appear to do out of kindness many things which seemingly arise out of exhibitionism rather than goodwill."[21] At the same time, he acknowledges that there was a place for such public benefactions in Rome's early history, since it was the only way to lay the infrastructure of a great city and the only way for the right kinds of men to gain public notice. The rule of thumb for Cicero is "to lend help above all to the person in greatest need," other things being equal.[22]

Benefits of all kinds, Cicero argues, create bonds of obligation, and the recipient should display his gratitude by fulfilling proper *officia*. No obligation is more powerful than the obligation imposed by the reception of a service or a benefit. That is to say, no obligation is more fundamental or important than gratitude, expressed in an eagerness to "repay in greater measure what we have received for our benefit." In this, the grateful person simply imitates nature: "Should we not follow the example of fertile fields, which yield much more than they have received?" Generosity flows both ways. The first moment of generosity is to bestow a kindness, the second is to repay it. The first is a free act, but "the failure to repay [a benefit] is not an option for a good man, so long as he can reciprocate without injustice to anyone."[23]

Gratitude is subject to measurement of a sort. We owe greater debts for greater benefits. But the attitude of the donor also needs to be factored in. We should "attach particular weight to the affection, enthusiasm, and goodwill of the donor."[24] Cicero celebrates the bond of friendship: "Of all bonds of fellowship . . . none is more pre-eminent or enduring than the friendship forged between good men of like character."[25] Yet he insists that the state's benefits to us are such that the obligations of patriotism outweigh all others. He quotes Plato's comment that "we are not born for ourselves alone, for our country claims a share in our origins,"[26] and asserts that while "parents are dear to us, and so are our children and relatives and friends," still "our native land alone subsumes all the affections which we entertain. What good man would hesitate to face death on her behalf if it would be of service to her?"[27] When obligations compete, "our country and our parents must take the first place," even over friendship. And the debt to country is finally weightier than the debt to parents.

At the same time, gratitude is not *identical* to repayment, a point Seneca makes more explicitly and systematically. A good but poor man "will certainly be a grateful man," Cicero says, "even if he cannot return the favor." Gratitude is simultaneously repayment and retention: "the man who repays gratitude keeps [the money he receives], and in keeping it has repaid it." Neediness makes a man grateful. In need, a man "is eager to show gratitude not only to the person who has merited it, but also to those from whom he anticipates future help, for he is in need of many things." A wealthy man's gratitude is his own, and may continue with his children, but "if you defend a man of slender means who is honest and unassuming" then he will "visualize you as a ready-made means of protection."[28]

Generosity is a matter of justice, and hence honorable. But the honorable is the useful, and in the later part of the treatise Cicero examines how generosity can be used well to advance one's interests, authority, and power. Men subject themselves to others out of fear of reprisal, hope of reward, and affection. The best way "to secure and to retain influence" among men is by "winning affection," and the worst way is to cause fear (as Caesar and Antony did).[29] Service is one of the ways to obtain goodwill from the masses and from the best men. Furthermore, "what strongly rouses the affection of the masses is the actual report and reputation which a person has for generosity, kindness, justice, good faith, and all the virtues associated with civilized and affable manners."[30] Both the bonds created by generosity and the reputation for generosity enhance one's public standing. Yet benefits are not merely self-interested. A carefully chosen gift to the right person is an aid to everyone. It is an act of justice that promotes the common good.[31]

Cicero is an old Roman Republican fearful of the new imperial system he sees taking shape, and as such he is an advocate for the traditional gift and gratitude system of patronage. Under his management, virtue and utility embrace, generosity and political expediency kiss one another. He aims to reform the system and to recover the hardy Roman virtues of yore. That there might be something more fundamentally amiss with Roman gratitude seems not to have occurred to him.

Benefits and Gratitude

Cicero lived in a tumultuous political era, when it was not yet clear what might replace the fraying Republic. By Seneca's time, the emergence of the emperor as the great benefactor had shifted the center of gratitude.[32] A powerful new alliance of reciprocity had appeared, one that traditional Romans viewed with skepticism and fear. Aristocratic Romans still operated by giving, getting, and restoring favors, but the emperor was a new single focal point to patronage.[33] Emperors often went over the heads of the existing patronage networks to win the loyalty of the Roman masses through gifts of bread and circuses. Shrewd emperors attempted to extend their own interests by making use of existing networks of aristocratic gift and gratitude. The shift precipitated by the empire, however, created opportunities for the expansion of a new form of power, that of the broker. Brokers often did not have wealth, land, or other resources of their own. What they offered clients was access, the benefits of their personal connections with the nobles who had such resources. Brokers were "friends of friends" willing to use their connections to patrons for new clients. This created a triangular relationship: the client would be bound to a new patron, and both would be bound in a debt of gratitude to the matchmaking broker who had brought them together.

Written in the first century of the Principate, Seneca's treatise *De beneficiis* is the most complete extant treatment of the topic from antiquity, and the most important single treatise on gratitude and ingratitude that has ever been written. Seneca remained well alive through the early Christian period, was known to and used by medieval theologians, was read by Elizabethans, and dropped from high regard only in the nineteenth century. Seneca summarizes the assumptions and operations of Roman gift and gratitude, but his treatise is also an effort to reform it according to Stoic principles. For Stoics, only the virtuous is "good" in the strictest sense; all the external variables are morally indifferent. Stoics also believed in the spiritual equality of all men. The use of benefits for personal gain and the inequities of a patronage system violated Seneca's philosophical commitments.

In contrast to Cicero, Seneca mounts a "frontal attack" on Aristotle.[34] Aristotle outlined a theory of gift and gratitude that was consistent with the independence and autonomy of the virtuous Athenian citizen. Seneca begins from the opposite premise: he lays out a theory of benefit and gratitude that will bind men together in mutual dependence. Seneca attacks the notion that one should give to attain and maintain a position of superiority, and rejects Aristotle's insistence that the magnanimous man recalls favors done more than favors received, which strikes Seneca as a form of ingratitude. He advises givers on how to give graciously and in a way that elicits gratitude; he advises givers on how to imitate the gods in their gifts; he advises recipients to receive in a way that will gratify the benefactor so that the benefits will continue to flow. This is the goal of philosophy in general: "Philosophy teaches us, above all else, to owe and repay benefits well."[35]

Benefits and return benefits are the main ingredients of the social glue that binds society together. Nothing binds a society together like benefits and reception of benefits.[36] At times, Seneca uses the image of the dance to describe the movement of gifts,[37] and likens the flow of benefit and return by reference to a ball game.[38] If gifts dry up, then the game is up. If gifts are received but not reciprocated, the dance of society might grind to a halt. Ingratitude is thus *the* great obstacle to social cohesion. Seneca despises the ungrateful, and ingratitude is as central a theme of his treatise as its positive opposite. Statements about ingratitude form an *inclusio* around the entire treatise. At the beginning, Seneca suggests that ingratitude is the worst of vices, and nothing is more "harmful to society" than ingratitude, while the final section urges that benefactors should imitate the gods by giving even to the ungrateful.[39] Many moral ills plague society—"homicides, tyrants, thieves, adulterers, ravishers, sacrilegious, traitors"—but "worse than all these is the ungrateful man." The only things that might be worse are the crimes that flow from ingratitude, "without which hardly any great wickedness has ever grown to full stature."[40] He says that his treatise has a threefold theme: to encourage readers to "give freely, receive freely, return freely."[41] But the central issue is more specific: how is one to encourage beneficence in a world full of ingrates? Throughout, he emphasizes the need for benefactors to imitate the gods by giving even in the face of ingratitude.[42]

This, along with his Stoic philosophical inclinations, is what determines Seneca's definition of a benefit. A benefit is "a well-intentioned action that confers joy and in so doing derives joy, inclined towards and willingly prepared for doing what it does."[43] By his definition, a benefit has to be intentional. Seneca tells the story of an assassin who accidently stabbed a king in a tumor and cured him of cancer, something none of the king's doctors could achieve. This is not a benefit, though it did the king good. A benefit has to be *well* intentioned. Again, an accidental benefit, or a benefit given when the intention is evil, is not a benefit. Seneca emphasizes too that there is a mutuality in the pleasure or joy of the exchange. The recipient receives pleasure in taking, but the giver also has pleasure in giving. That is all straightforward, but Seneca controversially adds that a benefit is not the thing that is given but rather the attitude and intention in which it is given. In the transaction of benefit and return, the "business is carried out within one's mind."[44]

Benefit exchange is not the action itself but the thing that is expressed by the action.[45] Seneca uses a sign/thing distinction to explain the relationship between the object or physical benefit and the actual benefit that is bestowed.[46] At other times he admits that the word "benefit" can refer to the object or action, or to the immaterial benefit in the strict sense.

Seneca has several reasons for this "spiritualization" of the benefit. One is the "relativity" of benefits. A more valuable object is not necessarily a more beneficial benefit. Someone who gives of his surplus is giving something less relatively valuable than the person who gives out of the little that he has (widow's mite). A farm is worth more than a loaf of bread, but to a staving man a loaf of bread is the greater benefit. If the benefit is the thing itself, Seneca thinks, it is difficult to make sense of this relativity. The most absolutely valuable thing would be the best benefit. He also acknowledges the "vulnerability" of benefits. He illustrates with the example of a man who is delivered from pirates (a common illustration in Seneca) by a benefactor, but then captured by someone else. Seneca insists that the benefit of the deliverance remains even though the enjoyment of the benefit has been lost. The rescued man still owes a debt of gratitude to his rescuer.[47] All benefits are vulnerable, but the obligation remains even if the physical benefit is removed. Most important, Seneca defines the benefit exchange as a thing of the mind in order to promote the free circulation of benefits. He does not want anything to interrupt that process. If the benefit is an object, and if a return benefit is owed, then those with few resources will be discouraged about return benefits. They may refuse benefits because they know they cannot repay. But if the benefit is a mental thing, it is as easy to return as thanks is.

Much of the treatise is about proper giving of benefits. Seneca advises benefactors not to give grudgingly or harshly or demandingly. He encourages the right tone of voice and the right facial expressions that are to be exhibited when giving a benefit. If someone gives with a tone of contempt, the benefit is not likely to be received well. He condemns benefactors who intend to use the benefit to control their beneficiary. Throughout his discussion of giving, the problem of ingratitude looms large. Seneca warns benefactors not to give in a way that inhibits rather than enhances gratitude.

He also addresses proper reception of gifts more directly and in great detail. The recipient should accept "with a cheerful acknowledgment of his pleasure," and this should "be made apparent to the giver so that he gets an immediate satisfaction." He adds that "seeing a friend happy is a good reason to be happy oneself, but making a friend happy is an ever better reason. We should make evident our gratitude by unrestrained expressions of emotions and we should express these feelings everywhere, not just in the presence of the donor." If one receives a benefit, then "receiving a benefit with gratitude is the first installment of its repayment."[48] Gratitude should be public, expressed not simply to the benefactor but to everyone. It is not the benefactor's role to publicize his generosity, but it is the recipient's role to do so: "The giver should only generate publicity about his gift to the extent that doing so will give pleasure to the recipient, but the recipient should hold a public meeting. . . . Some people express their gratitude secretly, off in a corner just whispering in the donor's ear. That is not diffidence; it is a way of denying the gift. Someone who eliminates witnesses before expressing thanks is actually ungrateful."[49] The praise offered should not be stingy and subdued, but effusive. Some receive benefits with disdain, suggesting that they have an "I don't need this" attitude. Others accept favors with passivity, and another "mumbles his thanks, barely moving his lips." None of these is a proper expression of thanks. Rather, "one must express one's gratitude with an intensity that corresponds to the significance of the gifts." Seneca offers some suggested responses: "You have put more people in your debt than you are aware" and "you don't know all that you have done for me" and "I will never be able to repay the favor."[50] The praise should not minimize the benefit given, but on the contrary maximize. Exaggerate the importance and value of the benefit, Seneca says, rather than the opposite. Among the public obligations of gratitude is the act of paying respect to the benefactor. One ought not be reluctant about showing up "to pay their public respects to those to whom they owe their life or their rank in society."[51] A recipient of a gift should always be dissatisfied with his expressions of thanks. No amount of effusive thanks is sufficient: "not being able to hope to match the benefit one has received, this is the mark of a truly grateful mind." One responds gratefully when one begins immediately to think about how to repay the debt. There may be a delay between reception and actual repayment, but there should be no temporal gap between reception and the eager search for a way to repay.[52]

Ingratitude has several sources.[53] It arises from pride, the belief that we deserve more than we have received. Greed fosters ingratitude, too. Seneca defines greed in temporal terms as a future orientation that is never satisfied with what has been offered and given in the past. Ambition is a species of greed. People who are intent on the future, he says, "have fragile memories," and memory is tightly bound to gratitude. Another source of ingratitude is envy, the habit of comparing the benefits we enjoy to the benefits that others have received. Perhaps the most important source of ingratitude, though, is simple forgetfulness. "Memory makes a person grateful,"[54] but the ungrateful person is one who has forgotten benefits received and the obligations that these benefits impose. The forgetful are never grateful.[55] The forgetfulness of benefits is not accidental; it is a culpable moral failure. The person who forgets a benefit has clearly failed to turn the favor over and over in his mind. Other desires for other goods have moved in and crowded out the memory of the benefit that has been received.[56] Seneca above all wants to emphasize that ingratitude is inexcusable. Returning a benefit is so easy, since the exchange takes place in the mind. To be sure, once thanks is given, and the obligations for the benefit is restored, one still has to return a thing. But that is technically separate, and reception with a kindly attitude is sufficient to pay the debt that the benefit imposes.[57] In all this, Seneca turns Aristotle upside down and gives him a good shake: the *benefactor* is to forget what he has given; the *recipient* is to nurse the memory of the favor, and return thanks loudly and often.

A cynic might read *De beneficiis* as ideology in the strictest Marxist sense, a treatise providing ethical cover for a patronage system that serves the interests of Seneca's own class. Seneca, though, has something else in view. He does not seek simply to understand the world. He aims to change it. His discussion in later books moves through a typically Stoic series of paradoxes. He addresses the paradox stated in Plutarch's *De communibus notitiis adversus Stoicos*, "On Common Conceptions," to the effect that ingratitude is impossible. Plutarch juxtaposes two statements of the Stoic philosophy Chrysippus: On the one hand, he says "nothing is useful to the base," while on the other hand "usefulness and gratitude extend to the indifferent things." If the first is true, then base men cannot be ungrateful because they have not received any benefit from a service done to them. It follows from this that ingratitude is simply impossible: good men are never ungrateful, but base men cannot be ungrateful. All this is against common sense, Plutarch says. In fact, the base receive many benefits, and insofar as they do not show gratitude they prove themselves ungrateful. The Stoic position must therefore be wrong.[58]

Seneca answers that "a bad person can receive certain things that resemble benefits (*beneficiis similia*), and if he does not return them he will be ungrateful." He cannot, to be sure, enjoy the goods of the mind, but bad people receive many bodily benefits and benefits of fortune, and "if he does not return them he is ungrateful."[59] To the rejoinder that someone who does not return a pseudo-benefit is guilty, at most, of pseudo-ingratitude, Seneca answers by returning to his fundamental subjective view of benefits and gratitude: if the base man *believes* he has received a benefit and does not respond as he should, he is ungrateful.[60] Throughout, Seneca subordinates theoretical concerns to the practical aim of keeping the wheel of benefits and gratitude spinning smoothly. His aim in raising the paradox is not to halt the proceedings but to purify giving, receiving, and grateful response. He eliminates theoretical dodges that might justify ingratitude, just as he attacks the practical dodges.

Seneca's purified patronage has a Stoic flavor. Gifts ought to be given for their own sake, even to the ungrateful, because virtue—in this case, the virtue of generosity—is its own reward. Givers ought to imitate the generous gods, and the generosity of nature that gives without distinguishing worthy and unworthy recipients. Similarly, gratitude ought to be expressed for its own sake. Gratitude arising from fear is servile; gratitude that seeks only future benefits is only flattery, not virtuous gratitude. If ingratitude is not renounced and avoided for its own sake, then fellowship will be removed from human society, and that is to destroy life itself: "Remove fellowship and you will destroy the unity of mankind on which our life depends."[61]

Seneca's Stoic "egalitarianism" is evident throughout the treatise. He probes the question of whether children can provide benefits to their parents, or servants to their masters. A long tradition had made the parent-child relation the paradigm of unrequitable benefits. Because parents give life to the child, and because life is the prerequisite for everything else the child might do, a child can never repay his parents adequately.[62] To be sure, "I could not have achieved anything unless benefits had been granted previously by my parents." Yet the fact that the parents give benefits first does not make later achievements less valuable than the benefits they gave. Seneca claims that he himself, not his father, is responsible for the good he made of his upbringing and education. After all, "there are some things whose beginnings depend on others but which nevertheless become greater than their beginnings."[63] A son can, for instance, enhance his father's reputation by his achievements. To his father, he says, "you gave me to myself as an unschooled and inexperienced person, and I have given you a son whom you can be proud of having fathered."[64]

He follows a similar line of argument in discussing a servant's capacity to benefit a master. A slave's normal work cannot be considered a benefit. It is merely service. But what of a slave who "has refused to betray his master's secrets" and "has done all he could to avert the suspicions of his interrogator"? How can anyone deny that a loyal slave such as this has benefited his master?[65] Again, Seneca's mental/intellectual conception of the benefit does some of his work for him: "What matters is not the legal status of the person who provides something, but his state of mind. Virtue shuts the door on no one."[66] Besides, social status is not of the essence of a man. Aristotle was wrong again: There are no natural slaves. There are only human beings, to which fortune has assigned different ranks according to the life of the body.

Whatever the state of his body, the mind of the slave remains free.[67] For Seneca, this is no theoretical point. He provides extended examples of benefits given by slaves to masters: "[O]ne slave gave his master life; another gave him death. One saved his master from perishing, and if that is not enough, saved him by perishing. One helped his master to die; another tricked him out of dying."[68]

If a slave can benefit a master, can a slave then put his master in his debt? And if a slave can benefit a master, what of a citizen with his emperor? Seneca certainly does think of the empire as a gigantic benefit-and-gratitude system: "He who takes care of everything and who protects . . . and who nourishes every part of the city as though it were himself . . . will be beloved, defended, and respected by the entire citizenry." An emperor who provides such benefits is "protected by his service" and is so fearless of opposition that his weapons have become mere ornaments.[69] Is a citizen's loyalty to the emperor a benefit?

Seneca's thesis opens this possibility, which would be a politically potent stance: a humble citizen might put the emperor into his debt. But Seneca shrank from the political import of his own argument. His political world presumes that the emperor is "always already there." He is always the first benefactor, and whatever loyalty citizens show is gratitude for a prior gift.[70] What if an emperor is *not* there? In his treason trial, C. Silius attempted to claim such a superior position to the emperor Tiberius. Designating his loyalty to Tiberius as a *beneficium*, he implicitly claimed that Tiberius was obligated to him, and in fact that Tiberius owed his throne to the loyal service that Silius had rendered. In response, Tiberius pointed to the fact that Silius had begun his career under Augustus, and thus owed gratitude to Tiberius' predecessor and through him to Tiberius. Silius had forgotten the beneficium he had received, had forgotten that his loyal service to Tiberius was a grateful response to Augustus' favors; he was guilty of the highest ingratitude. Silius committed suicide. The trial decided the theoretical question. Tiberius and Roman law agreed with Seneca: The emperor is always already there; he stands outside the exchange system. He imposes debts. Debts can never be imposed on him.[71] Gratia be to Caesar for all his many beneficia.

Conclusion

Seneca was a sensitive man, virtuous in a uniquely Roman and Stoic way. Yet in his "egalitarian" treatment of benefits and gratitude, mutuality of benefit finally hardens into rigid hierarchy, and he leaves open the possibility of a totalitarian state, to which all citizens owe unquestioned gratitude. Even at their most humane, the Greco-Roman circles of reciprocity have constricted diameters. Even at its most humane, Greco-Roman gratitude cannot provide the basis for a true *body* politic, a polity of *mutual* dependence, of multidirectional gift and return that run in every direction. Seneca sees such a body politic through a glass darkly, but it is better realized in the letters of his contemporary, the apostle Paul.[72]

THREE

Ingrates and the Infinite Circle

Christians exasperated Romans. They were sacrilegious atheists who defied the Roman gods. Bringing a new religion into the empire was well and good, for tolerant religious diversity was the genius of the empire. But proclaiming a god so large and jealous that he displaced all others was intolerable. Symmachus pled for "peace for the gods of our fathers, for the gods of our native land."[1] That the god was *new* added to the insult. Jews at least worshiped a God with an ancient pedigree, but this *Christos*, or *Chrestos*, or *Jesus* had only just turned up, and now his devotees appeared to be everywhere.

Christianity's religious distinctiveness supported a unique pattern of social life. They renounced all of the sacred customs and institutions of Rome. Everything that the Romans held sacred, they treated with contempt. Some pagans admired the piety of Christians, their peacefulness and charity. But others denounced them as antisocial. They were more loyal to the "brothers" of their sect than to their families, something that family-values Romans could look on only with horror. Wives disobeyed their husbands, husbands abandoned wives, daughters like Perpetua clung to Christ in the face of desperate parental appeals.[2] Christians had to be eliminated, Tacitus said, because they were "haters of mankind," and they were tearing up the solid foundations of Roman society.[3]

At every point, Christians proved themselves to be deeply ungrateful people. Roman worship was part of an ongoing circle of charis and gratia, a discharge of a debt incurred by reception of the favor and favors of the gods. Aristotle expressed an ancient (and modern) commonplace when he observed that children incurred an unpayable debt to their parents for the sheer gift of life,[4] and Romans agreed with the Socrates of Plato's *Crito* and of Xenophon's *Memorabilia*, who emphasized that citizens owed grateful obedience in exchange for the state's gifts of life, education, and safety. Christianity first appeared in the aftermath of the great Augustan age of grace, when Romans had brought peace and safety to the world. Christians could not have cared less, and instead seemed to be seeking another age of grace governed by another lord and benefactor, the criminal Jesus. Christians were willing to break all these bonds of gift and gratitude, ready even to break the bonds of patronage and benefaction, even while enjoying their fruits. When Diocletian learned that one of his favorites, Sebastian, was a Christian, the emperor shrieked, "Ingrate, I have given thee the first rank in my palace, and thou hast striven against me and my gods!" Then he sent the unfortunate Sebastian to be tied to a stake and shot full of arrows.[5] Diocletian's charge was more explicit than most, but the perception that the church was a community of ingrates was common among Romans.

On the face of it, it is an odd charge to level against a faith that places almost supreme value on thankfulness. According to the apostle Paul, thanksgiving was to be continuous among Christians. Paul exhorts his readers to "be thankful,"[6] and to "give thanks in all circumstances."[7] Thankfulness (*eucharistia*) is a marker of piety in contrast to impurity, greed, filthy talk, unholiness, and even idolatry.[8] For Paul, ingratitude is idolatry because it does not acknowledge God as the giver of gifts. Ingratitude is the original sin of Adam and Eve, who knew God but did not acknowledge him as God or give thanks.[9] To live in thankfulness is to live a "God-centered" life, which was, of course, Paul's aspiration for all.[10] Wealthy Christians from the first century on continued to engage in civic and social benefactions.[11] Paul expected Christians not to withdraw from civic life but to engage in euergetism in their towns and provinces, telling them they were right to expect civic gratitude in return.[12]

This high valorization of gratitude and condemnation of ingratitude remained a constant of Christian thought throughout the early centuries. In the fifth century, Salvian the Presbyter described Christian thanksgiving in terms that any Roman would have recognized: "We strive to compensate our Lord God in worship, honor and reverence for the benefits we have received from him." Because "we receive good things from him we return Him good things." For Salvian, the true reciprocal gift for divine favor was not the sacrifice of an animal but good works, joy, penitence, heart-felt thanksgiving.[13] Such "spiritualization" of sacrificial reciprocity had been common among the Roman elites for centuries, and it could hardly arouse the ire of an emperor.

Were then Roman perceptions and suspicions entirely groundless? I think not. The history of Western gratitude, like the history of Western intellectual life generally, originates in the clash and cooperation of two regimes of gift and gratitude—the Greco-Roman (especially Roman) and the Christian. Romans sniffed something new in Christian giving and gratitude, and to them it was putrid. The differences between Greco-Roman reciprocity and Christian giving must, however, be carefully worked out. Despite some statements of Jesus in the gospels, early Christian giving did not, as many moderns have suggested, flatten the circle of reciprocity into a straight line of selfless, agapic altruism. Moses, Jesus, and Paul all speak as much of circles of gift and gratitude as Homer and Aristotle, Cicero and Seneca. What Christianity did was to expand the circle of reciprocity and extend the field of gratitude until it covered everything and every circumstance. In the process of this expansion, they burst the smaller circles of Roman gift and gratitude and seemed to leave nothing in their place. Judged by the standards of the ancient world, Christianity introduced the possibility of holy *in*gratitude, and thus sowed seeds of a new form of social life in Greco-Roman soil.

Gifts and Thanks in Ancient Israel

Christianity grew from a Jewish root, and the later Christian pattern of gift and gratitude was evident already in the Scriptures of the Jews.[14] Generosity was incumbent on all Israelites. Israelites were specifically directed toward the poor, and especially the poor within Israel. "You shall not harden your heart, nor close your hand from your poor brother; but you shall freely open your hand to him, and shall generously lend him sufficient for his need. . . . I command you, saying, 'You shall freely open your hand to your brother,'" Moses instructed the people on the plains of Moab.[15] Every third year, a tenth of the land's production was devoted to those without means of support—Levites without inherited land, aliens, orphans, and widows.[16] Loans were to be cancelled every seven years and at the Jubilee. After seven years, loans matured into gifts.[17] Charity to the poor was woven into the agricultural practices of ancient Israelite farmers. They were forbidden to harvest to the corners of their fields and prohibited from going back to retrieve dropped sheaves. Those "gleanings" were instead to be left to the poor.[18] Though much of the economic instruction of the Torah reflects general ancient Near Eastern custom, Israel's system was uniquely oriented to providing for the needs of the marginal.[19]

As in ancient Greece, hospitality is a duty. Like Baucis and Philemon, Abraham and Sarah display righteousness by welcoming the strangers who turn out to be Yahweh and his angel,[20] and Lot exhibits an Abraham-like generosity to angelic strangers as well.[21] The Abrahamic pattern is written into the law. Israel is never to forget her experience as strangers in Egypt, and remembering that experience they are to sympathize with the strangers in their midst and treat them kindly.[22] The land of milk and honey is to be a land of hospitality, where strangers are welcome to feast on Israel's bounty, which is Yahweh's own bounty. Though the duty of hospitality is common to the Old Testament and Greco-Roman ethics, the context of the former gives it a distinctive coloring. In ancient and classical Greek civilization, hospitality was a means for establishing *xenia* relationships for political purposes. That motivation is muted if not absent in the Old Testament, and compassion comes to the fore.

Outside the Torah, too, generosity was a mark of the righteous man. One might say the same about Aristotle's virtuous, magnanimous man, whose life is marked by a virtuous use of wealth. But again the Israelite emphasis is distinctively on the righteous man's generosity to the poor. To qualify to enter Yahweh's presence, a man must work righteousness, which means, among other things, putting out loans without interest.[23] The righteous not only will have their needs supplied, but also will have enough to share: "All day long he is gracious and lends."[24] The wisdom literature promises a return on gifts: good comes to the man who lends graciously.[25] The sage of the Proverbs displays his wisdom in openhanded loans and gifts: "The generous man will be prosperous, and he who waters will himself be watered."[26] Generosity crosses the boundary between gift and commerce; it is the motivation for the one who sells on the market, for the righteous man sells rather than hoards his grain.[27] The theme is reiterated again and again: "He who gives to the poor will lack nothing."[28] "Blessed is he who is kind to the needy."[29]

In the Old Testament, "thanks" is often expressed with the word "bless" (Heb. *barak*).[30] If the generous man is "blessed," it suggests that he receives thanks in payment for his generosity. The passive form in these Proverbs, however, is a divine passive: *Yahweh* promises blessing to the openhanded, and so Yahweh is the one who "thanks." We return here to something like the ancient Greek notion of the "gratitude of the gods,"[31] but with a distinctively Israelite twist. The sovereign, single God of Israel repays with blessing those who are generous to the *needy*. This point above divine repayment, implicit in the terminology of "blessing," is explicit in many passages. When Israelites live by the generosity required by the Torah, they will enjoy the favor of Yahweh, which takes the form of material abundance. Israel gives tithes to the poor so that "Yahweh your God may bless you in all the work of your hand which you do."[32] The Proverbs reiterate the same theme: "He who is gracious to a poor man lends to Yahweh, and He will repay him for his benefits."[33] Israel's gifts operate within a circle of reciprocity, but, at least when gifts are given to the needy, this circle is not merely two-sided, not an exchange simply between a human giver and a human recipient. A third party is involved in every transaction, the generous God who guarantees that the circle of reciprocity will be closed by promising to reward those who share and practice his generosity. The promise of divine reward underwrites Israel's economy of generosity to those who cannot pay.

The emphasis on charity to the poor and the inclusion of God in the circle of reciprocity are unprecedented in ancient treatments of giving and gratitude.[34] Given the habits of ancient gift giving, the wealthy would be reluctant to give to those who are not likely to be able to repay in some fashion. Cicero and Seneca summarize ancient wisdom when he warns benefactors not to spread their wealth carelessly to the undeserving, defined as those who would be unable or unwilling to repay. Give to the just, because if the recipient does not repay in some form, no third party covers the debts. It is not all clear that Seneca would believe that someone *should* cover the obligations of gratitude. By contrast, the Torah relieves the wealthy Israelite of this anxiety, and thus dismantles the potential of stingy bookkeeping overwhelming generosity. Yahweh covers the debts of the poor by promising to reward the generous from his own infinite store of resources.

In archaic Greece, we identified two circles of reciprocity: mortals and immortals were bound in cycles of charis and return charis, and humans, especially aristocrats, were bound to one another by similar patterns of giving and gratitude. Greek civic life complicated the situation by adding other circles: the city itself was euergetes to its citizens, and within the city "private" friendships were sustained by mutual rounds of service. Roman patronage and benefaction operated in similar fashion, and, as in ancient Greece, these social circles of giving and response were "secular," parallel to the circle of divine-human exchange but separate. In the Old Testament, the divine-human circle is integrated with the social circle, at least when gifts are given to the poor. In place of the multiple circles of Greco-Roman religious and social reciprocity, the Old Testament imagines a single socio-religious circle initiated and completed by the generous gifts of the Creator. Thus, crucially, while the Hebrew Bible regularly exhorts the people of Israel to give gifts and to be generous, it includes no instructions about how the recipient should repay his benefactor. Normal social benefactions and gratitude do not come within the horizon of Torah or prophecy. There is no Mosaic or Isaianic *De officiis* or *De beneficiis*.

This is all the more remarkable because it is clear from many passages that ancient Israelites followed much the same practices of giving, reception, and return that Seneca enjoins on the Romans. As in the Greco-Roman system, gratitude is expected, and it is expected to take not only the form of verbal thanks ("bless") but also the form of material return. The characters in the biblical narratives know all about the obligation to give and repay.[35]

After Abram has defeated the four kings and rescued Lot, the king of Sodom offers to let Abram keep the plunder that he had recovered during the battle. Abram refuses in a display of magnanimity, citing an oath that he would not "take a thread or a sandal or anything that is yours, lest you should say, 'I have made Abram rich.' "[36] He is willing to be a giver of services, but refuses to receive in such a way that puts the king of Sodom in a superior position. Abram does not want to be bound, beholden to, or dependent on the king of Sodom. Abram's motives are unclear at this point in the narrative, but the sequel gives us a hint. He knows the character of the people of Sodom, that they are more apt to humiliate and rape visitors than they are to welcome them hospitably. Yet Abram receives from Melchizedek, the king of Salem, gifts of bread and wine, and returns a tithe to the priest-king.[37] Abram knows the dynamics of gift, debt, obligation, and return, and also about the care that needs to be taken in distinguishing those to whom he wishes to be bound from those he wants to keep at a distance. Cicero and Seneca would be proud, and perhaps even Aristotle would allow himself a slight approving nod.

Israel's patriarchs also know about gifts given to make peace. When he returns from his sojourn in Haran, Jacob sends ahead hundreds of animals in several waves to his estranged brother Esau with four hundred armed men.[38] He is transparent about his intentions: when Esau asks what all the falderal is about, he answers that he wants to "find favor in the sight of my lord."[39] Jacob knows that gifts have the power to pacify a murderous brother; long before Solomon, he knows that "a gift in secret subdues anger."[40] Jacob's "my lord" is revealing. Jacob recognizes that gifts can be a form of tribute to a superior to win grateful favor. The chapter ends with a gift negotiation, as Jacob convinces Esau to receive the gift "if I have now found favor in your sight."[41] If the gift is a bid for favor from a hostile other, Esau's reception of the gift provides assurance that his favor has been granted. Once the gift has been given and received, the two are bound. Esau displays his "gratitude" by putting aside earlier hostilities and welcoming Jacob back into the land.

Old Testament benefactors are indignant when their favors are met with ingratitude. David later operates by similar principles in his dealings with the fool Nabal.[42] While on the run from Saul, David and his men mingle with the shepherds who care for Nabal's flocks. His men do not interfere with or harass the shepherds. On the contrary, they provide protection. David naturally expects Nabal to be grateful for his service, and to express that gratitude concretely by supplying provisions for his men. When Nabal dismisses David, David's anger at the ingratitude is so intense that he marches toward Nabal's house with the intention of carrying out a war of utter destruction against him. He is arrested only by a gift from Nabal's beautiful, shrewd wife, Abigail. She brings a "blessing" (*berekah*) that pacifies David's rage. The conclusion to the story illustrates the flip side of Yahweh's promise to reward the generous. When David decides not to carry out "negative reciprocity" against Nabal, Yahweh steps in to repay Nabal for his ingratitude. Nabal's heart stops as he is relieving his bladder after a night of drinking.[43] This suggests that for the Hebrew imagination, the circulations of gifts and gratefulnesses are *never* simply intrahuman. God is always involved, not only in exchanges between rich and poor but also in those among the wealthy. Yahweh takes the side of the recipient of gifts to reward the generous; Yahweh also takes the side of the insulted to pay back the ingrate.

Greek writers as far back as Pindar emphasized the connection between gratitude and memory, and this is also evident in the biblical materials, and in some cases the expected memory for favors received is extremely long. When the Moabites and Ammonites attack Judah in the days of Jehoshaphat, the king delivers a prayer in which he reminds Yahweh of Israel's history with Moab and Ammon: "Now behold the sons of Ammon and Moab and Mount Seir [Edomites, descendants of Esau], whom Thou didst not let Israel invade when they came out of the land of Egypt (they turned aside from them and did not destroy them)."[44] Israel refused to attack Moab and Ammon at the time of the exodus in spite of the latter's provocation. Moab and Ammon "did not meet you with food and water on the way when they came out of Egypt" and went so far as to "hire against you Balaam the son of Beor from Pethor of Mesopotamia, to curse you."[45] Despite these provocations, Israel obeyed Yahweh and restrained from attacking. Now, hundreds of years after the exodus, Jehoshaphat reminds Yahweh of these circumstances, and then asks Yahweh to notice "how they are rewarding us, by coming to drive us out of the Thy possession which Thou hast given us as an inheritance."[46] Moab and Ammon should be grateful that Israel did not attack, grateful not only at the time of the nonattack but also forever after.

Many more passages might be cited, but despite the clear evidence that Israel operated according to widely accepted ancient customs of gift and gratitude, the Bible nowhere instructs or commands Israelites to *keep* these customs. The didactic portions of the Old Testament lay on Israelites the obligation to give, and there is perhaps an implied obligation to receive, but there is no explicit hint of an obligation to repay. In practice, Israelites repaid generosity by giving in return, and Israelites like David became enraged at violations of the system. But when explicit instructions are given, Israelites are always instructed to look past the human recipient to seek return payment from God, given in his own time and manner.

Given the Hebrew Bible's merging of liturgical and social circles into a single infinite circle, it is not surprising that most of the instances of the language of gratitude in the Old Testament are in liturgical contexts.[47] Thanksgiving is offered primarily and above all to Yahweh, and is offered for Yahweh's benefits toward Israel *as a people*. Thanksgiving is a communal act of covenant remembrance. It is as forward-looking as it is backward-looking. The Psalms recount God's benefits to Israel, and express hope that in the future he will continue his faithful care of his people.[48] Since Yahweh is seen as the ultimate Giver of all good, a failure to give thanks to him is idolatry, forgetfulness of the true God. Though the terminology of "ingratitude" is not often used, the narratives of Israel often describe their complaints and grumbling in the face of Yahweh's gifts.[49]

Gratitude thus typically takes form not only in verbal acts of thanks but also in ritual actions, that is, sacrifices (*todah*, thanksgiving). Hezekiah rededicates the priests so they can draw near to Yahweh to offer sacrifices and thanksgivings in the house of Yahweh, and Josiah repairs the altar to offer peace and thank offerings.[50] At the dedication of the wall, Nehemiah has the Levites offer thanksgivings with music.[51] Music accompanies the thanksgiving animal offerings. Jonah's promise to sacrifice with the voice of thanks combines thanksgiving and sacrifice.[52] The phrase "sacrifice of thanksgiving" is used in the Septuagint to translate *todah* in several passages.[53] When the Psalms talk about thanksgiving, the temple context often indicates that sacrifices of thanks are being offered.[54] This is clear too where vows and thanksgivings are spoken of together, since these are the two types of peace offerings.[55] In a number of Psalms, song is mentioned in connection with "thanksgiving," but is probably a description of two distinct liturgical acts, the offering of a thanksgiving peace offering and the joyful noise of song.[56]

The "thanksgiving offering" differs from other Old Testament sacrifices in a number of details.[57] This was the only animal offering that required bread in various forms: unleavened cakes mingled with oil, unleavened wafers anointed with oil, fried cakes of fine flour mingled with oil, as well as leavened bread. All this bread is said to be an offering to God (*qorban*), and a loaf of each form is given to the priest as contributions or "heave offerings" (*terumah*).[58] But most of the bread would be eaten by the worshiper and those who share the thanksgiving feast. An offering of thanksgiving was a feast, particularly a feast of bread. An Israelite who offers thanks prepares a "great bread" for those who celebrate with him. Thanksgiving is expressed by distribution of food. Ritually expressed, gratitude is not a circle but reception joined to dissemination.[59] Yet this dissemination is enclosed by the infinite circle, since a portion of the offering is returned to the God who is the "Patron" of the worshiper. At the temple, Israelite gratitude is social and liturgical at the same time, encompassing not only the benefactor and beneficiary but also the divine Benefactor, who is the ultimate giver of all good things.

Jews Bearing Gifts

Between the Old Testament and the appearance of Jesus, the ideology of gift and gratitude began to lean in the direction of Greco-Roman patterns of giving.[60] Examining the shifting patterns and descriptions of gift and gratitude highlights the ways that Hellenistic and Roman thought and social custom affected Jews of the intertestamental era and the first century. Here gift and gratitude provide a "stethoscope" to listen to the heartbeat of a culture in transition.[61]

A change is evident in the Apocrypha. Ben Sirach advises, "If you do good, know for whom you are doing it, and your kindness will have its effect. Do good to the just and reward will be yours, if not from him, from the Lord." On the other hand, "there is no bestowal of favor for one who supports an evil man."[62] Like the Torah and Proverbs, Sirach includes the Lord in the transaction. The reward might come from God rather than the recipient of the kindness.[63] But Sirach departs in significant ways from the Old Testament perspective. Unlike Moses or Solomon, Sirach urges the donor to be careful about the character of the recipient of his gift. He should give only "to the just," which implies that some inspection of the beneficiary is required before a gift is given. The beneficiary must qualify himself. Also unlike Moses or Solomon, Sirach exhibits some hope that repayment might come from the recipient. Also unlike Moses and Solomon, Sirach believes that part of the reason to select a just man as the recipient of largesse is that the just man is more likely than the wicked man to feel the pressure to repay the gift. A just man will be grateful and show his gratitude in returning goods or services in exchange for generosity. In all of these respects, Sirach inches away from Moses toward Seneca.

Josephus and Philo both adapt the language of Greco-Roman reciprocity in their explication of the faith of Israel. Josephus reimagines the covenantal relation between Yahweh and Israel on the model of the patron-client relation, preferring that terminology to the biblical terminology, and "much of Josephus's narrative . . . is profoundly concerned with the reciprocal relations between the Roman state and Jewish grandees."[64] All the elements of the biblical portrait are there, but they are colored by a Hellenistic overlay. Gratitude, which Josephus says is "in its own nature a just thing,"[65] thus comes into prominence in a way that it does not in Old Testament narratives. The law as a whole is a benefit to Israel, and Israel is to respond with gratitude, expressed in obedience. Josephus explains the prohibition of usury by pointing, as the Old Testament does, to the expectation that God will reward the generous, and he expresses this in terms of gratitude: "When thou hast been assistant to his necessities, think it thy gain if thou obtainest their gratitude to thee; and withal that reward which will come to thee from God, for thy humanity towards him."[66] Charity more generally is distributed in order to secure the gratitude of the recipient.[67] In his parting speech to Israel, Moses is made to speak of his role as a subaltern, a broker of Israel's relationship with God, a "minister in those matters wherein he was willing to do you good" (*euergetein*).[68] Because of this, the pious gratitude of Israel becomes a basis for the continuing relationship with God. When Abraham shows his willingness to offer Isaac, Yahweh determines that Abraham is a suitable partner, a client who responds rightly to the favors of his divine patron.[69] Solomon's prayer of dedication for the temple acknowledges that God needs nothing and is therefore beyond all recompense or repayment. It is therefore impossible for any human "to return sufficient thanks to God for his benefits." Yet man's superiority to the beasts is evident in his ability "to return thee thanks for what thou has bestowed upon our house, and upon the Hebrew people."[70] Throughout his writings, he imagined the God of Israel as a divine emperor, whose benefactions to Israel elicited the response of gratitude. Gratitude, in turn, ensured that God would remain favorable to his people.[71]

Josephus knew patronage firsthand. Prior to the Jewish war, he patronized the cities of Galilee, and after Jerusalem was destroyed, he became a client of the Flavian emperors, receiving citizenship and other benefits from Titus and Vespasian.[72] And he read both ancient and recent history in terms of those relations. "In story after story," Seth Schwartz notes, "Josephus emphasizes the social and political importance of the big man and his entourage."[73]

Philo, the first-century Jewish writer from Alexandria, likewise reads Israel's history with categories of patronage and benefaction. Philo emphasizes the infinite generosity of God, regularly describing the "maker of the universe" and "the Benefactor and King of kings."[74] So dependent are human beings on the gifts of the Creator that the only appropriate stance is a life of constant thanksgiving.[75] If God is the divine Patron and Benefactor, human beings are clients, recipients of his favor obliged to return to him both verbal and material thanks. Philo often speaks of divine-human exchanges in terms that explicitly evoke the system of patronage in the culture that surrounded him. He interprets the *aqedah* (the binding of Isaac) in such terms. Yahweh had given Abraham everything, and so Abraham repays by offering his son. The Lord returns the gift in turn by giving him back his son and then compounds the generosity by promising further gifts to his faithful servant: "God, admiring this man for his faith (πιστις) in him, giving him a pledge (πιστις) in return, namely, a confirmation by an oath of the gifts which he had promised him."[76]

Though Seneca and Cicero insist that benefits have to be repaid gratefully, they both also distinguish between the exchanges of social life and the transactions of the market. It defiles the social relation to adopt the mind of an accountant in giving and receiving gifts. Philo acknowledges a similar distinction, and satirizes the tendency to treat favors as sales.[77] Philo immediately adds that God does not give in this manner. He is "not like a seller vending his wares at a high price, but he is inclined to make presents of everything, pouring forth the inexhaustible fountains of his graces, and never desiring any return." This is so because God has "no need of anything," and because no creature is "competent to give him a suitable gift in return."[78]

For all his emphasis on divine generosity, Philo nowhere claims that God will reward the charitable for his charity.[79] Instead, his comments on gifts and responses to gift emphasize the horizontal social dimensions of exchange. Gifts create goodwill and affection. Those who refuse or neglect to repay a favor are perversely ungrateful. In his *Legatio ad Gaium*, Philo mentions the slanders that the emperor Gaius formulated against Marco, slanders that many credited as the truth. On the strength of these false accusations, Marco was eventually put to death with his wife. All of this is, Philo says, "the consequence of doing kindnesses to ungrateful people." Such people are not to be trusted with gifts, "for in return for the benefits which they have received, they inflict the greatest of injuries on those from whom they have received them."[80] In other places Philo injects the motives of Greco-Roman reciprocity into biblical passages that are differently motivated. In the Old Testament, interest-free charitable loans were supported by God's promise to reward the generous. Philo makes no reference to this promise and instead explains the prohibition of interest in terms of social reciprocity: "let the debtors be thought worthy of a humanity enjoined by the law, not paying back their loans and usurious interest upon them, but paying back merely the original sum lent. For again, at a proper season, they will give the same assistance to those who have aided them, requiting those who set the example of kindness with equal services."[81]

In the Torah, the relationship between wealthy benefactor and poor recipient is always a triangular one: Yahweh, as it were, secures both loan and repayment. Philo *de*-triangulates. He "secularizes" gift and gratitude. Philo undoes the single circle of Old Testament reciprocity and restores something closer to the multicircular patterns of Greco-Roman social life.[82] Along with Josephus, Philo represents the merging of Hebrew with Greco-Roman values that is the setting for the ministry of Jesus of Nazareth.

The Father Who Sees in Secret

Jesus was an ingrate.

He attacked the tradition of the elders. He encouraged disciples to leave, even to "hate," parents in order to follow him, and he spoke darkly of coming with a sword to divide family member from family member. He criticized the reciprocities of Jewish social life, and attacked the reciprocal expectations of Pharisaical piety. To the Jews of Jesus' time, to the pagans of Jesus' time, his innovations could be construed only as the actions of a madman, a man who had lost his mind in ingratitude.

His "ingratitude" is to some degree a matter of perception. He lived a life of continuous gratitude to his Father. To the Jews of his time, that no longer looked like gratitude. Jews had adopted Greco-Roman gift and patronage and the *philtimia* that motivated it.[83] By announcing the reign of God, Jesus aimed to detach giving and gratitude from the honor system in which it was embedded in Roman society and in Jewish life. He instructed his disciples to give generously and to receive with thanks but without participating in any honor competition. They are not to give in order to gain leverage or impose debts. Jesus assaulted the gift practices of his contemporaries. Jesus mocked hypocrites for blowing a trumpet when they gave alms.[84] For Jesus, a hypocrite is a Jew who gives to win honor from men. He is a Jew who gives but forgets that his reward comes from the Father of Israel. In a word, a hypocrite is a Jew who gives like a Gentile.

Jesus' opposition to the honor-driven system of gift and gratitude is radical. He does not, however, replace the circle of honor with a straight line of selfless altruism. Admittedly, he sometimes speaks as if giving is pure linear dissemination. "When you give, do not let your left hand know what your right hand is doing,"[85] and "Love your enemies, and do good, and lend, expecting nothing in return."[86] Yet whenever Jesus talks like this, he immediately adds that his disciples can hope for a reward from their Father. His attack on Jewish giving and gratitude was simultaneously a call to return to the triangular form of giving and gratitude found in the law and prophets.[87] Give alms in secret, not even letting one half of your body know what the other half is doing. But then he adds, "Your Father who sees in secret will repay (*apodidomi*) you."[88] Love for enemies is grounded in the same principle. Jesus' disciples can give up desire for revenge or "negative reciprocity" and love those who hate them because they know that "your reward will be great, and you will be sons of the Most High, for He Himself is kind to ungrateful and evil men."[89] As in the Hebrew Bible, the Father of Jesus is again included in the circle of reciprocity.[90] The force of this is evident in Jesus' jarring (to us) habit of introducing commercial language into religious talk. "Lay up treasures in heaven," Jesus says, in a context where giving to the poor is one way of building up one's heavenly bank account.[91]

Jesus' "eschatology," his confidence about the future, plays a crucial role in his teaching on gifts and gratitude. For Jesus, the rewards of generosity are not to be sought from the recipients of favors, and they are not to be sought necessarily within time. There is a judgment to come, and at the judgment all the good deeds of the righteous will be rewarded, as all the deeds of the wicked will be punished.[92] Be openhanded, be generous, Jesus can say: because the Father rewards at the last day. Within time, such gifts look like pure lines of altruistic self-sacrifice, but there is a time beyond time when all is repaid and restored.[93] For Jesus, generosity is at its root an act of faith; one gives not because one sees where the return is coming from but because one trusts one's Father to see in secret and to reward, perhaps in the unseeable and unforeseeable future.

Jesus' treatment of the duty of hospitality manifests the same pattern. Greeks and Romans knew the duty of hospitality, but they also used hospitality as a means for social and political advancement. An ambitious aristocrat used his invitations and guest lists and his conduct at the table to maintain and enhance his honor among his fellow aristocrats. When you invite an important person to your banquet, you are buying yourself an invitation to *his* next banquet. There is an expectation of a quid pro quo: if I invite him, he will invite me, and then I will really be in the inner ring, with the rich and famous. Similar habits of hospitality were at work in first-century Judaism.

Dining at the house of a Pharisee on a Sabbath, Jesus notes the hierarchical seating arrangements, the competition and striving for honor, the careful selection of prominent guests.[94] Jesus initially appears to give advice to help people avoid shame and gain honor: if you take a high seat, you may be required to move down, to your shame; but if you take a low seat, you can only go up. Jesus is not, however, offering tactical advice to social climbers. Rather, he assumes the stance of an honor-seeking Jew, and says that even on the Pharisaical premises, they should be humbling themselves. His more fundamental goal is to challenge the entire system. Competition for seats at the table becomes a parable of Pharisaical practice: Jews vie and compete for favor with the Divine Host, displaying their works and the strictness of their Sabbath observance and their utter ceremonial purity. God is not impressed. Disciples must follow Jesus' lead. He humbled himself, took the lowest seat, and therefore the Father exalted him to his right hand. Jesus thus instructs his disciples to renounce calculating hospitality.[95] Hospitality should imitate the hospitality of God, who gives generously to those who cannot repay him, who gives even though he needs nothing in return. Jesus does not condemn repayment. The issue is the source of the reward, and the timing. Those who seek honor from their peers in this age are wrong because they are too easily satisfied with honor and gifts that do not last. Jesus urges his disciples to look for "gratitude" or "blessing" from the Father, who rewards and repays in the age to come.

Throughout, the central theme of Jesus' teaching on gift and reciprocity is the revelation of the Father as the generous Patron of all his children. "Do not call anyone on earth your father; One is your Father, He who is in heaven."[96] Jesus' disciples have a single heavenly Patron who distributes gifts from his endless resources to all his children and who receives the thanksgiving of them all. Gifts and gratitude form a circle, but for Jesus as for Moses, God is the beginning and end, the alpha and omega of the entire system. Jesus aims not to destroy but to fulfill the infinite circle of the Torah.

For Jesus, this gospel liberates, and not only because it frees from sin. It liberates from the "principalities and powers," the social patterns and institutions that serve the powerful as the tools of enslavement and domination. In very direct ways, he promised, the practice of the gospel would loosen and undo the structures of Roman and Jewish oppression. Cicero warned his son not to dissipate his own family wealth by overly generous gifts, and Seneca told his interlocutor that a wise man gives to the just—that is, to those who can be expected to feel gratitude and return payment if possible. Jesus instructs his disciples not to act like Gentile "benefactors" (*euergetai*) who "lord it over" (*kurieuo*) their subjects.[97] As everyone well knew at the time, this was not sarcasm or hyperbole, but a perfectly scientific description of how Roman (and Jewish) rulers operated: they gave to impose debts and obligations of obedience on those beneath them; they gave with the expectation that repayment would come round. Jesus frees benefactors to give generously without anxiety about depleting resources or failing to get repaid honorably. The Father will take care of all that, Jesus says. The gospel likewise frees the recipient. Because givers look to the Father and not to the recipients for repayment, recipients are freed from debt burdens. They have repaid their debt when they give thanks to the Father who was the ultimate source of the gift in the first place. The only debts they owe are to love one another and to give thanks to God. Disciples thank God for one another, show gratitude for one another in God. But Jesus' kingdom is a kingdom without burdensome debts—not only a kingdom without financial debts but also a kingdom without social debts, where debts of gratitude are already covered by the all-generous Father.

It is a kingdom of freedom because it is a kingdom of "ingrates"—like Jesus.

Owe No One Anything

As in ancient Israel, thanksgiving had a liturgical form in the communities of early Christians. In talking about tongues, Paul says that one who does not know the tongue cannot join in the "Amen" at the eucharistia, since one cannot understand what has been said.[98] More important, the central rite of Christian worship involved a Eucharist, a thanksgiving prayer. Earlier, we examined the Old Testament's instructions regarding the peace offering of thanksgiving (*todah*), which forms one of the key ritual precedents for the Christian Eucharist.[99] Hebrews 13:15 exhorts believers to offer a continuous sacrifice of praise to God, and it naturally suggests verbal or sung praise (the verse ends by urging believers to offer "the fruit of lips that confess His name"). Yet "sacrifice of praise" (*thusia aineseos*) has more specific connotations as well. In the Septuagint translation of Leviticus, the phrase refers to the todah,[100] the bread feast of thanksgiving. "Sacrifice of thanks" is a name for the Christian Eucharist,[101] and Hebrews envisions a "continuous" (Heb. *tamid*) practice of the Eucharist.[102] The continuous eucharistic rite, along with the continuous offering of other sacrifices like generosity and hospitality,[103] replaces the continual rites of the new temple. In the temple, the tamid rites and patterns were all performed directly before God, but there was no continuous feast, no continuous thanksgiving, in Israel's temple. In the Christian temple, the church, temple rites are fulfilled in the continuous offering of the sacrifice of praise, the offering of thanks from the people of God. Thanksgiving, ritually enacted in the eucharistic feast, has replaced an entire apparatus of "continuous" actions and institutions as the liturgy of the Christian priesthood.

This, it seems, is behind Paul's claim that everything is "sanctified" (*hagiazo*) by thanksgiving.[104] Since all things are good and all are to be received with thanks, all things (*pan ktisma*) are gifts from the Creator. By giving thanks for all that comes to hand, the Christian correctly identifies the character of created things as created gifts. For Paul, thanksgiving has a performative effect on the things received. Receiving God's gifts with thanks does not merely identify them as gifts but also sanctifies them, consecrates them as holy things. The world is sanctified, made holy, through thanks.[105] To say that created things are "made holy" by thanks is to say that created things, already God's by virtue of creation, become specifically his possession by the prayers of the people of God. Given Paul's regular identification of believers as "holy ones" (*hagioi*), the logic seems to be this: Christians are holy ones, indwelt and anointed by the sanctifying Spirit of Jesus, priests to God and to Christ. As such, they ought only to touch, eat, and use holy things. If they receive anything that is impure, their priesthood will be defiled by it. Purity and holiness "taboos" continue to operate in the New Testament. Holy people must have holy things. But for Paul no elaborate rite of sanctification is required: only the giving of thanks. Once consecrated by thanks, a thing may be used only for God's purposes. Holy food could be eaten only by priests in the Old Testament, holy implements could be used only in the sanctuary, holy incense could be used only on the altar. If Christians consecrate whatever they receive by thanks, they are not only claiming it as God's own but also obligating themselves to use it in a particular way, to use it with thanks. Thanksgiving is thus the liturgy of Christian living. It is the continuous sacrifice that Christians offer. Gratitude to God is the continuous sanctification of the world.

Paul is the chief source of New Testament teaching concerning gifts, grace, graces, and gratitude.[106] Many of Paul's expressions of thanks are found in the opening sections of his letters, and in this respect Paul appears to be following a common, though not universal, practice of Hellenistic letter writing.[107] Like Josephus and Philo, Paul employs the patterns and terminology of Greco-Roman reciprocity in describing his own activities and the shape of the communities that he founds.[108] But Paul diverges from the normal practices of thanksgiving in the ancient world, and when he diverges he diverges just as Jesus did.[109]

Paul's gratitude is typically not for personal benefits but thanks to God for the recipients of his letters. "I thank my God through Jesus Christ for you all, because your faith is being proclaimed throughout the whole world."[110]

"I thank my God always concerning you, for the grace of God which was given you in Christ Jesus, that in everything you were enriched in Him, in all speech and knowledge . . . so that you are not lacking in any gift."[111] He offers thanks for the grace of God that is at work in others: *eucharisteo* for the *chariti* of God, expressed in the fact that they have received from God every *charismata*. For the benefit of "grace" and graces, he offers "good-graces." He thanks God for the response of believers to the gospel.[112] As in the Old Testament, Paul's thanksgivings are offered almost exclusively to God alone. He expresses gratitude toward the divine Patron, not for benefits done to *him* but for benefits done to *others*. What makes this odd is the expansion of gratitude beyond the narrow situation of direct benefit. Paul's indiscriminate gratitude expands beyond personal benefits, and that disrupts the small circles of traditional reciprocity. But his very indiscrimination is an offense. What place does *Paul* have giving thanks for the benefits that *another* enjoys? How, if at all, is it any different when *Paul* is the recipient?

The opening thanksgiving of Philippians answers that last question. The Philippians have assisted Paul in his ministry, and early in the letter Paul expresses his gratitude: "I thank my God for your remembrance of me."[113] By Greco-Roman standards, it is not adequate thanks. *Paul* was the one who received, the Philippians the ones who gave, and yet Paul's thanks are offered to a third party, the Father, the patron of both Philippians and apostles. Paul acts as if their gift was not directed to him at all; he calls it a sacrifice whose fragrant aroma is well pleasing to God.[114] And he certainly does not express any intention of repaying the Philippians. If they have needs, he directs them elsewhere: "My God shall supply all your needs according to His riches in glory in Christ Jesus."[115] Even when he acknowledges the favor, Paul studiously avoids the typical language of indebtedness that the Philippians would have expected from a recipient of their generosity. Instead of saying that the gift places a debt of gratitude upon him, Paul says that the gift elevates the Philippians into a "partnership" (*koinonia*) with Paul in the gospel.[116] Paul can return thanks to God for the Philippian gift because they are bound together in a single body of Christ, in a single work of the Spirit. Whatever goods come to the Philippians are Paul's too because all goods are commonly shared by the body. Even if the goods that the Philippians receive never come directly to Paul, he knows that they are benefits to the church as a whole, of which he is a member.

Still, one can hear the very Roman citizens of Philippi murmuring: we go to all the trouble, and *this* is the thanks we get—a thanks that is *no* thanks, a thanks that bypasses us to go to God? No wonder the Romans perceived Christians as ungrateful.

Elsewhere Paul sounds a somewhat Aristotelian note when he urges the Romans to "[o]we nothing to anyone but to love one another."[117] That is as much as to say, "Do not allow yourself to be put in a condition of debt to anyone." That does not mean, as it might seem, "Do not become a recipient of benefits." Paul knows that everyone is needy, dependent on God and on others for almost anything. "No debts" means that benefits are always finally referred to a single divine patron.[118] In the community of Jesus, the only debt is the debt of love. Thanks is owed, but it is owed *for* rather than *to* benefactors. Recipients of gifts are not indebted to the givers; they do not owe return payment. Givers do not impose burdens of gratitude on their beneficiaries; they cannot use their gifts to lord over recipients. The Father and his Son cover all debts, supplying all needs according to their riches. Thus, even when Paul does enter into something like a patron-client relationship, he flouts convention.

Paul subtly undoes conventions of patronage and clientage in his treatment of the charitable collection that he gathers from the Gentile churches for famine-ridden saints in Jerusalem.[119] His discussion turns on a series of word plays on charis, which, as we have already seen, is the key Greek term of gift and gratitude. In Paul's discussion, the word refers to the favor of God, to the active working of God's power in believers, to the concrete monetary contribution of the Corinthians, and, in an expanded form (eucharistia), to the thanks offered by the recipients in Jerusalem. By God's charis, he provides all that is necessary, makes the Corinthians sufficient for every good work, such that their bountiful generosity from the heart is itself a gift of God's grace. By God's charis, they give *chareis*.[120] Paul sees the churches bound together in mutual giving.

Jesus is the mold to which the Corinthians are to be conformed: being rich, Jesus became poor to make many rich.[121] That is the form that God's charis, embodied in Jesus, takes. Paul insists that if *that* Christ-formed grace is at work in the Corinthians, their lives will evidence that same self-impoverishing generosity. Yet Paul insists that God does not want to afflict the Corinthians with poverty so as to ease the Jerusalem church. Rather, he aims at equality (*isotetos*),[122] "equilibrium" or "balance" or even "reciprocity." Corinthians who supply the needs of the Jerusalem saints will someday find their needs supplied from the abundance of the saints from Jerusalem. The circulation of gifts from Corinth to Jerusalem and back is an epicycle on a larger circle that begins with God's grace to both Corinth and Jerusalem and ends with thanksgiving returned to God.[123] Within the infinite circle, communities of Christians form a mutually dependent, mutually needy body, a body in which each member community gives and receives in the confidence that the Father will balance it all out.

These connections of grace, mutual gift, and gratitude are fundamental to Paul's understanding of the church's pattern of communal life as a whole. The church is made up of those who have received the grace of God that comes from Jesus. Jesus is the great Benefactor of the church, the euergetes, the Lord who showers his favorites with gifts. He not only forms the church but also continuously supplies gifts necessary for the church to become more and more what it is. To build his church, the ascended Jesus, Paul says, gives pastors, teachers, evangelists, and other human gifts *charismata*, which contains the word "grace," charis.[124] As in the *todah* offering, proper reception of Jesus' gifts involves not only a direct return of thanks to God. Proper reception means multiplying and enlarging the gift, which is of course always itself also a gift. To receive a *charism* rightly is to use it, to disseminate it usefully in the body of Christ. Yet again this dissemination of gifts is enclosed within an infinite circle: a teacher receives the spiritual gift of teaching, disseminates it in the community, thereby encouraging someone with the spiritual gift of service to serve; the recipient of the gift of teaching gives thanks to God, who gave the gift. On the other hand, a woman with the spiritual gift disseminates her gift in service to a teacher; the teacher receives the gift, and gives thanks to God, who gave it.

Paul insists that this circle undoes any basis for rivalry and envy. The Lord gives as he pleases, giving the measure of grace and gifts. All have the same Lord, all receive from the same Spirit, and all are to rejoice in the gifts that each has. All are necessary for the functioning of the body, and those who are least favored receive more abundant honor. As with Jesus, so with Paul: eschatology, the view of the last things, plays a crucial role in his understanding of giving and reciprocity. Paul writes regularly of a final judgment to come, when each will be rewarded "according to what he has done in the body, whether good or evil." Those who persevere in doing good can expect to receive glory and honor and immortality.[125]

For all their apparent conservatism, Paul's ethics represent a revolutionary upheaval of the accepted patterns of gift and gratitude. In the Greco-Roman world, giving and reception established permanent hierarchies. Within the senatorial class, mutual favors and reciprocal benefits created a kind of equality. Yet the order of Rome depended on maintaining one-directional, hierarchical relations of gift and response. Givers were wealthy and well connected, and by their gifts they maintained their superior position; recipients were poorer and lower on the ladder, and their need for benefits was a mark of their permanent inferiority. Emperors displayed largesse in acts of euergetism, and the recipient cities and individuals could never make a return of sufficient value to balance the books. Ingratitude—that is, the refusal to make a return on a benefit—would destroy Roman order. So would inverting the flow of benefits and reciprocations. If someone could put the emperor in his debt, if patrons were as needy as clients, if clients could give equal benefits to patrons as patrons to clients, the world would be turned upside down.

This is precisely what the Romans accused the Christians of doing, because that is more or less what the Christians did. But the subversion of Roman order was more subtle than that characterization indicates. The world was not turned upside down; it is not as if the poor and the clients suddenly found themselves distributing gifts from above to their former patrons. Instead, the small circles of Roman reciprocity exploded into a network of mutual gift and reception. The exchange of gifts bestowed by and received by the Spirit worked against the emergence of a fixed hierarchy in the church. Within the church was to be a continuous exchange of gifts and honor in every direction—mutual patronage, mutual brokerage, mutual need, mutual supply.[126] This was to be no fixed hierarchy, but a seesaw.

Furthermore, Paul's goal was not merely to maintain a unified cohesiveness, even a differentiated and complex unity. Paul has something even more dynamic in view. Each gives and receives and gives again because all of them are engaged in a project of mutual *construction*. Each edifies (*oikodomeo*) others and builds up the community as a whole.[127] All are united in common need of the divine grace that circulates through the graces of the members. In the church, Seneca's vague dreams of community are, Paul says, to be realized. The church is truly a political body, where each member is dependent on the healthy operation of *all* the others. And it is a body growing up to maturity through the mutual exchange of gifts and the continuous offering of thanks to God.

Christianity's vision of the church is thus more socially and politically disruptive than the formation of an alternative society. Paul could have urged Christians to replicate Roman circles of gift and gratitude within the church. He could have flipped the Roman hierarchy upside down, ensuring the triumph of the meek. He could have created an ecclesial gift-and-gratitude system set apart from but parallel to the gift-and-gratitude system of Roman society, each running in small circles of benefactors and beneficiaries. Paul might, in short, have founded an Amish community. He did not. He instead envisioned a church whose "ingratitude," whose indiscriminate gratitude, broke open the snares of Greco-Roman reciprocity more fundamentally.[128] Paul's "no debts" rule gives each member of the society a degree of distance from the other members of the community. Paul snips the ligatures that bind one person to another in relations of debt; in place of debt he urges relations of love, patterned on the self-giving love of Jesus. Paul's infinite circle frees all from debt and thus creates individuals and a form of individualism.[129]

None of this could have been achieved by a simple redesign of the patterns of social behavior. The church's system of gift and gratitude makes no sense on purely sociological grounds. A community where everyone refuses to incur or acknowledge debts to one another seems to be a community headed for disaster. Such a society looks like the worst Marxist-postmodern caricature of democratic-capitalist-consumer society. The church's gift and gratitude nexus works only if there is *in fact* a single divine Benefactor and Patron to whom all the members are clients who owe grateful service, if all are fellow slaves (*douloi*) of the one Lord, Jesus. The church forms an "alternative society"—it is a *functional* society—only insofar as its gift exchanges are the product of a more basic koinonia in the Spirit.

Seeds of Ingratitude

Jesus was the first great ingrate in Western history, and he set the pattern for all later ingrates. With Jesus and Paul, a seed of ingratitude was planted in the European imagination, which grew to be one of our civilization's most important and enduring features. Most of those who draw from this early Christian instinct for ingratitude do not adopt Jesus and Paul wholely. They renounce tradition, but in the name of reason, not God's Word. They throw off the shackles of gratitude debts, not to give all thanks to God but to give thanks to none. In detaching Christian ingratitude from its theological basis, they create something quite new.

After all, Jesus and Paul look like ingrates not because they renounce gratitude. They look like ingrates because their gratitude is so big, so indiscriminate, that it confuses and destroys normal expectations about giving and receiving. They look like ingrates because they looked past every benefit to thank a divine Benefactor. Anyone who does not believe in that Benefactor is going to find Jesus and Paul deeply offensive, if not deluded. "Ingrate!" they will shout, like Diocletian, before calling for the archers.

FOUR

Patron Saints and the Poor

The fourth-century Christian writer Lactantius has been called the "Christian Cicero." That epithet is testament to his still-classical Latin style, but he deserves the title for his substantive contributions as well, for in a brief section of his *Divine Institutes*, he offers a Christian reformulation of the ethics of Roman reciprocity and patronage.[1] His discussion is premised on the Christian notion of spiritual equality. The God "who produces and gives breath to men" determined that everyone "should be equal" and thus "imposed on all the same condition of living." Everyone qualifies for wisdom, immortality, heavenly *beneficia*. Before God, social distinctions of master and slave evaporate, replaced by a family in which all are children of one heavenly Father: "No one is poor in the sight of God . . . no one is rich." He sounds like a Stoic: wealth and poverty are determined not by possessions but rather by virtue. If this is the true model of justice and *aequitas*, then it is clear that the Romans and Greeks, with their highly differentiated societies, could never be just.[2]

Lactantius' "spiritualization" of equality and justice might develop in a quietist direction: social and economic distinctions do not matter, and therefore everyone should simply be content with staying where he is. Lactantius, however, develops the point differently, insisting that the spiritual equality should be projected onto society, specifically through practices of mutual service. In distributing benefits, the truly just do not distinguish between worthy and unworthy recipients. Philosophers were right that hospitality is a virtue, but, Lactantius says, they erred by turning it to the purposes of utility: the houses of illustrious men should be open to the illustrious. Cicero said that liberality should be distributed to "suitable" persons. What, Lactantius asks, does "suitable" mean? Should not the houses of the illustrious be open "to the lowly and abject"? If he had the chance, Lactantius would upbraid Cicero: "You have erred from true justice . . . since you measured the offices of piety and humanity by utility." Neither euergetism nor payment of liturgies are truly beneficent acts, since they aim at making a show of liberality. They do not count as gifts, which are given only to those who do *not* "deserve to receive." Justice, piety, and humanity all demand that gifts be given to the blind, sick, lame, and destitute "without the hope of any return."[3]

Lactantius appears to replace the circle of Roman patronage and benefaction for a straight line of the pure gift. Christians are to give without any expectation or hope of any return at all. But Lactantius is still working with circles; he is working within the infinite circle of Jesus and Paul. Just benefaction to the poor is "a most acceptable sacrifice," and accordingly those who benefit those who cannot repay "will receive a reward from God." This is in fact the difference between a genuine benefit and a loan: if one expects a return "from men," then it is not "kindness" but instead "the lending of a benefit at interest." A true gift is given only if "the reward of this work and duty [is] expected from God alone."[4] The fact of miraculous heavenly return is most evident in the care of the dead. Pagan Romans saw no advantage in providing burial for strangers or the poor. Even virtuous pagans like Cicero allowed advantage and utility to set the limits of generosity, and death formed an impenetrable boundary, for no dead man pays interest. Christians, however, look to God for reward, the God who raises the dead, and so their beneficence can reach past the grave.[5]

Lactantius' beliefs were widely shared by early Christians. There are occasional expressions of pure altruism, an aspiration toward a linear "pure gift" without return. When Empress Verina visited the abbess Matrona in the late fifth century, for instance, she was surprised to find that the abbess refused any sort of payment: "Matrona asked for nothing whatsoever in return" for her service to the empress, even though she "was in no way prosperous."[6] Yet early Christians operated in a world of religious and social reciprocity just like their pagan neighbors. When they gave, they expected and hoped for a return gift.[7] Christians differed not because they renounced self-interest in giving but because they followed Jesus in looking to their heavenly Father for the return gift. They gave not in order to receive back the symbolic capital of human honor, not because they hoped that their names might appear on public placards, but rather to store up *heavenly* treasure. In each small Christian gift the cosmos shook in a drama that penetrated the boundary of heaven and earth. The "earthly language of exchange, commerce, and treasure" was extended to the heavenly world. For Christians, gifts "could be seen as loans to God" that God would repay at "unimaginable interest."[8] Gregory the Great could be so bold as to say that Christian giving put God in debt. Most were more circumspect. God is God, beyond human control or manipulation, and creatures cannot impose obligations on the Creator. Yet while strictly untrue, Gregory's extreme statement gave expression to the confidence of early Christians.

Not every gift could pierce the firmament. Exchanges in the market were earthbound. Gifts to God, though, made their way to heaven, and Christians believed they gave to God by giving to the poor. This was the most dramatic departure from Roman gift practices. As we saw in chapter 3, the Torah gave particular emphasis to generosity toward the poor, and Jesus and Paul recalled the Jews to these practices. Christians hoped to be repaid by the Father when they gave to the poor.[9] Christians reimagined the poor as "brothers" rather than distant "others," and thus in Christian giving, social lines were blurred as much as cosmic ones. The Old Testament characterized generosity to the poor in terms of justice rather than mercy. The just man gives generously, and the poor are not those who are materially bereft so much as the weak and vulnerable. Inspired by this Old Testament language, Christian leaders eventually pressed for structural and social changes on behalf of the poor. This definition of the Christian poor secured the triumph of Christianity in the cities of the Roman Empire because it implied that the church had to establish systematic justice rather than being satisfied with charitable relief. Increasingly over the early centuries, Christian writers denounced the political and legal structures that damaged the poor. In his writings on wealth, Ambrose evaded systematic oppressions like the Roman tax system, but later Christian thinkers concluded they could assist the poor only by aiming for a wider transformation of society.[10] Structural changes to secure rights and protections for the poor were at the heart of the early church's "Christianization" of the empire, which involved both a change in the external circumstances of the church and an internal transformation of the goals of Christianity itself. Concern for the poor was crucial to both shifts.[11]

If Christianity transformed Roman benefaction, Roman benefaction had a reverse impact on Christian practice.[12] Christian emperors gave legal sanction to Roman social hierarchies. The scope of Roman legal sanctions against ingratitude expanded in the fourth and fifth centuries, culminating in a decree of Justinian (530) that gave donors the right to revoke donations for ingratitude. Free clients, on the other hand, were denied the right to sue patrons who defaulted on their obligations to clients.[13] Patronage infiltrated the church. Pastoral power represented a new kind of powerless power, power without swords or troops, and the bishops managed wealth that was understood as a trust for the poor, a wealth without wealth. Even before the conversion of Constantine, which embedded the church's hierarchy firmly in the structure of the empire, signs of a "patronage" model of pastoral leadership are evident. Ambrose knew what he was about when he wrote *De officiis* for pastors. As the older aristocracies collapsed, the church shifted from "plebeian" to an "aristocratic" ideal of leadership. The change was hesitant and contested, but eventually triumphant.[14] By the end of the fifth century, the church was a wealthy institution in a world of scarcity, and bishops had taken the place of wealthy landowners as the magnates of countryside and big men of the city.

Bishops effectively became patrons, dispensing liturgical and charitable benefits to the people, who were expected to respond with grateful submission and obedience. Gifts were still thought of as benefits to the poor who cannot repay, but the role of the bishop was highlighted. According to the *Didascalia*, it is the duty of the people to give and it is the bishop's role to dispense gifts. The bishop is not accountable to the people for his dispensation, since he a servant of "the Lord God, who delivered the stewardship into his hands."[15] To every member of the clergy, it added, the laity are to "pay the honor which is right to him, by gifts and honors and with earthly reverence."[16]

According to the Carthaginian bishop Cyprian, not only material but spiritual benefits were in the hands of the clergy to distribute. Those who lapsed during persecution could be reconciled and readmitted only by the bishop, and they first had to prove themselves truly penitent by fasts, prayers, and alms. Whoever proves himself by "acts of submission" to the bishop and his *operibus iustus* in alms is welcome to return to the fold.[17] The same was expected of all the faithful. Submission to the bishop was the proper expression of gratitude for God's *beneficia* that flowed through him. Cyprian expected his subordinate clergy to play the role of clients as well. He demanded loyalty and considered them to be dependent on his favor. In fact they were. While lower clergy depended on the gifts of the faithful (*sportulae*), Cyprian himself provided the monthly *stipendia* to priests. This enabled the priests to devote themselves entirely to their ministry, but it also, importantly, left them indebted to the bishop's generosity.[18] To be sure, part of the rationale for administering alms through the church was to avoid shaming the poor or forcing them into patronal dependency on benefactors.[19] Yet the effect was to turn the bishop and priest into a patron, and as patronal patterns of gift and gratitude become more prominent in the church, the New

Testament's emphasis on a debt-free community joined in thanks to God becomes harder and harder to discern. The infinite circle that in the Bible included the giver, the recipient, and the divine Giver had contracted. God remained in the circle, but he was now accessible primarily if not exclusively through the ministrations of a broker-bishop who sponsored the donor in drawing near to God. The church became more a mirror image of traditional Greco-Roman gift and gratitude.

Expiation by Gift

Early Christian and medieval gifts were sometimes Christianized forms of euergetism, intended to enhance the prestige of the donor family. Gifts would purchase a prominent burial site in a cathedral or in the grounds of a monastery, and other social benefits would accrue to the donor. But gifts to the poor were emphasized in unprecedented ways, eventually supported by an ideology of wealth, generosity, and expiation formulated by Augustine. Some of the extreme Pelagians took aim at the wealthy, including the Christian wealthy, of the now Christianized empire. The wealthy, they thought, were not merely fools who spent their lives pursuing wealth that would rust and dissolve into thin air. They were wicked, and the only legitimate Christian response to wealth was renunciation. In response, Augustine defended the presence of the wealthy of the church, but simultaneously warned against pride: *tolle superbium, divitiae non nocebunt*—get rid of pride, and riches will do no harm.[20] The state of soul was more important than social or economic status. Practically, Augustine insisted that the rich could be justly rich only by sharing their wealth: "Let them be rich in good works. . . . This is not something you do behind closed doors. Either it is done, and is visible to all, or it is not done. . . . Let them be rich in good works, let them give readily, let them share (1 Timothy 6:18). . . . If rich people are like that, they need have no worries; when the Last Day comes, they also will be found in the Ark . . . they will not form part of the destruction brought by the Flood."[21]

Generosity to the poor was more than an obligation for wealthy Christians. It was a means of grace. Augustine insisted that prayers for forgiveness should be accompanied by alms, and the alms were something more than a sign of sincerity: "We should not only pray, but also give alms. . . . Those who work the bilge-pump lest the boat go down do so with their voices and working with their hands. . . . Let the hands go round and round. . . . Let them give, let them do good works."[22] The bilge at the bottom of the soul accumulates daily, and needs to be pumped out if the Christian is going to stay afloat. Good works, especially the good works of almsgiving, are rewarded with purification. But this is not quite a reward: God does not see the Christian giving and graciously pump out the bilge; the giving is already the bilge pumping. Again, the infinite circle of the New Testament is still operative here. God returns favors for gifts to the poor; specifically, generosity to the poor is answered by expiation of sin. But the infinite circle has become somewhat commercialized. While Augustine would deny that expiation can be purchased, generous Christians now know what they will get in return for their liberality. Gregory the Great's comment had become more literal: giving imposes on God a debt of gratitude.

The biblical accent on generosity to the poor also took on a new colorization as monasteries increasingly provided the keys that opened heaven to rich Christians. The Augustinian notion of gifts for expiation laid the foundation of medieval charity, most of which was not given directly to the poor but either to monasteries or to the church to be administered and distributed by monks or bishops.[23] Through the sixth century, "monks gradually came to eclipse the poor as the privileged others of the Christian imagination."[24] Monks had renounced material wealth and, just as importantly given the biblical notions of poverty, had given up social and political protections for a life of sustained vulnerability. As the professional poor, monks went through the needle's eye on behalf of everyone else. Gifts to monasteries were gifts to God's poor.[25] By giving land to monasteries, founding chantries, establishing foundations for colleges and other corporations, medieval noblemen were by definition doing acts of charity. The wealth of the monastery did not matter. Gifts to monks were by definition alms.

Legally, the property of a monastery did not belong to the individual monks or even the monastery as a corporation but to the dead saint. Charitable donation to the abbey was thus a donation to the saint. One gave in order to become a client of the patron saint, who served as a broker since he had a closer connection with God than the donor himself could hope for. Giving to a saint made the donor a friend of the saint, fictively a member of his kin group. Gifts to monasteries enabled the donor to become part of the monastic community itself, and a donor could hope to be given full burial rites and a grave among his monastic brothers. A gift won the giver a place among the friends of the friends of the saints, and it is always useful to have friends of friends of the powerful, especially if the powerful is the Most Powerful, Power Itself.[26]

Gifts, in short, were given *pro anima*, for the sake of the soul, or even for the sake of salvation.[27] Alms were intended as charity. These gifts were not considered payment, and in fact the language of religious gifts (*munus*) for most of the medieval period consistently emphasized that the giver, like Abel, was fundamentally giving himself (his *cor*, heart), rather than imitating

Cain in giving only the gift.[28] Still, alms givers expected spiritual returns on their gifts. Gifts to monasteries sometimes included specific terms that obligated the monks to offer prayer on behalf of the donor or the donor's family in perpetuity. Donations of land were often turned over to the monastery as the donor declined toward death, and the gift might come with a request for the monks to pray for the donor's time in Purgatory. Wealthy donors established chantries, where masses were said on a daily or weekly basis.[29] Through the liturgical activity of the monks, the dead relative of the patron was preserved in memory, memorialized before God until the final judgment.[30] Quotations from the Vulgate of the Old and New Testaments, along with the Apocrypha, encouraged alms as a means for winning salvation:

> Give alms; and behold, all things are clean unto you.
> Water quencheth a flaming fire, and alms resisteth sin.
> Redeem thou thy sins with alms.
> Alms deliver from all sin and from death.
> Give and it shall be given to you.[31]

Jesus' own words were crucial to the medieval mentality of gift: "Make friends with the mammon of unrighteousness, that when you shall fail, they may receive you into eternal dwellings." Failure to give was regarded as ingratitude. Because the clergy and monks provided the necessary social service of prayer, laymen felt obliged to show their appreciation with gifts.[32]

In all this, patterns of giving and gratitude that had originated in Greco-Roman (or Germanic) society affected the practice of almsgiving. Charity on a large scale was a Christian innovation, but it was pressed into preexisting social forms. Patronage invaded and partially colonized Christian charity.

The Largesse of Kings

"Feudalism" never existed.[33] Nor was there an early medieval "gift economy."[34] But there were gifts, and where there were gifts there were also obligations that accompany gifts.[35] Medieval society and politics were suffused with giving, receiving, and reciprocation. Few if any thought gifts were altruistic lines. Everyone gave expecting something in return. Small countergifts were often given in return for donations, functioning like receipts or surety, confirmation that the donation had been given.[36] There may have been no "feudalism," but there were fiefs, gifts of land either for past services or on promise of future service, gifts that were distinguished ritually from simple compensation.[37] Charlemagne gave gifts to the church and to diplomats, and received annual gifts (not taxes, which were slavish) from the nobles of his realm. The gifts themselves were important—horses, weapons, belts, and jewels were favorites—but the audience before whom the bestowal was performed was equally important. Kings earned the love of their people by showing their largesse, not only to nobles and bishops but also to the poor.[38] Generosity was a leading characteristic of a good ruler in the medieval period even more than the heroes of archaic Greece.[39]

Kings gave gifts to the church and to saints for the same reasons that nobles and other did—to gain forgiveness of sin—but also to make the saint a patron of their politics. When Clovis initiated his effort to drive the Arian Goths from Gaul, he ordered his men to refrain from any violence "out of respect to the blessed Martin" of Tours. "Where shall our hope of victory be if we offend the blessed Martin?" he asked. Avoiding offense was not enough, and Clovis sent a delegation with gifts to the church at Tours with the prayer that the Lord give him a sign of victory as he entered the church. When he arrived, "the first singer, without any pre-arrangement" sang the psalm: "Thou hast girded me with strength unto the battle." Assured of victory, and accompanied by still further signs, Clovis paid the vow and routed the Goths. The victory that began with gifts to the saint ended with "gifts to the holy church of the blessed Martin."[40]

Literature reinforced the image of the king's largesse. The good kings of *Beowulf* distribute rings, and the poem explicitly states that liberality in gifts is the chief way of securing loyalty in the future. The message is especially important for young warriors who need to look ahead to the time when they will be kings who need retainers to fight for them: "So must a young warrior bring it about by his goodness, by liberal gifts of property while under his father's protection, that in his old age there may afterwards remain with him eager retainers, a people who when war comes would serve him."[41] A very twelfth-century Alexander the Great in the old French *Roman d'Alexandre* displays his greatness by distributing a largesse to his nobles at his death bed.[42] Geoffrey of Monmouth commends Arthur, as do various versions of the Arthurian legends, for his generosity to his knights: "Once [Arthur] had been invested with the royal insignia, he observed the normal custom [*solitum morem*] of giving gifts freely to every-one. Such a great crowd of soldiers flocked to him that he came to an end of what he had to distribute. However, the man to whom open-handedness and bravery both come naturally may indeed find himself momentarily in need, but poverty will never harass him for long."[43] So too does the *Gawain* poet in the dazzling Christmas scene that opens the poem.[44] The fourteenth-century chronicler Pierre de Langtoft was still pointing to Arthur as the model of royal largesse. In contrast to Edward I, Arthur "shared generously [*largement*] his gain."[45]

Gifts are inexhaustible, some said. The *prudhomme* of the prose *Lance-lot* encourages expansive generosity on the ancient premise that generosity begets generosity: "Always give plenty," he says to Arthur, "and you will have plenty to give." A generous king will receive the love and generosity of his people in turn. Tireless giving wins "both worldly honour and the hearts of your people and the love of our Lord."[46] Others were more cautious. Aristotle may have been all but unknown, but his ethical mean was a standard for medieval liberality. William of Malmesbury criticizes William Rufus, William the Conqueror's son who reigned as William II, for allowing his giving to go beyond the proper mean. He distinguishes between prodigality and liberality: "The prodigal are such as lavish their money on those things, of which they would leave either a transient, or perhaps no memory in this world; neither will they gain mercy by them of God. The liberal are those who redeem the captive from the plunderer, assist the poor, or discharge the debts of their friends." Prodigality is a danger because it becomes a habit, and when a king runs out of goods to distribute he has to find more.

Gifts demanded reciprocation. A poetic Charlemagne speaks of the *dona* he distributes to Tassilo of Bavaria, his older cousin, and of the pledge of service that comes with it:

> Armrings with a great weight of gems and gold,
> A horse is offered gleaming under gold trappings,
> With these finest gifts of his lord the lad (*puer!*) is endowed
> And to him the king issued these words with placid speech
> "Receive these pledges of our perpetual service" (*perpetui servitus . . .*
>   *nostri*).
> Pouring sweet kisses on the king's knees
> The duke spoke these swift words from his breast:
> "King, to you may there be given a gift of well being in all things
> And I pay you service forever" (*ego servitium vobis per saecula solvo*).
> Thus having spoken, he withdrew to the fortress with the gift of the king.[47]

Kings should be generous. Lovers, too. Gratitude and ingratitude were central themes in the poetry of the courtly love tradition.[48] In his section of the *Roman de la Rose*, Jean de Meun has the Friend explain to the Lover how to use gifts:

> Many a reputation by fair gifts
> Has been sustained that else had fallen low.
> Many a prebendage has been secured
> By gifts of food and wine. Trust what I say:
> Good gifts give testimony of good lives;
> He's noble thought to be who noble lives.
> Presents cause givers gain and takers loss;

These forfeit freedom when to those they're bound.
What shall I say in summary? By gifts
One wins the favor of both men and gods.[49]

Writing poetry is a waste of time. Women will respond more favorably to money and shiny trinkets than to poetry, which they will read once and perhaps admire slightly.

In the courtly love tradition more generally, lovers complain and mourn loudly over the beloved's ingratitude at his attentions, and the instruction books for lovers all warn of ingratitude in the realm of love. John Gower names ingratitude as one of the servants of avarice, defining the ungrateful lover as the one who "begrudges giving anything in return" once he has had his pleasure.[50] In his formulation of the rules of courtly love, Andreas Capellanus condemned the fickle lover who enjoys a woman only to be drawn to the next beauty he sees, forgets "the services they have received from their first love," and "feels no gratitude for them."[51] Even in this romantic context, gratitude is viewed as part of a relationship of reciprocal service, though it is clearly moving toward becoming a sentiment. In Chaucer, kyndnesse, long associated with gratitude, becomes a sentiment.[52] While not unknown in the classical world, the emotional side of gratitude receives new emphasis in medieval love poetry, a portent of the future sentimentalization of gratitude. Gratitude has been dislodged from the dynamics of reciprocal giving, and has become more a matter of courtesy and proper etiquette.

Like Seneca, medieval poets, chroniclers, and thinkers recognized that gifts can go wrong. Largesse was, with courtesy, one of the wings by which one rises in esteem, wrote Raoul de Hodenc in his *Roman des eles*, but Raoul knew that it was possible to give a show of generosity while harboring avarice in the heart. Tardy gifts are dangerous because when one waits too long to give, "he who receives . . . will not feel any gratitude towards him."[53] Calculating one's gifts is also dangerous, likewise an expression of avarice. Withholding gifts to extract a specific service sows suspicion, and favors only the greedy, the easily bribed, the flatterers.[54] Gifts can be given in a way that encourages ingratitude.

Seneca and Cicero considered ingratitude the worst of vices and the seedbed of most other vices. Justice demands that everyone be given his due, and thus justice demands that the benefactor receive gratitude in return. According to Cicero, justice goes wrong in two ways, force and fraud (*aut vi aut fraude*). Fraud is a fox in its cunning, force a lion, but both are bestial actions beneath human dignity. For Cicero, though, fraud is the more contemptible (*fraus odio digna majore*), apparently because it includes an element of hypocrisy, since at the moment the fraudulent appears virtuous he is most false.[55] Precisely this Ciceronian scheme determines the arrangement of Dante's hell. *Inferno* 11.22–24 is a virtual translation of Cicero: "All malice meriting the hate of God / has, for its end, injustice. All such ends / afflict the sufferer by force, or fraud."[56] More clearly than Cicero, Dante explains that fraud is worse because it is "peculiar to mankind" (11.25–26; *de l'uom proprio male*), and Dante further distinguishes two forms of fraud, what Dorothy Sayers identified as "Fraud Simple" and "Fraud Complex." The former is fraud against a stranger, the latter and more vicious is fraud against "one who puts his faith in you" (11.53). Complex fraud is worse because it "forgets two bonds of love; / one made by Nature and one added on, / from which a special faith to keep is born" (11.61–63). As Dante well knew, forgetfulness was a dimension of ingratitude, and in placing the three traitors Brutus, Judas, and Cassius in the maw of Satan, Dante expressed a late medieval version of the Senecan and Ciceronian condemnation of ingratitude.[57]

In England, gratitude was treated as a fundamental principle of social life. Middle English translated gratitude as "kyndnesse" and punningly linked this virtue to "kin" and "kind." Being grateful was a way of acknowledging one's common humanity. Gratitude is kindness for kindness, which treats the other as kin. Thus, in his *Mirour de l'Omme*, John Gower treats ingratitude as a violation of nature.

> The ingrate who thus denatures himself
> is worse than a dog in his nature,
> for a dog, alive or dead,
> loves and defends its lord to its ability,
> but the ungrateful man at no time
> carries love or loyalty to you . . .
> Wherefore the ungrateful man is such
> that he is called "unnatural."[58]

Gower, however, is aware that social differences sometimes interfere with the formation of charitable bonds of gratitude. His *Confessio Amantis* tells the story of poor Bardus, who rescued Adrian, a Roman lord, from a pit. Adrian promises to give Bardus half of his goods in return for the favor: "Be hevene and be the goddes alle, / If that it myhte so befalle / That he out of the pet him broghte, / Of all the goodes whiche he oghte / He schal have evene halvendel." Bardus and his ass work to bring up the lord, but instead bring up an ape and a serpent who happened to have fallen into the same pit. Bardus is persistent, but when he finally draws Adrian from the pit, the lord forgets the reward and goes off with hardly a "grant merci." Unsurprised, Bardus tells his wife that night in bed, and says no more: "finally to speke oght more / unto this lord he dradde him sore, / so that a word ne dorste he sein." By contrast, the animals place themselves at the poor man's service, especially the serpent who "forth withal / A Ston mor briht than a cristall / Out of hir mouth tofore his weie / Sche let doun falle, and wente aweie." Good man that he is, Bardus is happy and goes on "Thonkende god." When the emperor hears about the precious stone that the serpent brought to Bardus, he also learns of Adrian's ingratitude and forces him to pay his debt. Bardus ends up with both the promised half of Adrian's goods and the gifts brought to him by the animals. Gower draws a lesson about "kindness":

> thus of thilke unkinde blod
> Stant the memoire into this day,
> Wherof that every wysman may
> Ensamplen him, and take in mynde
> What schame it is to ben unkinde.[59]

We shall meet this kindness/gratitude link in the following chapter in the plays of Shakespeare.

Age of *Gratitudo*

What the poets and chroniclers speak of more or less implicitly, the theologians of the later Middle Ages make explicit. The term *gratitudo* was coined in the scholastic period, and gradually replaced the classical and early Christian use of gratia for both gift and the return gift of gratitude. By the end of the thirteenth century, in fact, gratitude had replaced gift giving as a focus of detailed attention.[60] By the fourteenth century, gratitude had become something more than a fitting response in a binary exchange between a king and a nobleman, or between equally ranking aristocrats. It had grown up into a complete stance of the Christian before God. Children were drilled in the proverbial wisdom contained in the *Auctores Octo*: "Be not ungrateful to God if you wish to be graced . . . he is called 'ingrate' who is improperly grateful to a benefactor, by forgetting or by not rendering in return or by harming."[61] Johannes de Bromyard, an English Dominican of the fifteenth century, included lengthy entries on *Gratia* and *Gratitudo* in his 1485 manual of preaching, the *Summa praedicantium*. He linked ingratitude to avarice, and saw anxiety and sadness (*tristicia et anxietas*) as the causes of this disposition: "[J]ust as love makes a man generous, so sadness and anxiety of heart make him hard to God and to his family and friends. For a heart inwardly closed in sadness causes the purse to be outwardly closed, so that the man does not give alms. And it frequently happens that he who has received more from God gives less to him. But in behaving thus, these people harm themselves more than God or the poor."[62]

Scholasticism itself can be described as a form of academic gratitude. Scholasticism was defined by its social location—the scholastics were *school-men*, university theologians, rather than monks or bishops. But scholastics also aimed to provide a unified intellectual outlook for the whole of Christendom,[63] and in order to accomplish that task the scholastics had to prove the coherence of the Christian tradition. By careful linguistic and logical analysis, by their fine-grained distinctions, they were able to show that Augustine agreed with Gregory, and that both agreed with Moses, Jesus, and Paul. Degeneration into wooden traditionalism was a risk inherent in the project, a risk that later scholasticism did not escape. It was not clear that scholastics made room for the original disruption of Christian "ingratitude." At the time it emerged, however, it provided a powerful set of tools for theological reflection, powered by grateful reception, respect, and exposition of the entire Christian tradition.

Theologians sometimes found it necessary to correct common practice. Through much of the Middle Ages, wealthy families gave benefits to monasteries to fulfill the requirement of almsgiving. In his handbooks for preachers, Johannes de Bromyard, however, highlights more directly the need for the wealthy to give benefits to the actual poor. After telling of a caliph who died in his besieged capital with his gold because he loved it more than the people he should have been defending, Johannes draws this conclusion: "Demons occupy the rich and greedy if they refuse to hire mercenaries, the poor, that through them they may be delivered in the day of death."[64] Giving to the poor is the way that one can offer gratitude, the return gift, to God, and thus be saved.

The works of Vincent of Beauvais point to one of the factors that contributed to the rising interest in gratitude in the high Middle Ages. Shifting economic patterns and structures were remaking European society, and the scholastic theologians of the universities were keen to understand and evaluate the new trends. Scholastics condemned the practice of usury, sometimes on the grounds that usury interfered with the more charitable practice of doing favors without expectations of rewards. Geraldus Odonis states in a commentary on Aristotle's *Ethics* that "the usurer refuses to do free of charge what benefits another without loss to himself."[65] Without an act of self-sacrifice, a loan cannot be considered truly charitable. Vincent, however, regarded gratitude as a form of legitimate usury. Gratitude requires not only a recognition of benefits received but also return on those benefits, and Vincent cited Seneca's *Epistle 81* on ingratitude to reinforce his conclusion that "it is fraud to accept what one cannot repay." It is not enough to repay; repayment must contain an element of surplus. Anyone who refuses to return a gift in excess of the benefit (*cum usura*) is ungrateful (*ingratii*).[66] Thus, "*Gratitudo* . . . provides a metaphorical 'surplus' or category of profit even in loans of money where monetary profit was officially condemned as it was not in other kinds of exchange."[67]

The standard account of gratitude in the later Middle Ages was that of Thomas Aquinas. A summary of his comments on the subject circulated in the *Speculum morale*, regarded at the time as the work of Vincent of Beauvais but more recently recognized as an anonymous anthology.[68] For Thomas, gratitude is a virtue "annexed" to justice.[69] Justice is defined in terms of equality: "we call our deeds just if they return quid pro quo to others (e.g., the payment of wages due for services rendered)."[70] The equivalence required by justice can be of several kinds. In some cases, there is a natural equivalence, and this gives rise to natural right, but in other cases, the equivalence is established by consent, either by the consent of two contracting parties or by the general consent of a community. This latter category of equivalences is established by human will, and Thomas speaks of this as positive justice. This is valid, but the human will cannot, by itself, make something intrinsically unjust to be just. A community may agree that theft is lawful, but that does not make it just. Every virtue is "a habit that is the source of good acts," a habit being an innate, infused, acquired disposition toward a particular kind of action or behavior, and justice is no exception.[71] Since virtues are manifested in habits that produce good acts, and since virtues are defined in terms of the good acts that constitute the proper matter of the virtue, it is possible to say that "justice concerns things in relation to other things as its proper matter." Justice is located in the will, so that "acts of justice should be voluntary," and since virtues need to be enduring and not momentary, justice must be defined as an enduring disposition to act in a particular way. Again, "[t]he subject matter of justice consists of external actions insofar as they or the things we use through them are related to other persons, and justice directs us in relation to them. But we say that what is, in equal proportion, due other persons belongs to them. And so the proper act of justice consists only of rendering to others what is due them."[72]

Annexed virtues must have something in common with the principal virtue to which they are annexed. Thus, gratitude has something in common with justice—it renders a person what is due to him. All the virtues annexed to justice have this quality of being "directed to another person." But the annexed virtues fall short of the perfection of the virtue to which they are annexed. This happens in two ways: first, when a virtue falls short of justice with respect to equality (of persons or of things exchanged); second, when a virtue falls short "of the aspect of due." Religion is annexed to justice, but since we are not equals with God and cannot return to him what he has given us, piety is not justice. Filial piety falls short of justice in the same way. Gratitude falls short of justice because of an imperfection in the aspect of due. Due is of two kinds, legal and moral. Legal due "is that which one is bound to render by reason of a legal obligation." This sort of due is the proper matter of justice. Moral due "is that to which one is bound in respect of the rectitude of virtue." Gratitude falls into this latter category, and thus falls short of justice. Aquinas further distinguishes different senses of "due." Due is a kind of necessity, and it is a necessity in the sense that without it "moral rectitude cannot be ensured." This can be examined from the perspective of the debtor who owes the thing due, or from the perspective of the person to whom it is due. In the latter case, when we consider due by comparing the reward received with good things that have been done, we come to gratitude as annexed to justice. Citing Tully, he concludes that gratitude is "recollecting the friendship and kindliness shown by others, and in desiring to pay them back."[73]

Against this background, Aquinas details three features of gratitude, and conversely of ingratitude. Gratitude involves recognition, expression of thanks, and repayment "at a suitable place and time according to one's means."[74] Because the order of destruction reverses the order of generation, ingratitude develops in the opposite way: "the first degree of ingratitude is when a man fails to repay a favor, the second when he declines to notice or indicate that he has received a favor, while the third and supreme degree is when a man fails to recognize the reception of a favor, whether by forgetting it or in any other way." Ingratitude has three degrees, which again correspond to the three features of gratitude: "it belongs to the first degree of ingratitude to return evil for good, to the second to find fault with a favor received, and to the third to esteem kindness as though it were unkindness."[75]

For Aquinas, gratitude is not a purely psychological reality, but necessarily comes to expression ("thanks") and creates a debt that ought to be repaid, though the form and timing of the repayment vary. In a political setting, these features take on a somewhat different coloration, but Aquinas' triad is still workable. A populace is grateful to its rulers, for instance, when it acknowledges the benefits it receives from their government, when it gives public expression of thanks (which could take a variety of forms, from voting to patriotic celebrations), and when it repays those benefits (by, among other things, obeying laws and maintaining order). Shakespeare's ungrateful political figures fail at each of these three points—they fail to acknowledge receipt of benefits, to express thanks, and to repay for benefits received.

Aquinas argues that repayment of debts of gratitude should tend to exceed the original benefit. Gratitude should have an element of "usury," and that is because it is a just (equivalent) response to a gratuitous gift:

> [G]ratitude regards the favor received according to the intention of the bene-
> factor; who seems be deserving of praise, chiefly for having conferred the
> favor gratis without being bound to do so. Wherefore the beneficiary is under
> a moral obligation to bestow something gratis in return. Now he does not
> seem to bestow something gratis, unless he exceeds the quantity of the favor
> received: because so long as he repays less or an equivalent, he would seem to
> do nothing gratis, but only to return what he has received. Therefore grati-
> tude always inclines, as far as possible, to pay back something more.[76]

Grace is the appropriate repayment for grace received. While a gift imposes a moral obligation to make return, that obligation is best discharged in a way that highlights its gratuitous character. Though this tendency of gratitude to exceed the initial benefit is difficult to envision politically (how do citizens repay a general for saving their civilization from destruction?), it is at least clear that Aquinas does not regard arithmetic equality in gratitude as a good.[77]

Little of Aquinas' account is distinctively Christian. Believing as he does in creation, he recognizes that all things are gifts of God. He, of course, endorses the Pauline exhortation to "give thanks in all circumstances. Yet when he gives direct attention to gratitude, he follows Seneca and Tully to give a slightly Christianized version of ancient reciprocity. In his work the infinite circle of Christian gift and gratitude contracted, and this contraction was perpetuated into the following centuries.

Mystical Gratitude

Broad notions of gratitude appear among medieval writers. A notion of cosmic gift is inherent in the Christian notion of creation ex nihilo, but Anselm of Canterbury was one of the first to tease out the implications. Creation has an agent, God, but creation has no preexisting material cause. The "nothing" from which creation is made is an absolute privation. This is not a specific lack, which would be the case for something that existed but was wanting some good. The lack is not some potential awaiting actualization. Nothing but God exists before creation, and so nothing has any potential to be. Creation's lack is absolute, a privation so radical that only after the thing that was not comes into existence can we say that it lacked being prior to its being made. Creation is thus an absolute gift, a gift that has a recipient only in retrospect, only after the recipient receives the gift that gives it its existence.[78]

Following Seneca, Johannes Bromyard points out how animals are grateful to their owners, and claims that gratitude is also the ordering principle of plant life. Flowers take in the rays of the sun and "ceaselessly render back bright colors and scent." The visual and olfactory pleasures of flowers are the product of their gratitude. How much more do humans have reason to thank God, we who "day and night constantly receive benefits from God, both of consolation and tribulation." An ingrate is like a flower that says, "We do not wish to give off odor in the day but in the night." As a flower who refused to repay the sun acts "against nature," so too "the words and deeds of such ingrates are against reason."[79]

The implications of this creational cosmology were taken up among Christian mystics who repeated and developed the cosmic gratitude that we have already noted in Philo, Paul, and some of the early Christian writers. Meister Eckhardt saw creation and especially of the incarnate Son as unparalleled gifts to human beings. Behind these gifts to men is the nature of God, who is "of such a nature and of such an essence that he must give." "That man should receive God in himself is good, and by this reception he is a virgin. But that God should become fruitful in him is better; for the fruitfulness of a gift is the only gratitude for the gift." Enveloped by such gifts, one can respond rightly only in gratitude, and this gratitude produces the reality of God in the human soul. "If a human were to remain a virgin forever," he wrote, "he would never bear fruit. If he is to become fruitful, he must necessarily be a wife," and the word wife "is the noblest name that can be given to the soul, and it is indeed more noble than 'virgin.' That man should receive God in himself is good, and by this reception he is a virgin. But that God should become fruitful in him is better; for the fruitfulness of a gift is the only gratitude for the gift. The spirit is wife when in gratitude it gives birth in return and bears Jesus back into God's fatherly heart." Gratitude for the gift of Jesus is the means to the deepest union with God: "In the abstract Godhead there is no activity: the soul is not perfectly beatified until she casts herself into the desolate Deity where neither act nor form exists and there, merged in the void, loses herself: as self she perishes, and has no more to do with things than she had when she was not. Now, dead to self, she is alive in God."[80]

Other spiritual writers put gratitude and ingratitude in the center of their contemplation of God. Catherine of Siena instructs one Nanna to recall with gratitude the fact that Jesus bought her not with silver or gold but with his own life's blood. Contemplation of this truth is a protection against forgetfulness and arouses "holy and sweet gratitude" for the immeasurable love of God.[81] Unlike Eckhardt, Catherine does not view gratitude as the highest state of union with God. In the highest stages of love, "self-love is so lost that even gratitude is left behind, and man loves himself and God for the sake of God alone."[82] Mystics can ascend beyond the circle of gift and gratitude into a union where love becomes fully agapic, completely self-less.[83] On the other side, Teresa of Avila castigated herself for her "ingratitude and wickedness" toward God, because she had forgotten all his favors.[84] Her ingratitude was so deep that she "deserved hell" for it,[85] yet her very consideration of her "vileness and ingratitude" made her soul tender and brought her some consolation.[86]

In important respects, this mystical tradition captures the original Christian expansion of gratitude. Gratitude is not confined to one-on-one circular benefactions but embraces all of life. It is the movement of the soul to God. Yet at the same time, the mystics sometimes ended up in tangles similar to those of Aristotle.[87] As Aristotle's aspiration toward philosophical theoria eventually nullified the need for gift-and-gratitude relations with friends, so mystical flights tended to leave the church and fellow believers behind. In place of an infinite circle joining givers and receivers with the divine Giver, mystics tended to draw a small circle that encompassed only "me and God." For mystics, gratitude to God does not encompass but cancels the exchanges of ecclesial and social life.

Conclusion and Prospects

The medieval practice of donations, already questionable, became increasingly commercialized after the twelfth century, as gifts to monasteries became more and more calculated and contractual. Specific numbers and types of prayers and rites were specified when donations were made. The monks performed religious service for pay. In France, quid pro quo gifts to "God's poor" became increasingly common after the eleventh century.[88] During the last centuries of the medieval period, the church began to apply the principles of the new monetary economy to the supernatural system of salvation. What were once conceived as "gift exchanges" were increasingly viewed as purchases.[89] It was only a matter of time before someone would start singing about copper coins ringing in coffers to send souls springing from Purgatory.

PART II

⌣

Disruptions

FIVE

Monster Ingratitude

From its earliest emergence and throughout the Middle Ages, the Christian church's central religious rite was the Eucharist, a thanksgiving offering and meal, which became known as the Mass (from the dismissal at the end of the Latin mass, *ite missa est*). Medieval Christians viewed it as a gift exchange. In the early medieval period, it was an *oblatio* offered by the entire community of the faithful.[1] Laymen participated in the great eucharistic offering through the offertory, often enacted as a procession of gifts, including bread and wine, toward the eucharistic altar. When the Council of Macon (585) learned that some churches had deviated from the divine *mandatum* that required them to offer the "host" (*hostiam*) at the altar, it decreed that all men and women bring an offering of bread and wine each Sunday (*oblatio ab omnibus viris el mulieribus offeratur tam panis quam vini*).[2]

It was not a free linear gift. So long as the faithful offered the gifts in the spirit of Abel, offering their heart with bread and wine, they could be confident that through these offerings (immolations) they were obtaining remission of sins.[3] In the *Missale Gothicum* of the eighth century the gifts are offered with the prayer that God would sanctify and receive the gifts, and also to absolve sins (*per ea placates peccata nostra*).[4] Behind the practice of the Offertory was the Augustinian idea that the "whole redeemed community, that is to say the congregation and fellowship of the saints, is offered to God as a universal sacrifice through the great Priest who offered himself in his suffering for us." Through the gift, the church not only was cleansed of sin but also became the one body of the head, Jesus.[5] Christians may not have looked for a material countergift, but they expected spiritual benefit when they offered the sacrifice of the Mass.[6]

Two key changes took place over the course of the Middle Ages. On the one hand, the participation of the laity in the eucharistic rite declined to the vanishing point. The Offertory was slowly eliminated, and with the Gregorian reforms of the eleventh century a fissure opened up between the roles of laity and priest in the great Christian ritual of gratitude. Clergy alone began to eat the bread and drink the wine, and architectural and other liturgical changes reinforced clerical sacredness. Cloisters and choirs were marked off from clergy, the priest celebrated the Eucharist silently with his back to the congregation and often with no congregation present, the people no longer brought forward the bread and wine, and the host was changed from the bread of the "lay" table to specially prepared wafers. Communal offering *per sacerdotes* became a sacerdotal sacrifice *pro populo.*[7] Priests became quasi-brokers in a patronage system; they offered the sacrifice for the people, were able to win the favor of God, and were the conduits for the distribution of gifts to the entire people. The people no longer enjoyed a direct gift-and-gratitude relationship with God.

The other development was the commercialization of the Mass.[8] The Mass had long been conceived as a gift that evoked a countergift of forgiveness from God. Yet over the course of the Middle Ages, the rise of votive and private masses, as well as mass stipends, turned the gift exchange into something closer to a sale. Most masses of the Middle Ages did not take place in the gathered congregation, but in private, in monastic cells where monks chanted Mass after Mass on behalf of a paying patron. By their stipend, Christians could purchase a cleric's time to say Mass on their behalf. Masses were paid for to expiate particular sins, and penitential manuals specified how many penances could be removed by the performance of a mass. One mass could replace seven or twelve days of penitential fast, and the purchase of twenty masses could take the place of fasts over seven or nine months. Eventually, "precisely calculated price lists emerged."[9] The thanksgiving rite of the church was partially taken from the realm of the gift and placed in the realm of commercial exchange.

The transformation of the Mass was a result, a signal, and a cause of a revolution in Western religion. It centered on gifts and gratitude, in theory and in practice.[10]

Grace and Gift

Jesus was an ingrate. So were the Reformers. They rejected the church's settled tradition. They did not show gratitude to priests and bishops through whom the gifts of God were distributed. They brought innovation and confusion.

Reformers throughout the late medieval period raised objections to the narrow circle of Catholic reciprocity. Crassly commercial explanations of alms and donations to the church and monastery were condemned, and more subtle explanations of the circle of exchange were offered. Late medieval scholastics attempted to steer between a sacramental system that imposed a debt of gratitude on God himself and a system that seemed to leave nothing for humans to do. Gabriel Biel cut through the dilemma by developing a form of "covenant" theology using the analogy of the king's lead coin to explicate his doctrine of salvation. In times of economic crisis, when precious specie was rare, kings would issue coins made of lead. Though the lead had little or no value, a lead coin had economic value by the sheer decree of the king. Cheap lead coins counted as gold coins on the king's authority. Like lead coins, human works have no value in themselves before God and do not put God in our debt. No creature can ever make an adequate return on gifts received from the Creator and Redeemer. But God graciously accepts human works as an adequate expression of gratitude. In the covenant of redemption, he has promised to accept lead as the purest gold. Biel claimed that God does not deny grace to those who do the best with the leaden works they already possess.[11] Sophisticated theologies of this sort, however, barely penetrated the popular consciousness.[12] Closer to the popular consciousness was the legendary jingle of Jan Eck—as soon as the copper rings, the soul from purgatory springs. It was a jingle of reciprocity. Coins jingled in his collection can as they rolled around in a narrow late medieval circle.

Beginning with his *Ninety-Five Theses*, Martin Luther protested the sale of indulgences on the basis of a fresh understanding of grace and gift. The pope's pardons are not the same as "that inestimable gift of God by which man is reconciled to Him," and Luther warned that men had to be on guard against anyone who confuses the two.[13] The pope can relieve only the penalties of sacramental satisfaction, which are created by human beings in the first place.[14] Most fundamentally, the *verus thesaurus ecclesiae* is not the accumulated merits of the saints but "the Most Holy Gospel of the glory and grace of God."[15] Luther recognized that the gospel of sheer gift that he preached was fundamentally incompatible with the medieval church's theology and religious practice. Not only the sale of indulgences but also the theology and some of the practice of the Mass would have to be revised. In *The Babylonian Captivity of the Church*, Luther struck at the center of the medieval system, not by rejecting the gift but by radicalizing it. The Mass, he said, was no gift exchange, no human work performed to win favors from God. It is the gift of God to His people, to be received with faith and gratitude.[16]

Luther's mature theology was a gift theology from beginning to end. Some medieval scholastics had characterized creation in terms of "cause," but Luther, picking up a thread from both Anselm and the medieval mystical tradition, insisted that creation, like the eucharistic bread and wine, is sheer gift. It is not only creation that is given but also the Creator: "we see how the Father has given to us himself with all creation."[17] In an innovative formula, he described Christ himself as a *donum* to be *received* before he is an *exemplum* to be *imitated*: "The main teaching and central point of the Gospel is that before you take Christ as an example, you receive and recognize him as a gift and present, given to you by God and belonging to you—so that, when you see or hear that he does or suffers something, you do not doubt that Christ himself with such doing and suffering is yours, upon which doing and suffering you may no less rely than if you had done it yourself, indeed, than if you were Christ himself. Behold, that is what it means to have understood the gospel rightly, that is the abundant goodness of God, which no prophet, no apostle, no angel has ever fully expressed, which no heart can ever adequately marvel at or grasp."[18] In his Larger Catechism, he summed up the entire history of redemption as a story of God's self-donation:

> Here are the three persons and the one God, who has given himself entirely to us all, with all that he is and has. The Father gives himself to us with heaven and earth together with all creatures, that must serve and be useful to us. But through Adam's fall such a gift has become hidden in darkness and useless. On this account the Son thereafter also gave himself to us, granted us all his works, his suffering, his wisdom and righteousness, and reconciled us to the Father, in order that restored to life and righteousness, we might also know and have the Father and his gifts. Because, however, such grace would not be useful to anyone where it was so secretly hidden and could not come to us, the Holy Spirit thus comes and gives himself to us entirely: that One teaches us to know that benefit of Christ which has been shown to us, helps to receive and retain it, to use it profitably, to distribute it, to increase and further it.[19]

Despite what is often claimed, Luther did not turn the circle of biblical gift and gratitude into a linear divine gift, or human works into a pure dissemination. The grace of justification was wholly unmerited, but along with that grace God gave a gift that effectively made the sinner into a righteous person.[20] The Christ who indwells the believer is a living and active Christ, and when a believer responds to the gift of Christ in grateful faith, he produces good works. For Luther, faith fulfills the law because faith acknowledges God as God in obedience to the first commandment.[21] Luther was not an enemy of the fruit of works; what he attacked was the notion that a thorn bush can produce apples. Works do not make the Christian a Christian, but once made a Christian by the indwelling Christ, a person does works out of gratitude to God.

This "reciprocity" of gracious gift and grateful faith is evident in Luther's eucharistic theology. While rejecting every notion of eucharistic sacrifice as a self-justifying good work, he insisted that there is a return for the gift of the body and blood of Christ, a return made possible *by* the prior gift. It is not a return of things, but a self-offering in thanksgiving. "We offer bread and wine," Luther acknowledges, "solely for the purpose of giving thanks." Alternatively, he says that we offer "ourselves, and all that we have, with constant prayer." He can even speak of an offering of Christ to the Father, since the believer's self-offering is acceptable only insofar as he is in Christ.[22]

For Calvin, grateful reception meant distribution and dissemination. Not antinomian anarchy, but grateful obedience to God's law is the proper response to grace. As with Luther, this is enacted liturgically in the Lord's Supper. Those who receive the gift of the Eucharist are obliged to love one another. As in Augustine, the eucharistic meal forms a body of mutual service and ministry. Calvin emphasized indiscriminate and cheerful charity, and recognized the danger that gifts might "subjugate a person to whom you have done a benefit by making him obliged to you." Instead, Calvin insisted that one member of the body ought not be "obliged to work for the other parts because they are currently working for it."[23] Like Luther, Calvin emphasized the Eucharist as God's gift, a divine banquet that forms a community, and he complained in satiric tones about the "little sacrificers" who performed private Masses outside the presence of the community. Catholics, Calvin argued, not Protestants, are the ones who unleash the corrosive power of individual religion on the church.[24]

In social life, Protestants continued to operate by the etiquette of gift and gratitude, and this etiquette was reinforced theologically. When the Geneva Catechism asked, "Are we not to feel grateful to men whenever they have conferred any kindness on us," the answer was "Certainly." After all, God sends our benefactors so that "through their hands, as rivulets . . . blessings . . . flow from the inexhaustible fountain of his liberality." God himself thus "lays us under obligation," and God wants us to acknowledge benefactors with thanks. Whoever "does not show himself grateful to them by so doing, betrays his ingratitude to God."[25] Biblicist that he was, Calvin acknowledged the "reciprocity" texts in the New Testament, but there is a hint of defensiveness in his commentary. God is a rewarder of those who seek them, the writer to the Hebrews says, and for him this is a central dimension of genuine faith. Calvin affirmed that "no one will be in a suitable state of heart to seek God except a sense of the divine goodness be deeply felt," but under the contested circumstances of the Reformation, he added immediately that "many shamefully pervert this clause" by turning it into a text about "the merits of works" to reinforce their "conceit about deserving." True seeking of God involves "the conviction that he deserves eternal death" and a deep sense of "self despair."[26] Elsewhere, Calvin emphasized the eschatological structure of Christian reciprocity, encouraging hope for a promised reward to the end of time. Commenting on Jesus' promise that the Father who sees in secret will reward openly, Calvin notes that Jesus adds this promise because foolish men "think they have lost their pains, if there have not been many spectators of their virtues." On the contrary, "God does not need a strong light to perceive good actions." Jesus cures "the disease of ambition" by pointing his disciples to God and reminding his hearers that rewards will come "when the dawn of the last day shall arise, by which all that is now hidden in darkness shall be revealed."[27]

There is a shadow of Aristotelian individualism lurking in Calvin's claim that the strong members of the body benefit the weak, without expecting any return gift.[28] And Calvin occasionally sounded like an advocate of pure altruistic giving. Yet because Calvin stuck so close to the biblical sources, he continued to think in terms of a circle close to the infinite circle of the New Testament and the early church. Christians receive gifts gratuitously from God, pass on those gifts in serving others, which constitute a form of "sacrifice," and give alms as "a token of gratitude" toward God.[29]

Other Reformers dealt with the "reward" texts of the New Testament in a variety of ways. Pierre du Moulin pointed out that what Matthew calls a reward Luke calls "grace" (*charis*).[30] Miles Coverdale insisted on the Augustinian point that rewards given to the believer crowned only God's own works. The works that receive a reward are the Lord's works in the believer, who "useth us as instruments of his,"[31] and William Perkins made a similar point when he claimed that reward is not given to the one who works but "for Christs merits apprehended by faith," so that the correlation is not between "our merit" and the reward but because "Christs merit, and our reward."[32] Thomas Cartwright likewise insisted that the fact that there are degrees of reward in glory, as there are degrees of piety in life, "doth not overthrow the free and undeserved grace of God." Neither should be seen to open "the wicket for . . . blasphemous Merit to enter in by."[33]

But the affirmation of *sola gratia* put pressure on Protestant theologians to minimize or deny the circularity of the New Testament's teaching on grace. The tensions are especially apparent in the work of William Tyndale. While admitting that the Bible speaks of rewards, he effectively cancelled out the expectation of reciprocity. Whatever we do "must we do freely, after the example of Christ, without any other respect, save our neighbour's wealth only; and neither look for reward in the earth, nor yet in heaven."[34] Good works do not in any sense elicit a response from God, but only "testify" and "certify" that grace is at work in the believer. What is called a reward is actually only the natural result of good living.[35] Tyndale repeatedly returns to a linear conception of the gift: "he that worketh of pure love without seeking of reward, worketh truly."[36] In later Reformed theology, furthermore, concerns about eternal election swallowed up Calvin's own rich, and richly ecclesial, eucharistic piety, and as a result edged toward a linear conception of gift and gratitude. Calvinist theology often operates on a vaguely defined sacred-secular dichotomy that turns the medieval circle into a line: The sacred realm (Eucharist, justification) is the realm of divine gift and grateful human reception, but leaves no space for the worshiper to make a return gift; in the secular realm of daily life, givers give in a line that does curve around to become a return gift while recipients receive and express thanks but without incurring any obligation to return a countergift. In both realms, the circle of reciprocity is flattened. In both realms, thanks is reduced to an attitude of gratitude, unexpressed liturgically, or at best is expressed in obedience that is *not* considered a return gift.[37]

Treatises on the "arts of giving" were popular among the Puritans of the Reformed Church of England, and in these, as well as in catechisms and sermons, English Protestants emphasized the duty of generosity. In his sermon on Christian charity (1651), Edward Willan captured the precise sense of the infinite circle of the Bible: "Hee that giveth to the poore lendeth to the Lord, and hee that lendeth him shall again receive his owne with usury. The Lord himself is the poore mans surety and he that hath his suretyship is sure. Give then and it shall be given to you."[38] An overtone of threat hovers over most of these manuals. Most of the writers on gifts warn about the dangers of profligate gifts to unworthy recipients, and in the courtesy books of the same era Greek and Roman sources, including Seneca, are cited to support the early modern patronage system that engulfed English society.[39] A Protestant emphasis on one-sided gratuity and altruism also emerges in these treatises, a harbinger of the future ethics and theology.[40] While Protestants at times affirm the infinite circle of the Bible, there is a tendency to flatten it into a line of pure grace and altruistic giving.

Perhaps no one in the sixteenth century captured the conflict between Protestant and Catholic sensibilities about gift and gratitude as well as Rabelais in *Gargantua and Pantagruel*. The trickster Panurge revels in debt. Debt makes the world go round. It fosters charity, because lenders wish their debtors long life to ensure that they get repaid. If we gained nothing from others, we would be unlikely to risk life and limb to save life. Sun, moon, earth, and planets remain harmonious by mutual loans and debts, and the feet carry the body that the eyes guide because each part hopes to receive help from the others. As the blood circulates through all parts of the body, they all return the favor *en reconnaissance*, out of gratitude. Debt brings "Peace, Love, Delight, Faithfulness, tranquility, feasts, joy, jubilation; gold, silver, petty cash, chains, rings, and merchandise will skip from hand to hand." When all are indebted to all, "Will not this be the golden age in the reign of Saturn?"[41] It has psychological benefits as well, since being free of debts leaves everyone isolated and unwanted. Creditors pay regard only because of what is owed. Pantagruel will have none of it: "You shall owe to none, saith the holy Apostle, anything save love, friendship, and a mutual benevolence." Better to "work and win" than to borrow. Besides, in reality, universal debt does not the utopia that Panurge suggests. Lenders are frightening; debtors lie and cheat.[42]

The Very Modern Prince

As Rabelais' satiric debate indicates, the religious debates over gift, gratitude, and reciprocity were intertwined with wide-ranging social, political, and economic shifts. Democratic Athens provided some of the inspiration. In Athens, democracy was virtually defined as the separation of gift-and-gratitude networks from political power. But the nearer precedent came from the church, which in the eleventh century began a wholesale assault on the sin of simony, the purchase of church offices named for Simon Magus, an opponent of the apostle Peter. In the earlier Middle Ages, "access to high office was largely a matter of gift," but after the eleventh century the church began to purge out the simoniacs. Pope Gregory I had rigorously defined the sin of simony already in the seventh century. Not only cash payments but even gaining office by flattery and networking were condemned. He treated all forms of reciprocity within the church's hierarchy as sale. By the eleventh century, Gregory's strictures had become absolutized, joined with a demand for purity by an elimination of the impure influence of gifts.[43] Another Gregory, Gregory VII, revived Gregory I's strict notion of simony and used it to liberate the church from lay patronage and control and break the bonds between gratitude and office.

During the early medieval period, gifts were as fundamental to civic office as to church office, but following the church's lead late medieval towns applied something like the strictures on simony to their conferral of political power. The cities of the Swiss Confederacy drew a bright line between legitimate public gifts and illegitimate secret gifts. City officials kept thorough records of gifts received by the city and gifts given to visiting dignitaries, honorable citizens, and the like. Open gift giving was encouraged. Giving to visiting dignitaries was one of the main ways that a city gained prestige. At the public level, a variation of the old system of the honor gift was still operative. A generous city could depend on gaining a reputation for generosity. What was new, however, was the condemnation of *miet*, private gifts, which were thought to "soften" officials who should rule with hardy justice. Miet made rulers effeminate, and were metaphorically linked with sexual transgression, sodomy, and prostitution. Theologically, the secret gift was a Judas gift, a gift that seduced the recipient into a perverse form of gratitude, into treachery.[44]

Polities ruled by princes and kings were undergoing a shift in the sixteenth and seventeenth centuries as well. Largesse and liberality were no longer the main tools of power, as they had been from the time of *Beowulf.* The invention and spread of gunpowder undermined the value of large troops of horse. The age of the knight was over, and the age of the professional, paid soldier was beginning. Wages rather than largesse kept a king's armies happy. Flattering courtiers replaced fighting knights. Gifts and favors were still the currency of prestige at court, and courtiers cajoled to gain and retain their sovereign's good graces, but a courtier was no longer practically necessary as knights had been.[45] Benefits and gratitude in this setting lose some of their political heft; gratitude becomes a matter of court etiquette, rather than a part of a circle of political reciprocity. Early modern kings created their own administrative staffs, paid by the crown and loyal to it, and turned them into instruments of royal policy. The destruction of the gift-and-gratitude polity of the Middle Ages was not an accident or a quasi-natural decline. It was the result of deliberate efforts to centralize power with the king and to break the complex networks of loyalties that had formed much of medieval political life.[46]

Despite these political shifts, the dynamics of gift, benefit, and gratitude remained important for early modern political theorists. Machiavelli's reflections on gratitude and ingratitude were, as one might expect, Machiavellian.[47] Central to Machiavelli's outlook on politics were worries about the vicissitudes of time and a manly determination to overcome them. He admired the Romans, who would not have accepted the sixteenth-century advice to "bide the advantages of time." Rather, they "preferred those of their own valor and prudence."[48] Ambitious men like the Romans are made for great things. Nothing, he writes, is "more difficult and dangerous, or more doubtful of success, than an attempt to introduce a new order of things in any state."[49] One cannot rely on time, nor on benefactors. Anyone who remains subject to the "will and the fortune of those who bestowed great-ness upon them" is relying on "two most uncertain and variable things." Nor should a prince rely on his generosity to win friends: "Whoever thinks that amongst great personages recent benefits will cause old injuries to be forgotten, deceives himself greatly."[50] *Virtu*, boldness, cunning are neces-sary to achieve one's political aims.

Still, gratitude plays a political role in Machiavelli's political universe. He takes up the traditional view that gifts impose debts and win favors from the recipients. Princes need to beware of the alliances they make: "when a prince declares himself gallantly in favour of one side, if the party with whom he allies himself conquers, although the victor may be powerful and may have him at his mercy, yet he is indebted to him, and there is established a bond of amity." This is a position of strength, since "men are never so shameless as to become a monument of ingratitude by oppressing you." After all, "victories are never so complete that the victor must not show some regard, especially to justice." Gratitude paid dividends over generations. Machiavelli approvingly quotes a speech from a man who repays a debt of gratitude by giving an estate to the son of his benefactor: "in order that thou shouldst not only possess the estate which thy father left, but also that which my fortune and abilities have gained, I have never married, so that the love of children should never deflect my mind from that gratitude which I owed to the children of thy father."[51]

As traditional as Machiavelli's advice seems, his political instincts are quite different. The distance between Machiavelli and earlier writers on political reciprocity is clearest in his treatment of liberality.[52] Machiavelli admits that "it would be well to be considered liberal," but immediately warns that "liberality such as the world understands it will injure you." He clearly has in mind Christian generosity, which is to be performed in secret. A prince gains nothing by showing liberality in secret, since when liberal-ity is unknown "you will incur the disgrace of the contrary vice." To gain a *reputation* for liberality, the prince must commit himself to displays of generosity. But here lies a trap: "A prince of this character will consume by such means all his resources, and will be at last compelled, if he wishes to maintain his name for liberality, to impose heavy taxes on his people, become extortionate, and do everything possible to obtain money." A prince can be liberal from his own resources, from those of his people, or from the wealth of others. Machiavelli advises that he must be "sparing" in using his own wealth, but, especially if he is leading an army, he must be generous with other people's wealth. It is wise to "be very generous indeed with what is not the property of yourself or your subjects, as were Cyrus, Caesar, and Alexander."[53] In the *Discourses on Livy*, Machiavelli issues another warning against liberality. Conspiracies and seditions sometimes arise from a lack of generosity on the part of a ruler. But the opposite can happen too: many have become rebels "by an excess of benefits" as much as by an "excess of wrongs." In various Roman conspiracies, gifts stoked ambition to the point that "nothing seemed wanting to complete their power and to satisfy their ambition but the Empire itself." These efforts were failures. The conspirators got what "their ingratitude deserved."[54]

Given the dangers and uncertainties of liberality, Machiavelli concludes that the more prudent course is to risk appearing miserly. Over time, the careful prince will actually win a reputation for generosity because by preserving his wealth and refusing to burden his people "he is really liberal to all those from whom he does not take, who are infinite in number, and niggardly to all to whom he does not give, who are few." Miserliness is a vice, Machiavelli admits, but it is a necessary vice for those who want to maintain power: "A prince must care little for the reputation of being a miser, if he wishes to avoid robbing his subjects, if he wishes to be able to defend himself, to avoid becoming poor and contemptible, and not to be forced to become rapacious."[55]

In the *Discourses on Livy*, Machiavelli reflects on the differences between Rome and Athens with respect to ingratitude. Of these two "republican" polities, Rome displayed less ingratitude toward citizens than Athens, and the reason, he argues, is that "the Romans had less reason to suspect their citizens than did the Athenians." Ingratitude is linked here to suspicion, and he immediately links suspicious ingratitude to tyranny. Romans never lost their freedom, so "there was no great reason to be suspicious of them." Rulers had no reason to distrust the people. In Athens, however, liberty was taken by Pisistratus. When liberty was again restored, the Athenians took revenge for the loss and exiled "many excellent men." Out of this came "the practice of ostracism and every other violence which that City at various times took up against her Nobility." This contrast confirms the adage that a people that recovers liberty stings more severely than a people that retains it. The difference between the two cities, Machiavelli argues, has nothing to do with the character of the two peoples; there is no moral judgment to be made. If Romans had been deprived of liberty, they would have been as ungrateful as the Athenians.[56]

From this particular comparison, Machiavelli offers a more general reflection on the sources of political ingratitude and the question of whether the prince or the people is more likely to display this vice. Ingratitude's sources are greed and suspicion. When a commander of the army is successful on a military expedition, he deserves a reward from the people or prince.

If they are avaricious and refuse to honor him, "they make an error that has no excuse, but will leave behind for them an eternal infamy." The danger comes from the fact that "an injury is more apt to be repaid than a benefit," so that an unrewarded captain is a danger to the state. However burdensome gratitude might seem, it is little to pay to prevent revenge. Greed must be overcome and gratitude displayed.

Ingratitude that arises from suspicion is more excusable in Machiavelli's view. A captain who conquers territory for his lord gains glory and riches, and "of necessity acquires so much reputation with his soldiers, with his enemies, and with the Prince's own subjects, that that victory can be distasteful to the Lord who had sent him." The prince's suspicions are reasonable, and may even be exacerbated if the captain displays insolence and pride. The prince is enticed to find ways to parry the captain's rising reputation and power. He might send him off on a suicide mission, or diminish the achievement by trying to show that the victory was not the result of the captain's *virtu* but rather a result of chance, or the enemy's cowardice, or the skill of the subordinate officers. Suspicion is in fact so natural and powerful that the prince cannot defend himself, nor can the people. It becomes impossible "to show gratitude toward those who, by victory under their ensigns, have made great conquest." Natural as it is, the suspicion that breeds ingratitude is counterproductive and dangerous. A captain who is snubbed might well become vengeful, "as happened under Caesar who took by fore that which ingratitude denied him." The people are suspicious of powerful military officers because they want to preserve their freedom, but when that instinct for self-preservation inclines toward ingratitude, it inverts and establishes conditions for the tyranny it aims to avoid.[57]

Machiavelli offers a number of recommendations to princes to prevent the suspicions that lead to ingratitude. Rather than sending a subordinate to war, a prince "ought to go on his expeditions in person." If he wins, "the glory and the conquests are all theirs." There is no one to whom a debt of gratitude is owed. If others gain glory or they lose, it is clear that the prince is not able to gain glory except by extinguishing the glory of others. On these grounds, however, the injustice of the prince's gratitude will be plain to all, including himself, and he will be too shamed to act on it. The worst thing a prince can do is to remain behind while he sends a captain to fight his battles for him. If he does, he will invariably be stung by ingratitude, and a captain can defuse the danger of ingratitude by two methods: "either immediately after the victory he must leave the army and place himself in the hands of the Prince, guarding himself from any insolent and ambitious act, so that he (the Prince) despoiled of every suspicion has reason either to reward him or not to offend him, or if he does not please to do this, to take boldly the contrary side, and take all those means through which he believed that that conquest is his very own and not of his Prince, obtaining for himself the good will of his soldiers and of the subjects, and must make new friendships with his neighbors, occupy the fortresses with his men, corrupt the Princes (Leaders) of his army, and assure himself of those he cannot corrupt, and by these means seek to punish his Lord for that ingratitude that he showed toward him." These are the only options. If the captain is indecisive—if he is unwilling to leave his army behind after a battle, or cannot bring himself to be modest, or is unwilling to act aggressively to seize power—the delay and indecision will destroy him.[58]

Gratitude and ingratitude work differently within a Republican system. A prince can lead an army; a republic cannot. Machiavelli commends the practice of the Roman Republic: because of the Roman methods of government, the city was always full of "men of *virtu*" who could fight and win glory. Glory and praise were so diffused that the city had no cause to become suspicious of individual heroes. Thus, "not being able by such methods to generate suspicion, they did not generate ingratitude." In sum, "a Republic that does not want to have cause to be ungrateful ought to govern as Rome did, and a Citizen who wants to avoid its sting ought to observe the limits observed by the Roman Citizens."[59]

Machiavelli's work reflects the ambiguities and lacunae that we will see more fully in the next chapter's discussion of Hobbes and Locke. In political contexts, Machiavelli views gift giving and gratitude as practices and attitudes to be managed in the interests of the prince and to maintain the peace of the state. Given the manipulative thrust of much of what he writes on the subject, it is striking to note the effusiveness of his gratitude toward patrons. He opens *The Prince* with a preface to Lorenzo di Medici, where he reminds him that it is "customary for those who wish to gain the favour of a prince to endeavour to do so by offering him gifts of those things which they hold most precious, or in which they know him to take especial delight." Having no horses, arms, cloth, gems, or gold to offer the prince, Machiavelli offers the thing that is of highest value to him: "knowledge of the deeds of great men." He is certain that Lorenzo will receive the gift with favor, and is satisfied that "it is not in my power to offer you a greater gift than that of enabling you to understand in a very short time all those things which I have learnt at the cost of privation and danger in the course of many years."[60] While developing some of the same themes, the preface to the *Discourses on Livy* criticizes writers who through ambition and greed praise princes for virtuous qualities that are lacking rather than censuring them for their vices.

Rather than flatter, Machiavelli dedicates the book "to those who by their infinite good qualities" are worthy to be princes; he writes not for those "who could load me with honors, rank, and wealth, but rather to those who have the desire to do so, but have not the power." Still, Machiavelli views his writing in the context of relations of reciprocity. He offers the book as a countergift to Zanobi Buondelmonti and Cosimo Rucellai in return for "the obligations which I owe you."[61]

Try as one might, no one in the sixteenth century could escape networks of gift and obligation, patronage and gratitude. Gratitude's nets snare all, including those who imagine they possess the *virtu* to manage them.

Dramas of Ingratitude

The sixteenth century witnessed a wide-ranging disruption of traditional patterns of reciprocity. The old religious forms of gift and gratitude were disrupted by the Reformation, the rise of cities and of powerful princes and the development of military technology chipped away at medieval politics of gift, and the rise of the monetary economy recalibrated the balance of gifts and commerce in European economic life. The proliferation of written contracts was a sign that it was no longer possible to depend on traditional forms of obligation. In France, other social dislocations upended families. Economic growth and diversification gave children more choices than their parents had had, which created anxiety among parents who wanted more control over their family's future. Wills were manipulated to give reinforcement to familial bonds of gratitude.[62]

Some responded to these shifts and dislocations by renouncing what Montaigne called "the subtle science" of "benefit and gratitude." Montaigne insisted that men are freest when they can flee submission to obligations of any kind. It is necessary to "live by law and authority, not by reward and grace." One should be able to say with Virgil, "the gifts of the great are not known to me." For Montaigne and most Europeans of the seventeenth century, this "individualism" was still undergirded by theology. Montaigne wanted to be liberated from human bonds and to owe duty only to God.[63] Montaigne, Europe's first "individualist," is a very Pauline sort of individualist.

Writers of the English Renaissance responded with propaganda denouncing ingratitude and singing the praises of gratitude. They frequently cited Xenophon's account of ancient Persia's severity toward ingratitude,[64] and Seneca's *De beneficiis* was translated into English by Arthur Golding (1578) and Thomas Lodge (1614).[65] It was a Renaissance truism that ingratitude was irrational, monstrous, unnatural, and unjust, a vice and a fount of further evils, which could lead only to murder, theft, adultery, robbery, resentment, and vengeance.[66] Seneca's charges against ingratitude were repeated and repeated. The English medieval notion of kyndnesse, viewed as a central feature of social ethics, remained in place, and as a result ingratitude was not merely morally reprehensible but also socially destructive. "Concordia" or friendship was seen as "commodius to the weale-publicke," "the nursing mother of humane societie, the preseruer of states and politics,"[67] and thankfulness was in turn essential to the preservation of concordia. Benefits and gratitude for benefits were seen as the stuff of social bonds. Conversely, nothing, according to Arthur Golding's translation of Seneca, "dooth so much vnknit and plucke asunder the concorde of mankynd" as ingratitude,[68] and ingratitude was seen as the solvent of bonds between "children and the father, betweene brethren, kinsfolks & friends."[69] Ingratitude was often seen as a political evil as well. Political gratitude functions at various levels—binding the present generation to the past, the rulers to the ruled, citizens to one another—and thus ingratitude was recognized as a threat to the foundations of political life. And, since humanity is fulfilled in political community, ingratitude was seen as an assault on flourishing human life. Nicholas Breton charged that ingratitude turns men into "Machauilian fiends."[70] Ingratitude is analogous to treason,[71] and is itself an act of treason and a source of revolt.[72] Ingratitude is the vice common to the tyrant and the traitor.[73]

Ingratitude continued to be politically significant. In the second book of his 1531 *The Boke Named the Gouvernour*,[74] Thomas Elyot treats the vice of ingratitude, which he describes as "the most damnable vice and most against justice." Elyot places gratitude and ingratitude in the context of friendship, which is in turn concerned with the governor's selection of friends and favorites and the governor's need to be cautious about flatterers and false friends. Identifying ingratitude with "unkindness," Elyot provides a series of examples to define what this vice entails: "He is unkind which denies to have received any benefit that indeed he has received; he is unkind that dissimules; he is unkind that recompenses not." But the most vicious form of unkindness is forgetfulness. One who fails to return on a benefit still has some tokens of the benefit within, and these might later lead him to return thanks in time. The forgetful "may never be kind, since all the benefit is quite fallen from him." In short, "where lacks remembrance, there is no hope of any recompense."

Forgetful ingratitude makes men worse than beasts. Even beasts can remember a benefit after they have received it. A horse will allow the one who feeds him and keeps him to ride; but anyone else who tries to ride "though he be a king," the horse will throw. Animals in fact sometimes die in defense of their masters, a sign of their memory and gratitude. Elyot cites Pliny's story of a dog who "so assaulted the murderer of his master in a great assembly of people, that with barking and biting him, he compelled him at the last to confess his offense." Lions too show gratitude, though "of all other beasts . . . account most fierce and cruell," yet they "have in remembrance benefit showed unto him."

Gratitude is the bond of friendship, and these bonds should remain intact even if one or other of the friends advances in society: "How much are they repugnant and (I might say enemies) both to nature and reason that such one whom they have long known to be to them benevolent and joined to them in a sincere and assured friendship, approved by infallible tokens, ratified also with sundry kinds of benefits, they will condemn or neglect being advanced by any good fortune." Elyot lists several classical friendships, but laments that no such friendships are evident in his own day, where fair-weather friendships are the rule: "where at this day may be found such friendship between two, but that where fortune is more benevolent to the one than to the other the friendship wears tedious." Once one advances, one wants "to be matched with one having semblable fortune." If an old friend comes to misfortune, "he pities him, but he sorrows not, though he seem to be sorrowful, yet he helps not." Or, at best, he wishes to be seen to help, yet "travails he not," and though he wishes to be "seen to travail, yet he suffers not." Few "esteem friendship" to such an extent that they will "enter into the displeasure not of his prince but of them whom he supposes may advance his estimation toward his prince." It is a rare man who will "displease his new acquaintance equal with him in authority or fortune, for the defense, help, or advancement of his ancient and well approved friend." What kind of times are they when the best examples of virtue are found among beasts rather than men?

The anxieties of the age were represented dramatically in the plays of William Shakespeare.[75] *King Lear* is a chilling dramatization of the filial ingratitude of Lear's "wolfish" daughters, Goneril and Regan, who display a monstrous unkindness and ingratitude toward their aged father. The misanthropy of *Timon of Athens* is a form of ingratitude as well. Gratitude and ingratitude loom larger in Shakespeare's Roman plays than elsewhere,[76] and it is in these plays that the political and cultural dimensions of gratitude come to the fore. Dante might have written the lines about Brutus' "unkindest," because Shakespeare shared with Dante the belief that treachery was a political expression of ingratitude.

Shakespeare knew his Seneca, but for his Roman play *Coriolanus* he was directly reliant on Plutarch, who called attention to the way gratitude and ingratitude provided the impulse of the story. Having lost his father early in life, Coriolanus feels an unusual sense of filial gratitude toward his mother, Volumnia.[77] This is the key to the resolution of the story. When Coriolanus is exiled from Rome, his mother comes to woo him back to his mother city. She manipulates him with appeals to gratitude. Can it be wrong, she queried, for a great man to remember the benefits he has received from his parents? Coriolanus is not such a man; in fact he has proven himself an enemy of all ingratitude in his very attack on Rome's ingratitude: "Surely for no man were it seemly to cherish gratitude than for thee, who does so bitter proceed against ingratitude." But he has forgotten himself; while he punishes his country's failings, he falls into the same because he has "not shown thy mother any gratitude."[78] When he withdraws from Rome and returns to the Volscian camp, his Volscian enemies worry that he will win the affection of the men because "his earlier achievements secured him a gratitude which outweighed his later fault." To head off this danger, they interrupt his speech, crying out that Coriolanus was traitor and tyrant and not fit to live.[79]

Uncannily contemporary, *Coriolanus* is replete with the stuff of day-to-day political life: handlers, plots, propaganda, demagoguery, street riots, restive mobs, corrupt electioneering, and manipulations on all sides, all set against the background of a constitutional crisis and famine.[80] At a first reading or viewing, the whole play unfolds against the backdrop of the parable of the stomach, told to the assembled plebs by the patrician Menenius in the first scene.[81] All the organs of the body rebel against the stomach because, though "idle and inactive," it gets the first share of food. Deliberately and gravely and "with a kind of smile," the stomach explains, that he receives the food first only to send it through the inferior veins that keep the rest of the body in health (1.1.134–46).[82] Menenius' is a vision of a "mutually participate" social body, bound together by reciprocal benefit and assistance. Instead of enviously and ungratefully complaining against the patricians, the plebs ought, Menenius thinks, to recognize that their lives depend on the stomach of the Senate and that they are protected against the barbarous Volscians principally by the despised Martius. Menenius' parable initially seems to serve as an ideal by which the real Rome is measured, though ultimately we shall see that it has a more disturbing message.[83]

That Rome fails to live up to this ideal is evident in many ways, a fact evident not least in the repeated references to body parts that litter the play.[84] From one perspective, the play is a straightforward dramatization of

Menenius' fable, as it depicts the failure of the limbs to return gratitude for the stomach's benefits, the Roman populace's forgetful ingratitude for the service of her benefactor and protector(s). At the beginning of act 2, scene 2, an officer discussing Coriolanus' campaign for consul tells a fellow officer that Coriolanus' military accomplishments "deserved worthily of his country" and says that "for [the plebs'] tongues to be silent and not confess so much were a kind of ingrateful injury." They owe their voices/votes to Martius for past services rendered. In the following scene the "Third Citizen" offers a similar opinion: "[I]f he tell us his noble deeds, we must also tell him our noble acceptances of them. Ingratitude is monstrous, and for the multitude to be ingrateful were to make a monster of the multitude—of the which we being members, should bring ourselves to be monstrous members" (2.3.8–14). To be a "monster" means in Shakespeare's terminology to be unnatural. A literal monster does not share the nature of his parents, and metaphorically a monster renounces the common nature that he shares with others.[85] When the multitude fails to acknowledge Martius' contributions to Rome's prosperity and safety, Rome denies the nature that she shares with her civic "parent," and becomes monstrous.[86]

This speech opens two critical scenes in which Coriolanus seeks and appears to win the favor of the plebs, only to see his election seized from him through the machinations of the tribunes, who deftly exploit Martius' own flaws. Martius' campaign and its ultimate failure turn on the question of gratitude.[87] He asks for the "voices" of the people by speaking of the battle wounds that serve as memorial tokens of his service to the city. These tokens, he expects, will stimulate the memory of the plebs, who will thereby be stirred to support him in his run for the consulate. The tribunes, however, evoke remembrances of Coriolanus' contempt for the plebs (2.3.246–51), and this alternative recollection turns the populace from gratitude to hatred. Soon, prompted by the tribunes, they are calling for his banishment. When the tribunes describe Coriolanus as a disease, infection, poison, and gangrene that must be excised from the body of Rome, Coriolanus charges that the officers' fears have come true: Rome is a monster, a "Hydra" for whom the tribunes serve as "horn and noise of the monster's" (3.1.92, 94). Unkindness/ingratitude has turned the plebs at least into a thing unnatural, not of humankind.

In other plays, monstrous ingratitude turns cannibalistic,[88] and so it is for Coriolanus as well (see 2.1.1–12).[89] After the tribunes' plot has trapped Martius, Menenius prays that Rome would not be transformed into a cannibal mother: "Now the good gods forbid / That our renowned Rome, whose gratitude / Towards her deserved children is enroll'd / In Jove's own book,

like an unnatural dam / Should now eat up her own!" (3.1.288–92). Coriolanus will not abide the insult, and in his mind the ingratitude of Rome has
dissolved his bonds to Rome so completely that nothing obliges him any
longer to serve the city that gave him birth. Rather than endure contempt,
injury, and exile, he plans revenge, and at the urging of the Volscian commander Aufidius, determines to "pour war / Into the bowels of ungrateful
Rome" (4.5.131–32). Ultimately, the patricians join plebs in forgetful ingratitude (4.6.122–23), and Coriolanus despises them more deeply even than
the plebs, rejecting both his commander Cominius and his surrogate father,
Menenius, who appeal to him to abandon his assault on Rome. Rome chews
up its hero and spits him into exile. Rome fails at every point of Aquinas'
account of gratitude: Romans forget the benefits they owe to Martius' heroism, express hatred rather than thanks, and do not support him in grateful
repayment for his contributions to Rome.

This story of Roman ingratitude toward Coriolanus is crossed by the
story of Coriolanus' ingratitude toward Rome, and it is in the latter story line
that the more interesting insights into the politics of gratitude arise.[90] From
early in Shakespeare's play, Coriolanus' adherence to the code of benefit and
gratitude is, to put it mildly, open to question. Curiously, Martius' first word
in the play is "Thanks" (1.1.162), yet he immediately begins to chide the
plebs assembled in the public square as "dissentious rogues" who have nothing better to do than to rub "the poor itch of your opinion" so as to produce
"scabs" (1.1.162–64). His expression of gratitude is immediately subverted
by harsh attacks on the people.

Coriolanus, furthermore, refuses to *receive* benefits, which, while not
technically ingratitude, signifies his rejection of the rules of benefit and
return.[91] When his general Cominius commends his action at Corioli, Coriolanus complains that he cannot bear to be praised. Vickers sees this as com-
mendable humility, evidence that Martius is neither proud nor ambitious,[92]
but Cominius sees cruelty and ingratitude lurking beneath the apparent
humility: "Too modest are you, / More cruel to your good report than grateful / To us that give you truly" (1.9.52–54).[93] At the end of the scene, Martius reports that a poor man of Corioles "used me kindly" (1.9.82), but he
cannot even remember the man's name so that he can be repaid (1.9.89–91).
Wallace accurately suggests that Coriolanus takes Aristotle's magnanimous
man, rather than Seneca's grateful man, as his model. Like Aristotle's ideal,
Coriolanus remembers benefits conferred, and expects others to remember
them, but is indifferent to or forgets benefits received.[94] He is following part
of Aquinas' sequence of ingratitude: forgetful of a favor received, he also
treats the kindness of Cominius as an unkindness.

Aristotle would be proud: Martius has an aversion to dependence and the admission of inferiority that it involves, an aversion utterly consistent with both his outlook on Rome and his military tactics. A one-man army, he takes the city of Corioles without assistance, and later is able to boast "Alone I did it" (5.6.115).[95] Even when he moves from war to politics, he is a one-man show. To insert gratitude between the deeds and its reward is to insert the plebs, and Martius is repulsed by his reliance on their voices. He longs for a world in which there is no mediating populace between accomplishment and reward, where deeds are their own reward, where heroic honor can wriggle free of the community that valorizes it, where he can stand on his own without depending on the gratitude of the city. Before the tribunes turn the people of Rome against him, he has already separated himself from the body, preferring a kind of individualistic state of nature, acknowledging only those obligations that he chooses to acknowledge.

Intriguingly, though he scorns putting his wounds and deeds into the marketplace, he regularly employs the commercial language of merit, desert, and wages to describe the political value of his military successes. "I pray, your price o' th' consulship" (2.3.72–73), he says, to which the First Citizen replies that the price is to ask "kindly" (2.3.74). Provoked by the tribunes, he castigates the plebs as cowards, insisting that their "service / did not deserve corn gratis" (3.1.123–24). Evidently, Martius thinks of his own social bond with Rome, and Rome's obligation to the populace, as a matter of contract,[96] and he does not believe the plebs have fulfilled their end of the bargain. Rome certainly has no obligation to repay the plebs in excess of their contribution to Roman life, and when the plebs refuse to pay the respect they owe him, the contract becomes null and void. But his isolation is more radical still, for he not only renounces the economy of benefit and gratuity but also hesitates even to bring himself into the realm of exchange, whether economic or political. He acts as if he is a natural man liberated from the obligation of return because he has refused to accept. He turns his back on the city, declaring that "there is a world elsewhere" (3.3.134–35), and he ultimately utters an extreme statement of consensual social contract: "I banish you" (3.3.124).[97]

Martius' desire to escape the round of gift and return gift is for Shakespeare a sign of his inhumanity. At a number of points in the play, he, not the ungrateful multitude, is described as that paradigmatically isolated of all unkind and unnatural monsters, the dragon: "Believe't not lightly—though I go alone, / Like to a lonely dragon, that his fen / Makes fear'd and talk'd of more than seen—your son / Will or exceed the common or be caught / With cautelous baits and practice" (4.1.30ff.). Elsewhere, it is said that "he bears all things fairly. / And shows good husbandry for the Volscian state, / Fights dragon-like, and does achieve as soon / As draw his sword" (4.7.23ff.). When they return from their delegation to the Volscians, officials complain that "This Marcius is grown from man to dragon: he has wings; he's more than a creeping thing" (5.4.10-14). Even when he is serving the city, he is more a "thing" rather than a man, standing as he does outside the social compact of gift and exchange. Rome's ingratitude made it cannibalistic; Coriolanus responds with a similarly monstrous appetite to consume Rome.[98] Contrary to his fantasies, his titles and rewards do not rest only on his achievements on the field, but precisely on the grateful response of those who recognize his deeds. All he is depends on his participation in Roman society, and in particular depends on his inheritance of position, status, and title from his parents. Detached from the compact of gratitude that binds generations, he is without name, without class, without title. Isolated from the political community of Rome, he becomes "kind of nothing, titleless" (5.1.13).

The inhumanity of his position is especially evident in the internal soliloquies as he waits for Volumnia's arrival in the Volscian camp. He intends to resist the instinct to honor his mother and city. He will renounce filial attachments, and stand "As if a man were author of himself / And knew no other kin" (5.3.22–37). This is his dream: to be godlike, self-authored, without obligation to city or family. Renouncing kin, he becomes unkind.

When Volumnia arrives, she cajoles and manipulates him back to his obligations, and her victory is not merely a return to filial obligation. From her first appearance in the play, Volumnia has functioned as a personification of Rome.[99] She pushed him into combat, and urged him on to seek honor on the battlefield (1.3.5–17). She is the source of his valor, and the model of his contempt for the plebs. He drank all that he is from her breasts. To tread on Rome is to tread on the womb that gave him birth (5.3.120–25). Against this background, Volumnia's triumph over her son is a political as well as a familial victory, and Coriolanus' renewed recognition of the obligations he owes Volumnia is simultaneously a renewed recognition of his obligations to Rome. Time, history, heritage, mother, Mother-city reassert their claims, and Coriolanus' experiment in (un)natural individualism and independent freedom collapses.[100] But it is too late for him to be restored to the economy of gratuity. While his mother returns to the city in a triumphal procession like those that Martius once enjoyed, Martius returns to the Aufidius, and to the twenty-nine wounds he has received in battle, he adds the innumerable wounds inflicted by the Volscians in the marketplace of Corioli, where he again is the sole Roman in the city.[101]

The play thus traces Coriolanus' development from elevated magnanimous man, through the renunciation of obligations of gratitude that takes him close to a purely contractual understanding of his place in Roman political order, to a revival of political gratitude toward his M(m)other, the Womb/Rome that gave him birth. For Shakespeare, *Coriolanus* not only serves as a parable of the evils of collective and individual ingratitude but ultimately points to obligations deeper than consent. Rome is hardly free of political evils at the play's end. Martius saves Rome by his death, but he leaves behind a Rome infested with tribunes who manipulate the people for their own ends. Rome languishes still under the regime of "divided worship." But in that long silence when Martius reaches for his mother's hand, Shakespeare vindicates the fundamental premise of Menenius' parable, for his independent and isolated hero discovers that his consent does not exhaust his responsibility, that there is some deep, mysterious root for the compact of gratitude that binds city and citizen, past and present, Mother and son.[102]

Conclusion

The sixteenth and seventeenth were critical centuries for the story I am telling. The ancient and medieval circles of reciprocity that provided the shape of social and religious life had been disrupted and torn apart. It was not clear what exactly had been unleashed on the world. It was also not clear what, if anything, could rejoin the broken ends of the circle. Following Seneca, Shakespeare identified the new social pathology "ingratitude," and recoiled before the monster. Others in England, though, saw an opportunity to construct something new, something that might escape both the confinements of social reciprocity and the infinite circle of Christianity. That new thing we call modernity, and our account of its formation begins in the next chapter with a review of early modern political theory.

SIX

The Circle and the Line

The revolutionary changes in European society, politics, and church during the sixteenth century produced a "crisis in the economy of obligation."[1] Christians were divided on what they could expect from the Eucharist, or from the alms they offered. Neighboring towns no longer shared a common faith, and throughout Europe prince fought with prince in a chaos of blood. As Shakespeare discerns, the bonds of gratitude that had held European society together were frayed and European society seemed to be coming apart at the seams. Shakespeare had posed the problem with his usual clarity. One option was the "individualist" one: some found the collapse of gratitude debts liberating. Like Coriolanus, they would aspire to be self-created. But the self-created is the same as the dragon, and a man detached from obligations to his fellows is no longer human. He is a monster. On the other hand, Shakespeare knew that gratitude could be monstrous too: Rome with its demands for reciprocity was an unnatural, cannibalistic mother.

Early modern political theorists followed a third option: individuals could exist in a world of debt if their debts were *chosen*. Because individuals *willed* to be bound, they remained free even in their bondage; because they agreed to shoulder the debts of social life, society was still a possibility.

"Contract" or at least "consent" had been important for political thinkers before the early modern period, and some of the basic notions of social contract theories have deep roots in medieval political thought.[2] Post-Reformation theories maintained this emphasis, with consent, as in medieval theories, set within an overall theological framework. Man is naturally social, argues Robert Bellarmine in *De laicis sive saecularibus*, and

121

government comes from God. Yet even social life requires consent, since human beings have to "assemble and to ward off attacks with their combined strength,"[3] and in political life "it depends on the consent of the people to decide whether kings, or consuls, or other magistrates are to be establishing in authority over them" and the people are to determine whether "there be legitimate cause to change a kingdom into an aristocracy, or an aristocracy into a democracy."[4] Writing in 1594, Richard Hooker asserted that however natural society may be, societies do not emerge spontaneously in nature. Because "we are not by ourselves sufficient to furnish ourselves with competent store of things needful for such a life as our nature doth desire," which is a life suitable to the "dignity of man," we make up for our "defects and imperfections" by "seeking communion and fellowship with others" and "uniting themselves in political Societies."[5] Need and the possibility of mutual benefit provide a natural nudge into political society.

It is thus not contract or consent per se that sets early modern political theorists off from its predecessors. One of the things that sets them apart is their effort to construct a contract theory of the state with a deliberate methodological break from the past. Hobbes and Locke responded to the crisis of obligations by inventing a new science of politics. For them, a world of disconnected individuals is not a product of social disruption but the natural state of human life. Hobbes and Locke are innovative because they assume humans are originally autonomous rather than originally dependent. Like the early Christians and Reformers, they are innovative "ingrates," though they deviate from both because they break open not only the confining circular shackles of reciprocal social relations but also the infinite circle of Christian faith. As we shall see, Locke is the more innovative of the two, because he imagines he can construct a political order that has wriggled entirely free from bonds of gratitude.

Leviathan and the Laws of Nature

Enamored of the precision and apparent certainty of new scientific modes of knowledge and their ability to command nature, Hobbes was inspired to reconstruct political theory on a similar basis. Only a political theory that was as bold in rejecting past models as Galileo had been in rejecting Aristotelian cosmology and physics could meet the needs of the time.[6] In part, being "scientific" meant being clear-sightedly and coldly clinical in the assessment of political phenomena, a model of political thought for which mathematics was the ideal model. Hobbes' "turn" to Euclid was a crucial moment in the development of his mature efforts to formulate a geometry of political life.[7] In contrast to the scholasticism of the high Middle Ages, we might call

Hobbes' starting point a "methodological ingratitude." It is a term I shall have much occasion to use in the following chapters.

Despite his effort to break free of the past, traditional patterns of social life and traditional values still occupied a large place in Hobbes' political theory. He thought Aristotle's ethics and politics were too bound to words and hence to the passions that give words their inflections of meaning. He preferred Plato, whom he thought was able to move beyond conventional morality and political judgment to a more "scientific" politics because he ascended beyond words to ideas.[8] Furthermore, despite the effort of Hobbes to break free of the past, *Leviathan* assumes and reflects a traditional society marked by forms of hierarchy (master/slave, parent/child) and pursuit of honor. Hobbes does not advocate a patriarchal view of political society, yet he affirms the divine institution of familial authority and claims that obedience and honor to parents are a law of nature. He recognizes and affirms the reality of noncontractual relations and obligations, so much so that his vision of society has elements that might be called "feudal."[9] Competitions for honor and fear of shame motivate men in fundamental ways, and even when they engage in profitable enterprises they are as interested in wealth that enhances their vanity as in the way it embiggens their net worth. Hobbes acknowledges that the aristocratic concern for reputation is a natural right, and does not think that worry over one's reputation after death is absurd. He hated dueling and disparaged all cults of military glory, but these views do not necessarily reflect an antiaristocratic bias. Hobbes rejects dueling on grounds of nobility and, in any case, "the nobility had ceased to be a military class."[10] Given these attitudes, it is not surprising that Hobbes would commend "generous natures" who obey the laws of the sovereign not out of fear but out of virtuous hostility to "fraud or breach of promise" and out of "a glory, or pride in appearing not to need to break" one's word.[11]

Yet with his effort to view human nature and political life with the cold rationality of a scientist, Hobbes charted a new course for political theory. He famously concludes that the state of nature is a war of all against all. It cannot be otherwise, given the nature of human nature. Human beings seek to fulfill their own desires in all their actions. Among the central appetites is the appetite for superiority, which Hobbes names "vanity." "Continually to out-go the next before, is felicity," he says, and human life is a race that has "no other goal, nor other garland, but being foremost."[12] Hobbes does not mean this as a moral condemnation. It is simply the natural state of man that his own instincts and desires are nearer to him than anything else. Vanity cannot but lead to the "warre of every one against every one."

Then the fear of death intervenes, and this shocks man into reason. For Hobbes, the greatest good is self-preservation, and thus death is the greatest and supreme evil. From the instinct for self-preservation Hobbes infers a natural right to self-defense. In a world where the lives of people are solitary, poor, nasty, brutish, and short, the right of nature is "the liberty of each man to use his own power as he will himself for the preservation of his own nature; that is to say, of his own life."[13] In the state of nature, it becomes clear that everyone is always at risk. Faced with another who is striving, like me, to be foremost in the race of life, the most I can do is get rid of my rival by killing him. That is a short-term victory, however, since every man is striving in the same way to defeat me: I cannot kill *everyone*.[14] If I submit to the other who tries to dominate me, I have become his servant, a despotism that is the natural form of politics. As soon as rivals no longer view one another as enemies and begin to recognize that they have a common enemy, death, they are ready to consent to an artificial state, the perfected condition of political society. Far of death becomes the basis of concord and thus is the main "postulate of natural reason."[15] As Hobbes says at the close of *Leviathan*, the absolute Sovereign comes on the scene as the "King of the Proud," the one power sufficiently powerful to overawe the warring men in the state of nature and bring them to amicable community.[16]

Natural laws are valid already in the state of nature, derivable from the basic postulate of self-preservation. From this right of nature arise certain natural obligations. These obligations are ultimately obligations of obedience to God himself, Hobbes claims, but they can also be sussed out rationally from the state of nature and the natural inclination to protect oneself. A law of nature thus is a "precept or general rule . . . by which a man is forbidden to do what is destructive of his life." When the state of man is a war of all against all, the law of nature imposes on each man an obligation to strive for peace. This is the first law of reason or nature: "every man ought to endeavor peace, as far as he has hope of obtaining it," and to prepare for war if peace cannot be obtained. For Hobbes, the "first and fundamental law of nature" is "seek peace and follow it." The sum of the right of nature is "by all means we can to defend ourselves." Since all are enjoined to seek peace by the law of nature, they are also obliged to obey a second law: "that a man be willing, when others are so too, as far forth as for peace and defence of himself he shall think it necessary, to lay down this right to all things; and to be contented with so much liberty against other men as he would allow other men against himself."[17] The third law of nature is justice, by which Hobbes means that "men performe their Covenants made."[18] In all, Hobbes describes nineteen laws of nature.

Consistent with his egoistic conception of human behavior, Hobbes regards gifts as self-interested: "When the transferring of Right, is not mutu-all, but one of the parties transferreth, in hope to gain thereby friendship, or service from another, or from his friends, or in hope to gain the reputation of Charity, or Magnanimity; or to deliver his mind from the pain of compassion; or in hope of reward in heaven; This is not Contract, but Gift, Free-Gift, Grace: which words signifie one and the same thing."[19] For Hobbes, there is no free gift, no disinterested benevolence. No one gives up anything except on the hope that he will receive something for the exchange.

It is in this setting that Hobbes offers his most explicit discussion of gratitude, which he describes as the fourth law of nature.[20] The laws of nature make for peace, and gratitude is one of those laws. It is one of the constituent elements of human life that encourages men toward sociability. Like the third law, justice, gratitude is a response to a prior good; gratitude depends "on Antecedent Grace" as justice depends on "Antecedent Covenant." One acts with gratitude when he "receiveth benefit from another of mere grace endeavour that he which giveth it have no reasonable cause to repent him of his good will." Hobbes' reason for defining gratitude in this fashion is easy to see. "No man," he adds, "giveth but with intention of good to himself, because gift is voluntary; and of all voluntary acts, the object is to every man his own good." If a man could not expect to receive a grateful response—that is, a response in which the recipient "gives no cause to repent" his generosity—he will be reluctant to give at all. And that will be generally detrimental to human sociability. If men are ungrateful, givers will cease to give, and as a result "there will be no beginning of benevolence or trust, nor consequently of mutual help, nor of reconciliation of one man to another."[21] Gratitude has a linear structure: a grateful recipient does not return directly to his benefactor, but instead honors his benefactor in the way he uses the gift. Gratitude is dissemination, passing on the gift in right use.

Benefits can go wrong, especially if men are in a state of natural equality. If a benefit is given so that the benefactor can "triumph" over his dependent client, it is not genuine benefit and deserves no charity in return. It is *Warre* by another means. Even at their best, "benefits oblige," and "obligation is thraldome" that might be perpetual.[22] If we receive benefits from an equal, the obligation is hateful. But when we receive benefits from someone who is an acknowledged superior, we receive them with "cheerfull acceptation (which men call Gratitude)." This honors the giver, and satisfies the need for retribution for the benefit. When we respond to benefits with gratitude, it conduces to love and social bonding, even though we are left in a subordinate position. Even among equals, benefits can encourage love, "as long as there is hope of requital." For Hobbes, it is much in the interests of society to encourage "the most notable and profitable contention," the competition in giving gifts.[23] Ingratitude, on the contrary, has the opposite effect: without benevolence, men "remain still in the condition of war, which is contrary to the first and fundamental law of nature which commandeth men to seek peace."[24] In a natural state, gratitude might well demean; ingratitude promotes *Warre*. There is no solution as long as mankind remains in a natural condition.

Though for Hobbes gratitude appears occasionally as a topic throughout *Leviathan*,[25] it does not appear to loom large in Hobbes' thought. Furthermore, in his hands, gift and gratitude seem to be reduced to tools of self-interest. We seem to be back to the narrow circles of ancient patronage and reciprocity in which a superior does a service for an inferior in order to put the inferior in his debt and to ensure future service. Yet there is a more generous way to read Hobbes. For starters, though mentioned infrequently, gratitude plays a crucial role for Hobbes in explaining how human beings exist in the state of nature. One of Hobbes' most innovative notions is that a father derives his authority over his children from the children's consent. Hobbes is a patriarchalist, but, unlike other patriarchalists, he is a consent theorist at the same time. Children agree to be ruled by their father so that, as in the political order, family authority is based on consent. Gratitude is the link that joins choice with respect for parents. Because children are grateful to their fathers for life and nurture, they consent to his authority. Similarly, in the state of nature women are subordinated to men out of gratitude to men for not killing them.[26]

Furthermore, though Hobbes is an egoist who believes that men act to fulfill desires, he does not assume that these desires must be narrowly self-interested. Even on Hobbes' premises, it is possible to "choose to act for the sake of themselves, for the sake of others, for the sake of knowledge, for the sake of justice."[27] I might act, in short, out of a desire to promote the common good; that benefits me, but not *only* me. Gratitude is not simply a demand for reciprocal service to the generous donor; it ensures that benevolent service is performed throughout society. It ensures that gifts will continue to be given in the future, not only to me but to everyone. Virtues like gratitude thus push individuals beyond calculation of their own advantages; they act out of concern for the interests of society as a whole. Gratitude "greases" the machine of benefits, mutual service, gifts, and acts of kindness that make the world run smoothly. Gratitude in response to benefits binds human beings in peace.[28]

There is a catch. According to the first, encompassing natural law, we aim above all to preserve ourselves. A man need not make himself "prey" to those who are not seeking peace; he is not obliged to give if he knows that his gifts will be answered with ingratitude, nor to show gratitude if it leaves him vulnerable to control and manipulation by a benefactor. That is the crux of the problem. In the state of nature, natural law is "law" only in an attenuated sense. Natural laws are prudential rules; all are subordinated to the primary demand for self-preservation. If compliance with the laws of nature puts me in a vulnerable position toward my fellow man, I am not obliged to keep it. In the state of nature, no one can trust others to play by the rules.[29] Everyone lives in fear, and as a result the laws of nature cannot be realized. They are valid but are not effective.[30]

When men cede their natural authority and rights to the sovereign, natural law comes finally into its own. Civil society unleashes natural law from the rivalries and fears of the state of nature, and makes them not only valid but also effective. Because all agree that they will limit their natural liberty to bring an end to war, it is incumbent on each individual to divest himself of his natural right for the sake of the peace of all. Hobbes sees this as an application of the golden rule. When both parties transfer a right, the resulting relation is a contract. To be considered a "covenant," it is not enough for the parties to transfer the right to a thing. Rather, a covenant is established when the thing itself is transferred. But the social covenant is a mutual covenant: "both parts may contract now, to performe hereafter." In such situations, each party is naturally obligated to keep his promise. Natural laws that would be foolish to follow in the state of nature, when everyone is vulnerable to attack from ambitious others, become in civil society counsels of wisdom. Expectations are regularized. Creditors can be sure that their loans will be repaid, givers can expect gratitude, and recipients of gifts and benefits can respond with gratitude because they know that the movement of gifts is beneficial for all.[31]

Benefit and gratitude appear to function at an apolitical "social" level. The hierarchies of gift and gratitude that Hobbes knew in the society around him remain in place, but the political sphere itself seems to be wiped clean of the impurities of personal interest, with all power vested in an absolute sovereign something or someone. That is superficial.[32] The problem faced by Hobbes and all social contract theories is accounting for how the contract holds for people who did not enter it. Consent can explain the origination of a political society from a group of free and independent individuals. But how can the next generation be obligated to that covenant? They have not consented; why are they bound to the decisions of their predecessors? One can appeal to a theory of tacit consent or tacit promise. Hobbes himself appeals to a notion of "tacit covenant," but when Hobbes explains this, he appeals to the present situation of a person enjoying the benefits of civil sovereignty, especially the benefits of protection from war and from his neighbor's attacks. To explain the obligations of the descendants of the founders, Hobbes falls back on the law of nature, not on artificial obligations created by the social contract.[33] Any person who makes use of the benefits of the civil contract has implicitly consented.[34] In short, the duties toward the sovereign depend on present enjoyment of benefits, not on promises made earlier, and thus fall under the natural law of gratitude rather than the obligation to keep covenants. Though Hobbes describes the duties of citizens in covenantal terms, he appeals to the particular duties of the natural law when he wants to fill out the obligations and the basis for those obligations.[35] As noted earlier, he is a patriarchalist who works from an analogy between familial and political authority, and in both instances gratitude is the key to uniting consent with hierarchy.

Hobbes remains within the tradition by giving gratitude a prominent political role. He differs in emphasizing more overtly than most the self-interest at work in gift giving and gratitude, and, like Christian thinkers, he replaces the tightly dyadic conception of gratitude found in both classical and medieval writers with a linear dissemination of gifts. Where Hobbes departs most radically is in his detachment of political order from God. Scientific politics has no place for royal power descending from heaven, for the king's two bodies, for the magic of the king's touch. God has no essential role in political science, and so gratitude to God has no place either. Hobbes' contemporary critic, John Bramhall, attacked him for failing to mention gratitude to God among his laws of nature. In so doing, Hobbes neglected "the main and principal laws of nature, which contain a man's duty to his God, and the principal end of his creation."[36] This was hardly accidental. Hobbes said that "the right of nature whereby God reigneth over men, is to be derived not from his creating them, as if he required gratitude; but from his irresistible power."[37] God's relation to man, like the sovereign's to his subjects, is a power relation. Men owe obedience, not gratitude.

Hobbes dislocates gratitude by positing a clear distinction between the state of nature and civic society, by distinguishing between the natural condition of human life and the artificial sovereign constructed by the consent of the people. Gratitude is incorporated into the workings of the civic order, and even plays an essential role in binding the sovereign to his subjects. Gratitude can come into its own only when there is a sovereign power that awes or forces everyone to comply with expected patterns of benefit and repayment. But the natural/artificial distinction is there, and it is sharpened in Locke, for whom gratitude exists on one side of what has become a chasm between politics and gratitude.

Gratitude-Free Politics

Locke's earliest writings were written in the aftermath of the English Civil War, and that conflict remained in the back of his mind through much of his life. The Civil War attacked the fundamental tenets of social and political life. Early in the seventeenth century, one of the archbishop of Canterbury's lieutenants defined a commonwealth as "nothing more than . . . [a] mutual exchange . . . of benefits."[38] The lives of the gentlemen of the gentry were infused with the values of beneficence and gratitude. Like ancient Roman aristocrats, they were bound to one another by ropes wound of mutual favor, and they maintained their superior position in society by the same procedures. Their "beneficence cost little, and in return a price was tacitly demanded—in terms of deference, obedience and implicit recognition of the legitimacy of the prevailing social order."[39] The Civil War assaulted this social order in vital areas. Not only did Parliament overthrow and behead a king, but the army cast up all manner of radicals—Levellers and Diggers and other egalitarians who questioned the hierarchy founded on debts of gratitude.[40] Like the Reformation and the Continental wars that followed, the English Civil War created a crisis in the economy of obligations.

In reaction, many Restoration-era intellectuals and artists worked to shore up the order that had been assaulted. New writings on gentility emphasized the need for generosity, and buttressed their arguments with appeals to classical writers like Hesiod and Cicero. An English translation of Cicero's *De officiis* was printed and reprinted throughout the seventeenth century and was a standard text at Westminster, Eton, Cambridge, and Oxford. John Toland remarked that the book was "the common fashion at schooles," foundational to the education of "young Gentlemen." Ten editions of an abridged version of Seneca's *De beneficiis* were printed between 1678 and 1700. Shakespeare's tragedies of ingratitude were revived with revisions that highlighted the themes of gratitude even more starkly than Shakespeare. Nahum Tate's version of *Coriolanus* was retitled *The Ingratitude of a Commonwealth*, and in Tate's strangely popular version of *Lear*, gratitude is rewarded, as faithful Cordelia survives to marry Edgar and inherit Lear's throne.[41]

Locke was touched by this revival of gentlemanly benevolence and lower-class gratitude. He read and took notes on Cicero and Seneca, in whose letters Locke claimed to find "all the wisdome of the pagans."[42] Early on, he was influenced by the works of Robert Sanderson, who claimed to have read *De officiis* "not less than twenty times," so that he could repeat it "without Book."[43] In his *Essays*, Locke commended the ancient virtue of liberality, emphasizing that "heroic men in former times" gained divine honors by "toil, hazards, and liberality." Like Cicero, Locke advised a former student to maintain a balance of liberality and prudence. The aim was to be "provident and good natured."[44] He read and may have met Pufendorf, and commended his *De Officiis Hominis et Civis* as an important book for young English gentry because it emphasized the natural sociability of human beings and the role of services and grateful response in that sociability.[45]

Nor was this merely theoretical for Locke. Locke was himself a gentleman, and so was entirely enmeshed in the networks commended in these writings. He owed his admission to Westminster and Oxford to the favors of his father's patron, Alexander Popham, described by Locke in 1652 as "my god." He reiterated in 1660 that he was so much indebted to Popham that he was no more than a "utensill" in which Popham had "a Propriety."[46] He later enjoyed the patronage of the earl of Shaftesbury, who, though far wealthier than Locke, owed the latter a debt of gratitude because Locke had saved his life with an operation.[47] During the 1670s, Locke translated three of Pierre Nicole's *Essais de morale*, which developed a moral theory centering on service, obligations of gratitude, and love.[48] In his early writings (1660), Locke exults in the gift of peace brought by the restoration of the British monarchy. He no sooner entered public life than found himself "in a storm" of religious war. The calm that followed, he argues, "obliges me, both in duty and gratitude to be chary of such a blessing, and [to do] what lies in me to endeavour its continuance, by disposing men's minds to obedience to that government which had brought with it that quiet and settlement." Gratitude for the peace and order that government provides is, for the young Locke, the first plank of an argument in favor of state regulation of religion. The benefits that the state brings are so great that the grateful citizens owe it obedience even in matters indifferent.[49]

As important as benefit and gratitude were in Locke's life and in the works he studied and read, in his later political thought Locke eliminated gratitude from the foundation of political order. In the state of nature, he argued, all men have the authority to protect and defend their own property, which becomes theirs by the application of labor to nature, and to punish violations of crimes. Political power arises when men "give into the hands of the society, and therein to the governors" this twofold power—to protect property and to punish crime.[50] Locke acknowledges that even in the state of nature men are not equal in every respect, and that this inequality is evident in obligations of gratitude, respect, and honor:

> Though I have said above . . . "That all men by nature are equal," I cannot be supposed to understand all sorts of "equality." Age or virtue may give men a just precedency. Excellency of parts and merit may place others above the common level. Birth may subject some, and alliance or benefits others, to pay an observance to those to whom Nature, gratitude, or other respects, may have made it due; and yet all this consists with the equality which all men are in respect of jurisdiction or dominion one over another, which was the equality I there spoke of as proper to the business in hand, being that equal right that every man hath to his natural freedom, without being subjected to the will or authority of any other man.[51]

Children, for instance, are born dependent, under the "rule and jurisdiction" on parents. Having acknowledged the place of gratitude bonds in nature, Locke hastens to add that the bonds of this subjection are only so many swaddling clothes that the infant sheds as he grows: "Age and reason as they grow up loosen them, till at length they drop quite off, and leave a man at his own free disposal."[52] Even grown to the age of reason, Locke argues, children owe honor to their parents, as God's law commands:

> As He hath laid on them an obligation to nourish, preserve, and bring up their offspring, so He has laid on the children a perpetual obligation of honouring their parents, which, containing in it an inward esteem and reverence to be shown by all outward expressions, ties up the child from anything that may ever injure or affront, disturb or endanger the happiness or life of those from whom he received his, and engages him in all actions of defence, relief, assistance, and comfort of those by whose means he entered into being and has been made capable of any enjoyments of life. From this obligation no state, no freedom, can absolve children.

Yet "this is very far from giving parents a power of command over their children, or an authority to make laws and dispose as they please of their lives or liberties."[53] Familial life is infused with benefaction and gratitude, but political order rests on a very different basis. Even in civil society, human beings are dependent. In fact, dependency is "the original and foundation of all Law."[54] Yet this dependence is a different sort of dependence than that evident in families or society. It is a dependent need for direction and guidance from a superior.

Unlike Hobbes, Locke is no patriarchalist; because of his vigorous defense of maternal authority and his attack on the analogy between parental and political authority, he has been claimed to be a proto-feminist. His attack on patriarchy is central to his political theory. Locke's target in his

First Treatise is the *Patriarcha* of Robert Filmer, who used a model of paternal absolutism to argue for political absolutism, and Filmer remains a central target in the *Second Treatise* as well. To rebut Filmer's argument, Locke sharply separates filial obligations, and the obligations of gratitude and honor with which they are associated, from the duties of citizenship and the ordering of civil government: "It is one thing to owe honour, respect, gratitude, and assistance; another to require an absolute obedience and submission. The honour due to parents a monarch on his throne owes his mother, and yet this lessens not his authority nor subjects him to her government."[55] The obligation of gratitude does not entail the obligation to obey; benefits given do not ground the authority to command: "The power of commanding ends with nonage, and though after that honour and respect, support and defence, and whatsoever gratitude can oblige a man to, for the highest benefits he is naturally capable of be always due from a son to his parents, yet all this puts no sceptre into the father's hand, no sovereign power of commanding. He has no dominion over his son's property or actions, nor any right that his will should prescribe to his son's in all things."[56] Outside the realm of family obligations, the same sharp distinction applies. Honor and respect are due to the old and wise, parents owe protection to children, those with means are obligated to relieve the oppressed, and beneficiaries should show "gratitude to a benefactor, to such a degree that all he has, all he can do, cannot sufficiently pay it." Yet, these bonds and obligation "give no authority, no right of making laws to anyone over them from whom they are owing."[57] Traditional circles of gratitude function in social life. But they are not relevant to political organization.

Under "household" obligations, Locke includes not only the relations of children to parents but also the contractual relations of husband and wife and master and servant. These sorts of relations occupy a liminal position in Locke's theory. On the one hand, they are not relations grounded in actual physical relation. They are contracted and voluntary, and thus quasi-political. Yet these contractual relations do not involve the concession of freedoms and rights that the political order does. They are contractual, but the purpose of the contract is not general but specific: a man and woman enter a marriage contract for the narrow purpose of procreation, and the concession of natural rights extends only so far as that purpose. On the other hand, the obligations of gratitude that Locke sees operating in filial relations are not operative in these relations either. Gift and gratitude play no role in Locke's description of marriage or master-servant relations.[58] Locke follows Hobbes in making a sharp distinction between the natural state of human life and the artificial state of political order. What a child receives from his parents, and mutatis mutandis, what a beneficiary receives from his benefactor, "obliges him to respect, honour, gratitude, assistance, and support, all his life." These bonds are the bonds of "natural government," the chief example of which is the government of the family. But these natural bonds do "not at all" extend to the "ends and jurisdictions of that which is political."[59] By nature, men have liberty and power and self-possession, but in the political order these powers must be ceded to society and the governors charged with ordering that society.

The division of natural/familial and artificial/political, a division between the natural and the "made," corresponds to a distinction between justice and charity. Justice, Locke says, "gives every man a title to the product of his honest industry, and the fair acquisitions of his ancestors." Charity, by contrast, "gives every man a title to so much out of another's plenty, as will keep him from extreme want." It is uncharitable to use the occasion of charity to turn a man into a vassal or slave, to use the occasion of gift to lay a burden of gratitude on the poor.[60] Political authority, Locke argues in the *Second Treatise*, is for the purpose of protecting property, and thus is concerned with the realm of justice, not charity. The important point here for my purposes is that Locke thinks of justice as a public and political reality, while charitable gift giving is a private duty.[61]

That Locke is aware of the continuing power of gratitude obligations is evident, as in Machiavelli, in his obsequious prefaces. At the beginning of the *Essay Concerning Human Understanding*, he offers his patron "a present" and compares himself to a poor man giving a basket of flowers and fruit to a rich man, who accepts it with favor even though he has plenty of fruit and flowers of his own. His worthless book receives value because it is an offering "of respect, esteem, and gratitude." Locke is confident that his gift is "the richest present you ever received," but it is only fitting: "I am under the greatest obligations to seek all occasions to acknowledge a long train of favours I have received from your lordship," which however small are made great "by the forewardness, concern, and kindness, and other obliging circumstances that never failed to accompany them."[62] Locke's acknowledgment of a class system built on benefits and return gifts, reluctant as it may be, leaves his political theory in a state of unreality.[63] It is difficult to see how, in the real world, the wealthy could be prevented from using their powers of patronage to gain political power. And, of course, in the real world, Lockean liberalism has not prevented that at all. On this point, Rousseau is more cynical, perhaps more realistic: the social contract is a tool of the rich to exploit the poor.

Locke cannot quite escape gratitude in his political theory either. The Achilles' heel of contract models of political order is evident when we ask what obliges the generations after the founding generation to be loyal to the political order. Those who form the civil contract are obliged because they consented to the contract, but what of their children? What of people who never make a conscious decision to consent to the social contract? Locke manages to maintain a consent basis for political obligation fairly consistently, but eventually has to admit that people who had no part in the formation of a political order still are obliged to obey the laws because they enjoy the benefits of that order and because they simply are resident in the territory of that order.[64] They may not have been at the founding, and may never have taken an oath of citizenship, but by their sheer presence they have tacitly consented to the social contract. But while enjoying the benefits of a social order, and being resident in the territory of a particular polity, may generate some sorts of obligations, it is not evident that these obligations arise from *consent.* As John Simmons argues, "[C]onsent theory's big gun turns out to be of woefully small caliber."[65] If they do not rise from consent, however, it is not clear how Locke's theory can account for the persistence of political order through time. And Locke, having determined that gratitude works in the subpolitical realm of society but not in politics, cannot solve the problem by introducing gratitude as the basis of political obligation within the consensual state.[66] Ever since Locke, liberal political theory has been dogged by the same tension: gratitude remains a key political reality, but theorists all but ignore it.

Locke's work is a watershed in his consistent refusal to synthesize the bonds of gratitude into political theory, especially his theory of political authority. In doing this, he accomplishes something even more momentous for the future of political theory and practice: he constitutes a "private" arena of social life that is cleanly separated from the political sphere. Locke acknowledges that there are relations of benefaction and gratitude in families and in social networks. He regularly acknowledges his own debts to his patrons, and knows how to play the game of gratitude display well enough to keep his patrons' patronage. But in his theory none of this has any role in political life. It is not the foundation of political authority or political order, and it is not the dynamic power of politics. It is private social life rather than public life. What Locke accomplishes is not the "privatization" of gratitude, since that implies that there was a preexisting private sphere into which he stuffed gratitude. Rather, he theoretically constitutes a private sphere by claiming that gratitude, benefaction, debts incurred by favors, and so on are not the stuff of politics.

Gratitude as Moral Sentiment

With Adam Smith, we skip forward a century. That is purposeful. Smith knew Locke's work,[67] and he accomplished in economic theory what Locke accomplished in political theory—the constitution of a "private" space of gratitude separate from the public world of industry and finance.[68]

Adam Smith seems an unlikely figure to discuss in a survey of Western conceptions of gratitude. Superficially, he would seem to be villain number one in the destruction of the "gift economy" of medieval Christendom and the erection of the commercial economy of modern capitalism.[69] In *The Wealth of Nations*, to be sure, Smith says little about the role of gratitude and gifts in economic relations. That absence is itself revealing because it hints at an assumption that economic life is a distinct field of concern and analysis from the nexus of benefit and return. Yet Smith shared with other figures of the Scottish Enlightenment an obsession with the problem of social dependence that is traditionally associated with benefits and gratitude.[70] While *Wealth of Nations* says nothing about the role of gratitude, Smith's moral philosophy, contained in the *Theory of Moral Sentiments*, analyzes the morality of gratitude in a number of innovative ways.

Smith's moral theory redresses the individualism of utilitarian ethics that had grown out of Locke. Instead of seeing reason or interest as the sole motivator of human action or the sole ground of ethical life, Smith insists not only that sympathy is a universal human experience but also that sympathy lies at the foundation of the moral life. "How selfish soever man may be supposed," Smith notes at the outset, "there are evidently some principles in his nature, which interest him in the fortune of others, and render their happiness necessary to him, though he derives nothing from it except the pleasure of seeing it." Pity for the misery of others is a primordial human emotion, so much so that even the "greatest ruffian, the most hardened violator of the laws of society, is not altogether without it." When we see someone in piteous circumstances, we imagine ourselves in the same, and thus "become in some measure the same person with him," feeling his sensations in ourselves. Through the operation of imagination, self-interest thus flowers out in sympathetic compassions.[71]

Sympathy is the root of morals because sympathy and moral approbation are identical. When we approve another's passions, and consider them appropriate to their objects, we are saying that we sympathize with those passions. On the other hand, "not to approve of them . . . is the same thing as to observe that we do not entirely sympathize with them." Judgment by sympathy involves judgment by one's own lights, but this subjectivism is inevitable: "I judge of your sight by my sight, of your ear by my ear, of your reason by my reason, of your resentment by my resentment, of your life by my love. I neither have, nor can have, any other way of judging."[72] The judgment has to do with the match or mismatch between a passion and its object: anger is brutal and detestable, but anger that aims to redress injuries is "noble and generous resentment."[73]

Gratitude is one of the two chief sentiments that exhibit the sympathetic character of human existence. We may not benefit from another's faithfulness, but "we enter into their gratitude towards those faithful friends who did not desert them in their difficulties; and we heartily go along with their resentment against those perfidious traitors who injured, abandoned, or deceived them."[74] Like the other sentiments, it must be directed toward proper objects, but Smith's theory turns this moral point upside down. Because there is to be a match between sentiment and object, there is, by the same token, to be a match between object and sentiment. If we can judge sentiment by comparison with the object that gives rise to it, we can also assess the object by reference to the sentiment to which it gives rise. The use of gratitude and resentment as standards for judging merit is a natural consequence of Smith's sympathetic psychological moral theory: "Virtue is not said to be amiable, or to be meritorious," he writes, "because it is the object of its own love, or of its own gratitude, but because it excites those sentiments in other men."[75] The whole theory is underwritten by an unstated and undefended assumption that gratitude and resentment are more or less universal responses to certain kinds of actions. Smith assumes that there is a universal natural gratitude and resentment, and that this human consensus can serve as the basis of a moral theory concerning actions that are approved or disapproved. Beneficent actions require reward; they are meritorious. The reason, Smith says, is that "such alone are the approved objects of gratitude, or excite the sympathetic gratitude of the spectator."[76]

Smith admits that other passions arise in connection with the "happiness or misery of others," but none of these is so directly related to the quality of an action as gratitude and resentment. Both gratitude and resentment directly impose obligations on us. If someone does us a favor and receives a reward from elsewhere, "though it pleases our love, it does not content our gratitude." The debt of gratitude must be repaid by the debtor: "Till we have recompensed him, till we ourselves have been instrumental in promoting his happiness, we feel ourselves still loaded with that debt which his past services have laid on us."[77] So, negatively, with resentment: we are not satisfied that vengeance is taken on someone who has harmed us until we have been instruments of that vengeance. Because "gratitude and resentment . . . are the sentiments which most immediately and directly prompt to reward and to punish, they are properly the grounds for merit and demerit."[78]

Underlying gratitude and resentment are the fundamental sensations of pleasure and pain: "What gives pleasure or pain . . . is the sole exciting cause of gratitude and resentment."[79] Gratitude is a response to a kind of pleasure, resentment to a kind of pain. Human beings could not respond with gratitude or resentment without first being capable of the experience of pleasure and pain. Since animals can feel pleasure and pain, they are in a limited way capable of feeling and expressing both resentment and gratitude. Yet animal gratitude is imperfect, since gratitude desires not merely "to make the benefactor feel pleasure in his turn" but rather to commend the benefactor, "to make him conscious that he meets with this reward on account of his past conduct."[80] Gratitude aims to make the benefactor pleased with his conduct and "to satisfy him that the person upon whom he bestowed his good offices was not unworthy of them."[81] Proper gratitude does not attempt to "extort" favors, but it is interested in increasing the respect of the benefactor. Though rooted in the experience of pleasure, gratitude is not reducible to it. For an act or gift to be the proper object of gratitude, it must not only cause pleasure but also cause pleasure from design.

One would think that there is a difference between an act that rightly deserves gratitude and one that might elicit gratitude, and Smith acknowledges this at various points in the treatise. Praise and praiseworthiness are not the same, nor are blame and blameworthiness, nor loveliness and being loved. But the distinction between the two lies, Smith thinks, in the universality of the sentiment. I see only with my eyes, and thus compare your seeing with mine. Because his moral system is rooted in human sympathy, fellow feeling, human responses are the standard by which actions are judged. Thus, "he . . . appears to deserve reward, who, to some person or persons, is the natural object of a gratitude which every human heart is disposed to beat time to, and thereby applaud: and he, on the other hand, appears to deserve punishment, who in the same manner is to some person or persons the natural object of a resentment which the breast of every reasonable man is ready to adopt and sympathize with. To us, surely, that action must appear to deserve reward, which everybody who knows of it would wish to reward, and therefore delights to see rewarded."[82] There are occasions when we cannot enter sympathetically into the gratitude or resentment of another. "If we cannot enter into the affections which influenced his conduct, we have little sympathy with the gratitude of the person who receives the benefit," Smith argues.[83] But that means only that we cannot entirely approve the sentiment of gratitude.

In part, Smith is following the traditional notion that the motives and attitudes of the benefactor help to determine the degree and shape of the response. Cicero and Seneca said as much. But Smith's point is more radical. When we cannot sympathize with the gratitude of a recipient of a good turn because we suspect the motives of the benefactor, then we must conclude that the recipient's gratitude is excessive: "If in the conduct of the benefactor there appears to have been no propriety, how beneficial soever its effects, it does not seem to demand, or necessarily to require, any proportionable recompense."[84] We thus disapprove excessive gratitude—that is, gratitude with which we cannot entirely sympathize. On the other hand, we can share the gratitude of the recipient only if we fully trust the donor's motives. For this reason, Smith concludes that the "sense of merit" is a "compounded" sentiment consisting of both "a direct sympathy with the sentiments of the agent" and "an indirect sympathy with the gratitude of those who receive the benefit of his actions."[85] Resentment and the accompanying "sense of demerit" are also compounded. If we cannot entirely disapprove the motives of the one who does injury—if, for instance, we believe him partly justified—then we will not entirely sympathize with nor entirely approve the injured party's resentment. To sense demerit, we need to feel both direct antipathy to the sentiments of the agent and indirect sympathy with the recipient of the one who suffers.

Heir to centuries of Christian reflections on justice and reciprocity, Smith includes a theological element in his account. "We are equally grieved and enraged at the wrong that is done," he observes, but then "find it altogether out of our power to redress it." When justice fails on earth, we "naturally appeal to heaven" in hopes that "the great Author of our nature" will equalize the situation and bring relief. God's invisible hand balances social exchanges as much as the exchanges of the market.[86]

Important as gratitude and resentment are to Smith's moral theory, however, he carefully distinguishes between the realm where these sentiments operate and the realm of political life. Smith rings the changes on classical and Renaissance denunciations of ingratitude. It is "black" and "selfish" and deserves "the highest disapprobation." But, he adds, the ingrate "does no positive hurt to anybody." His failure to do good is not the same as doing evil. He becomes an object of hatred, but "his want of ingratitude . . . cannot be punished." Demanding and enforcing gratitude would be "still more improper than his neglecting to perform it." A benefactor who tries to force a grateful response suffers "dishonor," and no third person is capable of intervening to sort things out. If this is true of gratitude, which is "nearest to what is called a perfect and complete obligation," then it must be true even more of friendship, generosity, or charity.[87] Gratitude is a debt that needs paying, but no one has a debt of generosity or charity—at least, we do not speak as if they did. The realm of gratitude and benefaction must therefore be left to private persons, to the freedom of the wills of the participants. Even in the realm where warm sentiments like gratitude are operative, they are checked and subordinated to the sense of duty.[88]

If generosity and gratitude are consigned to the free interactions of social life, there is a virtue that must be "extorted by force" and whose violations are punishable. That is *justice*.[89] Smith notes the "remarkable distinction between justice and all the other social virtues . . . that we feel ourselves to be under a stricter obligation to act according to justice, than agreeably to friendship, charity, or generosity."[90] Justice is more precisely determinable than the softer virtues of generosity and gratitude, and this is partly because in many instances justice is "a negative virtue" that does not prescribe anything positive but "only hinders us from hurting our neighbor." Gratitude is one of the virtues where the rules are most precise, and admit of few exceptions. Yet, pushed slightly, it becomes evident that the demands of gratitude are far from precise.[91] Justice is different; its rules can be determined exactly, and its demands are subject to a calculus. It would be mere pedantry to insist on strict adherence to the rules of grateful reciprocity, but "there is no pedantry in sticking fast by the rules of justice." Justice and its rules are worthy of "the most sacred regard."[92] The man who keeps the bare minimum demands of justice is not necessarily admirable. He will not enjoy the affection of his fellow man. But he has a right to the same justice that he hands out: others must leave him be as he leaves others be. These precise rules of justice—which protect life and person, property, and personal rights—provide the firm foundation of society. Society can function without benefactions and gratitude. It is not a perfect society, but it is still functional. Not surprisingly, the model of this minimal society is the market, in which everyone acts out of self-interest and is punished only for impinging on the freedom of others.

It is important to clarify what Smith is saying. Seneca agrees that ingratitude ought not to be subject to legal sanctions or civil punishments.[93] Smith also speaks of the ways that society is enriched by mutual assistance: "Where the necessary assistance is reciprocally afforded from love, from gratitude, from friendship, and esteem, the society flourishes and is happy."[94] Yet, unlike Seneca or Aquinas, who defined gratitude as an "adjunct" of the virtue of justice, Smith sharply distinguishes gratitude-based social relations from the realm of justice, and likewise claims that even without benefits and gratitude, society could continue: "though among the different members of the society there should be no mutual love and affection, the society, though less happy and agreeable, will not necessarily be dissolved."[95] Society can survive without gratitude, but it absolutely needs justice. Justice alone suffices for social order: "Society . . . cannot subsist among those who are at all times ready to hurt and injure one another." For Smith, "benefi-cence . . . is less essential to the existence of society than justice. Society may subsist, though not in the most comfortable state, without beneficence; but the prevalence of injustice must utterly destroy it." Gratitude is decorative, an "ornament which embellishes" the stern, precise, impersonal founda-tion of justice, which is "the main pillar that upholds the whole edifice."[96] Along with other early modern and Enlightenment political and economic theorists, Smith is simultaneously constituting justice as legal and political that, unlike the Hebrew *zedekah* or Greek *dike*, is cleansed of every speck of benevolence, generosity, and mercy. Justice is the hardware, the energy powering the machine of the modern political economy. Justice is the gram-mar of social life, gratitude its rhetoric, its poetry. However exulting we might find elegance and sublimity in letters, Smith thinks we all know that these qualities are not essential to conversation or communication.[97]

Liberal Fantasy

Following Locke, Smith creates a realm of social life distinct from the realm of political economy, much as early modern theorists had created a realm of religious life distinct from social, political, and cultural life. Like Locke, Smith is not discerning a preexisting distinction. He theoretically imagines a distinction that simply did not pertain in the Roman world, the feudal sys-tem, or the courts of the Renaissance, when the benefit-gratitude nexus was the stuff of political life. He imagines a new ordering of sociopolitical life, one in which "state" and "society" and "economy" are identifiable as dif-ferentiated regions of human life. And at the heart of this new imagination is a constriction of the realm of gift and gratitude to "private" sociability.

Whether the world that Smith describes has *ever* existed is questionable. Graft and gratitude continued to be important in political practice long after 1776, and for all its celebration of self-interest the market has never been a gift-free zone.[98] Promotions are not always meritorious; deals and contracts are struck not merely for self-interest but because my college roommate's buddy knows someone who is part of a high-tech start-up. Everyone knows that gratitude is the lifeblood of politics. Senator negotiates with senator by calling in or imposing debts of gratitude: I will support your Medicare proposal if you lend aid to my tax plan. Congressman scratches the back of congressman so that he will later get a scratch himself. Legislators deliver truckloads of pork to constituents, who repay them with votes. Whatever their talents, a disproportionate number of Kennedys and Bushes rise to the top of American politics because voters and political patrons feel a sense of obligation toward the family. Quite apart from bribery, scandal, and corruption, this is how every modern democracy functions, and everyone knows it. More generally, gratitude is a central component of nationalism, arguably deliberately created and fostered to maintain the loyalty of citizens.[99]

Everyone, that is, except political theorists, who have spent the modern age carefully siphoning out gratitude from politics so as to constitute a "private" zone of gift and gratitude and a corresponding gratitude-free zone of public life. What modern politics aims at is a *structural* separation of gratitude from political life. Even if it is acknowledged that obligations of gratitude are central to the actual workings of politics, modern theory aims to erect a fictive wall of separation. Theorists try to convince everyone that they have identified something in the real world, and can be pretty convincing—until the next scandal breaks out. The world theorists claim to describe does not actually exist. The mythology of a political economy purged of the dynamics of gratitude is one of the defining mythologies of modern politics. Liberal theory is fantasy; works of liberal theory are fantasy fiction.[100]

Yet for all that, liberal theory is a Christian, or at least a post-Christian, fantasy. Locke was a Protestant, if a rather eccentric one. Lockean theory creates and guards the possibility of refusal, the possibility that a people might refuse an inherited political order and overturn it in a revolution, the possibility of individual resistance to state tyranny. This is Lockean freedom, Lockean individualism, and it is the freedom and individualism of the ingrate. From this angle, it appears that the deep foundation of Locke's theory is early Christian ingratitude, given new life by the Reformation. But if the pious (if unorthodox) Locke draws on Pauline and Puritan sources, it is only in part, for like Hobbes he detaches politics not only from the small circles of social reciprocity but also from the infinite circle of God and creation. Whether freedom and individualism can long survive outside the infinite circle is a question I shall address in the final chapter of part II.

SEVEN

Methodological Ingratitude

"She certainly did not hate him. No, hatred had vanished long ago." In its place was something more than respect, something beyond esteem. "It was gratitude.—Gratitude, not merely for having once loved her, but for loving her well enough to forgive all the petulance and acrimony of her manner in rejecting him." Instead of turning her away he did all he could "to preserve the acquaintance." A change of this magnitude in "a man of so much pride excited not only astonishment but gratitude." There was only one explanation: "to love, ardent love, it must be attributed."[1] Thus far the rambling thoughts of Elizabeth Bennet, tracking her changing feelings for the debonair Mr. Fitzwilliam Darcy.

For some, the private and sentimental gratitude created by the political and economic theorists of the seventeenth and eighteenth centuries was liberating. By erecting a market economy as a zone of pure self-interest, the political and economic theorists of the seventeenth and eighteenth centuries conversely freed the realm of social relations for pure altruistic generosity.[2] Liberalism liberated not only economic but also personal life by demonstrating that the proper place of friendship is wholly "outside" the calculating exchanges of the marketplace, and also "outside" the reciprocities in which friendship had been ensnared since Aristotle. Gratitude had become a soft and womanly virtue, a virtue of domesticity and feminine piety, falling within the province of novelists of romance and manners. The effort of political theorists and economists to confine exchange to the marketplace also opened up the possibility of the pure gift as its private counterpart. "Gift theorists" are as indebted to Locke and Smith as democratic capitalists.[3]

They are simply obverse sides of the liberal coin. Moralists continued, as we see ahead, to moralize about gratitude, but it was well on its way to being reduced to a sentiment, a matter of etiquette.[4]

Gratitude was, after all, no longer thought to be worthy of a central place in serious thought. After the Lisbon earthquake of 1755, anyone who proposed gratitude as a dominant stance in life looked hopelessly Panglossian if not positively evil.[5] Scientific advances made mystical notions of cosmic gratitude look quaint, and by the early part of the nineteenth century Darwin had posited natural evil rather than altruistic gift and grateful response as the dynamic of evolutionary development. We are the product of a competition for survival. It was a natural world in which benevolent reciprocity seemed to have no place, and for some this Hobbesian war spilled into social life. Economic and political developments also tarnished the usefulness of gratitude as a category of serious reflection. Industrial capitalism was beginning to take off, and a monetary economy had come to eclipse (though it never eliminated) whatever "gift economy" existed in early modern Europe. Politics was conducted not by kings and their knights, not by kings and courtiers, but by kings (or, in some cases, PMs) and salaried bureaucrats.

Christianity was the first eruption of "ingratitude" in Western history; the Reformation the second. The philosophers of the Enlightenment detonated the third ingratitude bomb. Indebted as it was to Christian and Protestant ingratitude, the Enlightenment was different. Jesus and Paul appealed back beyond first-century Judaism to recall the Jews to a form of gratitude they had all but forgotten. They were "ungrateful" toward the present in view of a past that they hoped to enact in the future. The Reformers likewise plundered the Bible and writers of the early church for standards by which to measure late medieval Catholicism. Both the early Christians and Reformers were ingrates toward the present order because they were grateful to God. By contrast, the philosophers appealed to no deep past; their ingratitude was not enclosed in an infinite circle of divine gift and human gratitude. They appealed to reason, and they claimed to be starting all over again.

The aspiration to begin again is most overt in the French Revolution. "Year 1 of the Revolution"—it was a potent symbol in Revolutionary France. After the National Convention abolished the monarchy on September 21, 1793, they created a new calendar in which September 22 became 1 Vendemiaire, year 1 of the Republic. It was the beginning of a new age, the beginning of a new world, built from a cleared ground. For observers like Edmund Burke, it was clear evidence that the revolutionaries were motivated by sheer ungrounded ingratitude. Burke's assault on the French revolutionaries turned on a theory about the obligations of political society. Social order is "indeed a contract," yet it was a different sort of contractual arrange-ment than "a partnership agreement in a trade of pepper and coffee, calico or tobacco," which are temporary and can be "dissolved by the fancy of the parties." The partnership of political society is not merely in certain "perish-able" or "animal" needs, but one "in all art, a partnership in every virtue and in all perfection." Such virtues cannot be pursued in one generation only. Society is thus a "partnership not only between those who are living, but between those who are living, those who are dead, and those who are to be born." There is a "great primeval contract of eternal society" that "holds all moral natures each in their appointed place." The contracts of each par-ticular nation are no more than a "clause" in this universal human contract, the law to which all are obligated, from which none can withdraw at their pleasure, to be dissolved "into an unsocial, uncivil, and unconnected chaos of elementary principles." Only a "first and supreme necessity" that "is not chosen, but chooses" can justify a resort to anarchy and a dissolution of a particular order.[6] That order is established by convention, and it requires long experience to be able to reform or revise the order wisely.

In his letter to the Earl of Lauderdale defending the pension granted to him by Prime Minister William Pitt, Burke explicitly charges that revolution-ary ethos is an ethos of ingratitude. "With them insurrection is the most sacred of revolutionary duties to the state. Ingratitude to benefactors is the first of revolutionary virtues. Ingratitude is indeed their four cardinal virtues compacted and amalgamated into one; and he will find it in everything that has happened since the commencement of the philosophic Revolution to this hour." It will never end. Any revolutionary who "pleads the merit of having performed the duty of insurrection against the order he lives in (God forbid he ever should)" will find others performing "the duty of insurrection against him." Anyone who "pleads . . . his ingratitude to the Crown for its creation of his family, others will plead their right and duty to pay him in kind."[7]

Cogito and New Beginnings

Behind the political year 1 was a philosophical year 1, which first took shape in the work of René Descartes.

Descartes included gratitude among the passions in his 1649 *Les passions de l'ame*. That classification itself is revealing. Instead of treating it as a vir-tue, an aspect of justice, as Cicero and Aquinas had done, Descartes included it among the passions. Within this context, much that Descartes says is quite traditional. A good deed done by another evokes "approval," and when that good is done for us specifically the approval of the goodness of the action is accompanied by gratitude.[8] Gratitude is defined as "a kind of love," which is aroused by an action that does good or at least was intended for our good. It "has the same content as approval," but beyond approval gratitude is "based on an action that affects us." The passion evoked is not merely one of love, but includes an element of reciprocation. We not only approve the action done, but because the action was done for our benefit, "we desire to reciprocate." It is this desire for reciprocation that gives gratitude more "strength" than merely approval, especially in those who have "noble and generous" souls.[9] Good deeds are one-half of the working of human social relations, but because gratitude seeks to reciprocate and close the circle of good deeds, it is "one of the principal bonds of human society."[10]

Descartes denies that ingratitude qualifies as a passion since there is no naturally implanted movement toward ingratitude. Rather, ingratitude is nothing but "the direct opposite of gratitude." It is not a passion but simply a vice. According to Descartes, three categories of people exhibit this vice: "Brutish" and "arrogant" people are ungrateful because they "think that all things are their due"; some are too "stupid" to take time to reflect on the benefits they receive from others; the "weak and abject" are obsequious in seeking help but then hate their benefactors. A weak man hates his benefactor because he "lacks the will to return the favour or despairs of his ability to do so." Certain that everyone is as greedy as he is and that no one does good without expecting reward, he thinks he has deceived his benefactor by taking a favor without any plan to return it.[11]

Drawing on a tradition that goes back at least to Epicurus, Descartes also claims that anger is "directly opposed to gratitude." Anger is a species of "hatred or aversion" that is directed specifically to "those who have done (or tried to do) not just to *someone* but to *us* in particular."[12] In contrast to indignation, which is "hatred or aversion" toward anyone who does evil to anyone,[13] anger is specified. In that respect, it is like gratitude: gratitude is a love that responds to a good done for me; anger is hate responding to evil done to me. Descartes distinguishes two varieties of anger. The first "flares up suddenly and is obvious from the outside," but the other "gnaws more at the heart." The second is the more dangerous because "its strength is gradually increased by the agitation that a burning desire for vengeance stirs up in the blood." Blood, mixed with bile from the liver and spleen, creates heat in the heart. This sort of anger opposes gratitude in a particular way: generous souls are the most grateful, and conversely the souls that are most vain, abject, and weak are the ones most susceptible to this slow-burning anger. The more vain a person is, the more intense his anger at wrongs done to him: to a proud person, any wrong done is an event of apocalyptic magnitude.[14]

It is here that Descartes contributes something innovative to the theory of gratitude and generosity. Generosity, Descartes says, has two elements: the conviction that one possesses nothing "except the free control of his volitions," and the determination to use that freedom for good purposes.[15] Vanity leads to excesses of anger because it causes us to exaggerate the wrongs done to us. Generosity has the opposite effect: it "makes us put a low value on all the good things that might be taken away" and a correspondingly "high value on the liberty and absolute control over ourselves that we cease to have when we take offense at something that someone else does." Generosity is "the best remedy" for excesses of anger. A generous man will not be aroused to extremes of anger; his generosity will keep anger in check, limiting it to contempt or "at most to indignation."[16] Generosity is thus not only a virtue in itself, but also the control switch on vices. It is not, however, a control only on anger. It arrests and limits the damage of vices generally. Generosity enables one to have command over jealousy and envy because the generous man finds worth only in those things that are completely within his control. It limits anger because the generous esteem everyone, and the generous are fearless because of their confidence in their virtue.[17] Generosity is "a kind of key to all other virtues and a general remedy for every disorder of the passions."[18] Where Aristotle and the scholastics had emphasized magnanimity or prudence as the chief virtue, Descartes' neo-Stoic ethic instead places generosity at the pinnacle of the hierarchy of virtues.[19]

Despite his traditional encomiums to gratitude and polemics against its opposite, something else is happening. Descartes advocates generosity because it reflects the stoic detachment from those things outside one's control, including detachment from any generous act on the part of others. Despite his affirmation of the virtue of gratitude, Descartes' understanding of generosity is a solvent of the passion of gratitude. Furthermore, Descartes links his account of gratitude to a dualistic anthropology in which the soul exists within the "machine" of the body.[20] He explains the heart's functions, the production of "animal spirits" in the brain, the movement of muscles, and the perceptions of the senses without reference to the soul, all of which "the body can do unaided."[21] The soul and body are intertwined, particularly in the pineal gland that Descartes identifies as the place where the soul is concentrated in greatest intensity. But the anthropology that locates gratitude in the soul militates against a developed notion of gratitude.

More important, Descartes' fundamental, foundationalist method of philosophy was as much a methodological ingratitude as scholasticism was methodological gratitude. Famously, he tried to restart philosophy on the basis of the undeniable truth of his own existence. Descartes' *ego cogito, ergo sum* is not original, at least in its form. It has origins in Augustine, who said in response to skeptics, "I have no fear of the arguments of the Academics. They say, 'Suppose you are mistaken?' I reply, 'If I am mistaken, I exist [*si fallor, sum*].' A non-existent being cannot be mistaken; therefore I must exist, if I am mistaken. . . . Then, since my being mistaken proves that I exist, how can I be mistaken in thinking that I exist, seeing that my mistaken establishes my existence [*quando certum me esse, si fallor*]?" But Descartes recognized that his use of this form of argument is quite different from Augustine's: "I do indeed find that [Augustine] does use it to prove the certainty of our existence. He goes on to show that there is a certain likeness of the Trinity in us, in that we exist, we know that we exist, and we love the existence and the knowledge we have. I, on the other hand, use the argument to show that this I that is thinking is an immaterial substance with no bodily element. These are two very different things." Indeed they are: in fact, Augustine and Descartes are further apart than this statement from Descartes indicates. Augustine's purpose in the larger context is to establish the continuing goodness of the world following the fall (against the Manichees). To this end, Augustine argues that "we recognize in ourselves . . . an image of God, that is of the Supreme trinity. It is not an adequate image, but a very distant parallel." And this premise leads to the conclusion that "we are human beings, created in our Creator's image."[22] For Augustine, the argument was part of an argument to support faith. For Descartes, it was part of a ground-clearing argument that would enable philosophy to start afresh on a basis of clear and distinct ideas, firmer than scholasticism.

Annoying Duty

Like those of Descartes, some of Jean-Jacques Rousseau's discussions of gratitude are quite traditional. In book IV of *Emile*, Rousseau lays out a theory of "sublimation" by which Emile's adolescent sexual desires can lay the basis for higher moral and aesthetic pursuits.[23] "As soon as he loves," Rousseau writes, "he depends on his attachments. Thus are formed the first bonds linking him to his species."[24] Initially, these bonds will be forged only with his students, friends, and closest fellows, but over time, as his nature is cultivated and after he reflects on the character of his attachments to his relations, "he will be able to get to the point of generalizing his individual notions under the abstract idea of humanity and to join to his particular affections those which can make him identify with his species." Leading a student to become sensitive to the bonds he has with others is a delicate process. A teacher is always in danger of exacting "obedience from him in return for the efforts you made on his behalf," which will only leave him oppressed at the obligations imposed without his consent: "He will say to himself that, while feigning to oblige him for nothing, you aspired to put him in debt and to bind him by a contract."

Reflections on the way teaching can backfire lead Rousseau into a general reflection on the problems of granting benefits: "Ingratitude would be rarer if usurious benefactions were less common. We like what does us good. It is so natural a sentiment! Ingratitude is not in the heart of man, but self-interest is. There are fewer obligated ingrates than self-interested benefactors. If you sell me your gifts, I shall haggle about the price. But if you feign giving in order to sell later at your price, you are practicing fraud. It is their being free that makes these gifts priceless." A fish has no debt of gratitude to the fisherman that offers him bait and then hooks him on his line. True benefaction does not come with a hook attached, and thus it never happens that "a true benefaction [will] produce an ingrate." Because gratitude is a natural sentiment, so long as a benefactor does not abuse his position, the pupil will be grateful. As soon as a giver "vaunts" his services, then they become "unendurable" for the recipient. Better for the benefactor to forget the benefits he has given, for that will make the recipient more apt to remember them.[25] All this could have been written by Seneca, who understood well that poorly given gifts can be onerous, that clumsy benefactions feed ingratitude. Elsewhere in *Emile*, Rousseau discusses the techniques a teacher can use to inculcate gratitude. The Savoyard Vicar encourages a teacher to give books to a student "to detach him gradually from his idle and vagrant life." He can even require the student to take extracts from the books he reads, but he will relieve the burden by "feigning to need these extracts," and by this same deception he will feed "the noble sentiment of gratitude."[26]

In personal life, Rousseau bristled at the constraints that obligations placed on him.[27] Rousseau's instinctive resistance to the constraints of social life included, explicitly, resistance to the obligations incurred by dependence on the favor of others. He reacted to reminders from friends about how much he owed patrons, and in a letter to Malesherbes he wrote, "every benefit demands gratitude; and I feel my heart to be ungrateful from the very fact that gratitude is a duty." The demand for generosity was equally irksome. In the sixth of his *Reveries du promeneur solitaire*, Rousseau describes how he gave a coin to a lame boy he met on a Paris street so often that it became "a kind of duty I soon felt to be annoying." To avoid the boy, he eventually stopped walking in the street. Though he recognized that he had broken an implicit contract of generosity and gratitude, he said that the injustice was "the effect of an independence the heart loves and pronounces only with effort." Bonds of generosity are as strong as bonds of gratitude. Giving poses obligations as much as receiving. Rousseau muses on the blessing of possessing a ring of invisibility that would allow him to be generous without incurring the obligation to anyone.[28]

Indeed, he bristled at constraints of any kind. Living according to the clock was a new experience for Jean-Jacques when he arrived in Paris, and he considered it an inhibition to his natural love of life. In his *Rousseau juge de Jean-Jacques*, he described himself as a man who "loves activity, but he detests constraint. Work is no strain on him provided he can do it at his own rather than at another's time."[29] The regulation of his bodily movements was bad enough, but Rousseau particularly resented the way that social constraints affected his soul. Gradually, he began to see that this kind of constraint was the essence of the deceptions of Parisian *politesse*: "I have been very warmly welcomed," a character in *The New Heloise* says. "People meet me full of friendship; they show me a thousand civilities; they render me services of all sorts." Yet the kindness rang false: "How can you become immediately the friend of a man whom you have never seen before?"[30] The pressure of politeness is relentless, and it is morally and intellectually damaging: "Endlessly, politeness makes demands, decorum gives orders; endlessly, we follow customs, never our own bent."[31]

On day in the summer of 1749, Rousseau was walking from Paris to visit Diderot when he read a newspaper ad concerning an essay competition on the question, "Has the restoration of the arts and sciences helped to purify morals?" He experienced something like an evangelical conversion, as in a moment everything rushed into him that would later be contained in his subsequent writings on the origins of inequality, the social contract, and education. His fundamental insight was a vision of the difference between *homme naturel* and *homme artificiel*, between natural man and man as society has remade him, between the freedom of man as he was made and as he existed in a state of nature and man as he has been enchained by the social contract and the demands of polite society. Seeing through the dazzling artificiality of Parisian society meant, in part, seeing through the obligations of gift and gratitude that constitute that society.

Rousseau needed a standard against which to measure eighteenth-century society, and he found it in the state of nature. Rousseau's state of nature differed from both the Hobbesian war of all against all and the natural freedom and equality of Locke. Hobbes considered gratitude one of the natural laws of human society, and Locke recognized the filial bonds of gratitude and honor as natural, though he denied that they formed the basis for political order. Rousseau's state of nature has no room for bonds of gratitude. Each man is author of himself, self-created. Rousseau was especially opposed to the interdependent natural state put forward by Pufendorf's *On the Duties of Man and Citizen*. A human being has "an intense concern for his own preservation," but because of his neediness he cannot fulfill this concern "without the help of his fellows." Thus, humanity is "well fitted for the mutual provision of benefits." Nature, Pufendorf insists, establishes kinship among men, and thus mutual goodwill is a natural law. Each man has unique skills, and thus each can be useful to others. If the benefit one has to offer costs nothing, withholding it is a "particularly odious act of ill will and inhumanity." If the benefit is costly, then giving it displays a "higher degree of humanity." Not only are all naturally equipped and bound to be generous, but gratitude too is written into the state of man: in return for a favor, "a man who has received a benefit should be grateful," which includes a show of appreciation, goodwill for the benefactor, and alertness to "an opportunity to make an equal or larger repayment, as he can."[32]

Rousseau would have none of this. In *Emile*, he argues that a teacher should be careful to keep a young student's imagination in check until the proper time. For a long time, Emile will be allowed to read only *Robinson Crusoe*, the "Bible of the new science of nature" that "reveals man's true original condition."[33] Crusoe has no assistance from any other humans, nor any help from civilized technology,[34] but still he pursues his own preservation and acquires "a kind of well-being." Rousseau knows that this is not the state of social man, nor a state in which Emile is likely to find himself. Still, "it is on the basis of this very state that he ought to appraise all the others." Crusoe's experience provides a means for "raising oneself above prejudices and ordering one's judgments about the true relations of things." One should test artificial social order from the viewpoint of how an isolated man would judge it.[35] Rousseau admits at the outset of his essay on the origin of inequality that such a state may never have existed. Still, it functions like the fall account in Christian theology: it sets a paradisiacal standard against which to measure the corruptions of the world, and it simultaneously gives one hope that the corruptions of the world are not simply written into the nature of things.

Inspired by the image of Crusoe, Rousseau's radical conception of the state of nature dispenses with the bonds of social life entirely. Natural men have no desires or passions except the most basic kind—to satisfy physical wants. He eats when he is hungry, drinks when he is thirsty, copulates when he is filled with sexual desire. There is no family gratitude in Rousseau's state of nature because there is no family. Men and women have random and nonbinding sex, and the children they produce survive or die depending on the strength of their constitution. Rousseau finds it "impossible to conceive why, in a state of nature, one man should stand more in need of the assistance of another, than a monkey or a wolf of the assistance of another of its kind: or, granting that he did, what motives could induce that other to assist him; or, even then, by what means they could agree about the conditions." The natural man wanders about "an equal stranger to war and all ties." Bonds of servitude arise from "mutual dependence of men on one another and the reciprocal needs that unite them," but those needs and that dependence arise only when one declines to a point where he cannot do everything himself, when he falls from his Crusoe Eden. That condition does not exist in the state of nature at all, since "every one is there his own master, and the law of the strongest is of no effect."[36] In the state of nature, there is no inequality except the sheer physical sort. No benefits are given, none received, none reciprocated. For Rousseau, of course, this is deeply liberating, because the debts of gratitude are irksome. The state of nature is Rousseau's fantasy of wish fulfillment.

There is one exception to the isolation and lack of passion of natural man: natural man experiences pity. Citing Mandeville's description of a parent watching a child torn to death by a wild animal, he observes that "men would have never been better than monsters, had not nature bestowed on them a sense of compassion, to aid their reason." Beyond Mandeville, Rousseau argues that compassion or pity is the source of all social virtues: "what is generosity, clemency or humanity but compassion applied to the weak, to the guilty, or to mankind in general." Giving benefits and relations of friendship are "only the effects of compassion." Rousseau is "certain that compassion is a natural feeling" that moderates love of self and thus "contributes to the preservation of the whole species."[37] What it does *not* do, importantly, is create bonds of reciprocal need and dependence. Pity is a passion of distance. Aristotle and Cicero would have hardly recognized a friendship built on compassion as friendship at all.

Obligations and relations come at a second stage. Over time, the savages wandering through the forest keep bumping into each other, and the repeated contact gives them a sense that they share something in common. Men and women decide to live together with their children under a single roof, forming little societies where "liberty and reciprocal attachment were the only bonds of its union." So long as men confined themselves to labor that each could accomplish alone, there was no need for mutual assistance, but "from the moment one man began to stand in need of the help of another, from the moment it appeared advantageous to any one man to have enough provisions for two, equality disappeared." Land had to be divided in order to be cultivated. Thus "natural inequality unfolds itself insensibly with that of combination."[38]

Division between "mine" and "thine" awakened envy, which awakened violence and acquisitiveness. At this point, Rousseau imagines something akin to a Hobbesian state of nature, but he sees this as the product of emerging society rather than as the natural state per se. Faced with these dangers, men have no choice but to join forces "to guard the weak from oppression, to restrain the ambitious, and secure to every man the possession of what belongs to him." Political institutions seemed to offer advantages, and so "all ran headlong to their chains." The aim, of course, was not to enslave themselves but to protect liberty, but in the event the formation of social and legal order "bound new fetters on the poor, and gave new powers to the rich." Government did not begin with arbitrary power ceded to the state, but rather became "depraved" and reverted to the "law of the strongest," just the law that society was formed to overcome.[39]

Rousseau issues a call "back to nature," but he does not see the formation of society as an entire loss. In the competition for honors that "inflames" civilized men to rivalry and enmity, he sees not only the worst but also the best, "both our virtues and our vices, our science and our errors, our conquerors and our philosophers."[40] Returning to nature does not mean undoing all the knots of obligation that society brings, but attempting to reform society so that it conforms more closely to the true nature of man, to his inherent freedom and equality.

Behind this is a conviction about the nature of obligation in general. Contrary to many interpretations, Rousseau is not opposed to law. In fact, the exaltation of law is at the center of his thought, as Kant (almost alone among Rousseau's readers) recognized.[41] But in society man gives his consent to the law, and finds in the law a charter of freedom. The best law is not heteronomous, an imposition from the outside, but the law of autonomy, a law that expresses the deepest instincts of man. As Rousseau says in *Emile*, "The heart receives laws only from itself. By wanting to enchain it, one releases it; one enchains it by leaving it free."[42]

Rousseau's ideal is clearly the republican government of Geneva. In the prefatory address to the magistrates of his home city that begins his essay on inequality, he praises the city and its government as the best possible one. He knows that he received much from Geneva, and most especially from his father. But Rousseau does not once express gratitude to the city, only zeal.

Even after the social contract forms men into a political society, gratitude plays little role. In *The Social Contract*, it is almost entirely absent. But in his discussion of civil religion toward the end of that treatise, Rousseau argues that the ideal republic needs a religion that is not politically divisive like Christianity nor a purely private religion, which contributes nothing to society. What is needed is a "purely civil" profession of faith that functions as a set of "sentiments of sociability, without which it is impossible to be either a good or loyal subject." Anyone who demurs will be expelled, not as for impiety but for antisocial behavior. The creed should include some positive dogmas—"the existence of an omnipotent, intelligent, benevolent divinity that foresees and provides; the life to come; the happiness of the just; the punishment of sinners; the sanctity of the social contract and the law." It has only one negative dogma: "No intolerance."[43] Civil religion opens a space that might be occupied by gratitude. An intelligent and benevolent deity who provides for the people might be a suitable object of grateful worship, which would function as one of the sentiments of sociability that keeps the city together. Rousseau's fears of the abuse of benevolence, however, over-take this option. If he opens a space for gratitude, it is a space that he leaves utterly empty.[44]

As much as Locke and Hobbes, Rousseau needs gratitude to secure his civic order. As much as Locke and Hobbes, perhaps even more, the thrust of his philosophy eliminates gratitude as a potent social power.

Sacred Duty

Like Descartes, Immanuel Kant posits a year 1. Kant frames his answer to the question, "What is Enlightenment?" as a demand for maturity. Enlight-enment, Kant says, "is man's emergence from his self-incurred immaturity." Immaturity he defines as "the inability to use one's own understanding with-out the guidance of another," and this immaturity is "self-incurred" when the cause is "lack of resolution and courage" to use one's understanding without guidance from outside authority. "Laziness and cowardice" are the two chief impediments to enlightenment, particularly laziness, since it is so easy to be immature and simply pay for someone to make decisions for us. Famously, he quotes from Horace, but the "sapere aude" does not mean "be wise" but "dare to be wise," and Kant's emphasis is on the daring as much as the wisdom.

For all the pyrotechnics of his programmatic essay, Kant expresses fairly traditional views on gratitude in his *Lectures on Ethics*. Echoing the Sen-ecan tradition, Kant says that ingratitude is among the vices that "are the essence of vileness and wickedness." He adds, "It is inhuman to hate and persecute one from whom we have reaped a benefit, and if such conduct were the rule it would cause untold harm. Men would then be afraid to do good to anyone lest they should receive evil in return for their good."[45] He argues too that a good man might deliberately refuse benefits offered so as to avoid the obligations they impose on him. Like Descartes, Kant has some innovative and interesting things to say about gratitude and especially about ingratitude. He links ingratitude with envy as a species of "human hate that is the complete opposite of human love." Kant distinguishes two sorts of ingratitude: "qualified" ingratitude is hatred of a benefactor, but the other and more common form of ingratitude is simple "thoughtlessness."[46] Ingratitude is common, and in Kant's view this commonness is not the result of a moral decline in society (as it is for the nostalgic Seneca). This commonality of ingratitude is a social evil because it undermines the motivation for giving, which is one of the bonds of society, and more deeply because in ingratitude love is "turned upside down." Ingratitude is not mere lack but "an urge to hate the person who loves us."[47]

These traditional views seem ungrounded. Kant complicates gratitude in a systematic way.[48] His deep admiration for Isaac Newton and the achievements of post-Baconian science was combined with anxiety about the cost of a mechanistic scientific outlook for human values, morality, and religion. To "make room for faith," he argued, he would have to "do away with knowledge." This he accomplished with a twofold limitation. Theoretical reason's province is limited to the realm of phenomena, appearances that are received through sense data. Things in themselves are outside our knowing, but this means, conversely, that freedom, immortality, and the reality of God are outside the realm of theoretical reason and are known only to reason in its practical operation, only in its answers to ethical questions about what is and what is not to be done. In making room for faith, Kant makes room for God, in some ways considerable room. Kant leaves two jobs for God to do. The first is a "regulative" function. The world appears to be governed by a wise ruler. We cannot know that the world is in fact governed by God, but we can act as if it is, and that helps to stimulate research and science. God's second and more central role is a moral one. We all face unconditional imperatives, duties that we need to accept against all desire and against our own happiness, and religion means simply to do your duty as if it were a divine command. Religion is ethics, and all the rest of religion, while it may be useful, is not the heart of religious life. Sacraments, worship, dogma, liturgy, hymns, prayer are part of "ecclesiastical" religion but do not constitute the religious life. Reason tells us that the content of religion is only ethics understood as God's voice speaking to us. If religions aimed at this goal, they would all agree: dogmatically, there is going to be disagreement; but there is universal *ethical* consensus among religions.[49]

The ethics that Kant arrives at in the *Grundlegung zur Metaphysic der Sitten* does not appear to leave much space for gratitude. In his effort to purify the realm of ethics, he argues that "[n]othing can possibly be conceived in the world, or even out of it, which can be called good without qualification, except a good will."[50] And the good will, for Kant, is a will that follows duty rather than its own inclinations or any expectation of happiness. The categorical imperative confronts us not with the offer of happiness but with a simple and absolute "Do this." This imperative arises out of the autonomy and the universal rationality of the human will. Since the will is self-moving, the good must lie in itself and not in any end it aims to achieve. Since rationality is universal, the imperative that confronts the will must be a universal one. From these premises, he draws the maxim that guides all moral conduct: "Act only according to the maxim by which you can will at the same time that it becomes a universal law"[51] or "Act that the maxim of your will could always hold at the same time as a principle in giving a universal law."[52] As Michael Waldstein summarizes, "I am autonomous when I will what I will without being motivated by any good or evil, that is, when I move myself according to the categorical imperative. I fall into heteronomy when I will something *because it is good*."[53] If Kant rules out doing good because it is good to do, he certainly rules out doing good in hopes of a return. Giving benefits for the sake of a return benefit violates the autonomy of practical reason. So does returning service because of a previous service given.

Kant's personalism ends at the same point. Kant argues with great power that human beings are not means but always ends: "It is only in man, and in many only as a subject of morality, that an unconditioned legislation concerning purposes can be found, which thus enables him alone to be a final purpose to which the whole of nature is teleologically subordinated."[54] Each person must be treated as the final end of nature. Kant can thus state the imperative of practical reason as this: "In the whole of creation everything one wants and over which one has any power can also be used merely as a means; a human being alone, and with him every rational creature, is an end in itself."[55] Such is the purity of Kant's system, though, that the acts of giving for the purpose of doing good, for the purpose of glorifying God, and in the hope of a return of thanks and a continuation of a relationship are all ruled out. All of these motivations treat the other as a means rather than an end. Kant rejects all circles of gratitude. Ethics is linear; doing good, giving benefits, is purely a matter of unrequited duty.

Kant's views on gratitude get more complicated when his later writings are taken into account. The widespread understanding of Kant as an ethicist of autonomy generally builds almost exclusively on the early *Grundwerk* and does not take sufficient account of Kant's more substantive discussion of ethics, especially in the second section of his 1797 *Die Metaphysik der Sitten*, "The Doctrine of Virtue." That is where he most explicitly and thoroughly explores gratitude and ingratitude.[56] Here more fully than elsewhere, Kant integrates the duty of love into his ethical scheme. Love in this context cannot be a sentiment, since sentiments cannot be commanded. Rather, love is a practical virtue. In addition to treating the duties of love, Kant examines duties of respect. The difference has to do with the effect that the fulfillment of a duty has on another. If an ethical action, a dutiful action, imposes an obligation on the one who is acted upon, then it is a duty of love. If the action does not impose such an obligation, it is a duty of respect. Duties of love are meritorious, since they are not strictly required. In this scheme, beneficence is a duty of love, and in fact is the leading duty of love, since it imposes on the recipient of the benefit a duty of gratitude.[57] Everyone is obliged to be beneficent by promoting "the happiness of others in need" and without "hope for something in return."[58] This is part of Kant's emphasis on the duty to advance the happiness of others, which takes a prominence in his late work that it does not have in the *Grundwerk*. Virtue aims at ends, and one's own moral perfection is one end of virtuous action, but in Kant's late work virtue also aims at the promotion of others' happiness as an end.[59]

Despite Kant's rigorous articulation of an ethics of duty, he finds some room for feelings and sentiments. As noted earlier, "love" means practical action, but the duty to love includes sentiments and feelings in a secondary position as accompaniments to the practice of practical love. Sentiments of love cannot be commanded, and so cannot rise to the level of duty. But the law can command the duty of *cultivating* such sentiments.[60] Similarly with gratitude: feelings of gratefulness cannot be imposed as duties, since sentiments are beyond the reach of moral law, but those who receive benefits have the duty to cultivate feelings of gratefulness toward their benefactors. Gratitude should be shown even to "predecessors, even to those one cannot identify with certainty."[61] Gratitude is an intergenerational virtue, a point at some tension with Kant's characterization of enlightened maturity as a liberation from tradition.

"The Doctrine of Virtue" leaves some loose ends dangling. Kant argues, in keeping with the tradition going back to Seneca, that gratitude includes the duty to "render equal services to the benefactor if he can receive them (if he is still living) or, if he cannot, to render them to others."[62] But it is not clear what sort of equality Kant means here, and if he means this principle to be taken strictly, then it is impossible to fulfill. He seems to ignore relevant considerations about the relative position and wealth of the parties. A poor client will only rarely have the opportunity to render "equal" services to a benefactor. Kant provides little indication of how he would resolve this dilemma. Though odd on the face of it, Kant's characterization of the duty of gratitude as a "sacred duty" is somewhat easier to resolve. According to Kant, a sacred duty is one

> the violation of which (as a scandalous example) can destroy the moral incentive to beneficence in its very principle. For, a moral object is sacred if the obligation with regard to it cannot be discharged completely by any act in keeping with it (so that one who is under obligation always remains under obligation). Any other duty is an ordinary duty.—But one cannot, by any repayment of a kindness received, rid oneself of the obligation for it, since the recipient can never win away from the benefactor his priority of merit, namely having been the first in benevolence.[63]

There are two standards here for identifying a sacred duty. First, Kant defines it negatively. A failure to perform a duty is a moral fault, but a failure to perform a sacred duty does wider damage because it undermines the chief duty of love, which is beneficence. Ingratitude dries up the springs of gifts at the source, and this is disastrous for everyone. Second, positively, a sacred duty is one that can never be discharged completely. Elsewhere, Kant makes the point even more emphatically: "[B]eneficence creates a debt that can never be repaid. Even if I return to my benefactor fifty times more than he gave me, I am still not yet quits with him, for he did me a good turn that he did not owe me, and was the first in doing so. Even if I return it to him fifty times over, I still do it merely to repay the benefit and discharge the debt. Here I can no longer get ahead of him; for he remains always the one who was first to show me a kindness."[64] A recipient of a benefit is duty bound to perform acts of gratitude forever. The reason, Kant indicates, is simply the temporal priority of the benefactor. His act was meritorious, because it was not done to fulfill a debt. But it imposes a debt obligation on the recipient, and it is a burden from which the beneficiary can never be released.

This is a hard saying. It seems as oppressive a system of reciprocity as any we have examined in earlier chapters. Yet Kant's argument is perfectly consistent with the traditional view of gratitude. Gratitude is not strictly speaking a debt, though the language of debt is often used. It is an unusual kind of debt, one in which the obligation is not discharged and relieved by repayment. Turn Kant around: suppose gratitude could be discharged by rendering "equal" services; then gratitude would seem to be no different from a loan. But everyone from Seneca on denies that benefits are to be treated as loans. More important, Kant's point is to indicate that gratitude is not directed at the benefit so much as at the benefactor: "We . . . are thankful not merely for the good we have received, but also for the fact that the other is well disposed toward us."[65] What sort of debt would gratitude be if a show of gratitude had a "paid in full" toward the giver? The recipient can certainly show gratitude, feel grateful emotions, and even repay service, but that does not end the bond that the original gift formed.[66] Gratitude is thus a sacred duty because generosity shown and received does not end the relationship between giver and recipient.

This late treatise goes some way to resolve the apparent tensions between Kant's emphasis on moral autonomy on the one hand and his emphasis on the obligation of gratitude on the other. Kant regards ingratitude with horror. He defines it as "displeasure or discontent at the obligation the other has laid on us, through the kindness he has shown towards us," and claims that it, like envy and malice, arises from the inherent spirit of rivalry that grips human beings. He sees ingratitude emerging from the inequality that benefits create, the threat that dependence poses to one's self-esteem and autonomy, and in some cases hostility to the benefactor himself. Gratitude, he observes, "seems to be contrary to our self-esteem, since it can almost never appear without the benefactor's worth being coupled with a demeaning of the value of the other party."[67] The key passage is this: "What makes such a vice possible is misunderstanding one's duty to oneself, the duty of not needing and asking for others' beneficence, since this puts one under an obligation to them, but rather preferring to bear the hardships of life oneself than to burden others with them and so incur indebtedness (obligation); for we fear that by showing gratitude we take the inferior position of a dependent in relation to his protector, which is contrary to real self-esteem (pride in the dignity of humanity in one's own person)."[68] This seems to imply that reception of benefits is an *actual* threat to self-esteem. Such an interpretation has a basis in Kant's ethical system as a whole. He argues for self-sufficiency, claims that it is a moral duty to do all that we can to avoid neediness, and severely limits the circumstances when it is appropriate to accept benevolence from others. Yet the foregoing passage indicates that ingratitude arises from a *mis*understanding of proper self-esteem. Though it is true that a benefit creates an inequality between the giver and recipient (and, according to Kant, a permanent inequality), this is not, Kant insists, a *moral* asymmetry. When we realize that self-esteem is dependent on the inherent dignity of human beings and not on our relative relation to others, we can combat the vice of ingratitude and receive benefits without fear. Besides, Kant says with some regret it seems, we cannot avoid dependence altogether: "To be able to rid oneself of all needs, one would have to be a higher being. . . ; [but human beings], in respect of their physical nature, are not capable of total self-sufficiency."[69]

Despite Kant's fuller account of gratitude in his late work, he has not escaped the effects of his basic ethical convictions. His inclusion of love and sympathy in his ethics runs aground on his insistence on autonomy. Having flattened the circle of reciprocity into a line of duty, he cannot resurrect the circle.

Conclusion

The Enlightenment owes its ingratitude, and even some of its specific expressions, to the original Christian disruptions. Paul as much as Kant wanted the human race to grow up; Paul as much as Rousseau was careful to avoid indebtedness. For Paul, of course, both of these themes were radically christological. Paul thought the race had grown up with the coming of Jesus, and that meant that "gratitude" to the fathers no longer would take the form of slavishly following their traditions and practices. Paul said, "no debts" because he insisted that Jesus had paid them all. The liberty to which Paul called the early Christians was a liberty in Christ. Descartes, Kant, and Rousseau attempted to extend the liberty while putting Christ to the side—honoring Him perhaps, but certainly not making him central to their program of illumination. In place of traditional circles and the infinite Christian circle, they offered an empty space for rebuilding or a pure line of duty. It is an unstable basis for social life, and in the event it was fairly rapidly overtaken by renewed circles, which arrived in the West from exotic realms across the sea.

PART III

Reciprocity Rediscovered,
Reciprocity Suspected

EIGHT

Primitive Circles

In the beginning there was Boas. Then there was Thurnwald. Then there was Malinowski. And in the last days there came one named Mauss to proclaim the good news of the gift, which descended from exotic Polynesia and Melanesia to the decadent capitalist West.

For centuries, Europeans and Americans had encountered "primitive" or "savage" tribes and puzzled over their practices regarding gifts and exchanges. Portuguese explorers came bearing gifts for the tribesmen they encountered on the coast of West Africa. Many conquistadors snickered at the folly of the "Indians" who accepted trinkets in place of real valuables. Gifts were exchanged as tokens of good will and signs of peace, and occasionally some observed that gifts played other social functions as well. Nicklaus Federmann led a large expedition of a couple of hundred to Venezuela and Columbia in 1530. Trading with the Caquetios, he realized that he could become rich by trading axes, knives, and hoes for the abundant gold that the Indians possessed, but he also observed that "they gave us so many gifts and presents from good will, and only to prove their magnificence to us, and not, as in the other hamlets and nations visited, from fear."[1] Already in 1764, Thomas Hutchinson of Massachusetts Bay Colony knew of the "Indian gift" as "a proverbial expression signifying a present for which an equivalent return is expected."[2] Eighteenth-century Europeans who visited New Zealand sometimes made the mistake of admiring a Maori pendant. The owner would force it on the admirer as a gift, and soon after would be smiling and speaking in praise of the recipient's coat or gun.[3]

163

With the rise of anthropology, such passing comments in travelogues, accounts from discoverers and colonists, and missionary accounts were given more systematic theoretical treatment. For our purposes, the result was a dramatic renewal of reciprocity. The circle was back.

Gifts before Mauss

In his studies of the Kwakiutl Indians who lived on the coast of British Columbia, Franz Boas described the institution of the potlatch that later became famous through Mauss' book.[4] Others had observed and recorded the potlatch ceremony before Boas, but none had analyzed its place in Kwakiutl society as he did and none had tried to discern the logic of what appeared to Western observers to be a tremendous waste of resources. Through intensive studies of social organization, myths, religion, and rituals, Boas discovered a regular oscillation in Kwakiutl social life. During the greater part of the year, the tribe was rigidly hierarchical, but during the winter the clans broke down into secret societies segregated by sex, and it was during this period that the tribe celebrated its potlatch ceremonies. Boas discerned the competitive edge of the giving and destruction of wealth during the potlatch, recognizing that the most excessive givers and destroyers enhanced their status in the tribe. He also described the potlatches as loan exchanges. A recipient of a potlatch gift was expected to return the gift at the next year's potlatch. Marriage customs were entwined with the potlatch as well. A man was able to gain the hand of a woman by potlatch exchanges with her family.[5]

In his studies of the Banaro tribe of New Guinea, Richard Thurnwald discovered a similar principle of reciprocity that explained the social order of the tribe down to the spatial arrangement of the families. The Banaro, he found, consisted of four villages, each of which could be subdivided into smaller "hamlets." Each hamlet had a "goblin hall" divided into two sections that represented the blood relations that needed to be reconciled. The goblin halls were homes to the spirit. Thurnwald was struck by "the symmetry in the arrangement of the goblin-hall," which he described as the "expression in space-terms of the principle of social reciprocity or the 'retaliation of like for like.'" Thurnwald was willing to generalize: reciprocity "pervades the thought of primitive peoples, and often finds its expression in their social organization."[6] Sexual life and marriage among the Banaro displayed the same principles. Women were fairly independent, but their sexual lives were ordered by a defined series of relations, not only with their husband but also with their husband's relations. A Banaro man had corresponding sexual encounters with his wife's relations.[7] As a result, Thurnwald argued, "all members of the tribe are connected with, and dependent on, each other."

Shared sexual partners functioned as "insurance against the disturbing influence of the emotions upon social life," insurance against envy and sexual rivalry in particular.[8]

Bronislaw Malinowski's studies of the Trobriand Islanders likewise highlighted the circulation of gifts in primitive cultures. Though he was influenced by the work of Karl Bucher, he contested Bucher's claim that "savages . . . have no economic organization." He believed that if he could prove that Polynesians ("taken as representative of the majority of the savage race now in existence") possessed "distinct forms of economic organization," then one would expect "to find more facts of economic interest than have been hitherto recorded." In fact, the Trobriand Islanders did have an economic organization; it simply was different from anything that Bucher recognized as an economic organization.[9] His best-known discovery was the *kula*, which he described as "a form of exchange, of extensive, inter-tribal character; it is carried on by communities inhabiting a wide rings of islands, which form a closed circuit." The kula trade involved two comparatively useless items— *soulava*, red shell necklaces, and *mwali*, white shell bracelets. The former moved from one person to the next in a clockwise direction around the archipelago, while the mwali moved counterclockwise. Gifts never stopped moving. Someone who received one of the gifts might possess it for a year or two, but then he had to trade it the next time a kula boat stopped at his island. The kula was an economic exchange in that goods changed hands, but it was also bound up with power relations among the islanders. Embarking on a trading mission, an Islander would be seeking "to attain his type of value, to follow his line of social ambition" and to share in an experience of epic dimensions. It was not, Malinowski insisted, a form of barter, and it was bound up with mythology, law, and magic. It was what Mauss would later call a "total social fact."[10]

Malinowski initially suggested that there was a spectrum of gift behavior among the Trobriand Islanders, everything from a pure altruistic gift to "real barter."[11] In his later work on *Crime and Custom in Savage Society*, the altruistic gift had dropped out of his analysis and reciprocity had become a "dogma."[12] Malinowski's purpose in *Crime and Custom* was to attack the widespread assumption that "savage" people obey custom without authority or specific legal regulations and defended instead the conclusion that a notion of law distinct from customary rules and without religious sanctuary existed among primitive peoples. In the process, Malinowski claimed that "reciprocity" is the basic pattern of tribal life. Social transactions and exchanges all possess an "inner symmetry" or "reciprocity of services" that is the organizational principle of tribal order: "symmetry of structure will be

found in every savage society, as the indispensable basis of reciprocal obligations."[13] Barter, he found, was not the main form of the exchange of goods;
instead, "most if not all economic acts are found to belong to some chain of
reciprocal gifts and counter-gifts, which in the long run balance, benefiting
both sides equally."[14] Even families among the Trobriand Islanders operate
by a "system of gifts, duties, and mutual benefits exchanged between the
husband on the one hand, wife, children and wife's brother on the other."[15]
Religion is "an obligation between groups and individual" and the religious expect that sooner or later they will receive "equivalent repayment
or counter-service, stipulated by custom."[16] When regarded from a legal
perspective, Malinowski claimed, "reciprocity, the give-and-take principle,
reigns supreme also within the clan, nay within the nearest group of kins-
men."[17] The binding force of Melanesian law, he concludes, is not custom or
religion but "the concatenation of the obligations . . . arranged into chains
of mutual services, a give and take extending over long periods of time and
covering wide aspects of interest and activity."[18]

Boas, Thurnwald, and Malinowski made it clear that tribal giving was
not like the private and often linear gift practices of modern friendship or
social relations. Giving was competitive, giving was done in expectation of
a return gift, and giving was bound up with the power and status relations
within the tribe. The difference between tribal and modern giving was stark,
and the cultural anthropologists were ready to use the primitive system to
mount a critique of modern society. As Thurnwald said, "[C]ivilized man . . .
is never an economic being alone, but in his desires and aims is 'disturbed' by
a great many other factors that have nothing to do with economics proper."[19]
Malinowski's use of anthropological data to critique modern society was
more pointed. For the natives, "to possess is to give—and here the natives
differ from us notably." Gift giving and return were not merely commerce
but a way of exhibiting the person and his rank: "A man who owns a thing is
naturally expected to share it, to distribute it; to be its trustee and dispenser.
And the higher rank the greater the obligation. . . . Meanness, indeed, is the
most despised vice, and the only thing about which the natives have strong
moral views, while generosity is the essence of goodness."[20]

The Gift

In formulating his highly influential theory of the gift, Marcel Mauss never
had to leave his study. He did no field work but summarized and theorized
on the field work of his predecessors, Boas, Thurnwald, and Malinowski. His
synthesis of the data was first published in 1925 as the major article in an
issue of *Annee Sociologique*, the journal started by Mauss' uncle and mentor,

Émile Durkheim. It is one of the crucial books of our history—indeed, one of the crucial books of twentieth-century intellectual history.

One of the key themes of Mauss' little book is the notion of a "total social fact," an institution, practice, ritual that embodied the entirety of a culture. Mauss argued that gift-giving and gift-receiving practices were not merely religious institutions, though they definitely had religious dimension. They were not merely about power, but there was a power element. They were supported by cosmological myths, so there was a mythological element to them. As he said, in a total social phenomenon or a total social fact, "all kinds of institutions are given expression at one and the same time—religious, juridical, and moral, which relate to both politics and the family; likewise economic ones, which suppose special forms of production and consumption, or rather, of performing total services and distributions."[21] Gifts were total also in the sense that they "impregnated" the whole society, as Malinowski put it.[22] In North America, the potlatch is "religious, mythological, and Shamanistic," but also has juridical, economic, and social structural dimensions; in New Guinea, the kula had the same spectrum of meanings.[23]

Mauss recognized that gift giving, though it involved valuable objects and goods and services, was not primarily concerned with those objects. The particular object might in fact be quite cheap. The point was *social* more than economic. By giving a gift, the giver enters into a bond with the recipient, and the recipient has obligations associated with the bond of the gift. Gifts form personal connections. He noted the difference from exchanges in market economies. Gregarious types learn the names of their waiter or the bank teller, but many of us do not enter into anything like a personal relationship with the people from whom we receive goods and services, or to whom we provide them.

As social exchanges, gift exchanges were embedded in power relations. Wealth contained a *mana*, a power of prestige and honor. But what surprised Mauss was that in these cultures it was not possession but generosity that enhanced the power, prestige, and honor of a big man of the tribe. It was not the richest man who was considered the big man. It was the one who was most willing to give away what he had. Among the Trobriand Islanders studied by Bronislaw Malinowski, the kula was an occasion for the display of honor-enhancing generosity. As Mauss observes,

> The act of giving itself assumes very solemn forms: the thing received is disclaimed and mistrusted; it is only taken up for a moment, after it has been cast at one's feet. The giver affects an exaggerated modesty: having solemnly brought on his present, to the sound of a seashell, he excuses himself for giving only the last of what remains to him, and throws down the objects to be

given at the feet of his rival and partner. However, the seashell and the herald proclaim to everybody the solemn nature of this act of transfer. The aim of all this is to display generosity freedom, and autonomous action, as well as greatness.[24]

The leading example of what he described as "competitive" or "agonistic" generosity was the "potlatch" practices among American Indians of the Pacific Northwest, from Vancouver up to Alaska.[25] The essence of the potlatch is the obligation to give:

> A chief must give potlatches for himself, his son, his son-in-law, or his daughter, and for his dead. He can only preserve his authority over his tribe and village, and even over his family, he can only maintain his rank among the chiefs—both nationally and internationally—if he can prove he is haunted and favoured both by the spirits and by good fortune, that he is possessed, and also possesses it. And he can only prove this good fortune by spending it and sharing it out, humiliating others by placing them "in the shadow of his name."

Without prestige, one loses one's soul, and prestige is maintained by generosity.[26] At the edges, the potlatch institutions turned into sacrifices, in which the big man engaged in "pure destruction of wealth." This was not, Mauss argued, a form of abnegation or renunciation of wealth. These "egoistic" displays have "the appearance of representing purely lavish expenditure and childish prodigality." Destruction is "for the pleasure of destroying," but even this is not "disinterested." Gifts and displays of wealth destruction establish hierarchies between "chiefs and vassals," because "to give is to show one's superiority, to be more, to be higher in rank, *magister*. To accept without giving in return, or without giving more back, is to become client and service, to become small, to fall lower (*minister*)."[27] Great men "hoard, but in order to spend, to place under an obligations, to have their own 'liege men.' On the other hand, they carry on exchange, but it is above all in luxury items, ornaments or clothes, or things that are consumed immediately, as at feasts. They repay with interest, but this is in order to humiliate the person initially making the gift or exchange, and not only to recompense him for loss caused to him by 'deferred consumption.'"[28] Power accumulated to the generous simply by the display of generosity. There was prestige in generosity itself.

Giving is not free. It is compulsory, if the giver wants to maintain prestige, power, connections, and peace. The giver always gives with the hope of achieving something in return. As Mauss observed, gifts were "apparently free and disinterested but nevertheless constrained and self-interested. Almost always such services have then the form of the gift, the present generously given even when, in the gesture accompanying the transaction, there is only a polite fiction, formalism, and social deceit, and when there is really obligations and economic self-interest."[29] This also was a surprise to Mauss—the discovery, as Mary Douglas summarized his point, that there are "no free gifts."

Gifts are not freely given because the second moment of this power game is the obligation to receive. Gift giving in these cultures is not linear giving but the first curve of a circle of gift exchange. As Mauss summarized, "The institution of 'total services' does not merely carry the obligation to reciprocate presents received. It also supposes two other obligations just as important: the obligation, on the one hand, to give presents, and on the other, to receive them."[30] The obligation to accept seems to be straightforward, but it is fraught. Since gifts were exercises of power, involving a claim of superiority, reception was naturally a willing subordination and acknowledgment of inferiority. To refuse a gift displayed a fear of having to reciprocate, and this refusal could be a provocation leading to war.[31] Once the gift is given, the recipient is not free merely to accept. He must also give back, return a gift of equal or superior value, sometimes return the very same gift. Mauss explained this using the Maori concept of the *hau*, the spirit of the giver that became the spirit of the gift and remained with the gift even after the giver had handed it over to another: "a power is present that forces gifts to be passed around."[32] From this Maori notion, Mauss generalizes that "souls are mixed with things; things with souls. Lives are mingled together, and this is how, among the persons and things so intermingled, each emerges from their own sphere and mixes together." In most cases, the reciprocal gift, the act of "gratitude," has to be returned with interest.[33]

This last power is the key to explaining how gift giving enhances the power of the giver. A chief imposes obligations, imposes even an identity, on someone by giving him a gift, especially a large and expensive one. He can expect countergifts, or services, or something in return. The more he gives and the more widely he distributes his gifts, the more men he has attached to him. There is a quasi-feudal idea here (and the idea of gift has been used to try to explain vassalage and feudal obligations in some recent scholarship).[34] Thus a kind of tyranny can be exercised through excessive generosity. The obligation to reciprocate a gift is so strong that the giver can sometimes specify the gift he wants in return. Given the power of gifts, and the obligations gift giving creates, gift giving was naturally part of peace treaties.

Few books have careers as successful as *The Gift*. It quickly became a classic in cultural anthropology, and has since spilled into virtually every other discipline. Social historians of antiquity and medieval and early modern Europe all cite the book. It is in the background, as we shall see, of the contentious debates about "pure gift" in contemporary philosophy, and it has spilled into Christian theology. It supports economic historians who want to trace the prehistory of capitalism back to "gift economies." It inspires utopians who want to restore the miraculous gift economies of the past in which shortages were unknown. If the test of a great book is its power to inspire other great books, Mauss' has to be ranked as one of the great books of the twentieth century.

Contested Gift

Classic though it is, *The Gift* has generated a great deal of critical attention. Some of Mauss' basic concepts have been challenged.[35] Marshall Sahlins, for instance, argues that Mauss misunderstood the central Maori concept of hau, on which Mauss based his theory concerning the spirituality of the gift and the primitive merging of person and property. For Mauss, the hau is the spirit of the gift bestowed by the giver. Because the object is endowed with that spirit, the gift makes its way back to the source. Mauss misconstrued what his Maori source told him, and misrepresented the source by excluding certain parts of his speech. When seen in its full context, the hau is not the spirit of the gift but the *yield* of a gift. The hau does not come into play with the original donation, but only at a second remove, when a third person is introduced. As Sahlins explains, "[I]f the second gift is the *hau* of the first, then the *hau* of a good is its yield, just as the *hau* of a forest is its productiveness."[36] At another level, though, Sahlins affirmed Mauss, arguing that he rightly discerned in the hau a "total concept." It was not a concept of spirituality or personality in gifts, but rather the principle of productiveness, fertility, fecundity. A gift has a hau because it produces a return gift.[37]

Sahlins argued that Malinowski and Mauss both missed the complexity of reciprocity. It is not merely one thing, not merely an act of balancing and returning to an original equilibrium. In addition to "balanced" reciprocity, primitive cultures evidence "generalized" and "negative" reciprocity. The former is a continuous exchange of goods and beneficial services. The value of these goods and services is not calculated or recorded, but all participants in the system expect that things will balance out over time. Every giver expects to be given as he gave, even though he does not necessarily expect the return to come from the recipient of his original gift. Negative reciprocity is an equivalent exchange, but it is not good for good or benefit for benefit, it is evil for evil, eye for eye, tooth for tooth. The play of these different sorts of reciprocity, Sahlins said, depends on kinship distance, sociability, and generosity. Generalized reciprocity is expected, for example, within a kinship group. I do not expect my brother to repay me directly for a service done, but I expect that over time our mutual services will be roughly equivalent. Outside the kin group, negative reciprocity is more likely to arise.[38]

Annette Weiner questioned Mauss' focus on alienable property, claiming that those things that cannot be given away are more important. In a sense, she confirmed Mauss' "spiritualization" of the gift by arguing that such property returned to the donor because it was invested with his personality. The anthropological obsession with reciprocity, she argues, is a matter of projection: reciprocity is a principle of liberal order,[39] and anthropologists project it onto the tribes they study where it does not belong. There is a give and take in tribal societies, she admits, but what drives it is a principle of keeping in the midst of giving. It is the "desire to keep something back from the pressures of give and take." What is held back is something that is essential to the identity of a group, and thus the retention of the gift in the midst of giving establishes "difference between one person or group and another." Not gift exchange but "keeping while giving" is crucial. Communal identity and difference are established through the mechanism of inalienable possessions.[40]

Others have refined the distinction between commercial exchange and gift exchange. Raymond Firth's elaborate study of *Primitive Polynesian Economy* concluded, against the biases of many anthropologists, that many of the principles of modern economic theory applied to primitive economies as well.[41] Firth did not conclude that primitive economies were proto-capitalist. The Tikopia among whom he did his field work had a "non-competitive" economy in that "there is no constant and admitted struggle between producers to offer their goods to sets of consumers" and also in the sense that "there is no attempt by producers to thrust themselves forward by generating new wants in consumers." More basically, for the Tikopia, economic relations are always social relations as well, so the economy of this tribe was inhibited by personal and psychological factors. In some contexts, religious factors determined the deployment of energy, tools, and resources. Firth recognized that the tribe operated by "a code of reciprocity" in economic transactions. The profit motive as known in capitalist economies does not operate among the Tikopia. Tribesmen pursue economic advantage, but "traditionally dictated patterns of behavior limit and define the lines of action along which economic advantage is pursued."[42]

In a sociological study of modern societies, David Cheal challenges Maussian gift theory from another angle. Instead of pointing out that "modern" elements of economic life are apparent in tribal economies, Cheal points to the self-evident fact that gift giving remains a major activity of modern social and economic life.[43] This fact has been neglected, he claims, because of the influence of two social science paradigms: anthropological elementalism and political economy. Mauss' reduction of giving to the "essence" of obligation to give, receive, and repay is a classic example of elementalism, especially as it has lent force to the claim that reciprocity as Mauss defined it is an essential feature of all human culture. Cheal responds that giving is not a fixed practice, not the same thing in all times and places. Gift giving can remain important without conforming to the norm established by anthropologists. Social scientists dominated by the model of political economy head in an opposing direction. Instead of finding the "essence" of tribal giving in every culture, political economists believe that there has been a caesura in Western history that reduced the role of giving to nil. Gift giving was important in early societies, but that is no longer the case after the "great transformation" to capitalist economy.[44] This transformation brought a sharp divide between public and private life, with gifts firmly on the private side of the wall of separation. Capitalism also brought a rationalization of economic activity that undermined the role of (presumably irrational) altruistic generosity. Cheal admits that the role of gifts in contemporary society is different from what it was in the tribal societies studied by anthropologists. Gifts are no longer "fetishized" as in earlier cultures, but they remain important in the "moral economy" where exchanges are done for socially desirable ends, transactions that allow "social ties [to be] recognized" and "balanced social relationships [to be] maintained."[45] Gifts manage small-scale social relations and, as "redundant" transactions, are "used in the ritual construction of small worlds."[46] Gifts "facilitate types of interaction that might otherwise be weakly institutionalized."[47]

Employing a Marxist apparatus, Pierre Bourdieu explores the subtle strategies and tactics of giving, receiving, and reciprocation. He takes his opening cues from Mauss' discovery that gift transactions "are based on obligation and economic self-interest." What intrigues him is the bifurcation between what is actually going on in gift exchanges and what we claim to believe is going on. Our subjective interpretation of the transaction diverges from the objective reality, and this act of bad faith regarding the gift is necessary to gift and return. What makes this mystification possible is the fact that there is always a delay between the gift and the return. If countergifts were returned immediately, everyone would recognize that an "economic" transaction was going on. When there is a delay, we can fool ourselves into thinking otherwise. Bourdieu writes that "[g]ift exchange is an exchange in and by which the agents strive to conceal the objective truth of the exchange, i.e. the calculation which guarantees the equity of the exchange. If 'fair exchange,' the direct swapping of equivalent values, is the truth of gift exchange, gift exchange is a swapping which cannot acknowledge itself as such."[48] In that gap, there is time for a thousand indecisions and decisions, a thousand stratagems and negotiations. Gifts enable one party to exercise control over another by imposing a social debt. But gifts also enable groups in modern societies to navigate through contested territory. Gifts bind groups together in the face of political and economy "insecurity."[49]

Others have argued that reciprocity is not a universal pattern in gift giving. Not all gifts are governed by the principle of reciprocity either. In China, gifts are relayed *up* the social hierarchy, from subordinates to superiors, without any expectation that the superior will return the favor. The gift is a bestowal of honor, and moves unilaterally. In such cases, the relation of giving and honor is the reverse of Mauss' competitive potlatch: it is not the giver who enhances his honor but the recipient.[50]

The most effective critiques of Mauss, however, go deeper. They challenge the "scientific" character of his work and the genealogy offered at the beginning of this chapter. Start with the genealogy. Mauss front-loaded his book with field work from colleagues working in the very young field of anthropology. But as his footnotes make clear, he was well aware of debates concerning gifts from more traditional disciplines and less exotic settings.

During the latter part of the nineteenth century, German economists of the "Historical School" attacked the neoclassical liberal view of *homo economicus* and its theory that all exchange is self-interested. They posed altruistic exchange as a alternative that emphasized mutuality and cohesion among the subjects of exchange. In the circles in which Mauss traveled, the work of German economists became part of the critique of the individualism of modernity and of the ideals of the French Revolution, an agenda pursued by Mauss' uncle Émile Durkheim.[51] Like other German economists, Karl Bucher, for example, objected to what he saw as abstract British economic theories, which attempted to universalize the historically specific British experience.[52] Beyond other theorists, and against liberal theorists like Smith and Ricardo, he argued that the very notion of a natural economic impulse was mistaken. Human beings, he acknowledged, naturally seek self-preservation and self-interest, but this takes different forms in different times and places: "estimating the degree of displeasure of not satisfying a need, estimating the displeasure of doing work to achieve an end, comparing the two forms of displeasure, and deciding which involves the lesser sacrifice"— these are learned habits of thought, not instinctive.[53] For Bucher,

> Economic man, and more important, the *values* of economic man, were the historical and logical beginning he wished to historicize. His aim was to stop projecting backwards from the mentality of one's contemporaries and instead

come to an empirical knowledge of the distinctive psychological make-up of economic actors in different times and places. Economic behavior as the rational exercise of choice between alternatives for a minimum effort and a maximum of gain was acquired behavior; entire societies had had to acquire it, and every child had to relearn it; mature adults in modern society followed it to different degrees.[54]

If this were the case, and "there was not a natural economic behavior intrinsic to human beings in all times and place," then it must be possible to trace a "history [of] the acquisition of this kind of activity." Bucher insisted that such a history had to be built on ethnographical observation rather than on fanciful "Robinsonade" models. Unfortunately, Bucher knew little of the ethnographic research that had been going on in Britain and France for decades, research that had already challenged simplistic models of economic and social development. Bucher's own history was thus quite as abstract as British theories had been, a variation of the liberal myth already found in Hobbes. The one difference was Bucher's "historicization of [Hobbesian] brutishness," which he saw as a product of historical development rather than an original natural condition.

Like British liberals, Bucher initially assumed that human beings are natural individualists.[55] His views began to change under the impact of Wilhelm Gaul's *Geschenk nach Form und Inhalt* (1914). Gaul laid out the contours of future theories of the gift in this remarkably prescient statement: "What is striking at once about the 'modern' gift is the much freer relationship between giver and receiver . . . which is based on the much freer relationship between individuals and a complete control over one's property. In both respects the subordinating force of normative as well as the economic expectations of older eras is foreign to modern times."[56] Like Adam Smith and unlike later theorists who hankered for a return to the gift economy, Gaul viewed the change as largely a gain.[57] Under Gaul's influence, Bucher came to recognize that "[g]ift giving plays a large role among primitive peoples everywhere. . . . But the gifts are never given without expectation of a response, in the expectation of a return gift, whose character the initial giver can help to decide." From there, Bucher began to sift through the premodern history of Europe to find evidence of primordial European "gift cultures": "In Germany itself the word *schenken* (meaning 'to pour,' and the root of *Geschenk* or 'gift') revealed the deep history of gift giving in the simplest gestures, such as offering drinks, in the ancient past. Going through folklore literature, he pointed out how common gifts had been for important life events in Europe, above all marriage."[58]

The sources of Mauss' theory were not only or in the first instance from tribal societies of the Pacific rim. *The Gift* was a landmark because he made these theories widely available, and because he made eclectic use of the work of the historical school. Though he generally adopted the evolutionary perspective, and saw *homo economicus* as a creation of postindustrial society, Mauss did not starkly polarize the older "gift economies" with the capitalist economies of the Western world. He recognized "survivals" of gift-and-gratitude systems within modernized economies. In any case, the basic triple obligation identified by Mauss (to give, to receive, to repay) was well known from European sources. The "gift economy" came not from a distant utopia, but from our own past.[59]

The Gift was a political treatise as much as a "scientific" one. Mauss never intended simply to illuminate tribal cultures or the Western past. Cultural anthropology was never simply a compilation and systematization of data. If Claude Lévi-Strauss is to be believed, cultural anthropology was a creation of Rousseau because of Rousseau's "extraordinarily modern view of the passage from nature to culture."[60] Perhaps Lévi-Strauss overstates his case. Regardless of whether the perspective was Rousseauian, cultural anthropology has never been an enterprise in pure science. It has regularly aimed to hold a mirror up to the West and to test the institutions and habits of Western man by what some have supposed to be the more "natural" habits of tribal men. Mauss was not an advocate of noble savagery, but he was a social democrat who advocated the introduction of "gift" elements into the capitalist societies of the West in the form of welfare.[61] Mauss was not an opponent of the market, and in an article on Bolshevism argued that the free market was a sine qua non of economic life. But he believed that market self-interest ought not infiltrate all of the relations within modern societies.[62] Mauss' vision of modern society softened by gift seems very similar to Catholic social thought since the late nineteenth century.

It is perhaps not surprising, then, as Sahlins points out, that Mauss roots his arguments in religious principles. Sahlins considered the political philosophy that animated Mauss, connecting the French thinker to the earlier primitivism of Rousseau and also to the concerns of Hobbes. Especially from a Hobbesian perspective, it appears that the purpose and need for reciprocity are not in the spirit of the gift but in the avoidance of war. Mauss himself acknowledged that the threat of war always hovered over the competitions of giving, and he implicitly agreed with what Hobbes makes explicit: "The compulsion to reciprocate built into the *hau* responds to the repulsion of groups built into society."[63] Citing Hobbes' fourth law of nature—gratitude—Sahlins argues that both Hobbes and Mauss recognize that the laws of nature are inadequate to ensure that Warre can be overcome. Men will not give without the expectation that they will receive in return; honoring the law of nature without the expectation and assurance that others will do the same is an abandonment of reason. Nature's laws, Hobbes makes explicit, are functional only in the context of an "artificial Power" and "Reason enfranchised only by Authority."[64] Mauss, Sahlins claims, took refuge in the irrational. What ensures peace is not the artifice of Leviathan's power, but the hau, the spirit that ensures that the gift will circle back to the giver.[65] However we finally sort through Mauss' relationship to Hobbes, it is clear that Mauss was continuing to work out the problems of European liberalism. *The Gift* seemed an exotic breakthrough only in a West that had (ungratefully?) forgotten its own ancient traditions of reciprocity, its own long history of reflection on gratitude.[66]

The Moral Memory of Mankind

With all this careful study of giving, reception, and reciprocity, it might seem that gratitude would rise to the surface of anthropological thought. Such is not the case, or at least such is not the case unless we equate reciprocity with gratitude. What most puzzled Mauss about primitive tribal giving was precisely the phenomenon that Seneca and Thomas Aquinas would have seen as an expression of gratitude, the repayment of a gift at a suitable time and place. To explain the obligation to make a return on a gift, Mauss resorted to the mystical concept of the hau. Whether it was a manifestation of sympathy (as Smith thought) or an expression of a unique emotional response of gratitude was not within his purview. Yunxiang Yan comments on the strange absence of attention to gratitude in anthropological literature:

> How shall we assess the role of sentiment or emotional response in systems of gift exchange? . . . Villagers regard gift giving as a means to express both their moral obligations and feelings such as concern, affection, gratitude, and sorrow. Gift giving may also express disaffection or anger. . . . When I read ethnographic accounts of gift exchange in other parts of the world, I am puzzled by the absence of such discussion. Most studies are preoccupied with discovering either the economic rationality or religious beliefs of the local people. We have detailed descriptions of the patterns of economic transactions, the working principles of reciprocity, the relations between gift giving and cosmology, or the interconnection between persons and things. Few studies have touched on the emotional world of ordinary people and the role that gifts play in expressing emotions.[67]

Anthropology has opened up new vistas, new integrated methods for exploring cultural and social phenomena. For all that, it appears to work within the
constraints of liberal modernity.

An exception to this forgetfulness of gratitude was the German sociologist George Simmel, who gives detailed attention to faithfulness and gratitude in an essay, describing faithfulness as "the inertia of the soul."[68] Less
impressionistically, faithfulness is "the peculiar feeling which is not directed
toward the possessor's eudaemonistic good, nor toward the other's welfare
as an extrinsic, objective value, but toward the preservation of the relationship to the other. It does not engender this relationship; therefore, unlike
. . . other affects, it cannot be pre-sociological: it pervades the relation once
it exists and, as its inner self-preservation, makes the individuals-in-relation
hold fast to one another."[69]

Simmel defined gratitude in contrast to contracted legal obligations.
Human contacts, he argues, "rest on the schema of giving and returning the
equivalence."[70] Where the required return is legally demanded, gratitude is
not operative; but where the legal obligation is absent, gratitude appears to
"establish the bond of interaction, of the reciprocity of service and return
service, even where they are not guaranteed by external coercion." Alternatively, Simmel describes gratitude as the return on an exchange where the
"interaction is lifted out of the spontaneous act of correlation through the
exchange of things."[71] He points out that gratitude might even move beyond
a response to specific favors, for we can be grateful to people we do not know
and be grateful for the sheer existence of another person.

In a striking aphorism, Simmel described gratitude as "the moral memory of mankind."[72] It is the continuance of a relationship built on an interaction of exchange (not necessarily of objects) into the present and future.
Gratitude connects human actions "with what has gone before, it enriches
them with the element of personality, it gives them the continuity of interac-
tional life." If grateful response were eliminated "society (at least as we know
it) would break apart."[73] Common gratitude toward a benefactor creates
bonds not only between the benefactor and recipients, but also among the
recipients. In a footnote, Simmel offers a compact account of the sociological
centrality of giving, emphasizing that the giving is necessarily an interaction,
an exchange, and never simply unilateral:

> [G]iving is by no means only a simple effect that one individual has upon
> another: it is precisely what is required of all sociological functions, namely,
> interaction. By either accepting or rejecting the gift, the receiver has a highly
> specific effect upon the giver. The manner of his acceptance, gratefully or

ungratefully, having expected the gift or being surprised by it, being satisfied or dissatisfied, elevated or humiliated—all this keenly acts back upon the giver, although it can, of course, not be expressed in definite concepts and measures. Every act of giving is, thus, an interaction between giver and receiver.[74]

Simmel recognizes that exchanges involving gratitude are not always, perhaps never, exactly equivalent, and suggests that the inequality of gift and return gift tends to move the gift-gratitude exchange in the direction of a purchase. A man shares his mind with another, and the other loves him in return; and Simmel sees in this the shadow of a "purchase" of love. But this shadow is dispelled once the specific realities exchanged are seen in context. "Man is not the merchant of himself," and his abilities "do not simply lie before him like merchandise on a counter." In giving his powers or abilities, he is giving himself "in the form of this single energy or attribute." Man is able to "offer and accept, by means of the apparently objective response to the gift which consists in another gift, all of the subjectivity of gift and giver."[75] Gratitude can be a response not to the thing or benefit given but to the relationship with the giver that comes to realization in the exchange.

Simmel reflects on the asymmetry between an original gift and a return gift. The first gift, he suggests, is free, but the second is coerced at least by the obligation of gratitude.[76] Simmel argues that the obligatory nature of the second gift, of gratitude, is one of the reasons people refuse gifts in the first place—they are refusing the bondage, the "character indelebilis" (Simmel's term, borrowed from scholastic sacramental theology!) that comes with receiving the first gift. And this obligation is "irredeemable" precisely because the recipient can never replicate the freedom of the first gift; his gift will *never* be equivalent, balancing the gift he's received. Gratitude thus has a unique force: "[G]ratitude is perhaps the only feeling which, under all circumstances, can be morally demanded and rendered. If by itself or in response to some external reality, our inner life has made it impossible for us to continue loving, revering, esteeming a person (aesthetically or ethically or intellectually), we can still be grateful to him, since he once gained our gratitude. To this demand we are (or could be) unconditionally subject: in regard to no fault of feeling is an unmitigated sentence as appropriate as in regard to ingratitude."[77]

Conclusion

The twentieth-century return of the circle was a momentous event in the history of Western gratitude, and Mauss' great and seductive book deserves its accolades. It does not, however, do what many think it does: it does not provide a viable alternative to the linear, gratitude-free politics of liberalism. In fact, what is curious is how thoroughly Mauss ignores his own ethnographic evidence when he offers his political prescriptions. The evidence shows that, while giving can sustain an uneasy peace, it can also be highly competitive and self-interested and can easily break into violence. Such giving is hardly a promising foundation for undoing competitive capitalism. There is a rhetorical sleight of hand: Mauss shows that "gift cultures" can be rather unpleasant places to be, but when he then offers proposals for modern socialism he uses "gift" in its gentle modern sense. It is not at all clear that a society, culture, or economy can function on what moderns mean by "gift"; it is very clear that we do *not* want a society that operates by the triple obligation that Mauss says is the essence of the "primitive" gift.

Mauss could get away with this because his theory does not offer a practical model of gift and gratitude but merely a formal construct of the gift, whose very abstraction and emptiness whisper of utopia. At least since Mauss, Valentin Groebner's dictum has held true: "To speak of gifts . . . is always to speak of utopia."[78]

NINE

Denken ist Danken

Anthropologists were not the only moderns to turn their attention back to the gift tradition of the West. In both Continental and Anglo-American philosophy, the past century has seen a comparatively small burst of interest in the topic.[1] Among philosophers working in the "analytical" tradition, the most ambitious treatment is Terrance McConnell's 1993 *Gratitude*.[2] He carefully sorts through the various conditions under which gratitude is obligatory. As Seneca said, not every good one receives from another is worthy of gratitude. Someone who cuts out a diseased organ while trying to kill me has not done me a benefit. According to McConnell, gratitude is owed if the benefit is voluntary and unforced, if the beneficiary has actually accepted the benefit (which he may not), and the benefactor must have sacrificed something to give the benefit.[3]

To the question "How is a debt of gratitude discharged?" McConnell's sensible answer is, "It depends." He thinks that gratitude is appropriate even for small favors, but the kind of return necessary varies according to the size of the benefit. A small favor may require only a verbal "thanks," but a more significant favor must be repaid more fully. But how it is repaid depends. It would be unreasonable if I repaid my parents for their support through medical school by giving them tuition plus interest. That would turn their benefit into a loan. The proper gratitude for parental favors is to use well the benefits received—in this case, to be the very best physician I can possibly be. In general, McConnell suggests that "a person discharges a debt of gratitude to another when she acknowledges and appreciates what the other has done, is prepared to provide the benefactor willingly with a commensurate benefit if the proper occasion for doing so arises, and does so because she (or a loved one) has been benefitted by the other."[4]

Feelings of gratitude are typically required when a benefit is received, but feelings of gratitude are not unambiguous. There are times when gratitude is unhealthily servile.[5] McConnell explores the ins and outs of debates between impartialists and personalists on the partiality of gratitude,[6] examines the place of gratitude in moral theories, and probes the question of whether and when children owe debts of gratitude to their parents.[7] It is all done with impressive care and control, all very sensible, much of it very traditional.

McConnell and other "analytic" analysts of gratitude have significant weaknesses. On McConnell's terms, the question of whether gratitude is owed can be answered only if the beneficiary has considerable knowledge of the benefactor's purposes, intentions, and even his character. The same objection, of course, could be raised against Seneca and Cicero, who also distinguish cases where return for a benefit is appropriate. For the Christian theological tradition, this is especially troubling because Christians are exhorted to give thanks for everything in all circumstances. Subjecting gratitude to a fine-grained moral calculus robs it of the spontaneity it has in the New Testament. For all their good sense, analytic philosophers make gratitude appear rather stingy, carefully corralled, bounded. Gratitude presents a nice occasion for rigorous ethical analysis, but really it is not something to make much fuss about.

By comparison, Continental philosophers have offered several expansive treatments of gratitude.

Gratitude for All and Everything

Søren Kierkegaard outlined a radically and expansively Christian conception of gratitude. As anyone who knows Kierkegaard's work knows, this is not because Kierkegaard failed to face the abyss of nihilism that opens yawning before human life. Nihilism comes from our sense that we have too little, or from the sense that there is too much suffering to bear. When one looks at "the anarchy into which everything seemed to have disintegrated," one may give into despair, thinking that "his eyes continually read an invisible handwriting in everything, that it was emptiness and illusion."[8] If there is at base only a "wild, fermenting force writhing in dark passions that produced everything significant or insignificant," then "what would life be then but despair?"[9]

Gratitude is not based on a "scientific" conclusion that the world is well run, that resources and talents are equitably distributed. It is not a nice expectation that everything will turn out well in the end; it is not teleologically determined. Rather, gratitude is rooted in the adoption of a hermeneutical principle, a determination to read everything in the register of love. Kierkegaard expressed it with typical sharpness: "Either God is love, and then it is absolutely valid absolutely to stake absolutely everything on this . . . or God is not love: and then, yes, then the loss is so infinite that any other loss is of no consequence whatsoever."[10] Suffering is an essential dimension of attachment to this love. Truly Christian gratitude is not thanks for the goods of this world, but rather thanks for the share and imitation of the suffering of Christ.[11] In his suffering, a character like the biblical Job discerns in the world an order of gift and the power of love. When he loses his children, he could chalk it up to dumb fate, but he instead speaks of children "given" and "taken," and in the absolute confidence that God is absolutely love, he blesses the Lord in the midst of loss and suffering. He saw written into the world not dark and stupid ferment but love, and so he can give thanks in all circumstances. Whether one has little, or one suffers, or one's desires are left unfulfilled, or one is wronged and insulted, no matter what, Kierkegaard's question is the Pauline one, "Did you thank God?"[12] After all, if God takes house and children, then Job was once in blessed possession of something that could be taken away.[13]

Though at the opposite end of the religious spectrum from Kierkegaard, Nietzsche shares the Danish philosopher's totalizing understanding of gratitude. In various texts, Nietzsche commented on the role of gratitude in human life. In *Menschliches, Allzumenschliches*, he explained "why the powerful man is grateful." The reason has nothing to do with gentle feelings to his fellow man. Rather, he recognizes that gratitude is itself a form of power, a way of enhancing power. By giving a benefit, the benefactor has "intruded into the sphere of the powerful man," and a man of true vigor cannot take that kind of intrusion lying down. He has to penetrate in turn into the "sphere of the benefactor," and he does so by an act of gratitude. Nietzsche identifies gratitude as "a milder form of revenge," necessary because without it "the powerful man would have shown himself powerless, and would have been reckoned as such ever after." All societies that affirm power place gratitude "among the first duties." He cites Swift's comment that "men were grateful in the same proportion as they were revengeful."[14]

For Nietzsche, gratitude is more than a stance toward a benefactor. It is a stance toward life as a whole, and that includes the pain that afflicts every life. Showing gratitude even to those who harm turns a person into a "gift-giver" with the overriding desire and purpose to bless others. Gratitude in the face of harm is the "essence" of "all of the *beautiful*, all of the *great* art."[15] It was the great virtue of the Greeks: "That which is so astonishing in the religious life of the ancient Greeks is the irrestrainable stream of GRATI-TUDE which it pours forth—it is a very superior kind of man who takes SUCH an attitude towards nature and life."[16] Gratitude was one of a knot of virtues that made up the "morality of the ruling class," which Nietzsche believed was so weak in his day:

> A morality of the ruling class, however, is more especially foreign and irritat-ing to present-day taste in the sternness of its principle that one has duties only to one's equals; that one may act towards beings of a lower rank, towards all that is foreign, just as seems good to one, or "as the heart desires," and in any case "beyond good and evil": it is here that sympathy and similar sentiments can have a place. The ability and obligation to exercise prolonged gratitude and prolonged revenge—both only within the circle of equals,—artfulness in retaliation, RAFFINEMENT of the idea in friendship, a certain necessity to have enemies (as outlets for the emotions of envy, quarrelsomeness, arrogance—in fact, in order to be a good FRIEND): all these are typical characteristics of the noble morality, which, as has been pointed out, is not the morality of "mod-ern ideas," and is therefore at present difficult to realize, and also to unearth and disclose.[17]

For Nietzsche, the life-affirming stance of gratitude stands in fundamental opposition to Christian morality. He acknowledges that in a certain sense "religion . . . is a form of gratitude." A self-confident nation will honor "the conditions which enable it to survive," those virtues that maintain its power, and will project those virtues "into a being to whom one may offer thanks."[18] Yet Christianity twists this into its opposite. Gratitude "affirms as instinctively as Christian morality negates. . . . The former gives to things out of its own abundance—it transfigures, it beautifies the world and makes it more rational—the latter impoverishes, pales and makes uglier the value of things, it *negates* the world."[19]

Gratitude's revenge is thus the revenge of the strong, in contrast to the revenge of *ressentiment*, the revenge of the weak, particularly of the Christian weak. Gratitude stands strong no matter what, and this is the true moral-ity: "While every noble morality develops from a triumphant affirmation of itself, slave morality from the outset says No to what is 'outside,' what is 'different,' what is 'not itself'; and this No is its creative deed. This inversion of the value-positing eye—this need to direct one's view outward instead of back to oneself—is the essence of *ressentiment*: in order to exist, slave moral-ity always first needs a hostile external world; it needs . . . external stimuli in order to act at all—its action is fundamentally reaction."[20] In contrast, the powerful spiritualize the energy of ressentiment into the direction of gratitude. Gratitude is not an acknowledgment of dependence but an affirmation of autonomy.

So foundational is gratitude to Nietzsche's stance in life that he supposes that religion itself is sensible only on this basis. John Caputo puts it brilliantly: "When life surges up all around us in a joyous dance of the elements, like the moon glistening on ten thousand waves in a midnight surf, then we look, if not 'up' in pre-Copernican wonder, at least 'around' for someone or something to thank, upon which we may expend our gratitude without reserve." In this state of divinization (*Vergotterung*), one should be "grateful for how things happen, for the dance the forces dance."[21]

Denken ist Danken

Heidegger's last word was "Danke." "Thanks."[22]

It was an appropriate ending for a philosopher who put gratitude back into play in philosophical reflection. That emphasis is particularly evident in the later Heidegger, after his *Kehre*, his "turn" in the late 1920s. Even earlier, in the arguments of his epochal *Sein und Zeit*, he was sketching a philosophical program that would bring giving and reception back to the center of human existence.[23] This arises in part from Heidegger's suspicions about the epistemological focus of modern philosophy after Descartes and Kant, the focus on the Ego and the war against skepticism. Knowledge, Heidegger observes, involves a relation of knowing between a knower and an object, and Heidegger has doubts about the way modern epistemology deals with each of these three elements. The negative thrust of *Sein und Zeit* is to overcome the various dualisms that dominated modern philosophy, including dualisms of knower and known, subject and object, self and world.[24] To accomplish this, he questions each element of the "epistemological situation."

What, for starters, is the knower?[25] For Western epistemology, it is the disinterested subject aiming for theoretical knowledge of the subject matter before him. One of Heidegger's central insights is that this kind of subject does not exist, since all human existence is "being-in-the-world," existence in a particular time and place. Humans exist in such a way that the human is codetermined by the world in which he exists. Heidegger coins the technical term *Dasein* to capture the embeddedness of human existence: human being is not just *Sein*, "being," but a *Da-Sein*, a "being-there." Heidegger also wants to know why "knowing" is privileged above other relations that we have with the world, and he concludes that knowing is not a single thing. There are multiple modes of knowing the world.[26] As for the objects, they are also not there just for the knowing. The knower always comes to the object with some prior classification, and, more important, some prior interest in the thing to be known.[27] Objects come to us in a context, with prior uses and assumed relations with us. Epistemology sees things as simple "present at hand," rather than as we really encounter them—"ready-to-hand," ready for a particular use. "It is," Michael Inwood summarizes, "easier to see a hammer as *vorhanden*, as a thing with certain properties or a bearer of predicates, if one ignores the engrossed carpenter hammering in a nail."[28] What we encounter and know is never an object stripped of its various associations and uses. We never know just a "hammer" or "just a table." The hammer is always a particular hammer, the table a particular table, and each of them is experienced in the first instance as something to be used. No one measures the dimensions of a table when first encountering it, as the scientific mentality would suggest. One instead wants to know if the table is suitable for writing, for eating, for laying out freshly picked apples. It takes an effort of abstraction to think of tables in general, and then of objects in general, and Heidegger thinks this imaginative effort has its uses. His goal, however, is to analyze the human encounter with the world as it takes place in "average everydayness" rather than in the rarefied conceptions of philosophers. The uses and purposes of objects, their relation to humans as "tools" or "equipment," are not a secondary overlay on the thing itself: "[W]hen I interpret something as a hammer I do not first see the entity as simply *present* at hand, as a length of wood with a piece of iron attached to it, and then interpret this as a hammer. I implicitly understand it as *zuhanden*, as equipment, from the start."[29] For Heidegger, then, Dasein lives in a world that is always already there, full of things with certain properties and uses, full of tools that are ready for man to use in his engagement in the world. Heidegger positions the human being within the world rather than, as in the Cartesian and even more in the German idealist model, above and outside it. We are embedded in the world and surrounded by things that we did not make. The first human stance is one of reception rather than domination, and reception is a hairbreadth away from gratitude.[30]

These themes focus more explicitly on gratitude following the famous "turn" in Heidegger's thought. Beginning in the late 1920s, Heidegger abandoned much of the difficult technical apparatus and terminology he had invented for *Sein und Zeit* and began to raise other questions using other concepts. Some have characterized the shift as one from a concern with Dasein to a concern with Sein, but that ignores the fact that already in his early work Heidegger was interested in Dasein largely because it was the pathway to the disclosure of Being itself. More important, the shift involved a more radical questioning of the philosophical tradition. Despite his attacks on the dualism of post-Cartesian philosophy, his earlier work continued to use traditional concepts in fairly traditional ways. When he distinguished between *existentialia* and *existentiell*, the echoes of the Aristotelian distinction of substance and accident were evident. Early on, he used the Kantian idea of "transcendental," which he abandoned in his later life.[31] More centrally, the later Heidegger became obsessed with language. He was obsessed with the workings of language in the methods of his later philosophy, and devoted considerable attention to poets, especially to Holderlin. His arguments were often based on questionable, if stirring, etymologies. For the later Heidegger, language is the "house of Being." Like J. G. Hamann in the eighteenth century, the later Heidegger trusts language to be wiser than men and thus explores the turns of language to arrive at the veiled unveiling event of truth.

The early Heidegger, the Heidegger picked up and exploited by French existentialists like Sartre, was a philosopher of authenticity and decision. In his later work, decision takes a back seat. In its place comes a fresh emphasis on receptivity: "He speaks more and more of listening, waiting, and complying."[32] It is no accident that he relies in his later work on Meister Eckhart, especially in adopting the latter's notion of *Gelassenheit*, "releasement" or "letting-be." What human beings are capable of doing is letting things be. This is the freedom that humans have beyond all inanimate and animal life. One sees hidden in this turn to receptivity a turn toward gratitude that becomes explicit at various points in Heidegger's later work.

This is evident in the way Heidegger elaborates a fresh idea of Sein in his *Contributions to Philosophy*. The key sentence is "das Seyn west als das Ereignis"—being essentially unfolds as appropriation.[33] Before we can grasp this statement, we need to grasp the meaning of Sein in Heidegger's work. Crucial to his late writing especially is a distinction between the ontic and the ontological, between the world of beings that we all inhabit and the reality of Being. Being is not the substance or essence that remains when the accidents of beings are removed, nor is Being another *thing* or person that gives existence to beings. That would make it just another being rather than Being itself. Being is neither a who nor a what. It is, in Richard Polt's words, the difference that it makes that there is something rather than nothing. Only human beings are aware of Being; only we ask the question of Being, the question that arises from our astonishment that there are beings.

Now, what would it mean for "Being" in this sense to unfold essentially as appropriation? The key terms here are *wesen* and *Ereignis*. As a noun, Wesen means "essence," but as an archaic verb it carries the connotation not only of what things are but what they do, how they work or how they exist. Richard Polt suggests that the English "transpire" is a close equivalent, but given the philosophical weight of the noun Wesen, "transpire" does not refer to historical accident but to the blossoming of Being in time. For Heidegger, though, Wesen is not something that happens to individual things. Beings *are*, but being itself "essentially unfolds" (*Das Seiende ist. Das Seyn west*). So we cannot treat Being as another being, nor can we ask what it is, because that would be to "take for granted" that things are. We might analyze beings through the avenues of different sciences, but those scientific endeavors bracket and ignore the question of Being and take for granted that things are. To pursue analyses that take the question of Being for granted puts us in danger of forgetting Being and the question of Being. Sciences, including philosophy, thus become instruments of the forgetfulness of Being that Heidegger wants to reverse. Heidegger was not opposed to science, but he wanted to return it to its origin—the sense of wonder that things are at all.

We can get a hint of what Heidegger means by saying that Being unfolds by appropriation if we glance at his analysis of the German phrase *Es gibt*. This is normally translated, colorlessly, as "there is," but in Heidegger's late etymological mood this will not do. *Gibt* is the third-person singular of *geben*, to give, and so *Es gibt* means, in a wooden literal sense, "It gives." And because language is the house of Being, this turn of phrase gives us a clue to the question of Being. If we ask, with Richard Polt, what is the "it" that gives, Heidegger's answer is Ereignis. Appropriation is what gives; it is the source of Being, not as a thing or person or cause from which Being comes, but rather the giving of Being itself, the event of giving. Heidegger says in the *Letter on Humanism* that Being is what gives Being. There is nothing beyond Being that gives it. Being is its self-giving. Polt suggests that "appropriation is Being's own way of happening."[34] Ereignis is not, however, simply "happening." It also connotes a kind of owning. It is a kind of owning because in the event of Being, something becomes mind. But the ownership works in reverse too: when Es gibt, when Being self-gives, Being seizes us. At certain moments, we are seized by the Being, by the wonder that there are things rather than nothing. In those moments of illumination we find the great moments of history.[35] But the appropriation is also a withdrawal that maintains the distance needed for letting be.[36]

All this sets us up for the insight that our primary stance in the world is one of receptive gratitude. If Being unfolds in the self-giving of Being, then we should receive. Heidegger sums up this claim by repeating the Pietist motto, *denken ist Danken*, a rare pun that works as well in English as in German: "To think is to thank." At a superficial level, we can see this as a comment about the role of language and the gift of a tradition. Without language, we would be incapable at least of sharing thoughts, and perhaps would be incapable of certain kinds of thought as such.[37] That is the direction that Gadamer took Heidegger's insights in his hermeneutical theory. Renouncing the Enlightenment "prejudice against prejudice," Gadamer insisted that projections and prejudices are inherent in the process of interpretation and that interpretation is everywhere. For Gadamer, language is not the prison house that it is in so much poststructuralist theory. Language seems a prison house only to those who still long for some way to escape creatureliness or for frustrated Platonists who want to shed time, place, and language to encounter ideas in their pure form.

For Gadamer, language is the condition of human freedom: "[W]herever language and men exist, there is not only a freedom from the pressure of the world, but this freedom from the environment is also freedom in relation to the names that we give things, as stated in the profound account in Genesis, according to which God gave Adam the authority to name creatures." Unlike animals, who are bound to environment, humans are capable of being free from environment, and that is because of language. Human beings experience the world through the medium of language, and language is inherently variable and flexible, offering multiple ways of accessing the complexities of the world. Speech is thus the source of human freedom: "Man can always rise above the particular environment in which he happens to find himself, and because his speech brings the world into language, he is, from the beginning, free for variety in exercising his capacity for language."[38]

One might characterize Gadamer's project as one of recognizing the virtue of necessity. We cannot understand the past, he points out, without involving ourselves in it; even if we could slice ourselves from our understanding of the past, then it would no longer be *we* who understand it. No matter how much we try to put ourselves into the shoes of an author or imagine a historical time period, it is *we* who are wearing the shoes and doing the imagining. That is obvious enough, though Gadamer is more forthright in acknowledging the obvious than many. What he rejects, though, is *regret* at the undeniable fact that we are we. Instead of wishing he could transcend himself in knowing, instead of worrying that our inescapable we-ness leads to relativism and skepticism, he points out that our we-ness is the condition of possibility for knowing anything at all. And this is obvious enough too, though much of the history of philosophy has been designed to avoid it: it is obvious because if we transcend ourselves in the act of knowing, then it is no longer we who are knowing it. Gadamer does not regret finitude. His is a philosophy at home in human skin, which means it is a healthy philosophy, since human skin is the only home we have.

That is all based on Heidegger, but Heidegger's use of *denken ist danken* is, however, more peculiarly his own. This is evident in his treatment of the theme in one of his lectures in *Was Heisst Denken?*[39] The argument once again begins from etymology: Greek *logos*, meaning "word" or "thought," is derived from the Greek verb *legein*, to gather up. Thinking is a matter of collecting, pulling together, assembling, and gathering, and this activity is necessarily an act of memory: "Memory is the gathering of thought,"[40] and "[t]hought is in need of memory, the gathering of thought."[41] Heidegger expounds the point with a further etymology, this time from Old English: "*thencan*, to think, and *thancian*, to thanks, are closely related; the Old English noun for thought is *thanc* or *thonc*—a thought, a grateful thought, and the expression of such a thought." Thus "the *thanc*, that which is thought, the thought, implies the thanks." To understand how thinking is a giving of thanks, it is necessary to see that the "thanc" was not "thought" in our sense of the word. What is named by "thanc, thought, memory, thanks . . . is incomparably richer in essential content than the current signification that the words still have for us in common usage."[42] It does not refer to "that thinking of the heart" to which Pascal referred, much less to the "mathematical" or "logical-rational" thought Pascal questioned. Rather, thanc encompassed both memory and thanks, memory not as the power of recall but as "the whole disposition in the sense of a steadfast intimate concentration upon the things that essentially speak to us in every thoughtful meditation." Memory in its original sense is close to the sense of "devotion"—that is, "a constant concentrated abiding with something." Through memory, past, present, and the hope of the future are all one in present being; memory is the gathering together of time, and thereby is the source of the images that flow from the soul. Thanc carried the same connotation of "the gathering of the constant intention of everything that the heart holds in present being."[43]

This is also what "thanks" means: "In giving thanks, the heart gives thought to what it has and what it is. The heart, thus giving thought and thus being memory, gives itself in thought to that to which it is held. It thinks of itself as beholden, not in the sense of mere submission, but beholden because its devotion is held in listening." That is what is called thinking, Heidegger says. Thinking is not merely taking interest or classifying and dividing, nor is it only the learning of skills. Thought attends to what is thought-provoking, and what is thought-provoking is what "gives us to think," a gift. The thought-provoking is Being itself, the uncanny recognition that there is something rather than nothing.[44] Thought happens when we have an idea in the original Greek sense, derived from the verb ειδω, to see, meet, encounter face-to-face. Thought is this encounter with Being.[45] This is why thinking includes thanking, why a thought is a thanc. It is true that thinking in this sense is reciprocity for being, and thought is beholden to being in the way a recipient is beholden to a patron: "Original thanking is the thanks owed for being." But that is not the deepest sense of thought as thanc, because thanking and thinking seen as "payment and repayment remains too easily bogged down in the sphere of mere conventional recompense, even mere business."[46] To think that thinking is repayment is to place thanks in the realm of economy, where it does not belong.

Denken ist danken at the deepest level:

> When we give thanks, we give it for something. We give thanks for something by giving thanks to him whom we have to thank for it. The things for which we owe thanks are not things we have from ourselves. They are given to us. We receive many gifts, of many kinds. But the highest and really most lasting gift given to us is always our essential nature, with which we are gifted in such a way that we are what we are only through it. That is what we owe thanks for this endowment, first and unceasingly.[47]

What form does this thankfulness for our own nature take? The thing given us is thought; Being provokes thought, and in what is thought-provoking "resides the real endowment of our nature for which we owe thanks." The proper and supreme thanks would thus be to think, and the "profoundest thanklessness" is "thoughtlessness."[48] The thinking that gathers, that recalls, is "true thanks" that is more than "recompense." The true thanks of thought is instead "an offering."[49]

We can tie this back to Heidegger's meditations on Es gibt and Ereignis. *Das Seyn wesen als Ereignis*—Being unfolds essentially as appropriation. That is, Being is pure giving, the sheer self-giving of Being itself. It is not something given by Somebeing beyond Being; there is nothing beyond or behind being, nothing beyond or behind the sheer giving that is Being. That anything exists is the mystery of Being; that I exist is part of that mystery. That *I* exist provokes the thought of the sheer givingness of Being. To think is to stand face-to-face with that givingness, to respond to the provocation of thought that Being presents to those beings that can think. George Steiner puts it well: "At its most penetrating, the exercise of thought is one of grateful acquiescence in Being. Inevitably, jubilantly, such acquiescence is a giving of thanks for that which has been placed in our custody, for the light [of Being] in the clearing."[50]

All this seems to be typical Heideggerian hot air, but for Heidegger it has concrete cultural import. It is bound up, for instance, with his suspicion of technology and his deep Teutonic agrarianism. In its original sense, Heidegger argues, *techne* was not simply an exertion of power over nature but a particular form of knowing. For the early Greeks, techne did not impose an alien form on the nature of a thing but rather brought that nature out more luminously. It included *poiesis*, "making," but also "poetry" that teased the truth out of things. Technology then involved a moment of illumination, an unveiling and truth telling, in the same way that art unveils the truth about the object of art and makes it more what it is than the thing itself.[51] Originally, technology, like art, was content to "let be." But modern technology is a corrupted form of techne, no longer a vocation that unveils truth about things but an adversarial position toward things. A dam does not let the river be; it harnesses water power to produce electricity and thus is a monstrous intervention into nature. Instead of making Being luminous in things, modern technology masks and hides it.[52] In contrast to this domineering Baconian stance, the proper response to the world is a response of thinking that is also a receptive thanking. Heidegger very explicitly sees the links between the rebirth of philosophy that he pursues and the salvation of the earth from technological exploitation. He aimed to overcome metaphysics because he saw Western metaphysics from Plato on as the villain that produced the scientistic and exploitive technological culture of modernity. Overcoming metaphysics was the key to overcoming modernity.[53]

In the end, Heidegger's formula undoes itself. Anticipating the teasings of Derrida, Heidegger is concerned with the danger of a circular return on the giving of Being and thought. The thinking that recalls "does not need to repay, nor be deserved, in order to give thanks. Such thanks is not a recompense; but it remains an offering."[54] Ereignis comes to the rescue to ensure that the gift of Being and thankful thought does not turn into a close circle of gift and recompense. The gift is withheld in the very giving; no gift ultimately "is," no gift appropriated by the recipient, so there is no-thing that can ultimately be returned. As Rebecca Comay puts it, "Thanking becomes simply the recursive, performative movement . . . which knows no object for the gratitude and thus has nothing with which to pay back."[55] *Denken ist danken* dissolves, and Heidegger's final *Danke* is perhaps nothing more than a *Danke fur nichts*—thanks for nothing.

Conclusion

In the end, we cannot avoid the vexed matter of Heidegger's Nazism, nor should we want to. Heidegger's way of thinking about thanking is deeply conservative, even reactionary. Thought is a moment of response to Being's Advent, and this easily becomes acquiescence in whatever is, whatever happens to appear. Especially if the happening is dramatic, especially if it appears dramatically to challenge the assumptions of decadent modernity, the Ereignis must be received with thanksgiving. There is little or no room for a moment of refusal, no space for critical ingratitude, whether inspired by the Christian gospel or by Enlightenment reason. It is dispiriting, but it seems no accident that the greatest modern philosopher of gratitude is also the philosopher of fascism.

TEN

Gifts Without Gratitude

Mauss' rediscovery of reciprocity challenged post-Enlightenment ethics and philosophy from various directions. Kantian ethics had advocated about disinterested good will, and benevolence especially had to be disinterested. If benevolence aimed at winning some reward from the beneficiary, it was no longer benevolence. From another angle, the fact that tribal cultures engaged in self-interested exchanges was a threat to the Rousseauist assumptions of cultural anthropology. If gifts in tribal cultures were so close to a form of "commerce," how were these tribal cultures useful as a foil for Western capitalism? One could read Mauss as a confirmation rather than a refutation of liberalism: everyone everywhere *does* pursue self-interest. Self-interest is not a learned behavior, inculcated by the institutions and norms of capitalist economy and society. Self-interest is a human tendency. Mauss might be leading us back by a tropical route to Hobbes and Adam Smith.

Contemporary philosophy has wrestled with these dilemmas at length.[1] In some quarters, it has become a central obsession. Some have attempted to defend what amounts to Kantian disinterestedness in a post-Mauss context, while others have sought for a bright line to distinguish gift exchange from commercial exchange. It is, however, important to recognize precisely where the debate centers. Though often seen as a debate about *The Gift*, that characterization misses the specific focus of debate. No one disparages gifts. Gift—especially in the singular, especially capitalized—is a hurrah word. Say it, and everyone nods and smiles. What rankles is not gift but the expected, obligatory *response* to the gift. What rankles is *gratitude*, the response to the gift that seems to shift the gift back into the realm of economy. As much as the Enlightenment philosophes, postmodernism is foundational, systematic ingratitude.

One of the intriguing features of the debate is that this has not been clearly seen even among the participants in the debate. That oversight is another indication of the modernity of postmodern thought. Even after the revival of reciprocity and the gift, Western intellectuals remain locked in a Lockean framework in which gratitude is a private sentiment or a matter of personal ethics, and is not a matter of serious philosophical or political concern.

I cannot hope to discuss the full range of contemporary thinkers who have contributed to the debate about "the gift"—which is a debate about gratitude. I have selected the two main contributors—Jacques Derrida and Jean-Luc Marion.

Given Time, the Gift of Death

Mauss' book is called *The Gift*, but Derrida provocatively claims that this is not the real subject of the book. On the contrary, the book "speaks of everything but the gift."[2] Mauss deals with exchange, economy, gifts, countergifts, sacrifice, and the obligation to give, to receive, to return. He speaks of "gift supplements" like the potlatch, of excessive and transgressive gifts, of giving back more than one receives, of "returns with interest." None of this constitutes for Derrida a discourse on the gift because all of it remains locked into the gift process that ultimately annuls the gift. All of Mauss' discussions of gift describe a circular process, sometimes explicitly, as when Mauss translates Malinowski's kula as "circle."[3] A circle, Derrida insists, is precisely what a gift is *not*.

He acknowledges that this circularity is what we normally mean when we talk about gifts. In normal discourse, to speak of the event of a gift is to speak of someone A intentionally giving something B to someone else C. Typically, too, C is assumed to acknowledge the gift, and etiquette and perhaps morality demand that C thank A for the gift. Such a commonsense notion of gift, Derrida claims, betrays a number of embedded presuppositions. It assumes that the donor A is unproblematically a "subject" with intentions, and that C is the same. If there is one thing that Derrida disagrees with, it is that there is any such thing as "unproblematic" anything. More radically, the commonsensical notion of giving assumes that exchange has an "Odyssean" structure, that it involves not only a gift but also a return.[4] Though this circularity is the condition of possibility of the gift, it is also simultaneously the condition of the impossibility of the gift. Derrida comes to this radical conclusion for a number of reasons.

Derrida proposes a strict contrast between gift and economy:

> One cannot treat the gift, this goes without saying, without treating this relation to economy, even to the money economy. But is not the gift, if there is any, also that which interrupts economy? That which, in suspending economic calculation, no longer gives rise to exchange? That which opens the circle so as to defy reciprocity or symmetry, the common measure, and so as to turn aside the return in view of the no-return? If there is gift, the given of the gift (that which one gives, that which is given, the gift as given thing or as act of donation) must not come back to the giving (let us not already say to the subject, to the donor). It must not circulate, it must not be exchanged, it must not in any case be exhausted, as a gift, by the process of exchange, by the movement of circulation of the circle in the form of return to the point of departure. If the figure of the circle is essential to economics, the gift must remain aneconomic. Not that it remains foreign to the circle, but it must keep a relation of foreignness to the circle, a relation without relation of familiar foreignness. It is perhaps in this sense that the gift is impossible. Not impossible but *the* impossible. The very figure of the impossible.[5]

Why *the* impossible? Because of the pervasiveness of gifts. Why the *impossible*? That, Derrida says, is because gifts inevitably fail to live up to the definition of gift. A gift requires that there be no "reciprocity, return, exchange, countergift, or debt. If the other gives me back or owes me or has to give me back what I give him or her, there will not have been a gift, whether this restitution is immediate or whether it is programmed by a complex calculation of a long-term deferral or *differance*." As Derrida says, this point is most obvious "if the other, the donee, gives me back immediately the same thing." For there to be a gift at all requires that "the donee not give back, amortize, reimburse, acquit himself, enter into a contract, and that he never have contracted a debt."[6] Overturning the classic tradition concerning gratitude as first of all recognition, Derrida insists that "it is . . . necessary, at the limit, that he not recognize the gift as gift. If he recognizes it as gift, if the gift appears to him as such, if the present is present to him as present, this simple recognition suffices to annul the gift." This is because "it gives back, in the place, let us say, of the thing itself, a symbolic equivalent." Recognition precedes gratitude, but for a recipient it is enough to perceive the "intentional meaning of the gift, in order for this simple recognition of the gift as gift, as such, to annul the gift as gift even before recognition becomes gratitude."[7] Thus, "At the limit, *the gift as gift* ought not appear as gift, either to the donee or the donor. It cannot be gift as gift except but not being present as gift."[8]

Not only the recipient but also the giver must refuse to recognize gift as gift: "[T]he one who gives it must not see or know it either; otherwise he begins, at the threshold, as soon as he intends to give, to pay himself with a symbolic recognition, to praise himself, to approve of himself, to gratify himself, to congratulate himself, to give back to himself symbolically the value of what he thinks he has given or what he is preparing to give." The gift loses its gift character as soon as it is recognized as such by the giver *or* the recipient; but without this recognition, the gift is not a gift either, because there is no intention of giving on the giver's part nor a recognition of reception on the receiver's part. Self-congratulation or "narcissistic gratitude" undermines the gift as much as any symbolic repayment of the recipient. Even "the simple intention to give, insofar as it carries the intentional meaning of the gift, suffices to make a return payment to oneself," and thus has to be excluded if there is to be a gift at all.[9]

In a tradition stretching at least from Seneca through Aquinas to the Renaissance, recognition and memory are intimately bound to gratitude. Derrida does not refer to this tradition explicitly, but he is clearly aware that memory is a component of "repayment" on a gift. For a true gift to be given, though, there must be an *absolute* forgetfulness on the part of both the giver and recipient. When Derrida says that the gift cannot be kept without ceasing to be a gift, he also means

> the keeping in the Unconscious, memory, the putting into reserve or temporalization as effect of repression. For there to be a gift, not only must the donor or donee not perceive the gift as such, have no consciousness of it, no memory, no recognition; he or she must also forget it right away [*a l'instant*] and moreover this forgetting must be so radical that it exceeds even the psychoanalytic categorality of forgetting. . . . [W]e are speaking here of an absolute forgetting—a forgetting that also absolves, that unbinds absolutely and infinitely more, therefore, than excuse, forgiveness, or acquittal.[10]

Yet this forgetfulness is not *nothing*, a mere "non-experience": "For there to be a gift event . . . something must come about or happen, in an instant, in an instant that no doubt does not belong to the economy of time, in a time without time, but also in such a way that this forgetting, without being something present, presentable, determinable, sensible or meaningful, is not nothing."[11]

Derrida's deconstruction of the gift appears to cut, if possible, even more deeply than this. There can be no subject giving a gift because, Derrida says, the subject is constituted by "dominating, through calculation and exchange" through "the mastery of this *hubris*." This might be taken to refer to the modern subject in particular, the target of postmodernism. But Derrida makes the point more radically: "[T]he subject and object are arrested effects of the gift. At the zero or infinite speed of the circle."[12] The subject and object are what appear when the strobe light of a gift event flashes.

Try a thought experiment to clarify the point: Sleepwalking Harry hands flowers to comatose Alice. Has a gift been given? There is an exchange, but both parties are unconscious of the exchange. We'd hardly think that there is a gift here, since we think of the intention to give as a constituent element of giving. So, the condition for the possibility of a gift is that Harry wake up and Alice come out of her coma; but as soon as they do that, they both recognize that a gift is being given, and this destroys the giftedness of the gift. So the conditions of the possibility of the gift are also the conditions of its destruction. The gift is impossible, *the* impossible. Gifts can be given only to those who are wholly other. If there is some preexisting bond—familial, political, economic, even friendliness—then the gift does not arise spontaneously as a gift. It is not free, and a gift that is not free is no gift at all. If there is any bond of exchange, including an exchange of gift and thanks, that follows the gift, the gift is once again destroyed.

The gift renounces self-interest. It refuses calculation, even reason. It seeks no return. It exists only in a momentary flash of madness.

Yet this madness is the deep-down truth of things. Following Heidegger's hints regarding es gibt, Derrida argues that this structure of the gift is also the structure of being and of time. Being "gives itself to be thought on the condition of being nothing (no present-being, no being-present)," while time "even in what is called its 'vulgar' determination, from Aristotle to Heidegger, is always defined in the *paradoxia* or rather the *aporia* of what is without being, of what is never present or what is only scarcely and dimly."[13] On the one hand, time destroys the gift "through keeping, restitution, reproduction, the anticipatory expectation or apprehension that grasps or comprehends in advance." On the other hand, time is the only true gift. The only gift that truly qualifies as gift, Derrida says, is the gift of nothing, and this means fundamentally the gift of time: the only present is the present moment, the nothing, the no-space, the not-duration that does not exist as the future makes its way into the past. Derrida speaks in terms of the gift and the event, and insists that the event that is gift, the gift that is event, must be unanticipated, unexpected, unconditioned, unforeseen to be gift; the gift event must be "irruptive, unmotivated—for example, disinterested. They are decisive and they must therefore tear the fabric, interrupt the continuum of a narrative that nevertheless they call for, they must perturb the order of causalities: in an instant." Gift and event "obey nothing, except perhaps principles of disorder, that is, principles without principles."[14] The gift is the Dionysian moment that breaks into and tears asunder the circle of exchange, the circulation of economy.

Derrida worries over Heidegger's es gibt. There is, on the one hand, the possibility of reification, which Heidegger himself, despite his insistence that Being was not someone or something giving something to someone, encouraged with his references to *das Es*. Derrida spotted a danger that "we arbitrarily posit an indeterminate power which is supposed to bring about all giving of Being and time."[15] Derrida raises other concerns with Heidegger's insistence on Hellenistic purism, his claim that the forgetfulness of Being requires moderns to return to the pre-Socratic sources, prior to the Socratic deviation of philosophy. Heidegger places all in the debt of the Greeks. *Denken ist danken*, fine; but what about the Hebrew, Christian, Latin, Romantic, African, or other inheritances that we have received. For Heidegger, Derrida fears, "Thinking now means thankfully-thinking-back on (Greek) Being, bound over in memorializing thinking-thanking (*denkendes Danken*, or *dankendes Denken*) which thinks on (*an-denken*) and ever forgets that to which thinking is bound in endless debt."[16] He finds it "horribly dangerous" because Heidegger's Ereignis serves as a guard against the unregulated dissemination implied by es gibt. There is the sheer giving, Being giving itself, giving giving, but Heidegger brings that back under control with the proprietary notion of Ereignis.[17] For these reasons, Derrida does not want his quasi-transcendentals—*differance*, or *Khora*—to be the recipients of gratitude. They are not principles of diffusion, not *exitus* that anticipates a later *reditus*. They are principles of pure dissemination, gift without return, gift without gratitude. As Caputo puts it, while "*Differance* gifts," we owe "no thanks to *differance*."[18]

In an essay on Levinas, Derrida discusses more explicitly the appropriate forms of thanks that might be offered to a thinker who has influenced him.[19] Derrida insists that the only way to give Levinas his proper due is to give him "faulty" thanks. Invoking Levinas' concept of the "Saying" versus the "Said" (Saying is the face-to-face encounter with the Other that cannot be captured by language of ontology—cannot be Said), Derrida argues that ingratitude is essential to his expression of thanks. He can do no more than celebrate the "Said" of Levinas' text, and this means that any thanks he gives violates Levinas' own notions of ethics—because he is not Saying to the living Other but only commending what has been Said in fixed texts. Derrida thus faces a dilemma: he can be silent out of respect for Levinas' ethical theory; or he can speak and give defective thanks, express his gratitude flecked with inescapable ingratitude.[20]

Derrida recognizes that his thanks is faulty in three ways. It "misdirects" thanks because it does not offer thanks directly to Levinas. This is necessarily the case since "the event [of gift] that obligates the response is no longer present at the moment in which thanks is given." He explains this in terms of a statement of Levinas concerning the obligation to respond to the Other: "He will have obligated" (*il aura obligé*), a future perfect that cannot be captured or located in time. Furthermore, Derrida's thanks is not pure thanks, but only a partial and hence ungrateful thanks. That is, Derrida does not simply repeat Levinas but criticizes and seeks to improve on him. He must do this if he is going to be thoroughly Levinasian, if he is going to open the Levinasian text to its "Other." But this means that his thanks cannot be undiluted, pure thanks, undiluted and uncritical reception. It has to include a moment of ungrateful critique. Finally, Derrida says that in "returning 'thanks,' he, in effect, returns property to Levinas and no longer gives a 'gift; of thanks.' " By committing a fault in thanks, Derrida wants to ensure that he does not simply return "the Same" to Levinas. But Levinas has already written in a way that disrupts the Same by the Other in an encounter of Saying. And this means that precisely by avoiding returning "the Same" to Levinas, Derrida is copying Levinas' method. Derrida sees a trap here: "Beyond any possible restitution, there would be need for my gesture to operate without debt, in absolute ingratitude. The trap is that I then pay homage, the only possible homage, to his work, to what his work says of the Work."[21]

Thanks might be given by praising the work of Levinas in a way that assumes a full context and a "dominant interpretation" of Levinas' work, but that is impossible because the horizon of context is in constant flux.[22] A dominant interpretation immanentizes the eschaton, encloses interpretation in a final context. And that means that the impossibility of gratitude drives ethics as much as the impossibility of gift. Derrida hems and haws his way through the question of thanksgiving to arrive finally at a stance of "radical ingratitude":

> Suppose that beyond all restitution, in radical ingratitude (but notice, not just any ingratitude, not in the ingratitude that still belongs to the circle of acknowledgement and reciprocity), I desire (it desires in me, but the it is not a neutral non-me), I desire to try to give to E.L. This or that? Such and such a thing? A discourse, a thought, a writing? No, that would still give rise to exchange, commerce, economic reappropriation. No, to give him the very giving of giving, a giving which might no longer even be an object or a present said, because every present remains within the economic sphere of the same. . . . That "giving" must be neither a thing or an act, it must somehow be someone (male or female) not *me*: nor him ("he"). Strange, isn't it, this excess that overflows language at every instant and yet requires it?[23]

What Derrida says about Levinas in this essay dovetails with the second part of *Given Time*, a dazzling exploration of Baudelaire's brief short story

"Counterfeit Money." By reflecting not only on the story itself but also on the existence of the story that Derrida reads, he raises another problem for the circular model of gift and gratitude. A text is a gift, yet there is no Baudelaire to whom we can return thanks for the gift. Baudelaire is dead, and even before he died his text had floated free of his personal presence. Most readers of Baudelaire never met Baudelaire to give thanks. More radically, Derrida suggests that there is no way to return thanks because the gift that Baudelaire gives—the gift of any writer—exceeds his intentions: "the structure of trace and legacy of this text . . . surpasses the phantasm of return and marks the death of the signatory or the non-return of the legacy, the non-benefit, therefore a certain condition of the gift—in the writing itself."[24] If the gift is something intended—as Derrida has insisted from the outset—then Baudelaire's text cannot be a gift, since it gives more than he intended. What is true of Baudelaire's text is true of all gifts:

> The gift, if there is any, will always be without border. What does "without" mean here? A gift that does not run over the borders, a gift that would let itself be contained in a determination and limited by the indivisibility trait would not be a gift. As soon as it delimits itself, a gift is prey to calculation and measure. The gift, if there is any, should overrun the border, to be sure, towards the measureless and excessive; but it should also suspend its relation to the border and even its transgressive relation to the separable line or trait of a border.[25]

A gift so controlled that it does not exceed intention is no gift, but a gift that gives more than intended seems something more than a gift. It seems a waste. That excess also means that there is no fitting way to judge the appropriate return. How does one calculate the debt of gratitude laid on a recipient of a gift whose giver cannot help but give more than he wanted to?[26]

Given Derrida's doubts about the possibility of gift and gratitude, it might seem that he would have little room for generosity. As we have noted earlier, however, his ethics is fundamentally an ethics of hospitality. We might equally say it is an ethics of the gift. The gift never arrives, never is present, but it is the intoxicating, gleaming absence that motivates and moves exchange. We will never give a gift, but still our desires are driven by the impossible. Because of Derrida's deconstruction, we will never be tempted to confuse the phenomenon of a present with the gift; there will always be an unrealized surplus, an impossible hope that drives our desire. To put it otherwise, we remain in the circle of exchange, and cannot escape it. Yet for Derrida the "transcendental illusion" of the gift raises the possibility of "overrunning the circle" precisely by means of the gift "if there is any." Derrida's failure in giving thanks does not lead to resignation but is an "incentive to undertake ethical Work."[27] The face-to-face encounter is what drives all ethical work in art, culture, and politics. This does not leave us outside the circle. As Derrida says, the overrunning "does not lead to a simple, ineffable exteriority that would be transcendent and without relation. It is this exteriority that sets the circle going, it is this exteriority that puts the economy in motion. It is this exteriority that engages in the circle and makes it turn."[28] By provoking desire, intention, the gift, though impossible, is the condition of possibility of thought in general. The desire to overrun the circle is the energy of the circle itself. It is not, as in Heidegger, that *denken ist danken*, but rather that the very impossibility of thanks opens space for thinking. Desire for the impossible gift loosens the circle enough to provide some space to think and breathe.

There is, besides, another mythology beyond the Odyssean one of economy, the mythology of Abraham. In his later treatment of the gift, *The Gift of Death*, Derrida takes up in part Levinas' challenge to Kierkegaard's reading of the story of Abraham and Isaac.[29] According to Kierkegaard, the narrative of Genesis 22 represents the difference between the religious and the ethical. Along the lines of Kant, Kierkegaard defines the ethical as a universal demand. What is ethical is what can be demanded of everyone everywhere all the time. But the ethical is not the be-all and end-all of human existence. Beyond the ethical is the religious sphere, in which a divine call brings a "suspension of the ethical." Abraham's sacrifice of Isaac is not exemplary for everyone. It shows instead that there is a realm of obligation beyond the universal. The knight of faith Abraham has a secret, a secret that cannot be brought into public to be judged by law or custom, and this secret, the response to the call of God, constitutes his unique individuality and unique purpose. Abraham's sacrifice is part of Kierkegaard's insistence that the particular transcends the universal.[30] Levinas disagrees. He points to the climax of the narrative, where the Lord intervenes to command Abraham not to slaughter his son. In that moment, the Lord turns Abraham back to the sphere of the ethical.

Derrida affirms Kierkegaard's insistence on pushing faith beyond calculation, to drive the cost of faith higher. But Derrida does not see the lesson as one for believers only. Rather, Abraham becomes paradigmatic of a non-Odyssean mythology of gift. Derrida follows Kierkegaard in arguing that Abraham has no expectation of return of favor. He gives without hope of a return gift, and so Abraham's willingness to sacrifice what he loves, to give death to Isaac, breaks the circle of exchange. But Derrida refuses to follow Kierkegaard in regarding this moment of rupture as a movement from the ethical to the religious. On the contrary, Abraham's experience of sacrifice is the experience of daily ethical life. Every time we act ethically, we offer Abraham's sacrifice afresh. We cannot aid one beggar without forgoing—and hence sacrificing—the aid we might offer to another beggar. Ethical action involves, inevitably, the sacrifice of ethics as universal obligation. For Derrida, this is not a response to the wholly other voice of God that transcends the voice of all others who cry out for aid. Instead, he concludes that "God" is a name worth preserving to maintain this ethical demand, that the voice of every other requires us to sacrifice ethics for the sake of that particular other. Derrida's pithy French formula captures the point. "God," he writes, "is to be found everywhere there is something of the wholly other. And since each of us, everyone else, each other is infinitely other in its absolute singularity, inaccessible, solitary, transcendent, nonmanifest, not originarily present to my ego . . . then what can be said about Abraham's relation to God can be said about my relation without relation to every other as wholly other."[31] In a word, *tout autre est tout autre*. Not only at the extremity of sacrificing one's only son, but in every ethical act, we must be "knights of faith."

It is in this final gift of sacrifice, this willingness to make a pure gift without hope of reciprocity, that Derrida locates the push that begins the circle of exchange. Abraham's gift is an instant. It is wholly disinterested, wholly outside the circle. It is a pure gift, the gift of death, the only pure gift there can be. He is ready to disseminate without hope of reciprocity. Yet in that very moment "God returns his son to him and decides sovereignly, by an absolute gift, to reinscribe the sacrifice in an economy that hereafter resembles a compensation."[32] So the circle is overrun, and by stepping out of the circle, Abraham sets a circle in motion.

Derrida contrasts Abraham's moment of ultimate sacrifice with what he regards as the circularity of Jesus, the Matthean Jesus in particular. Jesus offers rewards to those who give alms, pray, and fast in secret. This is doubly problematic for Derrida. On the one hand, it means that Jesus endorses a circle of gift and return gift that transcends the earthly sphere and incorporates heaven. Jesus' disciples are to give without hope of return from the recipient, but they can do this confidently because Jesus simultaneously promises that the Father will reward them. Disciples are to give without thought of earthly treasure, but in so doing they store up treasure in heaven, where their hearts are. Yet Jesus describes this form of circular exchange by contrasting it with the ways of the hypocrites—that is, the Jews. Ever sensitive to the sources of the Western "duel between Christian and Jew," Derrida questions the introduction of economy into the foundation of piety. Like Nietzsche, he questions the Pauline introduction of the terms of credit, debt, and payment into the very structure of the Christian theology of redemption.[33]

Being Given

Jean-Luc Marion has worked out his theories regarding gift, givenness, and exchange in two registers. On the one hand, he writes overtly theological essays and treatises, assuming the unsurpassable truth of Christian revelation. On the other hand, he writes philosophical treatises in the vein of phenomenology. To hear Marion discuss it, the two are sharply distinct, with no danger of confusion. When he does philosophical work on revelation, for example, he leaves completely open the question of whether any such revelation is available; when he writes theology, he works from the premise of the Christian account of revelation. Whether this is completely accurate is a vexed question, and not one that I intend to engage here.[34] It will be enough to note that the two projects run very much parallel, both of them aiming to liberate the subject matter (God or the phenomena) from prior conditions of human thought and language.[35] In both registers, he makes the categories of gift and givenness fundamental. We start from phenomenology.

Since Husserl, phenomenology has proceeded by a method of "bracketing" (*epoche*), or "reduction." The phenomenologist brackets the "reality" of phenomena (i.e., he does *not* ask the ontological question of whether they are existing things apart from consciousness), but also the possible "ideality" of phenomena (i.e., he does *not* determine whether the phenomena are fundamentally ideas). This phenomenological reduction is followed by a second "eidetic" reduction, which strips phenomena to their essential features, purifying them of anything that is accidental, so as to isolate what is truly essential to the phenomenon under investigation. As Husserl's thought developed, he described a third "transcendental reduction" in which the phenomena are grounded in the transcendent ego, the "I" that serves as the "horizon" within which phenomena appear. For Husserl, the ego as defined and described by Descartes "provides both the limits of what can be seen and how it is seen."[36] Husserl put it this way: "For me the world is nothing other than what I am aware of and what appears valid in such cogitationes (my acts of thought). The whole meaning and reality of the world rests exclusively on such cogitationes. My entire worldly life takes its course within these. I cannot live, experience, think, value, and act in any world which is not in some sense in me, and derives its meaning and truth from me."[37]

Marion likewise employs the "reduction," and also draws from Husserl a basic principle regarding the "givenness" of reality. Husserl suggested that "in its basis, every phenomenon surges forth as a gift, and therefore all phenomenality comes to pass as a donation."[38] Though Husserl did not develop this insight, Marion uses it as an opening to introduce "givenness," and from there the possibility of "revelation," into phenomenology. He wants to say not only that the phenomena appear to us but also that they *give* themselves. In order to achieve this, Marion embarks on a critique of Husserl and various formulations of phenomenological principles and methods. Husserl remains bound by metaphysics, partly because he limits givenness by what is available to sense experience or intuition. For Marion, "the pure given giving itself depends, once reduced, only on itself. Intuition in particular, thus also the transcendence of intentionality that it fulfills, can sometimes intervene, but it does not define the given." Intuition "suffers limits" but "givenness knows none. What gives itself, insofar as given in and through reduced givenness, by definition gives itself absolutely."[39] Husserl also remains bound to the metaphysical paradigm of the object, which Husserl virtually equates with being: "Immanent or absolute Being and transcendent Being are, of course, both called 'being,' 'object.'"[40] Husserl maintains the "privilege of primordial objectness" only by "the subsuming of what appears and is given in a category that is not given and does not appear." Marion maintains, on the contrary, that objectness is simply one mode of givenness: "objectness is reduced to givenness through appearing; it indeed ends up that givenness renders it [the object, or objectness] possible and defines it as one of its modalities."[41] Heidegger also ultimately fails to arrive at primordial givenness, first reducing being to givenness, but then abolishing givenness and the gift by reducing it to Ereignis, "advent."[42] Marion maintains that givenness remains the ultimate reality.

Marion embarks on a phenomenological analysis of a painting in order to show that it is not fundamentally an object but fundamentally a *given*, fundamentally a giving-of-itself. To treat a painting as an object, he argues, or a subsistence, is to miss what is primary in the painting. It cannot be reduced either to a "present-at-hand" or to a "ready-to-hand." A painting might be analyzed as a "manipulated ready-to-hand," and thus described in terms of the pleasure it gives, its economic value, its conformity to standards of excellence. But each of these analyses reduces the painting to a single determination and judges it by a single criterion. The reality of the painting exceeds all these reductions. Ultimately, the painting escapes this category because it "appears in, for, and by itself." To view the painting as an object, as a thing, is also not to get at the painting's reality: "to see it as a painting, in its own phenomenality of the beautiful, I must of course apprehend it as a thing (subsisting, ready-to-hand), but it is precisely not this that opens it to me as beautiful; it is as I 'live' its meaning, namely its beautiful appearing, which has nothing thinglike to it, since it cannot be described as the property of a thing, demonstrated by reasons, or hardly even said."[43] The essential character of the painting—its "beautiful appearing"—remains enigmatic if we try to bring it into the category of "being" or "object."

The key reality of the painting is its effect, what it gives: "What more does a painting give besides what it shows in showing itself as object and being? Its effect. What more does the painting offer besides its real component parts? Its effect. But this effect is not produced in the mode of an object, nor is it constituted or reconstituted in the mode of beings. It gives itself. The painting (and, in and through it, every other phenomenon in different degrees) is reduced to ultimate phenomenality insofar as it gives its effect. It appears as given in the effect that it gives."[44] Citing a comment by Cezanne, Marion says that the painting is "enchanting" because "its effect affects us more intensely and more enduringly than any being, ready-to-hand or subsistent."[45] It is only in the effect that the painting appears as painting. Marion concludes with a formulation indicating that appearances and phenomena come to us only as they *give* themselves: "Showing itself therefore amounts to giving itself." Givenness is a "fold," where the full reality is hidden, but when the phenomenon unfolds itself, it "shows the given that givenness dispenses. For the phenomenon, showing itself is equal to unfolding the fold of givenness in which it arises as a gift. Showing itself and giving itself play in the same field—the fold of givenness, which is unfolded in the given."[46]

Marion agrees with Derrida in wanting to isolate the gift in contrast to commercial transactions or two-way transactions of any sort. The gift as he has analyzed it is "twice opposed to exchange." This is true, first, because "it excludes the reciprocity that the other demands. It is accomplished perfectly with the disappearance of one of its extremes (giver or givee), without which the other would become obsolete. The gift does not consist in a real (ontic or objective) transfer even if it possibly tolerates some incidental objective support, while the other has no function but to make a thing pass from one owner to another. Here the gift contradicts exchange as economic." The second distance from exchange arises from "the very method of phenomenology": "While the gift according to exchange is stymied in the natural attitude, the gift in terms of givenness arises from the realm of the reduction. . . . if the nonintervention of either of the two extremes, or substituting for the object of the gift its receivability or its givability, makes progress toward gratuity (as is the case), they owe this, more essentially, to the reduction that makes them possible."[47] The difference between exchange and the gift in terms of givenness is the difference between the "natural attitude" and the "phenomenological act."

On the other hand, Marion wants to show, against Derrida, that there is a gift that escapes economy, a gift that fulfills something of Derrida's hope for a pure gift. He believes that it is possible, operating within the strict limits of phenomenology and not entering on the terrain of metaphysics or theology, to think the gift according to the mode of givenness rather than according to the mode of exchange. He accepts the challenge of Derrida's bracketing of the triple transcendence of the giver, the gift, and the recipient but claims that one can still arrive at an identifiable gift that does not "vanish in a cloud of smoke, the last breath of a fading concept."[48] The conditions of the im/possibility of the gift that Derrida lays out can yield a gift understood in the mode of givenness. Phenomena appear only insofar as they give themselves.[49]

Within this overall framework of "the given," Marion explores the nature of the gift. Accepting Derrida's claims that gift exchange is impure and "economic," Marion proposes as a practical matter to risk the gift despite the uncertainty of its possibility.[50] Theoretically, he wants to show that there is sufficient "trace" of the gift to elicit the risk. In place of Derrida's annihilation of the gift, Marion offers a reduction of the gift to pure givenness. This can be done by bracketing the various features of the gift situation: the giver, the gift itself, and the recipient. He speculates on the possibilities of gifts without givers, without recipients, and without an object given.[51] One by one, Marion eliminates the empirical features of the gift exchange—eliminates the giver A, the gift B, and the recipient C. None of them, it turns out, is essential to the gift. Any two of them will do at a pinch.

He begins with a discussion of the gift itself.[52] What, he asks, is a gift? It is not a transfer of property, because there are gifts in which the gift does not yield property to the recipient (a loan, a lease) and more important because "a gift sometimes does not consist in any object at all: in the cases involving a promise, a reconciliation, a blessing (or a curse), a friendship, or a love (or a hatred), the gift is not identical to an object but emerges only at the moment of its occurrence; rather than being identical with the gift, the object becomes the simply occasional support for the gift."[53] Indeed, the "richer" a gift, the less it is visible in the actual object given. Power is given in a crown, a *pallium*, and other insignia of power, but the objects do not give the power—they only symbolize it. Likewise, the wedding ring is a sign of the most precious self-gift, and yet the ring is not equivalent in value to the gift at all. Thus, "the gifts which give the most give literally nothing—no thing, no object; not because they disappoint expectations but because what they give belongs neither to reality nor to objectivity."[54] Thus, the disappearance of the object itself does not obliterate the gift, but helps us focus on the gift in the mode of givenness rather than in the mode of exchange.

What happens when we bracket the recipient? Like the gift, the reception does not lie in the object itself nor in being the end point of a transfer of property. Rather, reception lies in the act of reception itself, a point that can be illustrated by the phenomena of ignorance and refusal. A gift that is not known to be a gift is not a gift; it must be recognized as a gift. Similarly, a gift refused is not fulfilled as gift. It is not missing any *thing*, any object. What is missing is simply the acceptance. Reception occurs when a person makes up his mind to be a recipient. But reception is not easy. Receiving a gift means receiving obligation, and this is something we may well want to avoid. For Marion, this obligation is not a debt that the recipient owes to the giver. That would lead back to the gift in the mode of economy, which, Marion agrees with Derrida, would destroy the gift as such. What obligates is not the giver but the gift itself. The gift itself is a challenge to the autocracy of the recipient, his desire to be self-sufficient and autonomous:

> [T]he gift, by its own allure and prestige, decides the giver to decide himself for it—that is to say, decides (or determines) him to sacrifice his own autocracy, the autocrat of what is his own, in order to receive it. The gift decides about its own acceptance by deciding about its recipient. Thus, we will conclude that in the regime of reduction, the experience of consciousness in which the gift gives itself consists of the decision of the gift—the decision to receive the gift by the recipient but especially to decide the recipient of the gift by the gift itself.[55]

Again, the gift remains even in the bracketing of the recipient, but the gift emerges not according to an economy of exchange but according to the mode of givenness.

Marion furthers the argument that the gift remains even when the recipient is bracketed by bringing up specifically Christian standards of gift giving, from Luke 6. When gifts are given to enemies and ingrates, the gift is still a gift. He argues not simply that the gift remains when the recipient is bracketed, but that when the gift is given to an enemy who has no intention of returning a gift or an ingrate who refuses to recognize the gift, the sheer gratuity of the gift stands out in greater relief: "The simple fact that a gift is abandoned does not destroy it; on the contrary, it confirms it in its character of givenness—no reciprocity whatsoever; there is not even the recognition of this gift which would corrode its pure gratuity. The abandon indicates that the gift not only surpasses every counter-gift but that it surpasses every possible acceptance. The abandoned gift manifests, by its very disproportion, its givenness."[56] This is a crucial moment in Marion's argument. It is not simply that the gift remains when the recipient and his response of gratitude are bracketed. Marion thinks that the gift comes into its own and becomes most transparently itself when the recipient is siphoned from the process. Gifts are most gifty when there is no one to receive or give thanks for them. Marion is as enamored of the pure gift as is Derrida.[57]

Bracketing the giver likewise does not destroy the gift but shows the gift in its pure form of gratuity. A gift that comes from an anonymous or dead benefactor is one that escapes any countergift, since the recipient either is ignorant of his benefactor or has no benefactor to whom to respond. More fundamentally for Marion, the giver is not an absolute origin. A gift is the result of a predicate; it arises as soon as the giver considers it "for the first time, as gift, or, more exactly, as givable." Its givability does not depend on any intrinsic property of the gift itself, nor does the object itself change when the giver determines that the object is a gift. The gift arises when givability arises, and givability arises, Marion says, because the giver recognizes a prior debt, a prior obligation based on an anterior gift: "The gift begins and, in fact, is achieved as soon as the giver imagines that he owes something—a gift without thing—to someone, therefore when he recognizes himself not only in the situation of a givee but also and first as a debtor. The gift arises when the potential giver suspects that another gift (received but not yet perceived) preceded him, one for which he owes something, which he ought to repay, to which he ought to respond." This means that the giver is not the ultimate determiner of the beginning of a gift; the gift in a sense gives itself because the prior gift obliges the giver to give in the first place: "the gift resides in the decision to give made by the potential giver, but the latter can decide only insofar as he yields to givability, that is to say, recognizes that an other gift already obliged him."[58] Gifts decide the giver. Or, more specifically, "givability" decides the giver to give since the decision to give itself rests upon the obligation inspired by an anterior gift.[59]

Bracketing the gift, the gift-object, does not destroy the gift, but instead reveals the deepest reality of the gift, and the background of givenness that obliges the giver to give in the first place. It reveals the gift in the mode of sheer givenness. But in the process, gratitude is cancelled in the reduction. There is no exchange, no circle of any sort.

God Without Being

Marion thus responds to Derrida. His response to Heidegger appears in his more theological work, where, as noted earlier, he wants to show that Heidegger is wrong to take Being as the final horizon. Rather, Marion argues that the reduction reveals *givenness* as the ultimate horizon. Heidegger's assault on onto-theology provides a backdrop for Marion,[60] but Marion believes that Heidegger escapes one idolatry for another: "Beyond the idolatry proper to metaphysics, there functions another idolatry, proper to the thought of Being as such."[61] Because Heidegger subordinates God to Being, for him "any access to something like 'God' . . . will have to determine him in advance as a being."[62] Marion wants to formulate a theology that does not bind God to the ontic realm nor limit him by some prior thought of Being as such. When he says that we must think "God without being," Marion is not introducing a refined sort of atheism: "God is, exists, and that is the least of things."[63] But since God is not to be confined by any prior framework or system of metaphysics or ontology, he exists in a very different way than creatures exist. When he says that God is beyond the realm of human thought, he does not mean that we cannot speak or think of God, but that we must think and speak of him "otherwise" than we think and speak of everything else.[64] We must think of God in the categories of gift.

Marion fills out the distinction with a meditation on the differences between the "idol" and an "icon." An idol is created to satisfy our "gaze," and idols are ultimately mirrors, various forms of self-idolatry and self-deception. By contrast, an icon is not limited to what is visible on the surface, but "summons sight in letting the visible . . . be saturated little by little with the invisible." Christ himself is the "norm" of the icon. Like Christ, the icon is neither a sign of an absent reality nor a wholly present reality that can be mastered by the gaze. Instead, the icon is a trace of presence.[65] For Marion, the icon becomes a main example of a larger category of phenomena, which he described as "saturated phenomena," a phenomenon that contains more than what appears: "not everything is capable of being given perfectly," and this means that there is something beyond the limits of what is offered to the intuition by phenomena. Confronted by a saturated phenomenon, we are unable to subdue it to our mastering gaze, but are instead overwhelmed by it.[66] The reality of saturated phenomena like icons implies a decentering of the transcendental ego, which can no longer be considered the source of meaning. This disrupts a central phenomenological conclusion, and opens up the possibility of theology that is not mastered by philosophy.

Marion offers various strategies[67] for thinking and speaking of God without falling into idolatry. He "crosses out" the linguistic sign "God" as a reminder that, however God is present, his presence is never complete or under our control. This usage "does not indicate that Gxd would have to disappear as a concept, or intervene only in the capacity of a hypothesis in the process of validation, but that the unthinkable enters into the field of thought only by rendering itself unthinkable there by excess, that is, by criticizing our thought. . . . We cross out the name of Gxd only in order to show ourselves that his unthinkableness saturates our thought—right from the beginning, and forever." Crossing out the name of God reminds us that we do not possess God; he gives himself freely to us—we do not grasp him—and what he offers is "the only accessible trace of He who gives."[68] Marion focuses on *agape* as the name and character of God. While metaphysics is offended by a lack of limits, by any inability of a concept to encompass the reality, "love does not suffer from the unthinkable or from the absence of conditions, but is reinforced by them." That is, "love loves without condition, simply because it loves." Or, love "is not spoken, in the end, it is made. Only then can discourse be reborn, but as an enjoyment, a jubilation, a praise."[69] Love is connected not to understanding but to faith. Only bad lovers want to understand love before they love. As the God of agape, God gives himself as a gift for "no reason at all," and thus cannot possibly be limited and conditioned by metaphysics. If God is gift and love, then we ought to renounce every effort to domesticate him into our theories. Faith takes the place of knowledge; gift occupies the space once reserved for possession. God gives himself to us, but not in a way that makes him subject to us.[70]

Marion illustrates the difference between the economy of possession and the model of gift/love by a reading of the prodigal son. The prodigal begins the story requesting possessions, his *ousia*, which Marion takes, philosophically, as "being" rather than as "possessions." The prodigal "asks that one grant that he no longer have to receive any gift—precisely, no longer have to receive the *ousia* as gift: He asks to possess it, dispose of it, enjoy it without passing through the gift and the reception of the gift. The son wants to owe nothing to the father, and above all not to owe him a gift; he asks to have a father no longer—the *ousia* without the father or gift."[71] Such an ousia as possession does not last; it yields immediately to dispossession, as the son wastes all in riotous living, as it becomes "liquid" and slips through his fingers. In the process of losing the ousia, the possessed being, the son loses filiation as well—"I am no longer worthy to be called your son." Yet, in the end, the father returns him to his position as son. This is because the father's gaze is iconic rather than idolatrous; for the father, nothing is possession without gift. The game that allows a nonpossessive Being or being is itself gift.

In this way, Marion moves to a "God without being," a God who is gift. Being/beings does not determine the gift, but the opposite. The distance of giver and gift is a distance that unifies even as it separates: "This other model of the gift, since it unifies only to the extent that it distinguishes, can, precisely, distort Being/being . . . being remains in its appropriation to Being . . . but distance includes it in another apparatus, in another circulation, in another giving."[72] In short, Gxd does not need to be; "Gxd gives" is a sufficient confession.[73]

In Marion's theological as in his phenomenological work, gratitude does not fare particularly well.[74] In his philosophical work, Marion strips the gift of its triple structure in order to isolate the pure essentiality of the gift, but in doing so he insists that reception, acknowledgment, and return of thanks are inessential to the gift. In *God Without Being*, he proves to be as puritanical as Derrida when it comes to the gift. At times Marion focuses on the question of reception, but, like Derrida, he sees proper reception as pure dissemination without return. In an essay on Pseudo-Dionysius, he offers a positive alternative to the circle of economy that, with Derrida, he believes needs to be dismantled to save the gift. According to Denys' hierarchical vision of beings, God is the overflowing source of all beings. He gives the gift of existence to everything else down the hierarchy of beings. But the reception of the gift of being is not a return to God, who needs nothing at all since he is an eternal and infinite fountain of life in himself. Rather, proper reception of the gift involves an outpouring of gifts down the hierarchy. Proper reception repeats the gift.[75]

Marion's pictorial explanation is rooted in his phenomenological reduction of the gift to sheer giving. If the gift is not the object itself, but the giving act, then properly receiving it can take no other form than giving again: "Man does not receive the gift as such except in welcoming the act of giving, that is, through repetition by giving himself," so that "receiving and giving are achieved in the same act."[76] More fundamentally, the reception of the gift that is a repetition of giving bears a christological imprint. When Jesus delivers over the fulfillment of all hope and revelation, delivers over the secret hidden since the foundation of the world, he does it in the kenotic self-deliverance. Likewise, no gift is repeated or "received as a gift unless the recipient donor becomes integrally and in person—hypostatically—a gift."[77] This christological structure manifests a Trinitarian play of gift:

> Each person, and primarily the Son, trinitarily admits receiving himself from a paternal gift that he did not order. . . . [T]he Son receives from the Father not only everything that it comes down to him to concentrate in himself— that is, everything—but especially the very impetus of the gift, through which the paternal gift gives with neither reserve nor return. In his infinite and inconceivable dependence and poverty, the Son experiences the gift as gift, received in filial poverty and given from the overflowing anteriority of the Father. He in fact receives, in the dimensionless infinite that overwhelms him, only the givenness and the giveability of the gift.[78]

Marion thus returns to the insights of the Christian mystical tradition, according to which the highest form of gratitude is to give. Importantly, Marion at the same time achieves an account of reception that will satisfy (if anything can) Derrida's strictures on the gift: a receptivity that takes the form of pure dissemination must surely warm Derrida's heart. Yet Marion has recovered part of the Christian tradition while ignoring the circularity of Christian giving and thanksgiving. For gift exchange, he substitutes a line or proliferating labyrinth of dissemination. Nothing is ever returned to the God who initiates the process with his superabundant gift. Marion, as much as almost every other modern and postmodern writer, conducts his work outside the infinite circle of Christianity, even when he is working within an explicitly Christian framework.

Conclusion
Can a Gift Be Given?

Far and away the most powerful rejoinder to Derrida and Marion has been in the world of theologian John Milbank.[79] According to Milbank, modernity defines the gift purely in terms of freedom, its "non-compulsory" character. Gifts are considered private, in contrast to public contract. Yet even in modern societies, "many practices still fall ambiguously between gift and contract."[80] Thus, Derrida's and Marion's distinction of gift and contract does not hold, and the blurry lines between gift and commerce reflect the larger *aporia* of generosity—namely, that generosity is an obligation.

If gifts are part of an exchange, are gifts then reducible/deconstructible to contract?[81] Milbank says no, and he traces Derrida's "purism" to a particular understanding of agape: "This rigour takes the form of disassociating agape in turn from the giver's own happiness or well-being, then from *eros* or any kind of desire to be with the recipient of your love, then from justice or 'giving the other his due' . . . and finally from power, or the inescapable persuasion of the other involved in every offering." This rigor, he claims, is "unbiblical for all that it seeks to be super-biblical." It ends by depersonalizing gifts and, ironically, reaffirming the Cartesian subject and the domination of will. A disinterested gift can be given out only by a self-contained, self-controlled subject, but this subject is "suicidally sacrificial" in its giving. Derrida is also indebted to a "questionable Kantian understanding of the goodness of the gift as residing in purity of will or motivation."[82] Milbank rejects the opposition of agape and eros: "[H]uman generosity belongs within the context of prior attachments, or at the very least the making of such attachments." I do not give without concern for the relationship that the giving nurtures, a relationship that inevitably involves *me*. Instead of set-ting agape and eros in opposition, Milbank argues that "a reflection upon erotic love is not irrelevant to an elucidation of agapeic donation." Romantic gifts are mutual. A lover who gives and gives without reception or return from the beloved is called a stalker. Erotic love is mutual, or it is not love. Yet this mutuality is not commerce; it is not slavery. A romantic gift is "most free where it is yet most bound, most mutual and most reciprocally demanded."[83] Grateful reception and return do not contaminate a romantic gift. It is the response that a romantic gift aims to achieve: I *want* my beloved to notice what I give, and to give herself back to me.

Using the romantic gift as his paradigm, Milbank argues that a gift is characterized by a delay of return and a difference between the gift and the return. A gift is a matter of delayed nonidentical repetition, or nonidentical mimesis.[84] If you return a gift to me immediately after I give it to you, the gift ceases to be a gift and becomes a purchase; between a gift and its return, time passes. Milbank is clearly returning to an older, perhaps Thomistic, conception of gratitude. It is not merely verbal thanks or a sentiment of gratefulness. It is fulfilled in some sort of return gift—whether that gift takes the form of an object or the gift of one's attention, time, and friend-ship. Milbank thus breaks out of the confines of modern conceptions of gratitude, though even here he does not affirm the infinite circle of Christian exchange.

Gifts are not interchangeable, not equal. In the market, a $10 bill for $10 of groceries is appropriate, but gifts must include an element of sur-prise, novelty, asymmetry. Gift and countergift *must* not be identical. Given these features of gifts, Milbank concludes that Christian love as expressed in gifts is not linear altruism but a circle of "purified gift-exchange." Delay and nonidentical mimesis are the "necessarily creative self-expression of the genuine giver" that includes "a requisite attention to the other, her character, situation and mood." A gift is dependent not on purity of motive but on the suitability of the thing given, and thus the gift is not ruined by an impure motivation. Delight in giving also has a role here: "[O]ne can enjoy giving, not only in the mode of self-congratulation, but also as a kind of ecstasies, or continuation of oneself out of oneself." Desire for a response is not neces-sarily tarnished self-interest, but could be a "recognition of ineradicable con-nection with others and a desire for its furtherance." On this understanding, agapic giving becomes "a self-affirmation that is also a self-displacement, since it seeks to resituate self through the address of others towards me."[85]

To achieve this purified exchange, gifts must be purged of the competi-tive, agonistic, and honor-driven features that characterized gifts in ancient

and tribal societies. This is what the New Testament achieves. Paul teaches
we should owe no man anything save love, which "means that the infinite
debt is now a light burden and easy yoke, even where it involves repentance,
since all that is due is our own outgoing within which alone we are." The
exchange of gifts is what constitutes the church as a body made up of Jews
and Gentiles: The Romans "are exhorted to acknowledge the gift of the
announcement of God which they owe to the Jews and their law, not only
by words but also by material almsgiving to the poor in Jerusalem."[86] The
gospel, as it shapes the church, announces the possibility of purified gift
exchange: "We are . . . given the possibility to love because we are given the
true shape of love in the form of a love that is always already repeated."[87]
Thus the "new covenant fully sustains prophetic delay and non-identical repetition of the gift sufficient to characterize it as gift." The new covenant
fulfills the aspirations of local gift-exchange societies, and it fulfills them in
"perpetual Eucharist"—that is, a community "living through the offering
. . . of the gift given to us of God himself in the flesh."[88]

CONCLUSION

A Theistic Modernity

What a long, strange trip it's been, and it will be helpful to summarize at this point by returning to the illustration I offered in the introduction. Grandma has given you an ugly and useless soup tureen as a wedding gift. Should you put it away in a closet? Should you use it to feed the cat? Should you bring it out and serve soup from it when Grandma visits? Grandma's soup tureen provides a handy symbolic way of identifying different conceptions of gratitude across the centuries. WWAD? WWCD? What would Aristotle do? What would Cicero do?

- Aristotle would warn you that receiving the tureen puts you in a position of inferiority and that, if you want to be a virtuous and independent person, you should pay Grandma back with a bigger gift as soon as possible. Then forget you ever received the gift in the first place.
- Cicero would tell you to follow accepted custom, take the gift, look for a chance to reciprocate, and expect that your good offices will advance your political career.
- Seneca would encourage you to exaggerate the quality and beauty of the gift, to appear at Grandma's door every morning to accompany her on her way to the grocery store, loudly celebrating her generosity at every stoplight. He would encourage you to look for the right time and way to repay her.
- Jesus and Paul would tell you to honor and love Grandma, thank God with sincerity, and move on.

217

- The *Beowulf* poet would encourage you to pass out soup tureens to your employees to display your largesse.
- Aquinas would do his Seneca imitation. He would tell you to receive the gift, express gratitude, and look for the right time and place to requite her gift.
- Calvin and Luther would tell you to thank God, while recognizing you do not deserve the tureen or your grandmother's love. They would remind you that grace is a gift that can never be repaid.
- Hobbes would tell you that you should receive the tureen in such a way that Grandma will never regret having given it to you, which means,do not use it to feed the cat.
- Locke would say you should thank her and show esteem for her, so long as her gift was not an attempt to influence your decision to vote Democrat.
- Adam Smith would tell you that gratitude is a proper sentiment in response to something that gives pleasure, like a tureen.
- Kant would tell you that since Grandma gave first, you are obligated to her by a sacred duty, a debt that can never be repaid.
- Kierkegaard would remind you that we are to thank God even in suffering.
- Nietzsche would urge you to show gratitude *especially* if the tureen is ugly, to show Grandma how powerless she is to harm you.
- Heidegger would mumble something incomprehensible in German, hike up his lederhosen, and leave with a Nazi salute.
- Mauss would be at the head of a gaggle of anthropologists warning you that there is no such thing as a free gift, that Grandma might return later to reclaim her property, and that her display of generosity is likely a power play intended to put you in her debt.
- Derrida would say that you soiled the gift as soon as you said thank you.
- Marion would strip the tureen to its essence of pure givability, and you and Grandma would both disappear into phenomenological vapor.

Where Are We Now?

Where does all this leave us? Where are we with gratitude now, in the early twenty-first century?

There is a widespread sense that the "Enlightenment project" has run aground,[1] and there is a growing sense that the malaise of contemporary culture has something to do with our forgetfulness of gifts and our ungrateful marginalization of gratitude. Some see it as liberalism gone to seed. Liberal theory (expressed, for example, in the Declaration of Independence) posits an original gift, a bestowal, even a bestowal from a Creator. But the bestowal is a gift of *rights*, and over the centuries that bestowal has inspired only greater and greater demands for wider and wider rights. "Every day," José Ortega y Gasset complained in 1930, "a new luxury [is added] to their standard of living." In earlier ages, one's status and personal gifts "would have been considered one of fortune's gifts, inspiring humble gratitude toward destiny." Now, these have become rights, "not to be grateful for, but to be insisted upon."[2] Wealth has not satisfied, but led only to the expansion of desires, which has produced a "radical ingratitude" toward the very institutions that have satisfied his desires. Mass man is a "spoilt child" who acknowledges no limits, no duty, no necessity of self-restraint.[3] Ingratitude is evident in the very definition of national polities. The nation blames the state for all its ills, but it was the state that created the nation in the first place.[4]

For others, the crisis of modernity is capitalism gone to seed, and again gratitude arises as a central concern. Wilhelm Ropke lamented the infiltration of market mechanisms and valuations into arenas of social life where they did not belong. The idol of growth, argued E. F. Schumacher, is the fundamental error of modern economic systems. What measures economic health is the gross national product (GNP), and as long as the numbers stay steady, no one asks whether the products of our nation are in fact gross. Schumacher says that the economist "would lose all his certainties if he even entertained such a question: growth of the GNP must be a good thing, irrespective of what has grown and who, if anyone, has benefitted. The idea that there could be pathological growth, unhealthy growth, disruptive or destructive growth, is to him a perverse idea which must not be allowed to surface."[5] To my knowledge, Schumacher never describes this as "methodological ingratitude," but it might well be. It is this sense that our economics is dominated by ingratitude, discontent, greed, sheer self-interest, and accumulation that accounts for the popularity of the works of Wendell Berry. His economics arise from wonder at the nature of things, and from grateful respect for the specific contours of the world as it comes to us.[6]

For others, the ingratitude of contemporary culture arises from the idolization of the new and the denigration of the old, which has become the cultural companion of technological progress. Others see ingratitude as the dominant ethos of youth culture,[7] or a forgetfulness of the contributions of the dead.[8] Few voices of gratitude rise in the modern age, complains Robert Raynolds, and those that do are drowned out by a "legion" of resentful voices.[9] For critics of a religious bent, the underlying issue is a lack of thankfulness toward God. We have forgotten God, Solzhenitsyn said, and we know from Aquinas that forgetfulness is the most aggravated form of ingratitude. Though not always named as such, ingratitude is commonly recognized as one of the keys to understanding late modernity.

At the same time, and perhaps for the same reason, we are in the midst of something of a gratitude revival. Those who sense that our cultural pathologies are related to a gratitude deficit are doing what they can to fill that deficiency. We are surrounded by abundance, but we have convinced ourselves that there is no God to thank, and we can hardly give thanks to the market. We have an instinct for gratitude, but no one and nothing to which to direct it. We are in the grip of a gratitude hunger.[10]

Spearheaded by Robert Emmons and Michael McCullough, a branch of the "positive psychology" movement has embarked on a research program of "gratitude studies."[11] Psychology has produced highly ambivalent treatments of gratitude. Freud characterized the Oedipal desires of a son for his mother as the son's way of showing "gratitude." All of a boy's "instincts, those of tenderness, gratitude, lustfulness, defiance and independence, find satisfaction in the single wish to be his own father."[12] Theodore Reik traced all forms of sacrifice, including "offerings of homage, gratitude, atonement," to "the precautionary offering which is intended to ward off a threatening evil or an expected punishment, to assuage the anger of the God."[13] Ambivalence concerning gratitude turns to outright fright in the Freudian literary theory of Harold Bloom, who argued that rivalry rather than reception was the primary stance of poets toward their influential predecessors.[14] Not for nothing did Paul Ricoeur count Freud, along with Marx and Nietzsche, among the great modern "masters of suspicion."[15]

Working from a psychoanalytic perspective, however, Melanie Klein rehabilitated gratitude. Klein argued that envy was the greatest emotional inhibitor to feelings of love and gratitude. Envy and gratitude (and virtually every other emotional disposition) can be traced to the earliest experiences of an infant, specifically to the infant's contact with his or her mother's breast. If a child nurses well, he or she learns the rudiments of hope, trust, goodness, and gratitude. Deprived of this experience—whether because the mother has inadequate milk or because the mother does not provide emotional nourishment along with her milk—the child is impaired from the outset, set off on a life of hate, envy, or greed. Enjoyment of the breast produces grateful people, and only gratitude can counteract the destructive effects of envy. Gratitude, Klein insists, "is essential in building up the relation to the good object and underlies also the appreciation of goodness in others and in oneself. Goodness is rooted in the emotions and attitudes that arise in the earliest stage of infancy, when for the baby the mother is the one and only object."[16]

The contributors to *The Psychology of Gratitude* make the common modern assumption that gratitude is an "emotion." As such, it is integral to the promotion of personal happiness and well-being.[17] Gratitude curbs personally damaging emotions like resentment, regret, and envy,[18] and it even brings physiological benefits.[19] Yet the focus of their research is not narrowly psychological. They undertake their research against the background of the tradition of gratitude in philosophy and theology that my book has explored,[20] and many of the contributors take account of the moral dimensions of gratitude. Gratitude is a "moral affect" that has a variety of moral functions. Gratitude is a moral barometer that indicates "a particular type of interpersonal transaction"—namely, "one in which a benefactor contributes to a beneficiary's perceived well-being through some tangible or intangible benefit."[21] It is a moral motivator that encourages grateful people to act in altruistic and "prosocial" ways, and it is a moral reinforcer because a grateful response to an act of kindness encourages future acts of kindness.[22] In considering gratitude under the rubric of "fair exchange," the authors rejoin gratitude and justice, which have been severed since the eighteenth century.[23] Though written by psychologists and psychological researchers, *The Psychology of Gratitude* goes a considerable distance in recovering the ethical stature that gratitude has had through the centuries of premodernity. Though the authors consistently speak of gratitude as an "emotion," in practice they combat the post-Enlightenment reduction of gratitude to a sentiment. By treating gratitude as a *moral* affect, the authors challenge the habit of reducing gratitude to a matter of mere etiquette.[24]

Their moral analysis of gratitude shades into a consideration of the social and even political dimensions of gratitude. Since it is typically a response to a benefit given by another person (a human, or God), gratitude is a typically a social emotion that runs against the grain of the "individualistic" bias of modern society. A person who expresses gratitude signals that he recognizes he has been well treated by another, and this stimulates further "prosocial" behavior and attitudes in the future.[25] McCullough and Tsang go so far as to suggest that because "gratitude actually motivates people to behave prosocially, gratitude might be thought of as a social resource that is well worth understanding—and perhaps even cultivating—for the development of a society based on goodwill."[26] Political virtues such as civility and respect are also tied to gratitude.[27] On the other hand, because benefits and gratitude can be manipulated in order to dominate and control, gratitude needs to be rooted in a specific moral conception of the good, lest one be seduced into showing gratitude for a Hitler or a Stalin.[28]

Researchers in gratitude studies have also addressed questions about the religious aspects of gratitude. A number of research projects have found strong correlations between gratitude and regular participation in religious communities and activities.[29] Gratitude may be divided into two aspects: "thankfulness" in response to personal benefits and favors from another, and "gratefulness" as a sense of "gratuitous belonging."[30] The latter experience can be a response to perceived gifts from God, or can be a response to the sheer luck of a good life.[31]

Not every contemporary advocate of gratitude sees the necessity for theology. Ronald Aronson describes his experience of coming to the top of a hill on a spring day to hear the birds and bathe in the sun's warmth. His delight was not merely physical pleasure, not merely "gladness to be out here on this day." Alongside those experiences was "something else . . . curious and less distinct, a vague feeling more like gratitude than anything else but not toward any being or person I could recognize."[32] He insists that atheism does not empty the world of meaning, as Camus suggested. Appealing to Darwinian biology, he insists that meaning arises from the marvel of our natural and social interdependence. But then he cannot quite escape a substitute religion. We should be grateful to the sun, and perhaps even to microbes and distant basket weavers who are part of the global economic system that sustains and enriches our lives, and he finds in holiday gatherings a quasi-liturgy of thanks.[33]

Charles Eisenstein offers an ambitious proposal for resurrecting the original "mystical" dimensions of money as part of a program of "sacred economics." For Eisenstein as much as for Eckhardt or Johannes de Bromyard, life is sheer gift. "Our lives are *given* us," he writes, and thus "our default state is gratitude." Gratitude is "the truth of our existence." He knows enough of the Bible to allude, "in the beginning was the Gift," so that gratitude "is natural to us, so primal, so elemental." We have the "feeling of having received a gift, and the desire to give in turn."[34] One might ask, from whence the gift? To whom/what the gratitude? We are some ways into Eisenstein's encomium to gratitude before he answers those questions, somewhat in passing, by mentioning a source of the primordial gift, a "Giver" in whose gifts human gifts participate.[35] But it is clear that Eisenstein has no particular religion nor any particular Giver in mind. Religion is brought into the discussion insofar as it supports the Master of his system, the Gift.[36] Christianity, Buddhism, Jainism, and Judaism jostle happily on the page, all saying more or less the very same thing. Though he does not name Christianity explicitly as the culprit, Eisenstein argues that one of the chief factors eroding the sacredness of economics and property, the obstacle that stands in the way of the realization of an economy of gift and gratitude, is what he calls the "mind-set of Separation, of conquest, of overcoming evil."[37] All gods are invited to contribute to Eisenstein's sacred utopia, all but the *jealous* ones.

Aronson's book is a *vade mecum* for peripatetic atheists; it is something of a pep talk, a sermon assuring Aronson's church that they are not condemned to the empty lives that religious believers project onto them. His reflections on gratitude remain well within the confines to which modernity has consigned reflections on gratitude—sentiments of well-being, a small circle of friends at a holiday feast. Eisenstein's far more ambitious proposals do not wash as alternatives to modernity. He does not want to get rid of money, he insists. He only wants to restore it to its proper place, and to reenchant what has been disenchanted within the iron cage. With his bland and unbaptized Giver, his mishmash of "religion," he simply repeats the gestures of modernity. As a solution to a modernity built on a generic (and very, *very* Eurocentric) conception of religion, Eisenstein offers a renewed economics built on a generic (and very, *very* Eurocentric) conception of religion. Besides, undirected gratitude hunger holds considerable danger. In searching for somewhere to hang our gratitude, we might hang it almost anywhere on almost anything. The twentieth century was full of the corpses of those who fed their gratitude hunger on the largesse of Stalin and Hitler.

A more overtly theological and overtly political treatment of gratitude is found in Mark T. Mitchell's *The Politics of Gratitude*.[38] Building from a moral and theological account of gratitude, he sketches an avowedly conservative alternative to liberalism, what he calls a "politics of gratitude." Gratitude is an obligation we owe first of all to God, but also to parents, the state, nature, and our ancestors. He uses the tragedy of *King Lear* to illustrate the catastrophic social and political effects of ingratitude. A politics of gratitude involves a modesty about the ability of the state to solve social problems, an economy that works at a human scale, emphasizes localism, and protects property rights instead of pursuing limitless growth. A politics of gratitude leads to environmental politics that respect the earth as a creation, to social policies that protect the family, to educational reforms that root students in their surroundings rather than detaching them from their surroundings.

David L. Schindler provides a similar, profoundly theological sketch of a renewed gift-and-gratitude political economy. His "anthropology of gift and gratitude" begins from the premise that man is at home in the world by virtue of his relation to the Creator and to the rest of creation, especially to the community of human persons. This, rather than separation, is the basis of true individualism, since individual and community are not at odds but presuppose one another.[39] Relationships are inherent in any human action. There is no purely autonomous action, because we are dependent even in the midst of our independence. Schindler quotes George Grant quoting Paul: we are not our own, and because we are not our own we belong to ourselves only by belonging to others. "Creaturely ontology is best approached through reflection on the mother's smile," Schindler writes, alluding to a theme of Hans Urs von Balthasar. In the response to the generosity of the mother, the child is realized as his unique self. Such an ontology and anthropology places gratitude at the center of human life.[40]

These constituting relationships cannot be simply set aside in considering the production, exchange, and distribution of wealth. We are creatures of gift and gratitude, and any economy that works at cross-purposes with that human instinct is working cross-grained to human nature. What is produced is not simply the goods, the objects, or the commodities that are for sale. Rather, the intention and purpose of the producer, and the intended recipients of the production, determine the character of the thing produced. A home-cooked meal is not the same as a frozen dinner. A mother's love that produces the meal "is not merely a matter of an intention remaining external to the food." On the contrary, "her love *takes form* as food," and if the same food exists without that intention, it is simply a different thing.[41] Adam Smith was wrong. We must take account of the baker's beneficence or generosity if we are to assess his production accurately. If he produces bread only to make a profit, then the production "by definition entails instrumentalizing toward the end of profit everything that goes into the production." The baker is most interested in the "appearance of a certain quality of bread and bread-making." Worse still, the baker has instrumentalized himself, made himself only a tool of the bread-producing process, only a means for making profits. A baker who produces his bread out of generosity, however, implies a production process "undertaken for the sake of making what is intrinsically a good loaf of bread and for the sake of the person who will consume it." The latter intention lends "a different sense of time and measurement and aesthetics" to bread production. To say that the bread is simply the same implies that we have already decided to employ a "mechanical" standard of judgment, a standard that violates the anthropology of gift and gratitude with which Schindler started.[42]

In an economy of love, where producers produce for the sake of the thing produced and out of a desire to provide good things (to *give*) to consumers, an economy where consumers receive goods produced with gratitude, the reality of everything is deepened. The relations between producers and consumers are deepened and improved, because neither producer nor consumer sees himself as simply a cog in a machine of production, another instrument for the increase of the GNP. Gratitude is not ornamental to economy; it is constitutive of a healthy and humane economy.

Liberal order, and the economic system that accompanies it, rests on an entirely different anthropology and ontology. All production is reduced to profit making, and thus all production becomes instrumentalized. The anthropology of liberalism is an instrumentalist anthropology, and a materialist one. It cannot sustain its own achievements. Though it offers freedom, it ultimately undermines freedom. Its fundamental assumptions drive it toward a culture of death, because human beings are instrumentalized toward the end of profit. Freedom and wholeness come through relationships, and insofar as liberal order detaches individuals from those relationships, it inhibits rather than enhances freedom. Schindler detects a profound "ambiguity" in liberal society:

> The "rights" of the individual, freedom of choice, equality, the power of self-determination, the creativity of the self, community as mutual and enlightened self-interest, the capacities of modern science and technology, the institutionalized freedoms of market economics and democratic politics. . . . Each of these achievements—and each is a genuine achievement—insofar as it presupposes, however unconsciously, an onto-logic of abstract self-identity, *eo ipso* bears within it the seeds of its own undoing and indeed reversal.[43]

With much of Mitchell's and Schindler's program, I have great sympathy, but I wonder if they have grasped the radicalism of the New Testament's account of gift and gratitude. Is there room for Jesus the ingrate? Is there room for a Paul who refuses to acknowledge his indebtedness to the Philippians? Put another way, we can ask whether Mitchell's proposal will work even if God is not seen as the source and end of the infinite circle of gift and gratitude. Is his a theory *etsi deus non daretur*? Put in more political and historical terms, does either Mitchell or Schindler take adequate account of the fact that the freedoms of modernity are the product of a secularized Christian impulse?

Neither Schindler nor Mitchell acknowledges that "ingratitude" is one of Christianity's great contributions to Western civilization, precisely the contribution Christianity made to the formation of modernity. Paganism did not have to learn gratitude from Christians. Paganism knew all about gratitude, the oppressions of gratitude included. What was needed was a new impulse that broke through the past and opened the possibility of something new. Christianity displayed "ingratitude" toward traditions, religions, benefactors, but it was an "ingratitude" enclosed in comprehensive gratitude toward an infinite God who was the source of all good gifts but who also relativized all those gifts by the self-gift of his Son. A theological alternative to modernity that does not recognize the Bible's impulse toward ingratitude and its dissolution of debt is in danger of reinstating a traditional, but barely Christian model of social and political order. Those who dream Maussian dreams should remember that gifts can turn nightmarish. A theology that does not accept modernity, for all its flaws and distortions, as an achievement of Christianity, fails to that degree as a Christian theology. It runs the risk of failing as a social and political proposal, for, as Schindler acknowledges, the gains of modernity, especially its gain in human liberty, are genuine achievements. How they can be preserved in a narrowly circularized world of gift and gratitude is difficult to see.

～

Yet Schindler, Mitchell, and the other critics of modernity are, in my judgment, correct that the post-Enlightenment world cannot sustain itself. Modern society, conforming to the momentary relations of the market, aspires to social debtlessness. Locke's gratitude-free polity invades and colonizes the rest of society. Gratitude obligations are dissolved.[44] All the burdens of the past, all the hellish obligations to *les autres*, are erased. It is the dream of Rousseau and Diderot, year 1 every day. The social and economic pathologies that follow are evident. How, Dmitri Karamazov's prosecutor exclaims, can we survive if respect for fathers has to be *proven*, if debts of gratitude are not simply accepted as a matter of course? How can we survive once we raise the question, why should I love my father?

Yet modern society is a remarkable achievement, embodying, albeit in a distorted fashion, some of the communal vision of Jesus and Paul: "Owe no man anything. The certificate of debt has been cancelled. Forgive us our debts, as we forgive our debtors." Not even the most resolute opponent of modernity wants to undo that achievement. No one wants to return to kowtowing. No one wants to return to a social order where the way to say "thanks" is "I'm sorry—I am fully aware of my debt to you. I can never repay it."[45]

I have argued that the great thinkers on gratitude in the modern age pick up one or another fragment of the Christian infinite circle of gift and gratitude. Descartes and Rousseau represent the moment of ingratitude that allows a fresh start. Kant insists on gifts without expectation of return, and Derrida is a hyper-Kantian who thinks that even gratitude contaminates the gift. Locke separates the circles of social life from the uncorruptible linearity of politics, breaking bonds of gratitude in the name of fairness and justice.

Yet none of these fragments is coherent or realistic by itself. "Ingratitude" is a necessary moment of social and political life, without which there can be no progress, but when it is detached from circularity of every kind, it can only collapse or run aground. Liberal order is an achievement of massive historical importance, but in theory if not in practice, it depersonalizes politics by denuding politics of gratitude. An impersonal, mechanistic state is not the product of an unfortunate decline of liberalism. An impersonal mechanism is liberalism's genius. Yet it is a genius that exists more in theory than in reality. By his own admission, Derrida's "pure gift" is an elusive ideal that does not describe any actual human relationships. This is no basis for social life. Derrida wants to encourage generosity, as all strive to realize the impossible possibility of the gift. He is just as likely to condemn us to perpetual debt, to the perpetual guilt of falling short of an ideal purity, to the irredeemable burden of trying to live up to *the* impossible, to perpetual sowing without harvest.

Is there a way to cut through the dilemma—to retain the achievements of modernity's regime of gift and gratitude while escaping modernity's pathologies? If modernity is the product of fragments and shards of Christian tradition, then it seems reasonable to ask whether a whole Christianity might provide an antidote. Perhaps the solution is to put the infinite circle back together again. Let me illustrate by returning to the dilemmas posed in the introduction:

- The key to the infinite circle is the expansion of gratitude's "field of operation." Christianity infuses gratitude into every nook and cranny of human life. Because *all* comes from God, thanks is offered to him for everything. "Give thanks for everything in all circumstances" is as global a command as one can expect. Christianity satisfies the gratitude hunger of our age. Indeed, it more than satisfies; it provides a surfeit of gratitude.

- Only the infinite circle underwrites an ethic of self-sacrifice, which, for Christians, does not operate on the premise of "Those who lose their lives shall lose them" but the promise of "Those who lose their lives shall gain them." Only the infinite circle harmonizes self-interest and altruism, and thus only the infinite circle can underwrite the second great commandment that is the basis of all social life: you shall love your *neighbor* as *yourself.*

- Christianity reconciles personalism and freedom. The infinite circle of Christianity is personal from beginning to end. A personal God gives all gifts, often through human persons, and gratitude is offered to that same personal giving God. Yet the infinite scope of the circle of reciprocity gives room for refusal. I can thank God for a benefit without becoming indebted to the human benefactor. My thanks goes "over the head" of the human giver (in a somewhat Nietzschean fashion), and as a result I can simultaneously be grateful (to God) and ungrateful (rejecting enslaving bonds). At the same time, horizontal relations of need and dependency remain in place. Though my gratitude goes "over the head" of the human person, I am grateful *for* him, for his gifts and services, and I can acknowledge that I am dependent on him insofar as God has gifted him to gift me. As Paul says, I have no debts to my benefactor *except* the obligation to love him.

- Because Christianity's gratitude is global, it infuses the market as much as the nonmarket. As Schindler says, production for the market can be construed as a gift, as the provision of *good* and not merely the provision of goods for profit. As a consumer, I am to be as grateful for the goods I purchase with my own hard-earned money as for the unexpected check that arrives from an anonymous benefactor. It is all from God, and he is owed all thanks. In the Christian infinite circle, the opposition of commodity and gift breaks down somewhat (as Milbank notes). Social debts are "liquidated" as much as market debts, as I refer all gratitude to God. Yet the liquidation of debts in the market does not break my connection with suppliers any more than the liquidation of debts of gratitude breaks my connections with family and friends. I thank God for the goods that the manufacturer provides, and I thank God for the *manufacturer*. The persons, materials, operations, and processes that bring the goods to me are all also gifts from God, and I appreciate all these as his gifts. Again, I pay, and I owe no debts, *except* the debt of love. If I am to love the shopkeeper, who is my neighbor, I cannot think that my connection with him lasts only as long as it takes me to get my change. Markets are not necessarily impersonal machines of profit. Only the infinite circle can discipline the self-interest and acquisitiveness of the market without making "profit" a dirty word.

- According to the infinite circle of Christian faith, I am what I am in relation, but I am above and beyond all what I am in relation to God. There is an "individualism" inherent in Christianity, since our fundamental constitutive relationship is not to another human being, or to a human community, but to God. I can extricate myself (in modern fashion) from the small circles of gift and gratitude and remain and retain myself. This does not leave me outside all relation, since I remain in relation to God. And that relation confirms rather than subverts my relations with others. I owe no man anything, *except* the debt of love. Christianity offers an anthropological "individualism" that does not tend toward nihilism.

- Creation is God's gift, and I owe him thanks for its pulsing abundance. I owe the creation nothing but love. Yet within the infinite circle of Christianity there is a room for an "ungrateful" response to the creation. I am not obligated to leave it as it is. I can say, in *gratitude*, "We can make improvements on this gift."

- The globalization of gratitude in Christianity also opens up political space. Politics is inevitably personal, because all political actors are persons. Politics gets done through gifts and favors. Yet a political actor operating on the infinite circle of Christian faith will look for returns on service from his Father, not from his donors, constituents, or colleagues. A political actor who receives favors will be incorruptible insofar as he directs his thanks, and "ungratefully" refuses to acknowledge any debt *except* the debt to love. Gratitude can function as a public virtue without collapsing into cronyism only if it responds to gifts from a Patron who stands outside and above politics, the Father who sees in secret and rewards openly.

Conclusion

A social order that functions within the infinite circle of Christianity must take its cues from the church, which is the original community of absolute gratitude and focused ingratitude. If the church is going to play a central role in the renewal of modern society, it has to cultivate habits of ingratitude. Christians, and churches, must learn to renounce debts of gratitude, giving thanks only to God. If Chinese authorities loosen restrictions on house churches, for instance, Chinese Christians should be thankful to God for the freedom, but reject any offer of returning thanks to the state by moderating or adjusting their message. Of course, these habits of ingratitude exist within a global stance of gratitude, and so the church must also cultivate habits and practices of gratitude. We must all become Pentecostals (or Kierkegaardians), whose first instinct in every circumstance is to offer praise and thanks to the Father.[46] We must learn what it means to offer a continuous sacrifice of thanksgiving. Above all, the church must restore its ritual of gift and gratitude, the Eucharist, to its historically central place in worship, piety, and communal life, and Christians must learn how to practice a continuous Eucharist.

Only this, in my judgment, will preserve the achievements of modernity in a way that avoids its horrors. To retain, and to build on, modernity, atheistic modernity must be replaced with its only real alternative—a theistic modernity.

Notes

INTRODUCTION

1   "Why 'gift' exactly?" John Milbank asks. And he answers, "[G]ift is a kind of transcendental category in relation to all the topoi of theology, in a similar fashion to 'word.' Creation and grace are gifts; Incarnation is the supreme gift; the Fall, evil and violence are the refusal of gift; atonement is the renewed and hyperbolic gift that is forgiveness; the supreme name of the Holy Spirit is donum (according to Augustine); the Church is the community that is given to humanity and is constituted through the harmonious blending of diverse gifts (according to the apostle Paul)" (*Being Reconciled: Ontology and Pardon* [London: Routledge, 2003], ix).

2   I meant to refrain from the easy mockery of the self-help genre, but in a recent page-through of an Amazon.com search for books on gratitude, I came across this astonishing title, *Thank You Power: Making the Science of Gratitude Work for You*, by Deborah Norville (Nashville: Thomas Nelson, 2008). The title is doubly, unintentionally, Nietzschean: first, because it seems to express the subtle power of the weak, and, second, because it treats gratitude as an aggressive power. On Nietzsche, see chapter 9.

3   Margaret Visser says that English speakers say the word "thanks" a hundred times a day (*The Gift of Thanks: The Roots and Rituals of Gratitude* [New York: Houghton Mifflin, 2009], 8).

4   A starting point is found in John B. Carman and Frederick J. Streng, eds., *Spoken and Unspoken Thanks: Some Comparative Soundings* (Cambridge, Mass.: Center for the Study of World Religions, Harvard University, 1989).

5   Different as we are from Greeks and Romans, gift giving still runs in a circle in the modern West. At Christmas, we complete the circle of giving and return immediately, and when we give a gift or do a service in other circumstances, we usually expect at least an expression of thanks, which in many cases is enough to complete the circle. Typically, we also expect the person on the receiving end to remember the favor we have done and to act toward us in a way that expresses his or her gratitude. Parents, for centuries one of the paradigm cases of gratitude, expect their children to respect them for the sacrifices they make. Friends are affronted by friends who neglect to return grateful loyalty for favors they have done. One of the

puzzles of my story is that theorists of giving miss this circularity, and tell us that gifts ought to be lines stretching infinitely into the distance.

6   The term is Peter Brown's.

7   Jacques T. Godbout, "Homo Donator versus Homo Oeconomicus," in Antoon Vandevelde, ed., *Gifts and Interests* (Leuven: Peeters, 2000), 25.

8   Margaret Visser makes a heroic attempt to show that freedom, equality, individualism, and giving and gratitude constitute a "constellation" of values that are necessary for our society to function (*Gift of Thanks*, chap. 23).

9   This illustration brings up issues of the gratitude as a form of social deception that I have been unfortunately unable to pursue much further in this book. For some reflections, see the discussion of Rousseau in chapter 7.

CHAPTER 1

1   For the latter, see the description of Odysseus after Athena bestows charis on him.

2   There were other words for gifts—*doron*, for instance. But charis was the one most intimately linked with thanksgiving.

3   Sophocles, *Ajax*, 522.

4   Bonnie MacLachlan, *The Age of Grace: Charis in Early Greek Poetry* (Princeton: Princeton University Press, 1993), 4–11; J. W. Hewitt, "The Terminology of 'Gratitude' in Greek," *Classical Philology* 22, no. 2 (1927): 142–61; James R. Harrison, *Paul's Language of Grace in Its Graeco-Roman Context* (Wissenschaftliche Untersuchungen zum Neuen Testament 2 Reihe, 172; Tübingen: Mohr Siebeck, 2003), 1–210. MacLachlan (5) speaks of a "single movement of grace and response." While it is true that archaic Greek literature rarely includes explicit expressions of thanks, Hewitt can argue that there is no real attention to gratitude until Seneca only because he has predefined gratitude as a sentiment or a matter of verbal etiquette (J. W. Hewitt, "Some Aspects of the Treatment of Ingratitude in Greek and English Literature," *Transactions and Proceedings of the American Philological Association* 49 [1917]: 37–48). We should rather recognize that gratitude took a particular form in the Greek world, the form of return gift and service rather than the polite expression of thanks.

5   Claude Moussy, *Gratia et sa famille* (Paris: Presses Universitaires de France, 1966), 38–39, 174.

6   Moussy, *Gratia*, 77.

7   Moussy, *Gratia*, 53, 71.

8   Cicero, *De inventione* 2.66, 161, quoted in Moussy, *Gratia*, 280.

9   Moussy, *Gratia*, 293.

10   The word *ingratus* was ancient, but Tertullian was the first to use ingratus as a strict substantive, indicating an ungrateful soul (Moussy, *Gratia*, 185–86, 352).

11   Thanks to John Barclay for sharing some of his forthcoming work on *Paul and the Gift* (Grand Rapids: Eerdmans, forthcoming), which proved to be enormously helpful for me throughout this chapter.

12   *Iliad*, 1.470–90. On the role of Thetis in the epic, see Laura M. Slatkin, *The Power of Thetis and Selected Essays* (Washington, D.C.: Center for Hellenic Studies, 2011), pt. 1.

13   Homer, *Iliad*, 1.625.

14   Lucian, *On Sacrifice*.

15   Robert Parker, "Pleasing Thighs: Reciprocity in Greek Religion," in Gill, Postlethwaite, and Seaford, *Reciprocity in Ancient Greece*, 108–9: "one gift or act endowed with *kharis*, power to please, will call forth another, which will in turn evoke yet another."

16   See Jorg Rupke, *Religion of the Romans*, trans. Richard Gordon (Cambridge: Polity, 2007), 149: In some ways, "a sacrifice resembles a contract, it acquires a judicial

component—my gift commits the god, morally at any rate, to giving me in return something I value. The commitment is mutual; of course I will give thanks to the deity who has given me something by sacrificing in my turn again. There is thus a ceaseless cycle of obligation and gratitude, which the usual concentration on individual exchanges expressed by the phrase *do ut des* tends to obscure. There is a chain of actions, a reciprocity of gifts." Parker emphasizes that in both human-human exchange and human-divine transactions, "an exchange of *kharites* is not an exchange of goods, the value of one strictly calculated in relation to the value of the other, the exchange taking place automatically once a particular asking price has been met; it is an exchange of favours, a voluntary, if socially prescribed, expression of a relationship of friendship" ("Pleasing Thighs," 118–19). See also the comments on this issue in Barclay, *Paul and the Gift*.

17 Diodorus, *Library of History*, 3.56.3–5.

18 Dio Chrysostom, *Oration*, 1.40–41. On God as Patron and Benefactor, see Jerome Neyrey, "God, Benefactor and Patron: The Major Cultural Model for Interpreting the Deity in Greco-Roman Antiquity," *Journal for the Study of the New Testament* 27, no. 4 (2005): 465–92.

19 Seneca, *De beneficiis*, 4.7.1.

20 *Iliad*, 2.

21 *Iliad*, 8.238–41. See the discussion in Sarah Hitch, *King of Sacrifice: Ritual and Royal Authority in the* Iliad (Cambridge, Mass.: Center for Hellenic Studies, 2009), 97–98.

22 *Iliad*, 1.35–42.

23 Xenophon, *Oeconomicus*, 11.8.

24 Quoted in Harrison, *Paul's Language of Grace*, 54.

25 Quoted in Harrison, *Paul's Language of Grace*, 55.

26 Harrison, *Paul's Language of Grace*, 190.

27 Ζευς μοι χαριν ενδικως εχει, lines 767–68. On this theme of divine gratitude, see J. W. Hewitt, "The Gratitude of the Gods," *Classical Weekly* 18, no. 19 (1925): 148–51. Hewitt concludes with a neat summary of the difference between Greek and Christian conceptions: Greek religion, "which discovered no impassible gulf between god and man, the relations of man to man and god to god were supposed to hold between man and god." This means that "as man's own moral nature develops and he comes to recognize the duty of gratitude, and as, parallel with this, his view of the gods and of his relation to them develops along the lines of anthropomorphism and anthropopathism, he tends to explain the duty of the gods to make return for worship as he would explain his own obligations to make return for gifts or favors accorded to him." Christianity cannot accept "the thought of any obligation of god to man for services received." He adds, "Do whatever you may in the way of service to God, you cannot earn his thanks, any more than the servant who serves his master at meat expects thanks therefor. With our best endeavors we are still unprofitable servants and we cannot earn *charis* from God, in the sense of gratitude or thanks. What we do receive from God is *charis* in quite another and quite opposite sense—grace, something unearned and unearnable."

28 Lucian, *On Sacrifice*, 3.

29 Plato, *Laws*, 11.931. A number of the quotations in the following paragraph are found in Harrison, *Paul's Language of Grace*, 188–99.

30 Plato, *Euthyphro*, 14B.

31 Hewitt claims that "Xenophon is perhaps the earliest Greek writer to lay marked stress upon the thank-offering" (J. W. Hewitt, "On the Development of the Thank-Offering among the Greeks," *Transactions and Proceedings of the American Philological Association* 43 [1912]: 102).

32 Xenophon, *Cyropaedeia*, 8.7.3.

234 — notes to pp. 24–26

33   Plutarch, *Moralia*, 479F.
34   Lucian, *My Native Land*, 5.
35   Plato, *Euthyphro*.
36   Quoted in Parker, "Pleasing Thighs," 121–22. Parker suggests that most Greek worshipers would have said the same, but observes that "a normal worshipper, one not confronted by Sokrates, would not find it necessary to pose the question whether the gifts he was bringing to the gods were of any actual use." They would assume that their actions affected the gods.
37   Theophrastus, Περι ευσεβειας, 24.1–5.
38   Arrian, *Epict. Diss.* 2.17.24.
39   Musonius Rufus, Περι σκεπης, quoted in Harrison, *Paul's Language of Grace*, 193.
40   Plutarch, *Moralia*, 1102A.
41   MacLachlan, *Age of Grace*, 4–5 and passim.
42   Aristotle, *Nicomachean Ethics*, 5.1133a.
43   Seneca, *De beneficiis*, 1.3.2–1.3.10. I am using the translation of Miriam Griffin and Brad Inwood, *On Benefits* (Chicago: University of Chicago Press, 2011).
44   See Peter Brown, *Through the Eye of a Needle: Wealth, the Fall of Rome, and the Making of Christianity in the West, 35–550 AD* (Princeton: Princeton University Press, 2012); chap. 2.
45   In his book *The World of Odysseus*, Moses Finley notes that Greeks could acquire metal goods through force, but when force was not possible "an exchange mechanism was then the only alternative, and the basic one was gift-exchange. This was no Greek invention. On the contrary, it is the basic organizing mechanism among many primitive peoples, as in the Trobriand Islands, where 'most if not all economic acts are found to belong to some chain of reciprocal gifts and counter-gifts.'" Gifts are not disinterested in the ancient world: "[N]o one ever gave anything, whether goods or services or honours, without proper recompense, real or wishful, immediate or years away, to himself or to his kin. The act of giving was, therefore, in an essential sense always the first half of a reciprocal action, the other half of which was a counter-gift" (*The World of Odysseus* [New York: Penguin, 1979], 64; cf. 95–99). See also Finley, *Economy and Society in Ancient Greece* (New York: Penguin, 1983), 213–45; Oswyn Murray, *Early Greece*, 2nd ed. (Cambridge, Mass.: Harvard University Press, 1993), 48–49.
46   Hesiod, *Works and Days*, 185–89.
47   Hesiod, *Works and Days*, 349–50.
48   Pindar, *Isthmian Ode*, 7, 16–17. See Visser, *Gift of Thanks*, chap. 18.
49   The question of the historical value of the Homeric poems has been treated by many authors, often with a focus on the role of giving, receiving, and reciprocity. See Ian Morris, "The Use and Abuse of Homer," *Classical Antiquity* 5, no. 1 (1986): 81–138; Morris, "Gift and Commodity in Archaic Greece," *Man* n.s. 21, no. 1 (1986): 1–17; Walter Donlan, "Reciprocities in Homer," *The Classical World* 75, no. 3 (1982): 137–75. In addition to these, my interpretation of the poem is indebted to MacLachlan, *Age of Grace*, chap. 2; William Allan, "Divine Justice and Cosmic Order in Early Greek Epic," *Journal of Hellenic Studies* 126 (2006): 1–35; T. O. Biedelman, "Agonistic Exchange: Homeric Reciprocity and the Heritage of Simmel and Mauss," *Cultural Anthropology* 4, no. 3 (1989): 227–59; Walter Donlan, "Duelling with Gifts in the *Iliad*: As the Audience Saw It," *Colby Quarterly* 29, no. 3 (1993): 155–72; James Hooker, "Homeric φιλος," *Glotta* 65, nos. 1–2 (1987): 44–65; Norman Postlethwaite, "Akhilleus and Agamemnon: Generalized Reciprocity," in Gill, Postlethwaite, and Seaford, *Reciprocity in Ancient Greece*, 93–104. On the link between χαρις and glory (κυδος), see MacLachlan, *Age of Grace*, 15 n. 5. See also I. M. Hohendahl-Zoetelief, *Manners in the Homeric Epic*

(Leiden: Brill, 1980), chap. 4. For the sake of space, I confine my discussion to the "first" of the Homeric epics, but reciprocity and gifts play as crucial a role in the *Odyssey* as in the *Iliad*, though the focus is different. In the second epic, the plot turns not only on gifts badly exchanged among warriors but also on the uses and abuses of hospitality. Already in the proem, we are warned that there will be a violation of the rules of hospitality. Odysseus strives to bring his men back safely from the Trojan War, but their own recklessness destroyed them: because "they devoured the cattle of the Sun," the "Sungod blotted out the day of their return" (*Odyssey*, 1.9–10; Fagles translation). When the story begins, we are in Ithaca with Telemachus, where suitors besiege Odysseus' house to "bleed him white" and "eat him out of house and home." They have long overstayed their welcome, and only by the cunning of weaving and unraveling her father-in-law's funeral shroud has Penelope been able to keep them at a distance. This violation of hospitality is not merely a violation of the rules of etiquette. It is an attack on Odysseus' house and severely limits Telemachus' power to act. A chief's power comes from his wealth and his ability to distribute it to display the glory of his generosity and to win the grateful loyalty of the recipients of his largesse (cf. Donlan, "Reciprocities," 154, where he quotes Marshall Sahlins: "Redistribution is chieftainship said in economics"). By devouring the substance of Odysseus' house, the suitors are laying claim to chieftainship. The suitors' abuse of hospitality in the episode of the Cyclops, the one-eyed greedy monster, plays on the theme of hospitality over and over: the Cyclops shows no hospitality; he promises the guest gift to Nobody that he will eat Nobody last; he feeds on guests rather than feeding them; and Odysseus overcomes him with an excess of hospitality. For further discussion of the latter episode, see A. J. Podlecki, "Guest-Gifts and Nobodies in 'Odyssey 9,'" *Phoenix* 15, no. 3 (1961): 125–33.

50 See Jerome Neyrey, *Shame and Honor in Matthew* (Louisville: Westminster John Knox, 1998), 14–34, for an excellent summary of the ancient honor code. Also Gregory Nagy, *The Best of the Achaeans: Concepts of the Hero in Archaic Greece* (Baltimore, Md.: Johns Hopkins University Press, 1998).

51 *Iliad*, 12.374–81. I am using the translation of Robert Fagles.

52 *Iliad*, 11.935.

53 Hook and Reno point out that in some places κλεος is virtually synonymous with epic poetry itself (*Heroism and the Christian Life: Reclaiming Excellence* [Louisville: Westminster John Knox, 2000], 18).

54 For discussion of the commercial connotations of τιμη, see MacLachlan, *Age of Grace*, 16–17; Donlan, "Duelling with Gifts," 160: "Since the act of 'honoring' is always accompanied by a validating ceremony or gift, the idea of *time* is indistinguishable from its signs. Thus the abstract noun time is also used concretely to mean rank, for example, the office of *basileus*. So, too, *geras*, the 'prize of honor,' awarded to the leader as leader, is frequently a metaphor for his social position."

55 On this episode, see Walter Donlan, "The Unequal Exchange between Glaucus and Diomedes in Light of the Homeric Gift-Economy," *Phoenix* 43, no. 1 (1989): 1–15.

56 Biedelman, "Agonistic Exchange," 251–52 n. 6: "The Homeric epics spin out from an initially complex situation of debts. A marriage (between divine Thetis and mortal Peleus) demeans a goddess who is compensated by making her mortal son, Achilleus, destined for imperishable fame. This unequal wedding is attended by an uninvited guest, Eris or Discord, who brings a false gift (a golden apple). Paris awards this to Aphrodite who repays him by bestowing Helen, the wife of Menelaos. Her gift is accomplished by theft and deception while Paris is a guest but false friend to his host Menelaos. This is avenged by Menelaos, his elder brother Agamemnon, and others including Achilleus and Odysseus, who storm Troy. As

everyone knows, Troy is eventually taken and Helen recovered through another false gift of cunning, the great, hollow wooden horse. Hera and Athena give aid to the siege since they are offended that Paris gave the apple to Aphrodite and not to them."

57   *Iliad*, 1.138–40.

58   Donlan, "Reciprocities," 162.

59   Donlan, Reciprocities," 163. As Donlan puts it, "The *Iliad* begins with two gross violations of normal and expected reciprocity on the part of Agamemnon, paramount chief of the combined Greek army at Troy. First, he refuses to accept the generous gifts offered by Chryses, a priest of Apollos, as ransom for his daughter, who had been captured in a raid and awarded as a prize to the chief. Even though the Achaeans shout for him to respect the holy many and give back the woman, he sends Chryses away with harsh threats," which provokes Apollo to begin an attack on the Achaeans. His response to this is the second great violation of the wisdom, if not the rules of reciprocity: "[T]o compensate himself for the loss of Chryses' daughter, whom he now must give back, he threatens to take Achilles' spear-prize, Briseis, as compensation. . . . To seize a prize of honor, a *geras*, is an almost unthinkable insult, an act of 'negative reciprocity'" (Donlan, "Duelling with Gifts," 160–61).

60   *Iliad*, 1.142–48.

61   *Iliad*, 1.285–87. The Greek of the final clause is οτι αριστον Αχαιων ουδεν ετιας. MacLachlan translates "to the best of the Achaeans you gave no *time*," and comments, "Achilles was angered because Agamemnon had not awarded him his due share of time and indeed had gone further in stripping him of time. Leaning on the scepter in front of the assembly, Achilles turns to Agamemnon and takes a solemn vow. He will pull out of the righting, leaving the sons of the Achaeans to die at the hands of man-slaughtering Hector" (*Age of Grace*, 18). Marcel Widzisz points out that Agamemnon's failure is not simply in taking back a gift given, but also in the failure of timing, his demand to receive compensation for his lost war bride immediately ("Timing Reciprocity in the *Iliad*," *Arethusa* 45 [2012]: 153–75). Agamemnon's failure is not simply that he has become an Indian giver. The issue is also one of timing. When he has to give Chryseis back to her father, he compounds his error: "[N]ot only does he openly violate the norms of exchange (in that something that has already been given is asked to be returned), but he also runs roughshod over the possible *temporal* considerations of reciprocity." Achilles tells Agamemnon that he could actually come away with even more if he would simply wait until the fall of Troy. This is the strategy that Achilles uses. He briefly considers physical combat, but then restrains himself. He will wait and will reap more gifts.

62   *Iliad*, 9.146–49.

63   *Iliad*, 9.316–17. As Biedelman ("Agonistic Exchange," 236) points out, the word χαρις means "gratitude," and includes both verbal gratitude and material reward.

64   See Donlan, "Duelling with Gifts," 164–65, 168. See also Biedelman, "Agonistic Exchange," 237.

65   *Iliad*, 19.166–74.

66   *Iliad*, 19.177–78.

67   *Iliad*, 19.253–55.

68   John Gould, *Myth, Ritual, Memory, and Exchange: Essays in Greek Literature and Culture* (Oxford: Oxford University Press, 2003), 335–58, esp. 345–46.

69   Donlan, "Duelling with Gifts," 170, describes his giving as "reckless."

70   *Iliad*, 23.879–922.

71   Donlan, "Duelling with Gifts," 160, argues that Achilles is the superior Achaean all along, since he bests Agamemnon in giving.

72   John Gould, "HIKETEIA," *Journal of Hellenic Studies* 93 (1973): 74.
73   *Iliad*, 24.274–78.
74   For a moving novelistic treatment of this episode, see David Malouf, *The Ransom* (New York: Vintage, 2011).
75   *Iliad*, 24.592–99. Zanker, "Beyond Reciprocity: The Akhilleus-Priam Scene in *Iliad* 24," in Gill, Postlethwaite, and Seaford, *Reciprocity in Ancient Greece*, argues that the ending of the *Iliad* provides evidence that Greek gifts were not always self-interested but sometimes altruistic. Priam's gifts are an example of altruism to an enemy.
76   Herodotus, *History*, 5.90, 5.91.2, quoted by Anna Missiou, "Reciprocal Generosity in the Foreign Affairs of Fifth-Century Athens and Sparta," in Gill, Postlethwaite, and Seaford, *Reciprocity in Ancient Greece*, 187. For more on Herodotus, see David Braund, "Herodotos on the Problematics of Reciprocity," in Gill, Postlethwaite, and Seaford, *Reciprocity in Ancient Greece*, 159–80; John Gould, "Give and Take in Herodotus," in Gould, *Myth, Ritual, Memory, and Exchange*, 283–303. Gould argues that Herodotus makes reciprocity a principle of historical explanation: events happen because something or other was owed.
77   Xenophon, *Memorabilia*, 2.6.345.
78   Lynette Mitchell emphasizes the continuing impact of reciprocity on classical Athenian politics in *Greeks Bearing Gifts: The Public Use of Private Relationships in the Greek World, 435–323 BC* (Cambridge: Cambridge University Press, 1997).
79   Thucydides, *Histories*, 2.40.5, quoted in Missiou, "Reciprocal Generosity," 190–91.
80   Mitchell, *Greeks Bearing Gifts*, 142–47.
81   See the brilliant summary of Athenian "patronage-avoidance" by Paul Millett, "Patronage and Its Avoidance in Classical Athens," in Wallace-Hadrill, *Patronage in Ancient Society* (London: Routledge, 1989), 15–47, on which I have depended heavily in the following paragraphs.
82   Millett, "Patronage and Its Avoidance," 23–25. The democratic revolution was a revolt not only against gift debts but also against debt as such. It was a revolt against the oligarch of wealthy interests. Exactly how the system was altered is a matter of some debate. Richard Seaford characterizes the change as a shift from personalized reciprocity, the reciprocity of exchanges between kings and "vassals," to a situation where there was an impersonal, collective cult. The temple is the symbol of the move from personal to impersonal gifts, from reciprocity to solidarity. See Richard Seaford, *Reciprocity and Ritual: Homer and Tragedy in the Developing City-State* (Oxford: Clarendon, 1994). Christopher Gill challenges Seaford's account with the claim that reciprocity and solidarity are both found in both Homeric and classical Greece ("Altruism or Reciprocity in Greek Ethical Philosophy?" in Gill, Postlethwaite, and Seaford, *Reciprocity in Ancient Greece*, 313–14). In what follows, I follow Gabriel Herman, *Ritualised Friendship and the Greek City* (Cambridge: Cambridge University Press, 1987), though I acknowledge that Herman's arguments need to be qualified and supplemented by the findings of Mitchell, *Greeks Bearing Gifts*.
83   David A. deSilva, *Honor, Patronage, Kinship & Purity: Unlocking New Testament Culture* (Downers Grove, Ill.: InterVarsity, 2000), 102: "Only during the time of the Athenian democracy is there an attempt to move away from patronage as the basic model for structuring society."
84   Millett, "Patronage and Its Avoidance," 26.
85   Quoted in Herman, *Ritualised Friendship*, 76.
86   Herman, *Ritualised Friendship*, 78.
87   Thucydides, *Histories*, 2.13.1, quoted in Missiou, "Reciprocal Generosity," 186.
88   Quoted in Missiou, "Reciprocal Generosity," 194. Of Aristeides, Plutarch writes

238 — notes to pp. 33–35

similarly, "He walked the way of statesmanship by himself, on a private path of his own, as it were, because, in the first place, he was unwilling to join with any comrades in wrongdoing, or to vex them by withholding favours; and, in the second place, he saw that power derived from friends incited many to do wrong, and so was on guard against it, deeming it right that the good citizen should base his confidence only on serviceable and just conduct."

89   Herman, *Ritualised Friendship*, 157.
90   Herman, *Ritualised Friendship*, 160–61. See also Missiou's similar conclusions: "Recognizing that the demand of reciprocation was not in the interest of the new constitution . . . the Athenians realized that they had to break away from the ethos of the gift and abandon arguments relevant to the past" (Missiou, "Reciprocal Generosity," 188).
91   Herman, *Ritualised Friendship*. Tragedians were sensitive to the shift. Over and over, the extant Greek tragedies dramatize conflicts between *philoi*, between friends, violations of various forms of relationship established by gifts. Elizabeth Belfiore ("Harming Friends: Problematic Reciprocity in Greek Tragedy," in Gill, Postlethwaite, and Seaford, *Reciprocity in Ancient Greece*, 139–58) finds that only six of the thirty-two extant tragedies lack "a plot centring on harm to blood kin, *xenos*, spouse, or suppliant" (153). Within the city, personal relations established by reciprocal giving were precarious. On the other side, Aeschylus mythologized the deliberate break from negative reciprocity—revenge. Clytemnestra's murder of her husband in *Agamemnon* is both the culmination of a cycle of violence and a fresh origin for another cycle of negative reciprocation. By avenging his father by killing his mother, Orestes himself becomes the object of vengeance, until he finds refuge in Athens, where Athena establishes a court that tames the Erinyes, the blood-hungry Furies, and makes them part of a rationalized political system. On Euripides in particular, see J. W. Hewitt, "Gratitude and Ingratitude in the Plays of Euripides," *American Journal of Philology* 43, no. 4 (1922): 331–43; Mark Padilla, "Gifts of Humiliation: Charis and Tragic Experience in Alcestis," *American Journal of Philology* 121, no. 2 (2000): 179–211; Melissa Mueller, "The Language of Reciprocity in Euripides' Medea," *American Journal of Philology* 122, no. 4 (2001): 471–504.
92   "Invention" is from Herman, *Ritualised Friendship*, 78.
93   Missiou, "Reciprocal Generosity," 187.
94   Harry Neumann, "The Philosophy of Individualism: An Interpretation of Thucydides," *Journal of the History of Philosophy* 7, no. 3 (1969): 237–46.
95   In drama, the "ungrateful populace" became a standard trope of tragedy, all the way to Shakespeare and beyond. See Missiou, "Reciprocal Generosity," 188.
96   Plato, *Crito*, 52A3.
97   Xenophon, *Memorabilia*, 2.2.13.
98   Quoted in Paul Millett, "The Rhetoric of Reciprocity in Classical Athens," in Gill, Postlethwaite, and Seaford, *Reciprocity in Ancient Greece*, 228.
99   Quoted in Millett, "Rhetoric of Reciprocity," 230.
100 See Voula Tsouna, *The Ethics of Philodemus* (Oxford: Oxford University Press, 2008), 230–31; Martha Nussbaum, *The Therapy of Desire: Theory and Practice in Hellenistic Ethics* (Princeton: Princeton University Press, 2009), 249–51.
101 Desmond McNeill argues that classical Athens was more of a "gift society" than is usually thought. He quotes Marx quoting the *Nicomachean Ethics*: "Neither would there have been association if there were not exchange, nor exchange if there were not equality, nor equality if there ere not commensurability" (McNeill, "Alternative Interpretations of Aristotle on Exchange and Reciprocity," *Public Affairs Quarterly* 4, no. 1 [1990]: 55–68).
102 On the continuities between Homeric and political *arête*, virtue, see Alasdair

MacIntyre, *After Virtue: A Study in Moral Theory* (London: Duckworth, 1997), chaps. 10–12.

103   Aristotle, *Rhetoric*, 1367a28.

104   Aristotle, *Politics*, 1337b19–21.

105   Egon Flaig suggests that Aristotle reacted against the "euergetic ideologies" introduced into Athenian discourse by Xenophon's *Cyropaedia*. According to Xenophon's account, "And they [the Persians] bring one another to trial also charged with an offense for which people hate one another most but go to law least, namely, that of ingratitude; and if they know that any one is able to return a favour and fails to do so, they punish him also severely. For they think that the ungrateful are likely to be most negligent of their duty towards the gods, their parents, their country, and their friends; for it seems that shamelessness goes hand in hand with ingratitude; and it is that, we know, which leads the way to every moral wrong" (Xenophon, *Cyropaedia*, 1.2.7). Aristotle instead argued for a form of giving compatible with democratic independence. Thus, for him, "it is no longer the binding quality of gifts which is decisive, but rather the demonstration of superiority through giving and the superior giver's strict preservation of his freedom from commitments. Here, Aristotle paid tribute to the old ideal of autarchic aristocracy within new social conditions: The weak should be grateful, whereas the strong should defend themselves from being drawn into gratitude. With this, Aristotle removed the power of gift exchange to bind both giver and receiver, conceiving of giving instead as an agonistic social act" (Flaig, "Is Loyalty a Favor? Or: Why Gifts Cannot Oblige an Emperor," in Algazi, Groebner, and Jussen, *Negotiating the Gift*, 53–54).

106   Visser, *Gift of Thanks*, 216.

107   Aristotle, *Nicomachean Ethics*, 1221b–1222a.

108   *Nicomachean Ethics*, 1122b: "The magnificent man is like an artist; for he can see what is fitting and spend large sums tastefully. For, as we said at the beginning, a state is determined by its activities and by its objects. Now the expenses of the magnificent man are large and fitting. Such, therefore, are also his results; for thus there will be a great expenditure and one that is fitting to its result. Therefore the result should be worthy of the expense, and the expense should be worthy of the result, or should even exceed it. And the magnificent man will spend such sums for the sake of the noble; for this is common to the excellences. And further he will do so gladly and lavishly; for nice calculation is a niggardly thing. And he will consider how the result can be made most beautiful and most becoming rather than for how much it can be produced and how it can be produced most cheaply."

109   *Nicomachean Ethics*, 1122b13–14.

110   *Nicomachean Ethics*, 1122b19–1123a.

111   *Nicomachean Ethics*, 1122b–1123a.

112   *Nicomachean Ethics*, 1124b11–12.

113   *Nicomachean Ethics*, 1124b. The translator H. Rackham points out that Aristotle misinterprets Homer, who claims that Thetis had often reminded Zeus of her service to him (*Iliad*, 1.393ff.; 1.503–4).

114   *Nicomachean Ethics*, 1124b.

115   *Nicomachean Ethics*, 1125a11–12.

116   *Nicomachean Ethics*, 1158b, 1161–62.

117   *Nicomachean Ethics*, 1156a10ff. The translation is from W. H. Adkins, "'Friendship' and 'Self-Sufficiency' in Homer and Aristotle," *Classical Quarterly* n.s. 13, no. 1 (1963): 42.

118   This paragraph is indebted to the account in Adkins, "'Friendship' and 'Self-Sufficiency,'" 41–45. See also David Konstan, "Reciprocity and Friendship," in Gill, Postlethwaite, and Seaford, *Reciprocity in Ancient Greece*, 279–301. Adkins

emphasizes the continuity between Homeric and Aristotelian friendship: "In essentials, the concept of φιλια remains as it was in Homer. Nor is this surprising, for in essentially the conditions of life have not changed. . . . [T]he individual paterfamilias of fourth-century Athens is still in much the same position, and has much the same values, as the head of the Homeric οικος. His aim, as Crito's advice to Socrates shows, is to help his φιλοι and to harm his enemies, in accordance with the law or in defiance of the law, as occasion demands. These are the requirements of αρετη as commonly recognized. . . . [J]ust as in Homeric society, actions and results are needed, not emotion or intentions" (41). Adkins exaggerates the social continuity. Democracy affects the place and political role of reciprocity-based friendship.

119   *Nicomachean Ethics*, 1177a27.

120   Adkins, " 'Friendship' and 'Self-Sufficiency,' " 44–45.

121   Manipulation of gratitude in support of tyranny is common in modern totalitarian regimes. See Jeffrey Brooks, *Thank You, Comrade Stalin! Soviet Public Culture from Revolution to Cold War* (Princeton: Princeton University Press, 2001).

CHAPTER 2

1   Much of the discussion that follows examines theories of gratitude against the background of the Roman "patronage" system, briefly described and defined ahead. There is significant debate concerning the origins, terms, and contours of this system. See Wallace-Hadrill, *Patronage in Ancient Society*; Richard P. Saller, *Personal Patronage under the Early Empire* (Cambridge: Cambridge University Press, 1982); Saller, "Status and Patronage," in *The Cambridge Ancient History, Volume XI: The High Empire, A.D. 70–192*, 2nd ed., ed. Alan K. Bowman, Peter Garnsey, and Dominic Rathbone (Cambridge: Cambridge University Press, 2008), 817–54; Brown, *Through the Eye of a Needle*, chap. 3. On the related Roman practice of "benefaction" and the civic honors accorded to benefactors, see especially the collection of texts and inscriptions in Frederick W. Danker, *Benefactor: Epigraphic Study of a Graeco-Roman and New Testament Semantic Field* (St. Louis: Clayton, 1982), esp. 436–86. Some of the best summaries of the topic are from New Testament scholars, including deSilva, *Honor, Patronage*, 95–119; Helen Rhee, *Loving the Poor, Saving the Rich: Wealth, Poverty, and Early Christian Formation* (Grand Rapids: Baker, 2012), 1–26; G. W. Peterman, *Paul's Gift from Philippi: Conventions of Gift Exchange and Christian Giving* (Society for New Testament Studies Monograph Series 92; Cambridge: Cambridge University Press, 1997), 51–89; Stephan Joubert, *Paul as Benefactor* (Wissenschaftliche Untersuchungen zum Neuen Testament 2, Reihe 124; Tübingen: Mohr Siebeck, 2000), 17–72; Holland Hendrix, "Benefactor/Patron Networks in the Urban Environment: Evidence from Thessalonica," *Semeia* 56 (1991): 39–58; Neyrey, "God, Benefactor and Patron," 467–68.

2   Seneca, *De beneficiis* 1.42.

3   Flaig, "Is Loyalty a Favor?" 47. See Jacques Michel, *Gratuite en droit Romain* (Brussels: University Libre de Bruxelles, 1962).

4   See Charles S. Rayment, "The Suit for Ingratitude," *Classical Journal* 43, no. 7 (1948): 429–31; Rayment, "Late Imperial Extensions of the Suit for Ingratitude," *Classical Journal* 47, no. 1 (1951): 113–14. In his life of Claudius, Suetonius mentions that the emperor confiscated freedman who pretended to be Roman knights, and adds "Ingratos et de quibus patroni quererentur revocavit in servitutem" (*The Twelve Caesars*, V.25.1). Tacitus (*Annals*, 13.26–27) records the same situation in the reign of Nero, using the phrase *male meritos* instead of Suetonius' *ingratos*. Though he despised the ungrateful, Seneca warned that ingratitude should not be punished legally.

5   Dionysius of Halicarnassus, *Roman Antiquities*, 2.9.1. This section of *Roman Antiquities* has been published as an appendix to Wallace-Hadrill, *Patronage in Ancient Society*, 243–45.

6   *Roman Antiquities*, 2.9.3.

7   *Roman Antiquities*, 2.10.1–2.

8   On Dionysius, see Joubert, *Paul as Benefactor*, 60–62. It is possible he intended to set out an ideal to which he hoped Rome would measure up.

9   Andrew Drummond, "Early Roman *Clientes*," in Wallace-Hadrill, *Patronage in Ancient Society*, esp. 108–10.

10   See Danker, *Benefactor*.

11   Joubert, *Paul as Benefactor*, 31.

12   See Paul Veyne, *Bread and Circuses*, trans. Oswyn Murray (London: Penguin, 1990). Joubert, *Paul as Benefactor*, 51–58, gives a good summary of the dynamics of euergetism.

13   Dio Chrysostom, *Discourses*, 66.1–2.

14   Plutarch, *Moralia*, 822B, quoted in Joubert, *Paul as Benefactor*, 56n126.

15   Cicero's treatise has a long and impressive afterlife. Ambrose's *De officiis* was modeled on Cicero's, and applied the principles of leadership to the church. Much to his chagrin, Jerome was an ardent Ciceronian, and Augustine was fired for a life of philosophy by reading Cicero. The eleventh-century writer Hildebert of Lavardin's *Moralis philosophia de honesto et utili* employed Cicero's categories of the honest and the useful, Peter Abelard uses the four-virtue scheme outlined by Cicero, and John and Salisbury's *Policratus* includes an exhortation to Ciceronian virtue. Thomas Aquinas makes frequent use of Cicero in his treatise on justice. Erasmus published a commentary on *De officiis*, and Hugo Grotius drew on the treatise for his *De iurebelli ac pacis*. Cicero remained popular in the Enlightenment. Montesquieu testified that "La trate Des Offices m'avait enchante, et je le prendais pour mon modele"; Frederick the Great had the treatise translated into German and wrote to Voltaire, who also admired Cicero, "C'est le meilleur ouvrage de morale qu'on ait ecrit et qu'on ecrira." It was not until the nineteenth century that Cicero fell out of favor. A fuller review of the influence of the treatise is found in the introduction to the translation by Patrick Walsh (Oxford: Oxford University Press, 2000), xxx–xlv. Throughout the following summary, I rely on Walsh's translation.

16   *De officiis*, 1.20. Cicero is a strong advocate of the rights of private property, but he also argues that not all goods are or should be private. What costs nothing should not be withheld from anyone. He cites well-known Roman maxims: "Do not prevent access to running water" and "let all who want it take fire from your fire."

17   *De officiis*, 1.42.

18   "Undoubtedly the greatest boon of wealth is to be able to show generosity without plundering one's inheritance" (*De officiis*, 2.64).

19   *De officiis*, 1.46.

20   *De officiis*, 2.53.

21   *De officiis*, 1.44.

22   *De officiis*, 1.50.

23   *De officiis*, 1.48.

24   *De officiis*, 1.49.

25   *De officiis*, 1.55.

26   *De officiis*, 1.22.

27   *De officiis*, 1.57.

28   *De officiis*, 2.70.

29   *De officiis*, 2.23.

30   *De officiis*, 2.

31   *De officiis*, 2.63: "A gift bestowed on a man who is good and grateful gains its

reward both from the recipient and from everyone else; for so long as we forgo rash giving, generosity is highly popular, and most people praise it, because the kindness of eminent men is the common refuge of all. We must therefore ensure that we benefit as many people as possible with these kindly gestures, so that the recollection of them passes down to their children and to later generations, so that they cannot show lack of gratitude; for the whole world detests one who forgets a kindness, and counts such conduct as injustice inflicted on themselves, because it discourages generous giving; and they regard the perpetrator as an enemy to all the needier members of society."

32   In addition, Seneca had behind him a significant tradition of philosophical reflection on gifts. Brad Inwood writes, "Seneca had the advantage of a long tradition of philosophical discussion of social relations which frequently included serious discussions of such good deeds, their social function, and the norms which should govern them. Plato's works contain scattered remarks on the topic; Xenophon's Socratic and other works often reflect an enlightened layman's view; the Aristotelian corpus contains extensive discussion of good deeds in a number of contexts, most notably in connection with friendship; the topic features in the Academic and Peripatetic 'divisions' and in the Platonic 'definitions.' Books on good deeds or the related topic of gratitude are reported for Theophrastus, Demetrius of Phaleron, Stilpo, Dionysius, and Epicurus, among others; even the followers of Hegesias and the Annicereioi had views on the topic. . . . Cleanthes wrote a book on gratitude (*peri charitos*) and Chrysippus also wrote copiously on the topic." Inwood says that Zeno likely wrote on it, and adds that "Hecaton and his teacher Panaetius were much engaged with this sort of question" (*Reading Seneca: Stoic Philosophy at Rome* [Oxford: Oxford University Press, 2005], 66–68). See also the introduction to Seneca's treatise in Inwood and Miriam Griffin, trans., *On Benefits*, 1–14. In addition to Inwood, see Stephan Joubert, "Coming to Terms with a Neglected Aspect of Ancient Mediterranean Reciprocity: Seneca's Views on Benefit-Exchange in *De Beneficiis* as the Framework for a Model of Social Exchange," in John J. Filch, ed., *Social Scientific Models for Interpreting the Bible: Essays by the Context Group in Honor of Bruce J. Malina* (Leiden: Brill, 2001), 47–63; Miriam Griffin, "*De Beneficiis* and Roman Society," *Journal of Roman Studies* 93 (2003): 92–113; W. S. Watt, "Notes on Seneca, *De Beneficiis, De Clementia,* and *Dialogi*," *Harvard Studies in Classical Philology* 96 (1994): 225–39; Gerard B. Lavery, "The Adversarius in Seneca's De Beneficiis," *Mnemosyne,* 4th ser., 40, nos. 1/2 (1987): 96–107; Harold N. Fowler, "The Sources of Seneca *de Beneficiis*," *Transactions of the American Philological Association* 17 (1886): 24–33; Barclay, *Paul and the Gift.*

33   David Konstan recognizes a shift in the discourse of friendship beginning in the Hellenistic period: "While some of Isokrates' homiletics on the subject of friendship are reminiscent of the sayings ascribed to Menander . . . the advice to Demonikos envisages a quite different kind of addressee. Demonikos is in need of caution because unprincipled or duplicitous individuals may be disposed to insinuate themselves into the graces of a wealth and distinguished young man. The danger, then, is from those seeking to gain an advantage from an association with a powerful figure. The orator is worried not so much that unreliable friends may desert Demonikos in time of need, which is the emphasis in the Menandrean aphorisms, as that they may lead the youth astray and induce him both to squander his patrimony and abuse his authority. Isokrates' counsel presupposes that economic or social inferiors may pretend to friendship, and exert an unhealthy influence on the young man through flatter and deceit" (Konstan, "Reciprocity and Friendship," 295). In place of Aristotle's friendship between equals, we have asymmetrical friendship.

34   The phrase is Flaig's, "Is Loyalty a Favor?" 53.

35   *Epistle,* 73.9.

36   *De beneficiis*, 1.4.2. I am using the translation of Griffin and Inwood (Chicago: University of Chicago, 2011).
37   *De beneficiis*, 1.3.4.
38   *De beneficiis*, 2.17.3. For Seneca, the image is too "poetic" to be of much philosophical use, as are the allegories of the *Gratiae*.
39   *De beneficiis*, 1.1. The structural point is from Joubert, *Paul as Benefactor*, 41–42.
40   *De beneficiis*, 1.10.
41   *De beneficiis*, 1.4.3.
42   *De beneficiis*, 1.10.5, 7.31–32.
43   *De beneficiis*, 1.6.1.
44   *De beneficiis*, 1.5.2.
45   *De beneficiis*, 1.5.4.
46   *De beneficiis*, 1.5.6.
47   *De beneficiis*, 1.5.3.
48   *De beneficiis*, 2.22.1.
49   *De beneficiis*, 2.23.1.
50   *De beneficiis*, 2.24.2–4.
51   *De beneficiis*, 2.23.3.
52   *De beneficiis*, 2.25.3.
53   *De beneficiis*, 2.26ff.
54   *De beneficiis*, 3.4.2.
55   *De beneficiis*, 3.1.4.
56   *De beneficiis*, 3.5.1.
57   *De beneficiis*, 2.33.3, 2.35.1, cf. 2.28.1.
58   Plutarch, *De communibus*, 21. This example is discussed in Inwood, *Reading Seneca*, 74–85.
59   *De beneficiis*, 5.13.1.
60   *De beneficiis*, 5.13.4.
61   *De beneficiis*, 4.18.1–4.
62   A form of what I have called "tragic metaphysics" is at work in the notion that the origin is always superior to the supplement. On this, see my *Deep Comedy: Trinity, Tragedy, and Hope in Western Literature* (Moscow, Idaho: Canon Press, 2006).
63   *De beneficiis*, 3.29.3.
64   *De beneficiis*, 3.31.5.
65   *De beneficiis*, 3.19.2–4.
66   *De beneficiis*, 3.18.2.
67   *De beneficiis*, 3.20.1–2.
68   *De beneficiis*, 3.23.1.
69   Seneca, *De clementia*, 1.13.5.
70   See Flaig, "Is Loyalty a Favor?" 57.
71   Flaig, "Is Loyalty a Favor?" 59–61.
72   Contemporary, and supposed correspondent: from the fourth century, fictitious correspondence between Seneca and the Apostle Paul circulated throughout Christendom.

CHAPTER 3

1   Quoted in Brown, *Through the Eye of a Needle*, 106.
2   See Edward Gibbon, *Decline and Fall of the Roman Empire* (New York: Modern Library, 1932), chap. 16; Joyce Salisbury, *Blood of the Martyrs: Unintended Consequences of Ancient Violence* (New York: Psychology Press, 2004), 16–17. For a thorough and balanced discussion, see Robert Louis Wilken, *The Christians as the Romans Saw Them* (New Haven, Conn.: Yale University Press, 2003).
3   Tacitus, *Annals*, 15.44.

4   Aristotle, *Nicomachean Ethics*, 1158b–1162a. As we have seen, Seneca compli-
     cated this question both by suggesting that benefits can run from child to parent
     (and slave to master) and by insisting that many achievements are the work of the
     individual.

5   Jacobus de Voragine, *The Golden Legend of Saint Sebastian*, trans. Granger
     Ryan and Helmut Ripperger (New York: Longmans, Green, 1941), http://
     www.mcah.columbia.edu/medmil/pages/non-mma-pages/text_links/gl
     _sebastian.html (accessed December 8, 2012).

6   Colossians 3:15.

7   1 Thessalonians 5:18.

8   Ephesians 5:4; 2 Timothy 3:5. I believe Paul wrote the "Pastoral Epistles," but
     even if he did not the views expressed there represent early Christian views of
     thanksgiving.

9   Romans 1:21. On Romans 1 as a description of Adam's sin, see Morna Hooker,
     "Adam in Romans 1," *New Testament Studies* 6, no. 4 (1960): 297–306.

10   See David W. Pao, *Thanksgiving: An Investigation of a Pauline Theme* (Downer's
     Grove, Ill.: InterVarsity, 2002), 29.

11   Romans 13:1-7.

12   See Bruce W. Winter, "The Public Honouring of Christian Benefactors, Romans
     13.3-4 and 1 Peter 2.14-15," *Journal for the Study of the New Testament* 34 (1988):
     87–103. Peter Brown, *Through the Eye of a Needle*, 62–63, makes the same point
     about the postapostolic church.

13   Salvian, *The Writings of Salvian, the Presbyter*, trans. Jeremiah F. O'Sullivan (Wash-
     ington, D.C.: Catholic University of America Press, 2008), 182.

14   Throughout this section, I have relied on the superb summary in Peterman, *Paul's
     Gift*, 22–50; see also Pao, *Thanksgiving*, 53–64, 145–53. Like Seth Schwartz,
     I think that the ancient Israelite conception of gift and gratitude was different
     from that of other Mediterranean societies, but Schwartz is mistaken in thinking
     that the Torah rejects "reciprocity" in favor of solidarity and the "pure unrecipro-
     cated gift." See Schwartz, *Were the Jews a Mediterranean Society? Reciprocity and
     Solidarity in Ancient Judaism* (Princeton: Princeton University Press, 2012). For a
     brief critique, see Barclay, *Paul and the Gift*.

15   Deuteronomy 15:8-11. I recognize that many scholars reject the Mosaic author-
     ship of Deuteronomy. I accept it, but as with the Pauline letters the question of
     authorship is not essential to my historical use of these texts. Regardless of whether
     they come from Moses, they express the ideal of generosity to which ancient Israel-
     ites were expected to conform. I also acknowledge that the texts of the Old Testa-
     ment might reflect a developing sensibility concerning gifts and gratitude over the
     centuries of ancient Israelite history. For my purposes, those developments can be
     put to the side; it is the Bible as a whole that influenced Western conceptions of gift
     and gratitude.

16   Deuteronomy 14:28-29.

17   Deuteronomy 15; Leviticus 25. There is no evidence that the Jubilee was ever prac-
     ticed, and the only hints the Old Testament gives concerning the Sabbath years is
     a negative one: Israel goes into exile for seventy years to make up for the Sabbath
     years that they had failed to observe (2 Chronicles 36:21).

18   Deuteronomy 24:19-22.

19   This is one of the main findings of David L. Baker's excellent *Tight Fists or Open
     Hands? Wealth and Poverty in Old Testament Law* (Grand Rapids: Baker, 2009).

20   Genesis 18.

21   Genesis 19.

22   Exodus 15:15; 24:18, 22.

23   Psalm 15:5.

24 Psalm 37:26.
25 Psalm 112:5.
26 Proverbs 11:24.
27 Proverbs 11:26.
28 Proverbs 28:27.
29 Proverbs 14:21.
30 See A. Murtonen, "The Use and Meanings of the Words Lᶜbarek and Bᶜrakaʰ in the Old Testament," *Vetus Testamentum* 9 (1959): 158–77. Cf. Exodus 39:43; Deuteronomy 24:13; Proverbs 11:26.
31 See J. W. Hewitt, "The Gratitude of the Gods," *Classical Weekly* 18, no. 19 (1925): 148–51, and the foregoing discussion, chap. 1.
32 Deuteronomy 14:29.
33 Proverbs 19:17.
34 Peterman, *Paul's Gift*, 89: "Divine reward does enter not into Greco-Roman social reciprocity."
35 I leave to the side questions about gift giving in relation to marriage, on which see T. M. Lemos, *Marriage Gifts and Social Change in Ancient Palestine, 1200 BCE to 200 CE* (Cambridge: Cambridge University Press, 2010), esp. chap. 1.
36 Genesis 14:21-22.
37 Genesis 14:18-20.
38 Genesis 32:13-21; 33:1.
39 Genesis 33:8.
40 Proverbs 21:14.
41 Genesis 33:9-11.
42 1 Samuel 25. See Peterman, *Paul's Gift*, 30–32. For broader discussion of the passage in its context, see Peter Leithart, *A Son to Me: An Exposition of 1 & 2 Samuel* (Moscow, Idaho: Canon Press, 2003).
43 1 Samuel 25:37.
44 2 Chronicles 20:10.
45 Deuteronomy 23:3-4.
46 2 Chronicles 20:11.
47 Despite some denials, it seems clear that the Greeks also offered sacrifices as expressions of gratitude for benefits from the gods.
48 See Pao, *Thanksgiving*, 53–64, 119–44.
49 Pao, *Thanksgiving*, 91–98, 145–53. Pao points to Numbers 14 and Psalm 78 as texts that describe the ingratitude of the Israelites during their wilderness wanderings. Despite the miraculous provision of bread and water, they grumbled against the Lord. The Hebrew word for thanksgiving, *todah*, derives from the verb *yadah*, "praise," the root of the name Judah. Etymologically, the words for "praise" and "thanksgiving" are connected, and the verb form *yadah* is used regularly throughout the Hebrew Bible, translated as "thank," "praise," or "confess" depending on the context. The Psalms do not neatly divide into psalms of praise and psalms of thanksgiving, into psalms that celebrate Yahweh's character and attributes in themselves and psalms that celebrate Yahweh's acts on behalf of his people. Thanks and praise merge into one another in a theologically significant way, a sign that for Israel God's character is revealed in history and the world. Harvie Guthrie, *Theology as Thanksgiving: From the Psalms to the Church's Eucharist* (New York: Seabury, 1981). See also Jerome Neyrey, "Lost in Translation: Did It Matter if Christians 'Thanked' God or 'Gave God Glory'?" *Catholic Biblical Quarterly* 71 (2009): 1–23.
50 2 Chronicles 29:31; 33:16.
51 Nehemiah 12:27, 31, 38, 40.
52 Jonah 2:9.

246 — notes to pp. 64–65

53   Jeremiah 17:26; 30:19; 33:11; Amos 4:5.
54   Psalm 50:14, 23; 95:2; 100:3; 107:22; 116:17. Psalm 147:7 may also refer to a
      thank offering.
55   Psalm 56:12.
56   Psalm 69:30. This is probably also what is meant in Isaiah 51:3, which describes
      the restoration of Zion as the Edenification of a wilderness, where the joy, glad-
      ness, thanksgiving, and song again break out in the temple city. In a few passages,
      the word refers to verbal thanks. Joshua calls on Achan to "give thanksgiving" to
      Yahweh by revealing his sin (Josh 7:19). "Give thanks" is used in a more positive
      context in Ezra 10:11: Israel confesses God, speaks publicly of his works, and that
      is a form of thanks. That also seems to be the meaning of the word in Psalm 42:4,
      and Psalm 147:7 might also be referring to songs of thanksgiving rather than songs
      that accompany thanksgiving offerings.
57   See Pao, *Thanksgiving*, 98–103. The key text is Leviticus 7:11-15. Yahweh has
      given instructions for the rite for slaughter and burning of peace offerings in chap-
      ter 3. Chapter 7 returns to the different offerings, giving them in a different order,
      and expanding certain rules concerning each of the offerings. The law of the peace
      offering is the longest section, 7:11-34, and includes some rules about eating flesh
      and fat. Within this section, Yahweh distinguishes three types of peace offerings.
      One is the הדות, the second is the "votive" offering (נדר), and the third is the "free
      will" offering (הנדבה).
58   The requirement of bread and cakes and the fact that leavened bread is offered link
      the sacrifice of thanksgiving with several other rites in the law. When Aaron and his
      sons are ordained, the ram of filling is a kind of peace offering. When the ram of
      filling is sacrificed, the pieces are placed in Aaron's hands along with a cake of bread
      mixed with oil and a wafer from the basket of unleavened bread (Exodus 29:22-
      25). There is no "anointed" bread yet, because Aaron himself is not anointed. The
      cakes anointed with oil link with the priests. And at least we can say that offering
      a thanksgiving offering is analogous somehow to the ordination rite for priests. To
      give thanks is to be "ordained." Bread is also required when a Nazirite ends his vow
      (Numbers 6). The Nazirite brings unleavened bread, cakes of semolina mixed with
      oil, and wafers of unleavened bread anointed with oil. Leavened bread is usually
      prohibited. No leaven is allowed on the altar; during the feast of unleavened bread,
      no leaven is to be found in the homes of Israelites. The only place where leaven
      appears is at the feast of Pentecost, Weeks, a firstfruits festival that also celebrates
      the giving of the law. By including leavened bread in the thanksgiving offering, the
      worshiper is pointing to Pentecost; or, Pentecost is a feast of thanksgiving.
59   Edward C. Vacek helpfully emphasizes that gratitude cannot be simply dissemina-
      tion, since unless a gift is received no gift has actually been given ("Gifts, God,
      Generosity, Gratitude," in Keating, *Spiritual and Moral Theology* [Mahwah, N.J.:
      Paulist Press, 2000], 103–18). Though not making a specifically theological point,
      Lewis Hyde captures an important dimension of the biblical portrait of gratitude
      in speaking of the "labor" of gratitude: with "transformative gifts," the recipient
      of the gift "feels gratitude. I would like to speak of gratitude as a labor undertaken
      by the soul to effect the transformation after a gift has been received. Between the
      time a gift comes to us and the time we pass it along, we suffer gratitude. More-
      over, with gifts that are agents of change, it is only when the gift has worked in us,
      only when we have come up to its level, as it were, that we can give it away again.
      Passing the gift along is the act of gratitude that finishes the labor. The transfor-
      mation is not accomplished until we have the power to give the gift on our own
      terms. Therefore, the end of the labor of gratitude is similarity with the gift or
      with its donor. Once this similarity has been achieved we may feel a lingering and
      generalized gratitude, but we won't feel it with the urgency of true indebtedness."

Again, "The labor or gratitude is the middle term in the passage of a gift. It is wholly different from the 'obligation' we feel when we accept something we don't really want. (An obligation may be discharged by an act of will.) A gift that has the power to change us awakens a part of the soul. But we cannot receive the gift until we can meet it as an equal. We therefore submit to the labor of becoming like the gift. Giving a return gift is the final act in the labor or gratitude, and it is also, therefore, the true acceptance of the original gift" (*The Gift: Imagination and the Erotic Life of Property* [New York: Vintage, 1979], 47–51).

60   Contemporary scholars agree that "Hellenistic" Judaism is something of a misnomer, as is the polarization between "diaspora" and "Palestinian" Judaism. On the one hand, it was not only the Jews outside Palestine who were influenced by Greek language, culture, and customs. Palestinian Jews spoke Greek, reclined at the table like Greeks, employed Greek ideas. On the other hand, the influence was not in only one direction. As much as Jews were affected by their exposure to Greek civilization, Greek civilization felt the impact of the Jews. See Martin Hengel, *Judaism and Hellenism: Studies in their Encounter in Palestine during the Early Hellenistic Period* (Eugene, Ore.: Wipf & Stock, 2003).

61   The term comes from Brown, *Through the Eye of a Needle.*

62   *Wisdom of Ben Sirach*, 12:1–3. Elsewhere, Sirach rings changes on Greco-Roman themes: "Give to the good man and withhold from the wicked. Honor the pauper; give not to the scoundrel" (12:4–5); "When conferring benefits do not give reproach and in every gift pain of words" (18:15); "The wise man makes himself beloved with little but the favors of fools will be poured out" (20:13); "A gift of the foolish man will not profit you for his eyes are many in return for one" (20:14). Peterman, *Paul's Gift*, 41; Schwartz, *Were the Jews a Mediterranean Society?* chap. 3. Schwartz sees in the juxtaposition of Ben Sirach's Torah-based exhortations to piety and his advice on social relations a synthesis of "two competing value systems, the one based on the valorization of reciprocal exchange and the other on that of solidarity." He is similar to Stoics, but unlike the Stoics is never free from the anxiety about the dangers of reciprocal exchange, and he also reminds his readers "of the transcendental value of covenantal piety" as revealed in Torah (78).

63   "God is a God of reciprocity," Sirach says (32:12–13), alluding to Deuteronomy 16:16.

64   Schwartz, *Were the Jews a Mediterranean Society?* 80. Chapter 4 of Schwartz' book is devoted to Josephus, whom he describes as "the most important early translator of traditional Israelite or Jewish anxieties about reciprocity and related practices into a Roman world where such practices were beginning to assume a fundamental political importance" (81).

65   Josephus, *Antiquities*, 4.8.13. I am indebted throughout to Paul Spilsbury, "God and Israel in Josephus: A Patron-Client Relationship," in Mason, ed., *Understanding Josephus* (Sheffield: Sheffield Academic, 1998), 172–91.

66   Josephus, *Antiquities*, 4.8.25.

67   Schwartz, *Were the Jews a Mediterranean Society?* 105.

68   Josephus, *Antiquities*, 4.8.47.

69   Josephus, *Antiquities*, 1.13.4. Spilsbury writes, "God does not mind continuing to be Abraham's helper since Abraham has shown himself suitably grateful for the bounties he has already received. . . . Piety is rewarded with divine favour which elicits a response of gratitude and further acts of piety, which in turn secure God's continuing services as supporter and ally" ("God and Israel in Josephus," 187).

70   Josephus, *Antiquities*, 8.4.3.

71   Following the summary of Spilsbury, "God and Israel in Josephus," 190–91.

72   Josephus, *Life*, 76.

73   Schwartz, *Were the Jews a Mediterranean Society?* 108.

74 Philo, *Decalogue*, 41. See other citations in Peterman, *Paul's Gift*, 49 n. 120. See also Jason Whitlark, "Enabling χαρις: Transformation of the Convention of Reciprocity by Philo and in Ephesians," *Perspectives in Religious Studies* 30 (2003): 325–57; Harrison, *Paul's Language of Grace*, 114–33.

75 Philo, *De plantatione Noe*, 130–31: "It is the most appropriate work of God to confer benefits, and of created beings to show gratitude, since they are unable to give any requital of those benefits beyond gratitude; for whatever he might be inclined to give as a requital for the other things which he has received, will be found to be the private property of him who is the Creator of all things, and not of the nature which offers it. Having learnt therefore that there is only one employment possible for us of all the things that seem to contribute to the honour of God, namely the display of gratitude, let us at all times and in all places study this, with our voice, and with useful writings, and let us never desist composing encomiastic orations and poems, in order that both the Creator and the world may be honoured by every description of utterance which can be exhibited in either speaking or singing; the one being, as some has said, the best of all causes, and the other the most perfect of all created things."

76 Philo, *De Abrahamo*, 273.

77 Philo, *De cherubim*, 122: "[I]f you consider the matter, you will find that all men, and especially those who have been alluded to as giving gratuitously, sell rather than give; and that they, who we fancy are receiving favours, are, in reality, purchasing the benefits which they derive; for they who give, hoping to receive a requital, such as praise or honour, and seeking for a return of the favour which they are conferring, under the specious name of a gift, are, in reality, making a bargain. Since it is usual, for those who sell, to receive a price in return for what they part with; but they who, receiving presents, feel anxiety to make a return for them, and make such a return in due season, they in reality perform the part of purchasers; for as they know how to receive, so also do they know how to requite."

78 Philo, *De cherubim*, 123.

79 Peterman, *Paul's Gift*, 46.

80 Philo, *Legatio ad Gaium*, 60.

81 Philo, *De specialibus legibus*, 2.78.

82 Soteriologically, the result of this shift is the semi-Pelagian system that E. P. Sanders has dubbed "covenant nomism." Despite their deep hostility to Rome and its values, later Jewish rabbis "to some extent internalized the value of honor" understood as "social clout of dominance." On the other hand, they remind their readers that an honor economy is far from ideal and insist that "honor inheres especially in piety and in possession of Torah" (Schwartz, *Were the Jews a Mediterranean Society?* 117). Schwartz mentions a "remarkable passage in rabbinic marriage legislation" that imagines a Jewish community "in (presumably unconsciously) Aristotelian terms, as bound together by the regular and reciprocal pulsation of services and benefits through a social network." Other rabbinic texts express skepticism about human patronage, pointing to God as the only reliable patron. Yet others tell stories of successful patronage (170).

83 Herod acted like any Roman provincial governor, building theaters, amphitheaters, establishing athletic competitions, drama, and horse races. Josephus, *Antiquities*, 15.267–79, attributes Herod's projects to *philotimia*; Schwartz, *Were the Jews a Mediterranean Society?* 99–103. Despite the claim that Jews held honor in contempt, Schwartz argues that "wealthy Jerusalemites' desire for memorialization" is evident in monuments and mausolea of various kinds (104). Benefaction was important for the Jews, Josephus admits, but it was "only fully acceptable if combined with mildness of character and especially with piety." Gladiatorial games were out, gifts of food and votive offerings to the temple were legitimate (106).

84 Matthew 6:2-4.
85 Matthew 6:3.
86 Luke 6:35.
87 Many of Jesus' ethical instructions strike at the root of the honor system. Instead of responding slap for slap, restoring honor with negative reciprocity, he tells his disciples suffer not only the shame of of being slapped but also the double dishonor of not responding and being slapped again (Matthew 5:38-39). Imitating and sharing Jesus' own shame, the disciples participate in the divine righteousness that triumphs over the rivalrous honor system that creates injustice and conflict.
88 Matthew 6:4.
89 Luke 6:35.
90 Jesus' few prayers of thanks are modeled on the Old Testament as well. See George M. Soares-Prabhu, "Speaking to 'Abba': Prayer as Petition and Thanksgiving in the Teaching of Jesus," in Duquoc and Florestan, *Asking and Thanking*, 31–43.
91 Matthew 6:20.
92 See the "sheep and goats" scene in Matthew 25.
93 John Milbank, *Being Reconciled: Ontology and Pardon* (London: Routledge, 2003), 160–61.
94 Luke 14.
95 Luke 6:30-35.
96 Matthew 23:9.
97 Luke 22:25.
98 1 Corinthians 14:16.
99 On the thank offering as the background of the Christian Eucharist, see Dennis R. Lindsay, "*Todah* and Eucharist: The Celebration of the Lord's Supper as a 'Thank Offering' in the Early Church," *Restoration Quarterly* 39 (1997): 83–100.
100 Leviticus 7:12-15 uses θυσια αινεσεως.
101 Jacob Milgrom points out that the rabbis taught that the peace offering of thanksgiving is never offered for sin, but for deliverances of various sorts. It's the perfect model for the sacrifice that persists after the final sacrifice has been offered (*Leviticus 1–16: A New Translation, Introduction and Commentary* [New York: Doubleday, 1991]).
102 Hebrews 13 speaks of a "continuous" sacrifice of praise, and we can push the theology of thanks a step further by looking at the way the Old Testament uses the concept of "continual" ritual action (דימת). There were certain things that were supposed to be "continuous" in the tabernacle system. The lamps of the lamp stand were to burn continuously (Exodus 27:20; Leviticus 24:3, 4, 8). The high priest wore his breastplate so that the names of Israel would be memorialized before Yahweh continuously (Exodus 27:20; 28:29). The flower on Aaron's head was to be continuously there, so that he would be accepted before the Lord continually (Exodus 28:38). Lambs were to be offered on the altar to make a continuous burnt offering, which in this context meant every morning and evening (Exodus 29:39, 42; Leviticus 6:13; Numbers 28:3, 6, 10, 15). Along with this, there was to be a perpetual tribute offering (Leviticus 6:20; Numbers 4:16). Incense was to burn continuously in the holy place (Exodus 30:8). Importantly for our purposes, the bread of the face was also to be on the table before Yahweh perpetually (Exodus 25:30; Numbers 4:7). In the LXX, the Hebrew term is translated as δια παντος in many of these passages, literally "through all things" (Exodus 25:40; 27:20; 28:30, 38; 30:8; 34:10). By the time of the New Testament, that phrase had turned into a single word, διαπαντος. The demoniac was night and day in the mountains, διαπαντος (Mark 5:5). After Jesus ascended, the disciples were continuously in the temple (Luke 24:53). Their worship was the continuous temple worship of praise and blessing God, the new דימת. Hebrews uses the word twice, first to describe

the continuous ministry of the priests in the tabernacle (Hebrews 9:6) and then to describe the continuous sacrifice of praise that we are to offer to God, the continuous thank offering (Hebrews 13:15).

103 Hebrews 13.

104 1 Timothy 4:4-5.

105 It has been said that Jewish prayers of thanks have the opposite effect of "de-sanctifying" a gift. Creation is inherently holy, too holy for man to receive "raw," and so the gift must be transferred to the profane realm by prayer before it is received.

106 The statistics are revealing. Other than the Last Supper, Jesus rarely offers prayers of thanks, or talks about gratitude. The verb ευχαριστεω, its noun and adjective, along with the word "grace," which sometimes means "thanks," (χαρις) occurs sixty-two times in the New Testament. Of these, three-quarters are found in Paul's writings (Pao, *Thanksgiving*, 15). As we have seen, the most common expression of thanks in ancient Greek is the phrase εχειν χαρις, which uses the same word translated as "grace." Thanks is a kind of return of grace, a return of gift. Paul uses this expression frequently, with and without the verb (Romans 6:17; 1 Corinthians 15:57; 2 Corinthians 2:14; 2 Timothy 1:3). Thanks is a response to grace. It is ευχαριστια, good-grace. This word is used fifteen times in the New Testament, the vast majority in Paul (1 Corinthians 14:16; 2 Corinthians 4:15; 9:11-12; Philippians 4:6; Colossians 2:7; 1 Thessalonians 3:9). In Ephesians 5:4, Paul contrasts thanksgiving with filthy jesting and obscenity, and also contrasted to idolatry. To turn from idols to God is to turn from obscenity to thanksgiving. Colossians 4:2 is an exhortation to continue in prayer—a term used for 'continuous' in prayer, charity, etc. in the book of Acts. Paul tells Timothy to give thanks for all men (1 Timothy 2:1), and tells him that thanks is a universal sanctifier (1 Timothy 4:4-5). Thanks has a "Trinitarian" structure: it is offered to the Father for Jesus (Colossians 3:13-14) and also through him (Ephesians 5:20; Colossians 3:17).

107 This question has well nigh been beaten silly. See, for instance, P. Schubert, *The Form and Function of the Pauline Thanksgiving* (Berlin: Alfred Topelmann, 1939); Robert Jewett, "The Epistolary Thanksgiving and the Integrity of Philippians," *Novum Testamentum* 12, no. 1 (1970): 40–53; Jeffrey T. Reed, "Are Paul's Thanksgivings 'Epistolary'?" *Journal for the Study of the New Testament* 18, no. 61 (1996): 87–99.

108 The literature on this is large and growing larger. See Harrison, *Paul's Language of Grace*; Peterman, *Paul's Gift*; Pao, *Thanksgiving*; Joubert, *Paul as Benefactor*; Joubert, "1 Corinthians 9:24-27: An Agonistic Competition?" *Neotestamentica* 35, no. 2 (2001): 57–68; Joubert, "Religious Reciprocity in 2 Corinthians 9:6-15: Generosity and Gratitude as Legitimate Responses to *Charis tou theou*," *Neotestamentica* 33, no. 1 (1999): 79–90; David Briones, "Mutual Brokers of Grace: A Study in 2 Corinthians 1:3-11," *New Testament Studies* 56, no. 4 (2010): 536–56; Gerald W. Peterman, "'Thankless Thanks': The Epistolary Social Convention in Philippians 4:10-20," *Tyndale Bulletin* 42, no. 2 (1991): 261–70; Barclay, *Paul and the Gift*. On Hebrews, see David A. deSilva, "Exchanging Favor for Wrath: Apostasy in Hebrews and Patron-Client Relationships," *Journal of Biblical Literature* 115, no. 1 (1996): 91–116; and deSilva, *Perseverance in Gratitude: A Socio-Rhetorical Commentary on the Epistle "to the Hebrews"* (Grand Rapids: Eerdmans, 2000).

109 Pao, *Thanksgiving*, 20–21.

110 Romans 1:8.

111 1 Corinthians 1:4-7a.

112 Romans 6:17.

113 Philippians 1:3. The translation of the phrase μου επι τη μνεια υμων could refer

either to Paul's memory of the Philippians or to the Philippians' memory of Paul. Peterman (*Paul's Gift*, 93–99) makes a compelling case for the latter, and for the claim that this refers specifically to a monetary gift to the apostles, which Paul mentions explicitly in 4:10-20.

114 Philippians 4:18.

115 Philippians 4:19.

116 Philippians 1:5. See Peterman, " 'Thankless Thanks,' " esp. 270.

117 Romans 13:8; *medeni meden opheilete.*

118 Peterman, *Paul's Gift*, 149. Paul practices what he preaches here, and not only with regard to the Philippians. He refuses the offered gifts of the Corinthians because he believes that receiving them would inhibit the advance of the gospel. This is the argument of Peter Marshall, *Enmity in Corinth: Social Conventions in Paul's Relations with the Corinthians* (Tübingen: Mohr, 1987).

119 2 Corinthians 8. Earlier, in chapter 4, Paul speaks of persecution in a way that manifests the dynamics of grace and return. He endures for Christ's sake and for the sake of the church. "Death works in us [apostles], but life in you" (v. 12). He suffers all this for the sake of the Corinthians. In fact, he says that everything is "for your sake," and the purpose is that the grace (χαρις) of God, which is already increasing and abounding (πλεοναζω), will abound even more, exceeding all limits (περισσευω). This multiplier effect comes through the thanksgiving of man (δια πλειονων την ευχαριστιαν). The end of this is that the glory of God is enhanced—God's reputation increases, more people give honor to God. No doubt Paul's thought is reinforced here by the linguistic link between grace and thanksgiving, between χαρις and ευχαριστια. (This is even clearer in one of the classical expressions of thanksgiving, χαρις εχειν.) Thanks contains grace but expands it, makes it bigger. The thanksgivings of the church become a machine to produce superabundant grace, and to enhance God's glory.

120 There is a similar pattern in 2 Corinthians 9. In 2 Corinthians 9, Paul is directly dealing with questions of charitable giving in the Corinthian church. There is an eye-for-an-eye system in giving: you get as generously as you give (v. 6). What matters is not only the amount given, but also the attitude of the heart, since God does not look for grudging gifts or gifts of necessity but for cheerfulness in giving (v. 7). That is the good work that God makes them sufficient to achieve. At this point, Paul connects wealth and thanksgiving. Enrichment in all things to achieve bounty (*ploutizomenoi eis pasan aploteta*) works thanksgiving (*eucharistia*) to God. The riches of God's blessings, whatever they may be, work thanksgiving. The thanksgiving is not only on the part of those who receive abundance from God but also on the part of those with whom they share. When the saints have gathered an offering for famine relief, when they have performed that diaconal liturgy (*e diakonia tes leitourgas tautes*), it not only meets the needs of the saints who are suffering famine but also is multiplied, becomes abundant, by the thanksgiving that it provokes from the recipients. The liturgy of sharing evokes Eucharist. Paul is aware that he is employing the language of the liturgy to describe famine relief. Poverty relief is no more than an extension of the eucharistic liturgy of the gathered church.

121 2 Corinthians 8:9.

122 2 Corinthians 8:13-14.

123 Miroslav Volf captures the Pauline emphasis precisely: "The Corinthians do the giving, but God gets the thanks! Does that make sense? Only if its true that when the Corinthians give, it's God who gives. . . . Most likely [Paul] doesn't thank [the Philippians] because he believes he hasn't received gifts *from* them but *through* them" (*Free of Charge: Giving and Forgiving in a Culture Stripped of Grace* [Grand Rapids: Zondervan, 2005], 112).

124 Ephesians 4.
125 See Romans 2.
126 Briones, "Mutual Brokers," reaches a similar conclusion from an examination of 2 Corinthians 1:3-11.
127 Here I draw on John Barclay, "Manna and the Circulation of Grace: A Study of 2 Corinthians 8:1-15," in Wagner, Rowe, and Grieb, *Word Leaps the Gap*, 423–25.
128 This is dramatically evident in the Pastoral Epistles. Beneath their surface "conservatism" is a radical assault on the assumptions of Greco-Roman society. Reggie Kidd argues that "one of the principal concerns of 1 Timothy is to help rich Christians understand their place in the household of God and to help the church, in turn, learn how to make room for such people." The role of the wealth, Kidd thinks, is to "devote themselves to *euergesia*." That seems to replicate Greco-Roman reciprocity relations, but Kidd adds that in the Pastorals "[t]he assumption that wealth is an index of moral worth is dismissed out of hand" and "the notion that a wealthy person's future can be secured through the shrewd cultivation of 'friends'—i.e., people obligated to return favors—is not even given a hearing." The wealthy as much as the poor are utterly dependent on the kindness of God, united with the poor in need. Kidd notes too that eschatology disrupts the pattern of social relations: "[T]he whole web of human reciprocity is dismantled if it indeed in the next age rather than in this one and from God himself rather than from earthly friends that the wealthy can expect a return on their beneficences" (*Wealth and Beneficence in the Pastoral Epistles: A "Bourgeois" Form of Early Christianity?* [SBL Dissertation Series 122; Atlanta: Scholars Press, 1990], 155–57).
129 It is, I think, the sine qua non of modern Western individualism, which is, however, a "secularization" of the Christian version. On this point as on others, gratitude is a stethoscope for diagnosing Western civilization's inner developments and deviations. See chapter 4.

CHAPTER 4

1 For a summary, see Rhee, *Loving the Poor*, 135–37.
2 Lactantius, *Divine Institutes*, 5.15.
3 *Divine Institutes*, 6.11–12.
4 *Divine Institutes*, 6.12.
5 *Divine Institutes*, 6.12.
6 Quoted in Daniel Caner, "Towards a Miraculous Economy: Christian Gifts and Material 'Blessings' in Late Antiquity," *Journal of Early Christian Studies* 14, no. 3 (2006): 329–77.
7 See Brown, *Through the Eye of a Needle*, xxv: During the fourth through the sixth centuries, "we are in a society where—for pagans, Jews, and Christians alike—religious giving was thought of as a religious transaction." On reciprocity in 1–2 Clement, the Didache, and Ignatius, see Frederick W. Danker, "Bridging St. Paul and the Apostolic Fathers: A Study in Reciprocity," *Currents in Theology and Mission* 15, no. 1 (1988): 90–94.
8 Brown, *Through the Eye of a Needle*, 85.
9 Generous benefactions to the poor were not merely theoretical. Prudentius depicted the frenzied charity of Saint Lawrence while the latter was a deacon at Rome: "He runs about the city gathering into one flock the companies of the infirm and all the beggars who cry out for alms. . . . There a man showing two eyeless sockets directs his straying, faltering footsteps with a stick; a cripple with a broken knee; a one-legged man. . . . Here is one whose limbs are covered with running sores. . . . Such people he seeks out through all the public squares, used as they were to being fed by Mother Church. . . . There stood the company of poor

men in their swarms, a ragged sight. They greet the Prefect with a roar for alms" (*Peristephanon*, 1.141–81, quoted in Brown, *Through the Eye of a Needle*, 77–78).

10 Brown, *Through the Eye of a Needle*, 80.

11 Early Christians also developed the Pauline emphasis on continuous thanks, along with the Philonian cosmology of gift and gratitude, reflected in writers like Justin Martyr. Like Philo, he insists that thanks is the proper form of response, the true form of sacrifice: "What man will not acknowledge that we are not atheists, but declare that He has no need of streams of blood and libations and incense; whom we praise to the utmost of our power by the exercise of prayer and thanksgiving for all things wherewith we are supplied, as we have been taught that the only honour that is worthy of Him is not to consume by fire what He has brought into being for our sustenance, but to use it for ourselves and those who need, and with gratitude to Him to offer thanks by invocations and hymns for our creation" (*First Apology*, 13). In the early fifth century, Augustine had concluded, based on biblical materials, that the pattern of gift exchange even defined the life of the Triune God. Scripture speaks of the Spirit as the "gift of God," and Augustine reasoned that this gift was not just a gift from God to men but a gift exchange in the inner dynamics of the Trinity. The Spirit was the Father's gift to the Son, and likewise the return gift of the Son to the Father. This is the first move in the development of Augustine's well-known triadic notion of Triune love. Gift giving requires a giver, a gift, and a recipient who is also a giver of returns; love is a form of gift that also requires three (like Seneca's three graces)—the Giver, the Gift, and the Giver again who keeps the circulation of the gift in motion. Love, he argued, "is *of* some one that loves, and *with* love something *is* loved." In love, therefore, we can see three things, "he that loves, and that which is loved, and love." Love itself must therefore be "a certain life which couples or seeks to couple together some two things, namely, him that loves, and that which is loved." All this applies to fleshly loves, but the structure of love becomes even clearer when we "tread down the flesh and ascend to the mind." In loving a friend, one loves the mind and there one sees more clearly that there are three things: "he that loves, and that which is loved, and love" (*De Trinitatis*, 8.10). Augustine does not speak of "gratitude" here, but the cycle of reciprocity would have been familiar to the Latins of his time. Such a Trinitarian theology of gift goes far beyond even the exalted ethics and metaphysics of gratitude found in Philo. For Philo, gratitude was the *creature's* response to the Creator's gift. Augustine implies that gratitude has been elevated into a divine responsiveness, God's return gift to God. One might extend this much further than Augustine, as recent theologians of gift have done. For them, the creature's response of thankfulness to the Creator is precisely the creature's inclusion in the thanks of the Son to the Father, which the Son offers through the Gift, the Spirit, which he has shared with his people. Given the historical focus of this study, we will, with reluctance, leave these ecstasies to the side.

12 For the sake of simplicity, I speak here only of the impact of Greco-Roman patronage on Christian conceptions. In moving beyond the boundaries of the empire to Christianize the barbarians, the church encountered another form of giving. Tacitus had already remarked on the gift practices of the barbarians: "It is a national custom for gifts of cattle or agricultural produce to be made to the chiefs, individual citizens making voluntary contributions for this purpose. . . . They take particular pleasure in gifts received from neighboring states." Hospitality is highly valued, with "no distinction . . . between acquaintance and stranger." Guests have a right to any parting gift. In general, though the Germans "take delight in presents," they do not practice Roman-style gift and gratitude: "they expect no repayment for giving them and feel no obligation in receiving them" (*Germania*, 15, 118).

13   Rayment, "Late Imperial Extensions," 113–14. The decree made its way into the *Institutes* of Justinian, which stated, "sciendum tame nest, quod, etsi plenissimae sint domationes, tamen si ingrate exsistant homines, in quos beneficium collatum est, donatoribus per nostrum constitutionem licentiam praestavimus certis ex causis eas revocare."

14   Brown, *Through the Eye of a Needle*, 529.

15   *Didascalia*, 9.

16   *Didascalia*, 9.

17   *Epistles*, 19.1. On Cyprian, see Rhee, *Loving the Poor*, 143–47; C. E. Straw, "Cyprian and Matthew 5:45: The Evolution of Christian Patronage," *Studia Patristica* 18, no. 3 (1989): 329–39; A. Stewart-Sykes, "Ordination Rites and Patronage Systems in Third-Century Africa," *Vigiliae Christianae* 56, no. 2 (2002): 115–30. Titular churches were named for nonclerical patrons; on such patronage in the church at Rome, see J. Hillner, "Clerics, Property and Patronage: The Case of the Roman Titular Churches," *Antiquite Tardive* 14 (2006): 59–68.

18   Rhee, *Loving the Poor*, 146–47, quotes C. A. Bobertz, "Cyprian of Carthage as Patron: A Social Historical Study of the Role of Bishop in the Ancient Christian Community of North Africa" (Ph.D. diss., Yale University, 1988): "Cyprian believed that in making the confessors clients, he would in turn have a prior claim on the spiritual resources they might control." Rhee writes (146), "In dispensing and controlling both spiritual and material *beneficia* as the imitator and administrator of God's benefaction, Cyprian consistently stressed the recipients' (clients') submission to the bishop (patron) as a quintessential condition and expectation in reciprocity" and "the episcopal distribution of clerical *beneficia* (e.g., gifts and payments) put them under the line of Cyprian's patronage, and their reciprocal loyalty was therefore expected in return even as they distributed material *beneficia* as (proxy) patrons to those in need under the direction of and on behalf of the bishop." We do not follow the story, but quasi-Roman models of patronage remained important to the church throughout the medieval period. Benefits from the Roman bishop to other churches and monasteries, for instance, were one of the main sources for papal power, according to R. W. Southern, *Western Society and the Church in the Middle Ages* (New York: Penguin, 1970), 113–15: "The popes, like other rulers, simply gave what they could to those who asked and could pay for what they asked, in return for loyalty and obedience" (114).

19   Niel Bronwen, "Models of Gift Giving in the Preaching of Leo the Great," *Journal of Early Christian Studies* 18, no. 2 (2010): 225–39. Bronwen argues, among other things, that early Christians made "discriminate giving" the norm.

20   Brown, *Through the Eye of a Needle*, 349.

21   Quoted in Brown, *Through the Eye of a Needle*, 352.

22   Quoted in Brown, *Through the Eye of a Needle*, 363.

23   Joel T. Rosenthal, *The Purchase of Paradise: The Social Function of Aristocratic Benevolence, 1308–1485* (London: Routledge & Kegan Paul, 1972), 10.

24   Brown, *Through the Eye of a Needle*, 517. On the rise of the monasteries and their services to medieval society, see Lester K. Little, "Monasticism and Western Society: From Marginality to the Establishment and Back," *Memoirs of the American Academy in Rome* 47 (2002): 83–94, esp. 89.

25   Stephen D. White, *Custom, Kinship, and Gifts to the Saints: The Laudatio Parentum in Western France, 1050–1150* (Chapel Hill: University of North Carolina Press, 1988).

26   Stephen White explains the logic: "Gifts to saints, who were God's friends and would intercede with him for the givers, were to be made through the mediation of monks, without whose intercession friendship with God or God's saints could not reliably be established. . . . [M]onastic benefactors were often represented as hoping

that if they granted a portion of their ephemeral earthly inheritance to one of God's close, sainted friends, the saint and his monastic dependents on earth would then recognize these lay people as friends or even as kin of a sort and intercede on their behalf with God. God would then forgive them their sins and ultimately give them an enduring inheritance in the kingdom of heaven" (*Custom, Kinship, and Gifts*, 29). Megan McLaughlin likewise notes that prayer was "associative" and was offered "to identify the dead as members of the Christian community, as friends of the clergy and as clients of the saints on earth and therefore in heaven." The aim in the high Middle Ages was "in creating and maintaining close bonds with potentially powerful intercessors" rather than in "specifying the kinds and quantities of prayers to be performed for them after death" (*Consorting with Saints: Prayer for the Dead in Early Medieval France* [Ithaca, N.Y.: Cornell University Press, 1994], 254–56). See also Penelope D. Johnson, *Prayer, Patronage, and Power: The Abbey of la Trinité, Vendôme, 1032–1187* (New York: NYU Press, 1981); Barbara H. Rosenwein, *To Be the Neighbor of Saint Peter: The Social Meaning of Cluny's Property, 909–1049* (Ithaca, N.Y.: Cornell University Press, 1989); Samuel K. Cohn Jr., *Death and Property in Siena, 1205–1800: Strategies for the Afterlife* (Baltimore, Md.: Johns Hopkins University Press, 1988); Constance Brittain Bouchard, *Holy Entrepreneurs: Cistercians, Knights, and Economic Exchange in Twelfth-Century Burgundy* (Ithaca, N.Y.: Cornell University Press, 1991); Wendy Davies, *Acts of Giving: Individual, Community, and Church in Tenth-Century Christian Spain* (Oxford: Oxford University Press, 2007).

27 Philippe Jobert, *La notion du donation. Convergences: 630–750* (Paris: Les Belles Lettres, 1977). See the summary of Jobert's work in Arnoud-Jan Bijsterveld, "The Medieval Gift," in Cohen and de Jong, *Medieval Transformations*, 128–29.

28 Bernhard Jussen, "Religious Discourses of the Gift in the Middle Ages: Semantic Evidences (Second to Twelfth Centuries)," in Algazi, Groebner, and Jussen, *Negotiating the Gift*, 173–92.

29 Rosenthal, *Purchase of Paradise*, chaps. 2–3.

30 Quoted in Bijsterveld, "Medieval Gift," 134. See Little, "Monasticism and Western Society," 89: "The monks said prayers not just for themselves but for all, and not just for the living but also for the dying and the dead. They had the names of the deceased for whom they undertook an obligation to pray inscribed in registers called books of life, *libri vitae* (after those lists of the elect mentioned in the Book of Revelation) or *libri memoriales*. The necrology of the Cluniac nuns of Marcigny-sur-Loire lists 10,000 names, and that of Reichenau four times as many. The persons named were to be remembered during the mass, but as there was no way all the names could be read out each time, the book was placed upon (plugged into, as it were) the altar. In this complex ancestor cult, the principal intermediaries, who had the task of trying to save the deceased, were the saints, whereas the intermediaries between the living and the saints were the monks. Any contact with the holy had to be made through them." Little adds that donations were given to pay for "these indispensable services rendered": "Great quantities of land were handed over to monastic communities by lay people anxious to secure their own access to salvation. The accumulation of huge monastic patrimonies is attested to by the large cartularies that document them, by the wealth, prestige, and political power that went with an abbot's role as landlord, and by the size and splendor of abbey churches."

31 This combines Luke 11, Daniel 4:27, and Tobit 4:11-13, quoted in White, *Custom, Kinship, and Gifts*, 154–55.

32 McLaughlin, *Consorting with Saints*, 146.

33 Or, if there was a feudal system, its heyday was, as William Maitland quipped, the mid-nineteenth century (quoted in the landmark article of Elizabeth A. R.

Brown, "The Tyranny of a Construct: Feudalism and Historians of Medieval Europe," *American Historical Review* 97, no. 4 [1974]: 1064). In addition to Brown's article, see Susan Reynolds, *Fiefs and Vassals: The Medieval Evidence Reinterpreted* (Oxford: Oxford University Press, 1996), who provides a genealogy of the concept of feudalism as a social system founded on the concepts of fief and vassal. F. L. Ganshof, *Feudalism* (New York: Harper, 1964) is one of Reynolds' and Brown's main targets. Appreciative yet critical reviews of Reynolds came from Fred Cheyette (originally in *Speculum*) and Paul Hyams (originally from the *Journal of Interdisciplinary History*), both available at www .fordham.edu/halsall/source/reynolds-2%20reviews.asp (accessed December 14, 2012). See also the review by Stephen D. White in *Law and History Review* 15, no. 2 (1997): 349–55.

34   That for two reasons: first, because commerce and gift giving coexisted throughout the medieval period and, second, because the lines between gift and sale, though acknowledged in law and elsewhere, were not always crystal clear. On the first point, see Florin Curta, "Merovingian and Carolingian Gift-Giving," *Speculum* 81, no. 3 (2006): 671–99; on the latter, Wendy Davies, "When Gift Is Sale: Reciprocities and Commodities in Tenth-Century Iberia," in Davies and Fouracre, *Languages of Gift in the Early Middle Ages*, 217–37, and William Ian Miller, "Gift, Sale, Payment, Raid: Case Studies in the Negotiation and Classification of Exchange in Medieval Iceland," *Speculum* 61, no. 1 (1986): 18–50. For the view that the early medieval economy was largely a "gift economy," see Georges Duby, *The Early Growth of the European Economy: Warriors and Peasants from the Seventh to the Twelfth Centuries*, trans. Howard B. Clarke (Ithaca, N.Y.: Cornell University Press, 1974); Philip Grierson, "Commerce in the Dark Ages: A Critique of the Evidence," *Transactions of the Royal Historical Society* 5th ser., no. 9 (1959): 129–40; Lester K. Little, *Religious Poverty and the Profit Economy in Medieval Europe* (Ithaca, N.Y.: Cornell University Press, 1978), 3–18.

35   Arnoud-Jan Bijsterveld writes, "Although the mechanism of gift-giving adopted no forms in changed circumstances, apparently it preserved its force and capacity to create, maintain, and restore relations between individuals or groups of people all through the Middle Ages. Also, the basic religious beliefs and doctrines underlying the gift-relationship remained much the same" ("Medieval Gift," 143).

36   On the "launegild" in Lombardy, see Chris Wickham, "Compulsory Gift Exchange in Lombard Italy, 650–1150," in Davies and Fouracre, *Languages of Gift in the Early Middle Ages*, 193–216. In her essay in the same volume, Davies details the use of countergifts that blurred the distinction between gift and sale.

37   See Stephen D. White, "Service for Fiefs or Fiefs for Service: The Politics of Reciprocity," in Algazi, Groebner, and Jussen, *Negotiating the Gift*, 63–98, and White, "The Politics of Exchange: Gifts, Fiefs, and Feudalism," in Cohen and de Jong, *Medieval Transformations*, 169–88.

38   For Charlemagne in particular, see Janet L. Nelson, "The Settings of the Gift in the Reign of Charlemagne," in Davies and Fouracre, *Languages of Gift in the Early Middle Ages*, 116–48.

39   According to James Hooker, despite the similarities between archaic Greek and early medieval gift giving, the Homeric poems never identify good kings explicitly by their generosity, as medieval texts do ("Gifts in Homer," *Bulletin of the Institute Classical Studies* 36 [1989]: 79–90).

40   Gregory of Tours, *History of the Franks*, 2.37.

41   *Beowulf*, lines 20–24, translation in Andrew Galloway, "The Making of a Social Ethic in Late-Medieval England: From Gratitudo to 'Kyndnesse,'" *Journal of the History of Ideas* 55, no. 3 (1994): 366. I have drawn heavily on Galloway's superb article throughout this section of the chapter.

42 Stephen D. White, "Giving Fiefs and Honor: Largesse, Avarice, and the Problem of 'Feudalism' in Alexander's Testament," in Maddos and Sturm-Maddox, *Medieval French Alexander*, 127–41.

43 Geoffrey of Monmouth, *The History of the Kings of Britain*, trans. Lewis Thorpe (London: Penguin, 1966), 212, quoted in Galloway, "Making of a Social Ethic," 367.

44 *Sir Gawain and the Green Knight* is in fact all about gifts and returns. The Green Knight offers his neck to anyone who wants to strike it off, his macabre version of a Christmas gift. When he chases down and picks up his head, which has been rolling about being kicked like a football, the mouth invites Arthur's boldest knight to find him in the Green Chapel the following year for a return gift. While Gawain stays in Bertilak's castle, the seductive Mrs. Bertilak tempts him with gifts, including the magically protective green girdle. See Britton Harwood, "Gawain and the Gift," *Proceedings of the Modern Library Association* 106, no. 3 (1991): 483–99.

45 Thomas Write, ed., *The Chronicle of Pierre de Langtoft*, 2 vols. (London: Longmans, 1898), 2.296, quoted in Galloway, "Making of a Social Ethic," 367.

46 Quoted in White, "Service for Fiefs," 74.

47 Quoted in Nelson, "Settings of the Gift," 145.

48 On the problems of the notion of "courtly love," see C. Stephen Jaeger, *Ennobling Love: In Search of a Lost Sensibility* (Philadelphia: University of Pennsylvania Press, 1999). C. S. Lewis' claim that courtly love marked a sea change in Western sensibilities, in comparison to which the Renaissance was "a ripple on the surface of literature," is perhaps overstated, but in my view more true than false (*The Allegory of Love: A Study in Medieval Tradition* [Oxford: Oxford University Press, 1985]). The classic statement of the maximal interpretation of courtly love's impact is Denis de Rougement, *Love in the Western World*, rev. ed. (Princeton: Princeton University Press, 1983). Once gratitude and ingratitude got into romance, they stayed, as we will have occasion to note again in chapter 6.

49 Guillaume de Lorris and Jean de Meun, *Romance of the Rose*, 8197-214.

50 William George Dodd, *Courtly Love in Chaucer and Gower* (Boston: Ginn, 1913), 70.

51 Andreas Capellanus, *Art of Courtly Love*, trans. John Jay Parry (New York: Columbia University Press, 1990), chap. 5.

52 Galloway, "Making of a Social Ethic," 381: Chaucer "avoids applying 'kynd' and 'kyndnesse' altogether to general social ethics, using these instead to mean either simply 'natural' or 'kind' in the more modern, sentimental sense, limited almost entirely to the experience of lovers."

53 Quoted in White, "Service for Fiefs," 76.

54 On bad gifts, see White, "Service for Fiefs," 81–86.

55 Cicero, *De officiis*, 1.41.

56 "D'ogne laizia, ch'odio in cielo acquisita, / ingiura e 'l fine, ed ogne fin cotale / o con forza o con frode altrui contrista." I am using the translation of Anthony Esolen (New York: Modern Library, 2002).

57 Dante gives a more philosophical analysis of ingratitude in *Convivio*, 12, and following Roman tradition links it to treachery and other vices. He begins from the premise that "every goodness proper to a thing is deserving of love in that thing." To love masculinity, one must love beards; to love femininity, one loves beardlessness. Those aspects of a thing that are more proper to it are the most deserving of love, so that the thing that is most deserving of love in a man is what is most human, which is "justice, which resides in the rational or intellectual part, that is, in the will." Conversely, whatever is most opposite to justice is most inhuman, and thus hated most of all, "as, for example, treachery, ingratitude, falsehood, rapine, deceit, and the like." On gratitude and ingratitude in Dante's thought, see Allan

Gilbert, *Dante's Conception of Justice* (New York: AMS Press, 1971), 29, 53–54. For other poetic treatments of gift and reciprocity, see Adelheid L. J. Thieme, "Gift Giving as a Vital Element of Salvation in *The Dream of the Rood*," *South Atlantic Review* 63, no. 2 (1998): 108–23; Andrew Galloway, "Layamon's Gift," *Proceedings of the MLA* 121, no. 3 (2006): 717–34.

58   *Mirour de l'Omme*, 6673–85, quoted in Galloway, "Making of a Social Ethic," 377.

59   Gower, *Confessio amantis*, 5156–60. In William Langland's *Piers the Plowman*, even more than in Gower, kyndnesse/gratitude becomes a social norm. In his poem, Wit charges that Christians have failed to show proper kindness to their own:

> Sholde no Cristene creature cryen at the yate [gate]
> Ne faille payñ ne potage [lack bread or stew], and [*if*] prelates dide as thei sholden.
> A Jew wolde noght se a Jew go janglyng for defaute [complaining of want]
> F
> or alle the mebles [goods] on this moolde [earth], and [*if*] he amende it myghte.
> Allas that a Cristene creature shal be unkynde til [to] another!
> Syn [since] Jewes, that we jugge [deem] Judas felawes [companions],
> Eyther helpeth oother of that that hym nedeth.
> Whi nel [won't] we Cristene of Cristes good [with Christ's goods] as kynde be
> As Jewes, that ben oure loresmen [teachers]? Shame to us alle!
> The commune for hir unkyndenesse, I drede me, shul abye [pay].
> (9.80–89)

The translation is from Galloway, "Making of a Social Ethic," 380. Galloway comments, " 'Kyndenesse' here implies a social and economic contract on the 'natural' basis of religious, and we may suppose, cultural unity, since Jews had been expelled from England a century before. Wit makes the ideal of 'kyndnesse' more specifically political still by advocating it to the 'commune,' that elusive late-medieval word for either the 'common people' or the entire citizenry." In the speech of the Samaritan, "immediate social exchanges [are] more important for defining a sacred community than any institutional religious forms or practices. Worship God and love your kindred Christians, the Samaritan advises both poor and rich, and the Holy Ghost will literally glow through you onto those who deal with, producing a united community in a way that no mere documentary promises or external observances can" (380–81). See also Galloway, "A Fifteenth-Century Confession Sermon on 'Unkyndness' and Its Literary Parallels and Parodies," *Traditio* 49 (1994): 259–69.

60   Andrew Galloway writes that "[d]iscussions of gratitude at first compete with and then, increasingly, supersede discussions of gift-giving; from the late thirteen century on, the formulas and proverbs of the one slowly replace those of the other" (Galloway, "Making of a Social Ethic," 368, 370).

61   *Auctores Octo* (London, 1514), quoted in Galloway, "Making of a Social Ethic," 370.

62   *Summa praedicantium* (Basil, 1485), art. 7, quoted in Galloway, "Making of a Social Ethic," 371.

63   See R. W. Southern, *Scholastic Humanism and the Unification of Europe: Foundations* (London: Wiley-Blackwell, 1997).

64   *Summa praedicantium*: "demones obsident modo divites et avaros qui si noluerint sibi stipendiarios conducere, i.e. pauperes ut per eos liberentur in die malo morti."

65 Geraldus Odonis, *Sententia ex exposition cum quaestionibus super libros Ethicorum* (Venice, 1500), quoted in Galloway, "Making of a Social Ethic," 370.

66 Vincent, *Speculum doctrinale*, 4.53–55, quoted in Galloway, "Making of a Social Ethic," 369.

67 Galloway, "Making of a Social Ethic," 370.

68 Galloway, "Making of a Social Ethic," 369.

69 Aquinas, *Summa Theologiae*, II-II, 107.

70 *Summa Theologiae*, II-II, 57.

71 *Summa Theologiae*, II-II, 58.

72 *Summa Theologiae*, I-II, 100, 1.

73 *Summa Theologiae*, II-II, 80.

74 *Summa Theologiae*, II-II, 106.

75 *Summa Theologiae*, II-II, 107.

76 *Summa Theologiae*, II-II, 106.

77 The notion, for instance, that we owe taxes only because of the public services we might receive violates the trajectory of gratitude, turning political obligations into narrowly economic transactions. On Thomas' account, loyal attachment to a benefactor would be one possible form of "repaying" the debt of gratitude, though there would no doubt be others and there would no doubt be other grounds for loyalty.

78 On Anselm, see Kenneth L. Schmitz, *The Gift: Creation* (The Aquinas Lecture 1982; Milwaukee: Marquette University Press, 1982), 28–34. David Hart argues that "gift theology" is at the root of Anselm's much-criticized account of the atonement; see "A Gift Exceeding Every Debt: An Eastern Orthodox Appreciation of Anselm's Cur Deus Homo," *Pro Ecclesia* 7, no. 3 (1998): 333–49. For other medieval theologians on the reality of creation, see Zachary Hayes, *The Gift of Being: A Theology of Creation* (Collegeville, Minn.: Michael Glazier, 2001), 45–51.

79 *Summa praedicantium*, quoted in Galloway, "Making of a Social Ethic," 372.

80 Quoted in Hyde, *The Gift*, 54–55. John of the Cross describes the return gift that the soul makes to the God who gives himself to the soul. God gives himself to the soul, and thus when the soul seeks to return a gift to God, it "gives to God, God himself in God." When the soul "in this gift to God offers him the Holy Spirit . . . it gives God something of its own that is suited to him." How suited? On the one hand, "the soul cannot give God again to himself, since in himself he is ever himself," yet "God who could not be paid with anything less [than himself] is considered paid with the gift of the soul." God himself "accepts it gratefully as something it gives him of its own" (*The Living Flame of Love* [Garden City, N.Y.: Image Books, 1962], 78–80).

81 Catherine of Siena, letter to Nanna, *Letters*, available at http://www.gutenberg.org/cache/epub/7403/pg7403.html.

82 Catherine, letter to Brother Bartolomeo Dominici, in *Letters*.

83 A similar sort of mysticism is one of the moving forces behind Derrida's advocacy of pure gift. See John D. Caputo, *The Prayers and Tears of Jacques Derrida: Religion without Religion* (Bloomington: Indiana University Press, 1997), and chap. 10.

84 Teresa of Avila, *The Life of the Holy Mother Teresa of Jesus*, www.ccel.org (accessed February 26, 2013), 4.15.

85 Teresa of Avila, *Life of the Holy Mother Teresa*, 7.14.

86 Teresa of Avila, *Life of the Holy Mother Teresa*, 10.2.

87 See chapter 1.

88 McLaughlin, *Consorting with Saints*, 169.

89 Esther Cohen, *Gift, Payment, and the Sacred in Medieval Popular Religiosity* (Wassenaar: Netherlands Institute for Advanced Study in the Humanities and Social

Sciences, 1991), summarized by Bijsterveld, "Medieval Gift," 145. Richard Keyser agrees that after 1350 "le don pieux se conforme a un modele comptable 'accumulatif.' . . . Cette reciprocite religieuse est comme le commerce, precise, systematique et largement objective" ("La transformation de l'echange des dons pieux: Montier-la-Celle, Champagne, 1100–1350," *Revue Historique* 305 [2003]: 794).

CHAPTER 5

1 A ninth-century document declares, "Non solum sacrificial quae a Sacerdotibus super altare Domino consecrantur, Oblationem fidelium dicuntur, sed quaecunque ei a fidelibus offeruntur." Quoted in David Granz, "Giving to God in the Mass: The Experience of the Offertory," in Davies and Fouracre, *Languages of Gift in the Early Middle Ages*, 20.

2 The decree is quoted in Granz, "Giving to God," 21.

3 The decree is quoted in Granz, "Giving to God," 21.

4 Quoted in Granz, "Giving to God," 24.

5 Augustine, *De Civitate Dei*, ed. and trans. Robert Dyson et al. (Cambridge: Cambridge University Press, 1998), 10.6.

6 Arnold Angenendt, "Donationes pro anima: Gift and Countergift in the Early Medieval Liturgy," in Davis and McCormick, *Long Morning of Medieval Europe*, 133: "In the Middle Ages, the material component came to the fire and, understood entirely as reciprocity, brought with it the expectation of a countergift from God."

7 J. A. Jungmann, *The Mass: An Historical, Theological, and Pastoral Survey*, trans. Julian Fernandes, ed. Mary Ellen Evans (Collegeville, Minn.: Liturgical Press, 1976), 64–70. See also a fuller treatment of the significance of the Gregorian reform in Leithart, "The Gospel, Gregory VII, and Modern Theology," *Modern Theology* 19, no. 1 (2003): 5–28. On the shifts in the theology of the Eucharist, see Henri de Lubac, *Corpus Mysticum: The Eucharist and the Church in the Middle Ages* (Notre Dame, Ind.: University of Notre Dame Press, 2007).

8 This was one of Luther's central objections to the Catholic rite. The Lord's Supper is fundamentally a gift, and Luther renounced the "commercialism" and "bartering and dealing" that he discerned in the Mass ("Admonition Concerning the Sacrament," quoted in Piotr J. Malysz, "Exchange and Ecstasy: Luther's Eucharistic Theology in the Light of Radical Orthodoxy's Critique of Gift and Sacrifice," *Scottish Journal of Theology* 60, no. 3 (2007): 306 n. 42. Malysz' article challenges William Cavanaugh's interpretation ("Eucharistic Sacrifice and the Social Imagination in Early Modern Europe," *Journal of Medieval and Early Modern Studies* 31, no. 3 [2001]: 585–605), who claims that Luther created a dualism of exchange and gift that turned the gift into a supernatural disruption of the normal transactional patterns of social life. Malysz responds, in part, by pointing out that "the mass of the late Middle Ages contributed to the progressive contractuality of social relationships, rather than simply being undermined by the social processes" (304). On the Reformers' charge of commercialization, see also Brad S. Gregory, *The Unintended Reformation: How a Religious Revolution Secularized Society* (Cambridge, Mass.: Belknap, 2012), 262–63.

9 Angenendt, "Donationes pro anima," 141–43.

10 Natalie Zemon Davis, *The Gift in Sixteenth-Century France* (Madison: University of Wisconsin Press, 2000), 100: "In a profound sense, the religious reformations of the sixteenth century were a quarrel about gifts, that is, about whether humans can reciprocate to God, about whether humans can put God under obligation, and about what this means for what people give to each other." Writing specifically of Calvin, Davis captures the wide range of reform, the shifting of the center of gratitude in sixteenth-century France: "No more exchange between the living and

the dead, as Purgatory disappears. No more systematic exchange between laity and clergy; all believing Christians are priests and now pastors are paid regular salaries. No more confraternities circulating gifts among the brothers and sisters; Christians have no particular fellowship other than their parish. Fewer things can serve as gifts, as candles lose their religious role, and fewer holy days exist that might occasion special gift exchange" (119).

11 On Biel, see Heiko Oberman, *The Harvest of Medieval Theology* (Grand Rapids: Baker, 2000).

12 "The popular view of the mass was distinctly mechanical. The layman was taught to believe that he could increase the effect of Eucharistic prayers by the simple process of multiplying them and making them more elaborate. The benefits which the living and dead received varied in direct proportion with the number of masses said and the amount of offering made at each" (B. L. Manning, *The People's Faith in the Time of Wyclif* (Cambridge: Cambridge University Press, 1919), 72, quoted in Rosenthal, *Purchase of Paradise*, 13.

13 Thesis 33.

14 Thesis 34.

15 Thesis 62.

16 Luther, *Three Treatises*, 2nd ed. (Minneapolis: Fortress, 1990).

17 Quoted in Oswald Bayer, "The Ethics of Gift," *Lutheran Quarterly* 24 (2010): 447–68, 455.

18 Quoted in Bayer, "Ethics of Gift," 455.

19 Quoted in Bayer, "Ethics of Gift," 456. Calvin's theology took off from a similar starting point. Even before he begins talking about the Eucharist, Calvin's theology is deeply eucharistic. God the Father is a kind and loving Father, who gives all good things to his children. Despite their sin, he is determined to bring them to salvation, to share in his life at his table. He calls them to grateful reception of his gifts, which means that they are to receive his gifts fruitfully, living in obedience to their Father and in union with the Son. See Brian Gerrish, *Grace and Gratitude: The Eucharistic Theology of John Calvin* (Eugene, Ore.: Wipf & Stock, 2002).

20 See Stephan K. Turnbull, "Grace and Gift in Luther and Paul," *Word & World* 24, no. 3 (2004): 305–14.

21 Luther, "Faith of a Christian," in *Three Treatises*. The first commandment is the root of all the others, so when one believes in obedience to the first commandment, fulfillment of the other commandments becomes easy.

22 Luther, *Small Catechism* and "That These Words of Christ, 'This Is My Body' Still Stand Firm Against the Fanatics" (1527), quoted in Malysz, "Exchange and Ecstasy," 305–7. Malysz emphasizes that for Luther the Eucharist does not merely form a pattern for Christian society, but actually forms that society in the gift of the incarnate Son.

23 Calvin, *Institutes*, 2.6.55; 3.7.6–7. To see how these charitable principles were worked out in practice, see Ronald Wallace, *Calvin, Geneva, and the Reformation* (Eugene, Ore.: Wipf & Stock, 1998); Robert Kingdon, "Social Welfare in Calvin's Geneva," *American Historical Review* 76 (1971): 50–69. It was a truism among the Reformers that funds that had been used by the Catholic Church to support indolent monks or to decorate lavish churches ought instead be devoted to the poor.

24 Calvin, *Institutes*, 4.18.17. See Gerrish, *Grace and Gratitude*, 150–51.

25 *Catechism of Geneva*, q. 237. In the light of our discussion of Jesus and Paul in chapter 3, it is clear that this catechism answer misses the disruptive force of early Christian "ingratitude." As described by the catechism, Genevan society replicates the pattern of benefaction and gratitude-debt found in Roman society, now reinforced and made transcendent by theological principles.

26   *Commentary on Hebrews*, 11:5–6.

27   *Commentary on a Harmony of the Gospels*, at Matthew 6:4.

28   Something of Seneca too. Calvin's first published work was a commentary on Seneca's *De Clementia*, and Calvin continued to use Stoic categories and to evidence Stoic inclinations throughout his life. On this, see Leithart, "Stoic Elements in Calvin's Doctrine of the Christian Life," *Westminster Theological Journal* 55, no. 1 (1993): 31–54; 55, no. 2 (1993): 191–208; 56, no. 1 (1994): 59–85.

29   Calvin, *Institutes*, 4.18.16.

30   Pierre du Moulin, *The Buckler of the Faith* (Newberry, 1631). Moulin appears to be reading a Protestant doctrine of grace into the term *charis*. As we noted in chapter 1, the word was the normal Greek term for a return gift, pleasure returned for the pleasure of an initial benefit.

31   Miles Coverdale, *A Spiritual and Most Precious Pearl* (1550; repr., Cambridge: Cambridge University Press, 1844), 147.

32   William Perkins, *A Golden Chain* (1590; repr., Cambridge: Cambridge University Press, 1612), 104.

33   Thomas Cartwright, *A Confutation of the Rhemists Translation, Glosses and Annotations on the New Testament* (1618; repr., New York: Da Capo, 1971), 59.

34   Tyndale, *Doctrinal Treatises and Introductions to Different Portions of the Holy Scriptures* (1525; repr., Cambridge: Cambridge University Press, 1848).

35   Tyndale, *Doctrinal Treatises*, 66.

36   Tyndale, *Parable of the Wicked Mammon* (London, 1528).

37   For a helpful corrective to contemporary linear conceptions of the gift, especially as seen in the Reformed versions of "Sonship theology," see Kelly Kapic, *God So Loved, He Gave: Entering the Movement of Divine Generosity* (Grand Rapids: Zondervan, 2010).

38   Quoted in Ilana Krausman Ben-Amos, *The Culture of Giving: Informal Support and Gift-Exchange in Early Modern England* (Cambridge: Cambridge University Press, 2008), 250n22.

39   Ben-Amos, *Culture of Giving*, chaps. 5–7. See also Felicity Heal, "Food Gifts, the Household and the Politics of Exchange in Early Modern England," *Past and Present* 199 (2008): 41–70.

40   Ben-Amos, *Culture of Giving*, 273: The discourse on gifts "elevated giving as a form of gratuitousness—a sort of altruistic, sacrificial benevolence and love that sought no reward, alongside the kind of offering that carried benefits and reciprocities."

41   *Gargantua and Pantagruel*, book 3, 3.IV. The notion that this debate reflects a conflict of "Protestant" and "Catholic" mentalities comes from Davis, *Gift in Sixteenth-Century France*, 121–23.

42   *Gargantua and Pantagruel*, book 3, 3.V.

43   See Timothy Reuter, "Gifts and Simony," in Algazi, Groebner, and Jussen, *Negotiating the Gift*, 157–68.

44   Valentin Groebner, *Liquid Assets, Dangerous Gifts: Presents and Political at the End of the Middle Ages*, trans. Pamela E. Selwyn (Philadelphia: University of Pennsylvania Press, 2000). See also Groebner, "Accountancies and *Arcana*: Registering the Gift in Late Medieval Cities," in Cohen and de Jong, *Medieval Transformations*, 219–43; Groebner, "The City Guard's Salute: Legal and Illegal, Public and Private Gifts in the Swiss Confederation around 1500," in Algazi, Groebner, and Jussen, *Negotiating the Gift*, 247–67.

45   On this development, see Norbert Elias, *The Civilizing Process: Sociogenetic and Psychogenetic Investigations* (London: Blackwell, 2000); Helmuch Berking, *Sociology of Giving* (London: Sage, 1999), chap. 8.

46   On this process, see Charles Tilley, ed., *The Formation of National States in Western*

Europe (Princeton: Princeton University Press, 1975); Tilley, *Coercion, Capital and European States: AD 990–1992* (London: Wiley-Blackwell, 1992).

47 Thanks to my research assistant, Donny Linnemeyer, for help in assessing Machiavelli's views on this topic. Donny's research was crucial for me throughout this chapter and the following two.

48 *The Prince*, chap. 3. I am relying on the translation of W. K. Mariott (Chicago: Encyclopedia Britannica, 1952).

49 *The Prince*, chap. 6.

50 *The Prince*, chap. 7.

51 *The Prince*.

52 *The Prince*, chap. 16.

53 *The Prince*, chap. 16.

54 *Discourses on Livy*, 3.6. I am using the translation of Christian Detmold, available at http://oll.libertyfund.org/?option=com_staticxt&staticfile=show.php%3Ftitle=1866.

55 *The Prince*, chap. 16.

56 *Discourses on Livy*, 1.28.

57 *Discourses on Livy*, 1.29.

58 *Discourses on Livy*, 1.30.

59 *Discourses on Livy*, 1.30.

60 *The Prince*, Preface.

61 *Discourses on Livy*, Introduction.

62 For all this, see Davis, *Gift in Sixteenth-Century France*, 67–72. Davis speaks of "obligation anxiety" as a characteristic of sixteenth-century French life.

63 Montaigne, "On Vanity," in *Essays*, available at http://oregonstate.edu/instruct/phl302/texts/montaigne/montaigne-essays--6.html.

64 Catherine Dunn, *The Concept of Ingratitude in Renaissance English Moral Philosophy* (Washington, D.C.: Catholic University of America Press, 1946), 3–8.

65 Dunn, *Concept of Ingratitude*, 9.

66 Dunn, *Concept of Ingratitude*, 10.

67 Pierre Charron, *Of Wisdome* (English translation 1608), cited in Dunn, *Concept of Ingratitude*, 26.

68 Cited in Dunn, *Concept of Ingratitude*, 28–29.

69 Peter de la Primaudaye, *The French Academie* (1594), cited in Dunn, *Conception of Ingratitude*, 29.

70 "A True Description of Unthankfulnesse," cited in Dunn, *Concept of Ingratitude*, 15.

71 "For like as treason is no other thing than a breach of faith and dutie; euen so ingratitude is no other thing, than a breach of the band and dutie due vnto a man, by reason of a pleasure receiued" (Remigio Nannini, *Civill Considerations upon Many and Sundrie Histories* [1601], cited in Dunn, *Concept of Ingratitude*, 47).

72 William Bullein compares the ingratitude of Judas to "all Traitours agaynste Prynces, by whome they haue receiued Benefites" (*The Bulwarke of Defense against All Sicknesse* [1579], cited in Dunn, *Concept of Ingratitude*, 48), and Robert Dallington describes the defection of two Italian vassals from the king of France as an act of "vngratefull reuolt, from so magnificent a Prince" (*Aphorismes Civill and Militarie* [1629], cited in Dunn, *Concept of Ingratitude*, 49).

73 Hewitt, "Some Aspects of the Treatment of Ingratitude," 42–47.

74 Available online at http://www.luminarium.org/renascence-editions/gov/gov1.htm. The following paragraphs summarize chapter 13 of Elyot's second book.

75 Recent Shakespeare scholarship has emphasized not only his interest in contemporary Elizabethan politics but also the theological setting in which those political interested have been developed. Debora Shuger writes, "[I]f it is not plausible to

read Shakespeare's plays as Christian allegories, neither is it likely that the popular drama of a religiously saturated culture could, by a secular miracle, have extricated itself from the theocentric orientation informing the discourses of politics, gender, social order and history." Quoted in Jeffrey Knapp, *Shakespeare's Tribe: Church, Theatre and Nation in Renaissance England* (Chicago: University of Chicago Press, 2002). In his 2002 *Shakespeare's Tribe*, Jeffrey Knapp argues that scholars do not go far enough. While they stress "the centrality of religion to the study of Renaissance drama," they accept part of the secular theater thesis they are opposing since they assume that "Renaissance playwrights [are] 'Christian' only cognitively or subliminally, rather than purposively and devotionally." Thus not even recent revisionist scholarship "allows the possibility that Renaissance plays may have been intended and received as contributions to the cause of true religion," nor have scholars considered the possibility that "Shakespeare and his contemporaries were capable of envisaging their profession itself—their acting and playwrighting—as a kind of ministry." For his part, Knapp argues that "English theology and ecclesiology shaped the drama at a fundamental level, in helping to determine the conceptualization of the player and the playwright as professions, and of the theater as an institution; these self-images in turn disposed theater people toward the enacting of certain confirmatory plots, themes, and characters on stage; and thus religion had a crucial say in the creation of plays, in their content, and, by extension, in their presumed social effects." In short, "religion had a more direct role in the production of plays than as the deep structure of dramatized ideology; it provided the rationale and even motives for acting and playwrighting." Along similar lines, Julia Reinhard Lupton argues that Shakespeare's dramas "stage the sacramental marriage, civil divorce, and dangerous liaisons between politics and religion in the West, probing the intersection between the founding metaphors of diving sovereignty and modern forms of social organization based on the economic contracts of individuals. Shakespeare's plays, I suggest, are preoccupied by the strange cohabitation of the saint and the citizen" (*Citizen-Saints: Shakespeare and Political Theology* [Chicago: University of Chicago Press, 2005], 12).

76   Clifford Ronan, *"Antike Roman": Power Symbology and the Roman Play in Early Modern England, 1585–1635* (Athens: University of Georgia Press, 1995), 81: "[T]his theme is not at the heart of most Tudor-Stuart tragedies with Christian settings, even if Macbeth is a striking exception." Rather, "most studies of *ingratitude*—lack of *grac*ious acceptance—are to be found in tragedies with a pagan setting: in other words, beyond the customary sphere of *gratia*." Though "Roman dramas constitute 30 percent of Shakespeare's œuvre . . . concordances suggest that these five plays and *Timon* contain fully 60 percent of the dramatist's four dozen uses of words like *ingrate, ungrateful,* and *ingratitude*." Ronan concludes that "Shakespeare and his fellow dramatists seem to have viewed the Ancient world, particularly Rome, as stained with a cruel pride—self-interested, ungenerous, contentious, murderous. In fact, the Renaissance as a whole makes more of Roman ingratitude than Antiquity did" (emphasis in original). The importance of ingratitude in Coriolanus has been recognized at least since Dunn, *Concept of Ingratitude*, 31–32. See also Clifford Chalmers Huffman's *Coriolanus in Context* (Lewisburg, Pa.: Bucknell, 1971), 207–11. Peter F. Neumeyer, "Ingratitude Is Monstrous: An Approach to Coriolanus," *College English* 26, no. 3 (1964): 192–98, offers an interpretation of the play very near my own.

77   Plutarch, *Life of Coriolanus*, 3.3–4.

78   Plutarch, *Life of Coriolanus*, 36.2–3.

79   Plutarch, *Life of Coriolanus*, 39.3–4.

80   In defending Coriolanus' status as a tragic hero, Brian Vickers is particularly good at describing how every faction of Rome tries to turn the military hero into a

puppet who will advance their interests in Vickers, *Shakespeare: Coriolanus* (London: Edward Arnold, 1976), passim. The play has often been read and produced as a dramatization of political ideology as well, though the particular ideology represented by the play has varied wildly across the political spectrum. A production at Drury Lane in 1789 embodied the strongly anti-Jacobin politics of its producer, John Philip Kemble, idealizing the patrician characters and representing the plebs, in R. B. Parker's words, as "clownish, ineffectual dolts." Nazis produced the play during the 1930s to expose the evils of democracy and to celebrate Hitler as a conqueror greater than the Roman Martius (Coriolanus). So powerful was the play's resonance with Nazis that it was banned in the first years of Allied occupation. On the other hand, many productions offer leftist interpretations that highlight the distasteful pride of Coriolanus and present the tribunes as champions of democracy. Eastern European productions during the 1930s turned the plebs and tribunes into heroes and condemned Martius as a tyrant, while Bertolt Brecht's unfinished adaptation thoroughly reinvented the story. In Brecht's version, instead of being fearful and demoralized by Martius' attack on Rome, the tribunes organize the plebs into a defense force so powerful that Martius withdraws of his own accord. This summary is taken from R. B. Parker's introduction to the Oxford edition of *The Tragedy of Coriolanus* (Oxford: Oxford University Press, 1998). Cathy Shrank offers a fine summary of the political uses of the play: "That interpretations of Coriolanus have been—almost without exception—politicized is as true for modern productions and critical appraisals as for seventeenth- and early-eighteenth-century adaptations. Almost every constitutional crisis in post-Restoration Britain prompted a rewriting of the play. Nahum Tate's *The Ingratitude of a Common-Wealth* (1681) places Coriolanus within the context of the Exclusion Crisis; John Dennis's *The Invader of His Country* (1719) draws explicit parallels between Martius and James Stuart, the Old Pretender, evoking Stuart's failed attempts to invade England in 1708 and 1715; and James Thomson's *Coriolanus* (1749) aligns Martius with Charles Stuart, the Young Pretender, in the wake of the Second Jacobite Rebellion in 1745. The play has similarly reflected the political upheavals of twentieth-century Europe: in the Mussolini-like death of Laurence Olivier's *Martius at Stratford* in 1959, or in the English Shakespeare Company's production of 1990, directed by Michael Bogdanov, set against the collapse of Communism in Eastern Europe" ("Civility and the City in Coriolanus," *Shakespeare Quarterly* 54, no. 4 [2003]: 406). Left and right seem to have equal claim to the play. It is not difficult to turn the play into a critique of aristocratic elitism: "What's the matter, you dissentious rogues, / That, rubbing the poor itch of your opinion, / make yourselves scabs?" are Coriolanus' first words in the play, and set the tone for his other speeches to the plebs. He condemns them as cowardly hares and geese; at his banishment, he dismisses them as a "common cry of curs"; and he often complains of their body odor and bad breath. His politics are profoundly antidemocratic. He wonders at the "double worship" of Rome's famously mixed political system, a political system in which "gentry, title, wisdom / Cannot conclude but by the yea and no / Of general ignorance" (2.1.144–46). Could Shakespeare have expected his groundlings to warm to such a tragic hero, or to be moved to pity and fear by his death? On the other hand, it is difficult not to feel the force of Martius' opinions. Is it not in fact better for the wise and informed to make political decisions than to subject them to the veto power of the ignorant and apathetic? Furthermore, Shakespeare does not go out of his way to make the people of Rome sympathetic (a point made with particular force by Vickers, *Shakespeare*, 16–17). They do not know what is good for them, repeatedly demonstrating the truth of Coriolanus' assessment. They gleefully banish their Hector, not stopping for a moment to ask what it will cost them. The tribunes cynically manipulate the plebs as much as they do Coriolanus himself, and are as dictatorial and contemptuous of the people in their own way as Coriolanus is.

81 John M. Wallace makes a similar point when he examines the connections between Coriolanus and Seneca's *De beneficiis* in "The Senecan Context of *Coriolanus*," *Modern Philology* 90, no. 4 (1993): 465–78. On the uses of analogy, and particularly the analogy of the human body, in Renaissance political thought, see James Emerson Phillips, *The State in Shakespeare's Greek and Roman Plays* (New York: Columbia University Press, 1940), chap. 4.

82 Wallace speaks of the "ironies and contradictions" and "meaninglessness" ("Senecan Context," 467), yet however falsified by the play, the tale itself is a standard bit of early modern social theory and was probably meant to be a model of social life.

83 Shakespeare's Roman plays are all overshadowed by an ideal of unified political order, and in each case Rome fails to live up to its ideal. Rome is always double Rome, though the doubling of Rome differs from play to play. In *Julius Caesar*, Rome is initially divided between the remaining adherents to Pompey and the plebs who celebrate Caesar (1.1). The division of Rome in *Coriolanus* is institutionalized by the distinction between the Senate and the tribunate, who represent the plebs. For a general treatment of the unnerving underbelly of Menenius' parable, see Roy W. Battenhouse, *Shakespearean Tragedy: Its Art and Its Christian Premises* (Bloomington: Indiana University Press, 1969), 341–55.

84 Zvi Jagendorf provides a helpful catalogue: "legs, arms, tongues, scabs, scratches, wounds, mouths, teeth, voices, bellies, and toes" ("*Coriolanus*: Body Politic and Private Parts," *Shakespeare Quarterly* 41, no. 4 [1990]: 458).

85 This is sometimes supported by a punning theoretical riff on the word "kind": those who refuse to receive or return kindness prove that they are of a different kind/genus, monsters in human shape rather than humans. Besides the obvious words for gratitude used by Shakespeare, "kindness" and "unkindness" were often used as synonyms of "gratitude" and "ingratitude," respectively, and "churl" also carries the specific connotation of "ingrate," with the additional suggestion that the ingrate is a non-noble person, whatever the person's actual social status (Dunn, *Concept of Ingratitude*, 13, 86–91). See also "unkind" in *The Oxford English Dictionary* (Oxford: Clarendon, 1933), 11:249, and "churl" and "churlish" in the same dictionary (2:409–10).

86 Brother Anthony of Taize, "Shakespeare's Monsters of Ingratitude," *Shakespeare Review* (Seoul) (1990): 1–10, available at www.ccsun7.sogang.ac.kr/~anthony/Ingrate.htm (accessed February 26, 2013).

87 The ingratitude of the people is manifest both on the battlefield and within the walls of the city, for in both settings they abandon Martius to fight it out for himself. See E. A. M. Colman, "The End of *Coriolanus*," *ELH* 34, no. 1 (1967): 1–20, 10.

88 Brother Anthony of Taize, "Shakespeare's Monsters of Ingratitude." Also, Terence Eagleton, *Shakespeare and Society: Critical Studies in Elizabethan Drama* (New York: Schocken, 1967), 99–104, on the self-defeating or self-consuming character of Rome.

89 See Stanley Cavell, *Disowning Knowledge in Six Plays of Shakespeare* (Cambridge: Cambridge University Press, 1987), 150–51.

90 This is the way that Seneca read the story of Coriolanus, and there is reason to think that Shakespeare was familiar with Seneca's treatise: "Coriolanus was ungrateful, and became dutiful late, and after repenting of his crime; he did indeed lay down his arms, but only in the midst of his unnatural warfare" (*De beneficiis*, 5.16).

91 Eagleton, *Shakespeare and Society*, 104, makes a similar point in regard to Martius' reluctance to seek the voices of the plebs: "Coriolanus . . . envisions no reciprocity:

he sees this mutual relationship of plebeians and patricians as circular, destructive, self-defeating." Eagleton compares him to Achilles, seeking "self-creation without reference to society" and rejecting any "need for social verification."

92   *Coriolanus*, 23–24.

93   Like all heroes, Martius is caught in a fundamental dilemma: his status as hero is a matter of reputation, and thus depends entirely on the approval of his fellows, yet in the agonistic setting of an honor-shame ethic he is striving to rise above his fellows. Martius attempts to struggle free of the dilemma by refusing the plaudits of his commanding officer, but is resentfully aware that he depends on them for his fame.

94   Wallace, "Senecan Context," 476 n. 15, quoting from Joshua Scodel. The same point is developed at greater length in Battenhouse, *Shakespearean Tragedy*, 362–74, and even more thoroughly and precisely by Carson Holloway, "Shakespeare's *Coriolanus* and Aristotle's *Megalopsyuchos*," unpublished paper provided by the author.

95   Here, and at several other points, Shakespeare has modified Plutarch to emphasize the hero's isolation. As Jagendorf points out, he thinks of himself not as a limb or organ of Rome but as a whole, isolated body to himself, and it is fitting that he is named after the city that he conquered: "La ville c'est moi" (Jagendorf, "*Coriolanus*: Body Politic," 462–63).

96   Terry Eagleton describes Coriolanus as "perhaps Shakespeare's most developed study of a bourgeois individualist," one of those modern "new men" with pretensions to self-creation, who "prefigures the time—not far off from Shakespeare's England—when a whole society would fall prey to the ideology of self-authorship, when all individuals will be only begetters of themselves, private entrepreneurs of their bodies and sole proprietors of a labour force" (*William Shakespeare* [Oxford: Blackwell, 1986], 73–74).

97   Eagleton suggests that Coriolanus refuses to be "object" in relation to Rome, insisting instead on remaining "subject." Coriolanus thus joins Timon of Athens (and, of course, Caliban) as one of Shakespeare's great depictions of man in a state of nature. It is noteworthy that Coriolanus and Timon at least enter the state of nature by renouncing political society. Isolation is not an originary state, but a corrupted state. And it seems quite clear that, for all his suspicion of the abuse of authority and law, and for all his proto-Freudian sense of the pathologies of civilized life, Shakespeare was convinced of the classical and medieval axiom that man is a social and political animal.

98   Marjorie Garber puts the matter well: "More than almost any other Shakespearean hero, he aims at a status that is less like that of a man and more like that of a dragon, a god, or a machine—someone or something, in other words, that does not feel. . . . [T]o be human is to suffer, and that to be aloof from suffering is to turn one's back on humanity, and to be merely a thing, a tin god" (*Shakespeare After All* [New York: Anchor Books, 2005]).

99   So Menenius: "This Volumnia / Is worth of consuls, senators, patricians, / A city full; of tribunes, such as you, / A sea and land full" (5.4.53–55).

100 Eagleton is thus mistaken to say that Coriolanus "is basically no more a Roman than Aufidius is a Volscian" and that he renounces Romanness as soon as it conflicts with his self-definition (*Shakespeare and Society*, 112). Eagleton accurately describes Coriolanus' aim, but his capitulation to Volumnia shows that he cannot achieve it. This is the tragic horror of his self-discovery, that he is intractably Roman after all. Clifford Chalmers Huffman is on the mark in saying that Martius' decision to abandon his revenge "reflects his alliance with traditional values that deny total freedom to man's will" (Huffman, *Coriolanus in Context*, 215).

101 Cavell, *Disowning Knowledge*.

102   Wallace, who has written the most complete essay on political gratitude in Cori-
       olanus, is more pessimistic than Shakespeare about the possibility of a political
       and social order rooted in gratitude. Harold Goddard has it right: The parable
       of Menenius is "the Pauline doctrine that we are all members one of another,"
       and *"Coriolanus* is a poetic demonstration of this truth, and its hero, with all his
       virtues, made, by his own confession, the capital mistake of trying to live 'As if a
       man were author of himself / and knew no other kin.'" Being an individual is thus
       "not enough to be one's self," and Martius' melting before his mother, wife, and
       son means that "for the first time he lets his various 'parts' become members one
       of another and becomes himself something like the complete man he never was
       on the battlefield for all his valor. The dragon reverts to the butterfly" (Goddard,
       The Meaning of Shakespeare, 2 vols. [Chicago: University of Chicago Press, 1951],
       2:233–34).

CHAPTER 6

1   The phrase is from Marin Terpstra, "Social Gifts and the Gift of Sociality: Some
       Thoughts on Mauss' *The Gift* and Hobbes' *Leviathan*," in Vandevelde, *Gifts and
       Interests*, 191–208, 202.
2   On the medieval roots, see Francis Oakley, *The Medieval Experience: Foundations
       of Western Cultural Singularity* (Toronto: University of Toronto Press, 1988);
       Brian Tierney, *The Idea of Natural Rights: Studies of Natural Rights, Natural Law,
       and Church Law 1150–1625* (Grand Rapids: Eerdmans, 1997). Older histories of
       political theory acknowledge the medieval precedents: Otto von Gierke, *Develop-
       ment of Political Theory* (New York: H. Fertig, 1966); Gierke, *Political Theories of
       the Middle Age*, trans. Frederick William Maitland (Cambridge: Cambridge Uni-
       versity Press, 1987); J. N. Figgis, *Political Thought from Gerson to Grotius, 1414–
       1625* (n.c.: Forgotten Books, 2012). Relevant texts are found in Oliver O'Donovan
       and Joan Lockwood O'Donovan, eds., *From Irenaeus to Grotius: A Sourcebook in
       Christian Political Thought* (Grand Rapids: Eerdmans, 1999).
3   Bellarmine, *De laicis*, V. On Bellarmine, see Gary Glenn, "Natural Rights and
       Social Contract in Burke and Bellarmine," in Frohnen and Grasso, *Rethinking
       Rights*, 58–79. I have also been assisted by Glenn's unpublished paper, "In the
       History of Social and Political Contract, Whatever Happened to the Sixteenth
       Century?" presented at a panel of the Society of Catholic Social Sciences, a copy of
       which was provided to me by the author.
4   *De laicis*, VI.
5   Hooker, *Laws of Ecclesiastical Polity*, 1.10.1.
6   Sheldon Wolin, *Politics and Vision*, expanded ed. (Princeton: Princeton University
       Press, 2004), 219. Hobbes did not, however, endorse the experimental scientific
       endeavors of scientists like Boyle, since he thought such laboratory study of par-
       ticulars could never rise to the level of natural *philosophy*. On Hobbes' opposi-
       tion to Boyle, see Steven Shapin, *The Scientific Revolution* (Chicago: University of
       Chicago Press, 1996), 110–11, as well as, far more expansively, Steven Shapin and
       Simon Schaffer, *Leviathan and the Air-Pump: Hobbes, Boyle, and the Experimental
       Life* (Princeton: Princeton University Press, 2011).
7   Leo Strauss, *The Political Philosophy of Hobbes: Its Basis and Its Genesis*, trans. Elsa
       M. Sinclair (Chicago: University of Chicago Press, 1952), 137–38. On the inherent
       "impurity" of scientific endeavor, see Steven Shapin, *Never Pure* (Baltimore, Md.:
       Johns Hopkins University Press, 2010). I leave Shapin's Puritan-style subtitle to
       the reader to discover.
8   Strauss, *Political Philosophy*, 139–41. Strauss argues that Hobbes was flatly wrong
       in his assessment of the two ancient philosophers: "[I]n truth, it is precisely Plato

who originally 'takes refuge' in speech, and Aristotle was in so far only his disciple and successor. . . . Plato, much more than Aristotle, orientates himself by speech" (141).

9   The term is from Keith Thomas, "The Social Origins of Hobbes's Political Thought," in Brown, *Hobbes Studies*, 189. This entire paragraph is indebted to Thomas' article.

10 Thomas, "Social Origins," 199.

11 Quoted in Thomas, "Social Origins," 202–3. Thomas points out that "in the seventeenth century 'generous' retains its original meaning of being well-born, noble, having a good lineage. According to the dictionaries of the period 'generosity' means 'gentlemanlike courage,' or 'noblesse of minde, or of bloud.' It can even be regarded as synonymous with 'gentility,' meaning, 'gentry, nobilitie, gentlemanship'" (204). Laurie Bagby (*Thomas Hobbes: Turning Point for Honor* [Lanham, Md.: Lexington Books, 2009]) is right in saying that Hobbes looks for a source of political obligation other than honor, that he substitutes fear, and that he is uncertain about the virtue of fortitude. In the state of nature, honor runs aground. Still, Hobbes has more of a foot in traditional society than is often suggested.

12 Hobbes, *Elements of Law*, 1.9.21.

13 Hobbes, *Leviathan*, chap. 14.

14 *Leviathan*, chap. 13.

15 This summary is dependent on Strauss, *Political Philosophy*, 13–29.

16 *Leviathan*, chap. 28.

17 *Leviathan*, chap. 14.

18 *Leviathan*, chap. 15.

19 *Leviathan*, chap. 14.

20 The role of gratitude in Hobbes' thought has been strangely neglected. It has become standard procedure to name only the first three of Hobbes' laws of nature (John Hallowell, *Main Currents in Modern Political Thought* [1950; repr., Lanham, Md.: University Press of America, 1984], 75: "there are three principal laws of nature") or to rapidly rattle off the laws of nature and move on to the question of sovereignty, as if the laws of nature no longer played a role in Hobbes' model of civil order. Feminist political theorists have begun to focus attention on gratitude as a political concern; see Nancy J. Hirschmann, "Gordon Schochet on Hobbes, Gratitude, and Women," available online at www.rci.rutgers.edu/~schochet/Hirschmann_Schochet-to-Me.pdf and republished in a revised form in Hirschmann and Joanne H. Wright, eds., *Feminist Interpretations of Thomas Hobbes* (University Park: Penn State University Press, 2013), 125–45. Caleb Goltz and Joan C. Tronto trace this neglect to the influential interpretation of Ferdinand Tonnies, who fits Hobbes into his own paradigm contrasting *Gemeinschaft* (community, traditional society) with *Gesellschaft* (society, individualistic and modern). In Tonnies' view, Hobbes' description of the state of nature fails as a description of "the antagonistic character of this unleashed modern society." Hobbes was wrong to believe that *Gemeinschaft* had disappeared entirely, but otherwise he agreed that Hobbes was a theorist of modern individualistic *Gesellschaft*. For Tonnies, gratitude had its place in family life and in the quasi-kin relations of neighborhoods and small villages, but was absent from the mechanized politics of modernity. On this, see Goltz and Tronto, "Politics and Gratitude: Rediscovering Hobbes's Fourth Law of Nature," an unpublished paper kindly provided to me by Joan Tronto. Tonnies' work has been published in English translation as *Community and Society*, trans. Charles P. Loomis (Mineola, N.Y.: Dover, 2011). The foregoing quotation is from Tonnies, *Hobbes Der Mann und der Denken*, quoted in Goltz and Tronto. For a Tonnies-influenced treatment

of Hobbes, see, for instance, C. B. Macpherson, *The Political Theory of Possessive Individualism* (Oxford: Clarendon, 1962).

21 *Leviathan*, chap. 14.

22 On the assumption that men are naturally unencumbered, equal, and free, "[f]avours no longer produce, and gratitude obligations no longer perpetuate, any relations of recognition. They merely limit the freedom of the will and the scope for personal interest: in short, they call forth illegitimate dependence that is damaging to the subject's self-esteem" (Berking, *Sociology of Giving*, 125).

23 *Leviathan*, chap. 11.

24 *Leviathan*, chap. 15. This is not an isolated comment. In *Elements of Law* (90), Hobbes writes, "It happeneth many times that a man benefitteth or contributeth to the power of another, without any covenant, but only upon confidence and trust of obtaining the grace and favour of that other, whereby he may procure a greater, or no less benefit or assistance to himself. For by necessity of nature every man doth in all his voluntary actions intend some good unto himself. In this case it is a law of nature, *That no man suffer him, that thus trusteth to his charity, or good affection towards him, to be in the worse estate for his trusting.* For if he shall so do, men will not dare to confer mutually to each other's defence, nor put themselves into each other's mercy upon any terms whatsoever; but rather abide the utmost and worst event of hostility; by which generall diffidence, men will not only be enforced to war, but also afraid to come so much within the danger of one another, as to make any overture of peace. But this is to be understood of those only, that confer their benefits (as I have said) upon trust only, and not for triumph or ostentation. For as when they do it upon trust, the end they amed at, namely to be well used, is their reward; so also when they do it for ostentation, they have the reward in themselves. But seeing in this case there passeth no covenant, the breach of this law of nature is not to be called injury; it hath another name (viz.) INGRATITUDE." Later in the same treatise (*Elements of Law*, 100), he offers biblical justification for gratitude: "men ought to be grateful, where no covenant passeth, Deut. 25, 4: *Thou shalt not muzzle the ox that treadeth out the corn*, which St. Paul (I Cor. 9, 9) interpreteth not of oxen, but of men." In *De cive* (3.29), he links gratitude with the second great commandment to love our neighbor as ourselves: "because they who love God cannot but desire to obey the divine Law, ingratiand they who love their Neighbours cannot be desire to obey the morall Law, which consists as hath beene shewed above in the 3. Chapter, in the prohibition of *Pride, ingratitude, contumely, inhumanity, cruelty, injury*, and the like offences, whereby our Neighbours are prejudic't, therefore also *Love* or charity are æquivalent to *Obedience*." See also *De cive*, 3.8 (gratitude as the "third" law of nature); 4.6 (again providing scriptural proof).

25 See chapter 26, where it is listed with equity and justice among the laws of nature, and chapter 42, where gratitude is the motive for the church's support of its ministers.

26 See Hirschmann, "Gordon Schochet on Hobbes," 141–43; also Gordon J. Schochet, "Thomas Hobbes on the Family and the State of Nature," *Political Science Quarterly* 82, no. 3 (1967): 427–45, esp. 444. Hobbes also sees gratitude as a continuing obligation for children even after they are free from their parents' direct authority (*Leviathan*, chap. 30). See in slight contrast Nathan Tarcov, *Locke's Education for Liberty* (Lanham, Md.: Lexington Books, 1999), 38, who rightly says that Hobbes does not base a father's authority "*simply* on gratitude" but fails to see how gratitude functions as a support for a form of consent.

27 David Boonin-Vail, *Thomas Hobbes and the Science of Moral Virtue* (Cambridge: Cambridge University Press, 1994), 185, quoted by Goltz and Tronto, "Politics and Gratitude," 7.

28 Goltz and Tronto, "Politics and Gratitude," 6. "Grease" is their term. They argue that Hobbes overcomes the "dyadic" character of traditional notions of gratitude in favor of a "pay-it-forward" model. On this account, Hobbes is in this respect closer to Paul than Cicero.

29 Norberto Bobbio, *Thomas Hobbes and the Natural Law Tradition*, trans. Daniela Gobetti (Chicago: University of Chicago Press, 1993), 45–46.

30 Bobbio, *Thomas Hobbes*, 46.

31 Mary Dietz writes, "Gratitude is second only to justice in Hobbes's articulation of the code of conduct that is the means toward peace. A grateful citizenry is one where 'benevolence or trust' as well as 'mutuall help' can take root; for if givers enjoy the gratitude of receivers, they will be inclined to proffer assistance again on future occasions . . . [Gratitude] is literally the reward that inclines the giver to keep on giving. Mutuality and reconciliation of one man to another is the result. Hobbes made gratitude a civic virtue because it is the quality that keeps men disposed toward human reciprocity; it is the linchpin that sustains the contract" (Dietz, "Hobbes's Subject as Citizen," in Dietz, *Thomas Hobbes and Political Theory*, 105, quoted in Goltz and Tronto, "Politics and Gratitude," 7–8).

32 Here I follow Howard Warrender, *The Political Philosophy of Hobbes: His Theory of Obligation* (Oxford: Clarendon, 1957). See also the exchange between Warrender and John Plamenatz in Brown, *Hobbes Studies*, 73–100.

33 Warrender, *Political Philosophy*, 236. As Warrender puts it, "[T]he person concerned will be obliged . . . to act in such a way that his protector [the civil sovereign] could not reasonably wish that he had never protected or spared him" (51). More generally, he insists that for Hobbes the laws of nature are not shed off when human beings enter civil society: "These laws of nature are regarded by Hobbes as constituting obligations for man both in the State of nature and civil society" (52).

34 Hobbes, *De cive*, 14.12.

35 Warrender says, "[W]here he is forced to supplement the principle of covenant, all the additional principles employed by him are covered by his account of the laws of nature or the articles of peace." But if this is true, does Hobbes need the civil covenant at all? Warrender argues that the role of the civil covenant is to specify where those obligations are to be expressed: "[R]eason cannot indicate which person or persons we should obey, and the determinate obligation to obey a man or group of men as sovereign requires an agreement to recognize a particular man or group for this office. Thus in virtue of the equality of men, an obligation upon one man to obey the commands of another, always depends upon his covenant" (*Political Philosophy*, 244). Warrender summarizes, "The political covenant, the device whereby the sovereign acquires his power, is essentially a means by which the citizen takes an obligation upon himself to obey the commands of the sovereign. . . . From his general duty to observe natural law and the valid covenants which he makes under its provisions, the individual becomes bound by the civil law to which he is contracted, and the power of the sovereign is primarily the reluctance of his subjects to break natural law." In all covenants, there are for Hobbes two principles involved: "that of keeping a promise and that of gratitude for the consideration involved" (317).

36 Quoted in Helen Thornton, *State of Nature or Eden? Thomas Hobbes and His Contemporaries on the Natural Condition of Human Beings* (Rochester, N.Y.: Boydell & Brewer, 2005), 118.

37 *Leviathan*, chap. 31. See A. P. Martinich, *The Two Gods of Leviathan: Thomas Hobbes on Religion and Politics* (Cambridge: Cambridge University Press, 2003), 95–96.

38 Quoted in John Marshall, *John Locke: Resistance, Religion and Responsibility* (Cambridge: Cambridge University Press, 1994), 159.

39 Keith Wrightson, *English Society: 1580–1680* (New Brunswick, N.J.: Rutgers University Press, 2003), 42.

40 See Christopher Hill, *The World Turned Upside Down: Radical Ideas during the English Revolution* (New York: Penguin, 1991); also Hill, *The Century of Revolution, 1603–1714* (New York: Psychology Press, 2002); Hill, *Puritanism and Revolution* (New York: Random House, 2011).

41 Marshall, *John Locke*, 161–65. In a brilliant essay on "Individuality and Clientage in the Formation of Locke's Social Imagination," John Dunn describes three forms of relation evident in Locke's correspondence: patron-client, familial, and the egalitarian discussion groups of his friends in Oxford and elsewhere. For all his skill, he could not have had the illustrious career he eventually had without "the sustained capacity to display appropriate gratitude" to patrons. Locke distrusted and resented those on whom he was dependent, but his "intellectual imagination" was focused particularly on the problems of social dependence (Dunn, *Rethinking Modern Political Theory: Essays 1979–1983* [Cambridge: Cambridge University Press, 1985], 13–33).

42 Quoted in Marshall, *John Locke*, 164.

43 Quoted in Marshall, *John Locke*, 162.

44 Quoted in Marshall, *John Locke*, 168.

45 See Marshall, *John Locke*, 201–4, for a summary of Pufendorf and his influence on Locke.

46 Quoted in Marshall, *John Locke*, 163.

47 Marshall, *John Locke*, 172.

48 See the summary of Nicole's work and its influence on Locke in Marshall, *John Locke*, 178–89.

49 Locke, *First Tract on Government*, in *Locke: Political Essays*, ed. Mark Goldie (Cambridge Texts in the History of Political Thought; Cambridge: Cambridge University Press, 2006), 7.

50 Locke, *Second Treatise*, 171. The *First* and *Second Treatises* exist in many readily available editions. The citations here refer to standard paragraph numbers.

51 *Second Treatise*, 54. Marshall calls this "an extremely important but shamefully neglected paragraph of the Second Treatise" (*John Locke*, 298).

52 *Second Treatise*, 55.

53 *Second Treatise*, 66.

54 Quoted in Dunn, *Rethinking*, 24. The rest of the passage reads, "A dependent intelligent being is under the power and direction and dominion of him on whom he depends and must for the ends appointed him by that superior being. If man were independent, he could have no law but his own will, no end but himself. He would be a god to himself and the satisfaction of his own will the sole measure and end of all his actions."

55 *Second Treatise*, 66.

56 *Second Treatise*, 69.

57 *Second Treatise*, 70.

58 *Second Treatise*, 77–94.

59 *Second Treatise*, 170.

60 Locke, *First Treatise*, 42.

61 Ivan Kenneally, "Thanksgiving," *New Atlantis*, http://www.thenewatlantis.com/publications/thanksgiving (accessed September 20, 2012) overstates his case: "Locke's interpretation of the human person is remarkably abstract and generally unencumbered by any real dependence on others. . . . In place of natural gregariousness and mutual dependence, Locke substitutes self-interested reason and atomistic independence."

62 Locke, *Essay Concerning Human Understanding*, Introduction.

63   This point was driven home by discussions with my research assistant, Donny Linnemeyer. See also John Dunn's comments earlier.

64   *Second Treatise*, 119.

65   A. John Simmons, *Moral Principles and Political Obligations* (Princeton: Princeton University Press, 1979), 93. Simmons offers a devastating critique of Locke's idea of tacit consent on pages 79–100.

66   The point can be made forcefully by noting the stark contrast between Locke's labored efforts to explain the obligations of second-generation and marginal groups and that offered by Locke's friend, the "Whig" philosopher James Tyrrell, with whom Locke lived for a time when he was writing his two treatises. Sojourners "may well be lookt upon as under an higher Obligation in Conscience and in Gratitude to his Government, than Strangers of another Contry, who onely staying here for a time to pursue their own Occasions and having no Right to the same privileges and advantages of the Commonwealth do onely owe a passive obedience to its laws" (quoted in Melissa A. Butler, "Early Liberal Roots of Feminism: John Locke's Attack on Patriarchy," in *Feminist Interpretations of John Locke*, ed. Nancy J. Hirschmann and Kirstie M. McClure [University Park: Penn State University Press, 2007], 101). Tyrrell, who is close here to Locke's arch-nemesis Robert Filmer, links gratitude with political obligation in a way that Locke never does. The question of gratitude as a basis for political obligation has been revived recently. A. D. M. Walker, "Political Obligation and the Argument from Gratitude," *Philosophy and Public Affairs* 17, no. 3 (1988): 191–211; Walker, "Obligations of Gratitude and Political Obligation," *Philosophy and Public Affairs* 18, no. 4 (1989): 359–64. For crucial views, see George Klosko, "Four Arguments Against Political Obligations from Gratitude," *Public Affairs Quarterly* 5, no. 1 (1991): 33–48, and Simmons, *Moral Principles*, 157–90.

67   With Shaftesbury, Mandeville, Hutcheson, and Hobbes, Locke is on Smith's list of "some late philosophers in England, who have begun to put the science of man on a new footing." Quoted in Ian Simpson Ross, *The Life of Adam Smith* (Oxford: Oxford University Press, 2010).

68   One of the gaps in the foregoing chapters is a consideration of the history of Christian views of usury, which is bound up with views of friendship, gratitude, and gifts. Protestant theologians loosened medieval restrictions on usury, and in the seventeenth century political theories of privatization confined charity loans to the private realm. This was already an achieved reality by the time Smith wrote, an important aspect of the construction of modern economic order. For the history, see Benjamin Nelson, *The Idea of Usury: From Tribal Brotherhood to Universal Otherhood*, 2nd ed. (Chicago: University of Chicago Press, 1969); and Bartolome Clavero, *La Grace du don: Anthropologie catholique de l'economie moderne* (Paris: Albin Michel, 1996). Clavero takes as his starting point a statement from a seventeenth-century treatise on price and usury, "Si le gain n'est pas donne immediatement en raison du pret mais par amitie ou reconnaissance, alors il n'y a pas usure," and describes the terrain of his work as divided into two series of concepts: "gratitude, amitie liberte d'un cote, obligation justice et egalite de l'autre."

69   For discussions of Smith's theory of gratitude, see Vernon L. Smith, "The Two Faces of Adam Smith," *Southern Economic Journal* 65, no. 1 (1998): 1–19; Jon Elster, "Two for One? Reciprocity in Seneca and Adam Smith," *Adam Smith Review* 6 (2012): 152–71; Estrella Trincado, "Adam's Smith's Criticism of the Doctrine of Utility: A Theory of the Creative Present," in Montes, *New Voices on Adam Smith*, 313–27, which ties Smith's ideas on gratitude to his views of time. For a treatment of gratitude and disinterestedness prior to Smith, see Pierre Force, *Self-Interest before Adam Smith: A Genealogy of Economic Science* (Cambridge: Cambridge University Press, 2003).

70   Dunn, *Rethinking*, 196 n. 59. On the Scottish Enlightenment generally, see Gertrude Himmelfarb, *The Roads to Modernity: The British, French, and American Enlightenments* (New York: Knopf, 2004), chaps. 1–2. On Smith and Hume, see Glenn Morrow, "The Significance of the Doctrine of Sympathy in Hume and Adam Smith," *Philosophical Review* 32, no. 1 (1923): 60–78. A few passages from Scottish writers on gratitude illustrate Dunn's point. In *A Treatise on Human Nature* (1739–40, 3.2.5), David Hume argues that it is best to do "but few actions for the advantage of others, from disinterested views" because "we are naturally very limited in our kindness and affection" and "because we cannot depend upon their gratitude." In *An Enquiry Concerning the Principles of Morals* (1751, 3.1), Hume imagines a prelapsarian world in which there would be no need for deed or written contract because everyone would be prompted "by the strongest inclination" to seek everyone else's happiness. Gratitude is among the private duties of "probity or justice," according to Adam Ferguson in his 1786 *Institutes of Moral Philosophy* (5.2). It is a duty particularly incumbent on children. Gratitude, writes Ferguson, is "return made for favours received." Such returns cannot be calculated by any "precise measure," nor are they extracted by force. In fact, what counts is more the "intention of the benefactor" than the value of the benefit received. Ingratitude is offered as an excuse for "neglecting good offices," but that is flimsy: "it is the business of a man to perform his own part, not to answer for the returns which others may, or may not, be disposed to make." All this could have come from Seneca, or Thomas. More broadly, Ferguson raises the problem of dependence early in the treatise in an examination of "disparity and rank" (1.10). For his part, John Millar wrote an entire treatise cataloging his *Observations Concerning the Distinction of Ranks in Society* (1771), in which he argues that gratitude is the source of filial affection.

71   Smith, *Theory of Moral Sentiments*, 1.1.1.
72   *Theory of Moral Sentiments*, 1.2.3.
73   *Theory of Moral Sentiments*, 1.2.5.
74   *Theory of Moral Sentiments*, 1.1.1.
75   *Theory of Moral Sentiments*, 3.2. On this basis, Smith argues that merit and demerit must be defined and explored on the basis of the underlying sentiments of gratitude and its opposite, resentment. Smith defines merit as "deserving reward" and demerit as "deserving punishment," but when he expands on those definitions he does so in terms of sentiments roused by actions: "[T]hat action must appear to deserve reward, which appears to be the proper and approved object of that sentiment, which most immediately and directly prompts us to reward, or to do good to another. And in the same manner, that action must appear to deserve punishment, which appears to be the proper and approved object of that sentiment which most immediately and directly prompts us to punish, or to inflict evil upon another. The sentiment which most immediately and directly prompts us to reward, is gratitude; that which most immediately and directly prompts us to punish, is resentment" (*Theory of Moral Sentiments*, 2.1.1).
76   *Theory of Moral Sentiments*, 2.1.1.
77   *Theory of Moral Sentiments*, 2.1.1.
78   *Theory of Moral Sentiments*, 2.1.1.
79   *Theory of Moral Sentiments*, 2.3.1.
80   *Theory of Moral Sentiments*, 2.3.1.
81   *Theory of Moral Sentiments*, 2.3.1.
82   *Theory of Moral Sentiments*, 2.1.2.
83   *Theory of Moral Sentiments*, 2.1.3.
84   *Theory of Moral Sentiments*, 2.1.4.
85   *Theory of Moral Sentiments*, 2.1.5.

86   Walter Nord, "Adam Smith and Contemporary Social Exchange Theory," *American Journal and Economics and Sociology* 32, no. 4 (1973): 421–36, 429.
87   *Theory of Moral Sentiments*, 2.2.1.
88   *Theory of Moral Sentiments*, 3.4: "A benefactor thinks himself but ill requited, if the person upon whom he has bestowed his good offices, repays them merely from a cold sense of duty, and without any affection to his person. A husband is dissatisfied with the most obedient wife, when he imagines her conduct is animated by no other principle besides her regard to what the relation she stands in requires. Though a son should fail in none of the offices of filial duty, yet if he wants that affectionate reverence which it so well becomes him to feel, the parent may justly complain of his indifference. Nor could a son be quite satisfied with a parent who, though he performed all the duties of his situation, had nothing of that fatherly fondness which might have been expected from him. With regard to all such benevolent and social affections, it is agreeable to see the sense of duty employed rather to restrain than to enliven them, rather to hinder us from doing too much, than to prompt us to do what we ought. It gives us pleasure to see a father obliged to check his own fondness, a friend obliged to set bounds to his natural generosity, a person who has received a benefit, obliged to restrain the too sanguine gratitude of his own temper."
89   On the distinction of gratitude and justice, see Fonna Forman-Barzilai, " 'Smith on Connexion,' Culture, and Judgment," in Montes, *New Voices on Adam Smith*, 101–2.
90   *Theory of Moral Sentiments*, 2.2.1. Some have argued that *Wealth of Nations* is a specific application of Smith's moral theory in the realm of economics. I find much more persuasive Vernon Smith's reconciliation of Smith's "two faces": Smith's insight was to see that "humans are simultaneously other-regarding and self-regarding," and these two aspects are reconciled when we distinguish "between personal and impersonal exchange" (Smith, "Two Faces," 16–17). Where I find Smith suspect is in his acceptance of Adam Smith's claim that "the propensity to truck, barter, and exchange" is universally human.
91   "If your benefactor attended you in your sickness, ought you to attend him in his? or can you fulfill the obligation of gratitude, by making a return of a different kind? If you ought to attend him, how long ought you to attend him? The same time which he attended you, or longer, and how much longer? If your friend lent you money in your distress, ought you to lend him money in his? How much ought you to lend him? When ought you to lend him? Now, or to-morrow, or next month? And for how long a time? It is evident, that no general rule can be laid down, by which a precise answer can, in all cases, be given to any of these questions" (*Theory of Moral Sentiments*, 3.4).
92   *Theory of Moral Sentiments*, 3.4.
93   Smith does allow for a degree of state promotion of benevolence: "The laws of all civilized nations oblige parents to maintain their children, and children to maintain their parents, impose upon men many other duties of beneficence," and it is right for laws to "command mutual good offices to a certain degree" (*Theory of Moral Sentiments*, 2.2.1). See James E. Alvey, "Adam Smith's Higher Vision of Capitalism," *Journal of Economic Issues* 32, no. 2 (1998): 441–48. It is also clear that he believes that a moral life includes both justice and benevolence (see Donald J. Devine, "Adam Smith and the Problem of Justice in Capitalist Society," *Journal of Legal Studies* 6, no. 2 [1977]: 399–409). Yet in his social and economic theory, he keeps them apart, separated into the two realms of public justice and private benevolence.
94   *Theory of Moral Sentiments*, 2.2.3.
95   *Theory of Moral Sentiments*, 2.2.3.

96   *Theory of Moral Sentiments*, 2.2.3.

97   Not surprisingly, as we will see in the next chapter, gratitude becomes the province of novelists of romance and social realism.

98   See David Cheal, *The Gift Economy* (London: Routledge, 1988), who elaborates the obvious fact that gift giving is big capitalist business.

99   See Joseph Anthony Amato, *Guilt and Gratitude: A Study of the Origins of Contemporary Conscience* (Westport, Conn.: Greenwood Press, 1989), passim; Benedict Anderson, *Imagined Communities: Reflections on the Origin and Spread of Nationalism*, 2nd ed. (New York: Verso, 2006). Amato recounts the Soviet and Nazi manipulations of gratitude. On the former, see Brooks, *Thank You, Comrade Stalin!*.

100   Ilana Krausman Ben-Amos has shown that patronage was on the rise in the very century when Locke was attempting to expunge it from the foundation of political order, and also demonstrates that networks of kin and friends were economically and politically significant. Informal networks were increasingly distinguished from the formal institutions of markets and parliaments, especially in the discourse of the time (Ben-Amos, *Culture of Giving*, 9, 70–78). Locke's theory imagined a society that did not exist, and perhaps has never existed.

The fantastic, fabulous character of liberal theory is inherent, I think, in the notion of a prepolitical state of nature. If men once existed in natural conditions and then consented to form a sovereign to overawe them, or ceded rights for the protection of property, they must already have had a common language, which means they must already have formed a community. We acquire a common language by common descent, or education, or interaction with speakers of another language. If natural man did not acquire his common language in that fashion, it is not clear that he was human as we know humans. The fantastic character becomes even more overt in later liberal theory, such as that of Rawls. The most cogent rejoinder to this charge is Augustine's: "Both 'civil' and 'fabulous' theologies are alike fabulous and civil" (Augustine, *De civitate Dei*, 6.9). Liberal theory will flourish only if it acknowledges its mythical basis, and, on good liberal premises, competes with other mythologies to persuade citizens concerning its vision of the good society.

CHAPTER 7

1   Jane Austen, *Pride and Prejudice* (1813; repr., New York: Norton, 1966), Part 3, chap. 2. Gratitude is frequently a stage toward love in Austen's work.

2   Allan Silver, "Friendship and Trust as Moral ideals: An Historical Approach," *European Journal of Sociology* 30, no. 2 (1989): 274–97, 290.

3   Jonathan Parry, "The Gift, the Indian Gift, and the 'Indian Gift,'" *Man* 21, no. 3 (1986): 453–73.

4   See, e.g., Maaja Stewart, "Ingratitude in 'Tom Jones,'" *Journal of English and Germanic Philology* 89, no. 4 (1990): 512–32, and the discussion of gratitude and ingratitude in the novels of Robert Challe and Marivaux in Patrick Coleman, *Anger, Gratitude, and the Enlightenment Writer* (Oxford: Oxford University Press, 2011), chaps. 2–3. Helmuch Berking makes the point very well: "Gratitude is a *modern* feeling, a quite recent mode in the history of civilization which is due to the gradual disencumbrance from obligations to be grateful. . . . [G]ratitude as a feeling and expression of 'pure' appreciation can arise only insofar as obligations to be grateful have been dispelled or transferred to other, partly more effective, modes of social control" (*Sociology of Giving*, 24). Berking acknowledges, of course, that gratitude was expressed in other forms in premodern cultures; but it is isolated as an emotion only under conditions of modernity. Alternatively, gift and gratitude were the province of Romantics, who appealed to earlier pastoral forms

of social order as a countermodel to industrial capitalism. For a careful exploration of gratitude as an emotion, see Visser, *Gift of Thanks*, chaps. 19–21.

5   On the place of the earthquake and other disasters in the development of modern Western thought, see Susan Neiman, *Evil in Modern Thought: An Alternative History of Philosophy* (Princeton: Princeton University Press, 2002), esp. 131–38 on Voltaire.

6   Edmund Burke, *Reflections on the Revolution in France* (New York: Macmillan, 1890), 107–8.

7   Edmund Burke, "Letter to a Noble Lord," available at www.ourcivilisation .com/smartboard/shop/burkee/tolord/index.htm. Burke's nemeses included Thomas Jefferson and Thomas Paine. Jefferson remarked that the dead have no rights since they are nothing, and Paine insisted in *Rights of Man* that he was defending the rights of the living against the attempted usurpations of the dead (quoted in Allain Finkielkraut, *L'Ingratitude: Conversation sur notre temps* [Montreal: Quebec Amerique, 1999], 135). Burke defended the British social order of benefit and reciprocity as well as the conventions of the British constitution. In fact, in his long parliamentary battle concerning the administration of India, Burke attacked Warren Hastings precisely for undermining the zamindars, whom Burke regarded as the Indian equivalent of the English gentry. When gifts were exchanged among Indians on the basis of homage, respect, hereditary connections, relations between "the protector and protected," then there was no moral quandary: "[I]t did not look like a submission to man, but in confirmation to the order of Nature itself." He continued, "When the Lord is identified with the Vassal, with the force of a recognized relation. His dignity is their pride.—His wealth is their opulence.—His entertainments are their Festivals. His funeral rites are the common consolation. His onerous Visits their Hospitality.—His religious rights and pilgrimages their own favourite revered cherishd superstition. On his best favourable aspects wish that he was a father and protector who had a common concern with his people." The Revenue Settlement of 1772, quoted in Harry Liebersohn, *Return of the Gift: European History of a Global Idea* (Cambridge: Cambridge University Press, 2010), 18. Ironically, yet, in his speech on the impeachment of Hasting (1788), Burke castigated the profiteering of Britain's Indian administration: "By the vast sums of money acquired by individuals upon this occasion, by the immense sudden prodigies of fortune, it was discovered that a revolution in Bengal was a mine much more easily worked and infinitely more productive than the mines of Potosi and Mexico. It was found that the work was not only very lucrative, but not at all difficult." Though Burke views the system of benefits and gratitude as a basic reality of social life in both England and India, he attacks the incursion of gift exchange into the British government of India, even though such exchanges were common in Mughal India. Reacting to the Hastings scandal, James Mill made Burke's assumption explicit: "[C]ustom, the custom of a country, where almost everything thing was corrupt, affords but a sorry defense" (quoted in Liebersohn, *Return of the Gift*, 22). A modern distinction between gifts and bribery was imposed on the Indian situation, where it did not really pertain. What the Indians regarded as marks of honor and investiture were construed as commercial transactions. Hastings was eventually acquitted in 1795, but the attacks had their effect: afterward, the British administration kept careful records of the monetary value of all gifts offered.

8   Descartes, *Passions of the Soul*, 64. I am using the translation of Jonathan Bennett, available at http://www.earlymoderntexts.com/pdf/descpass.pdf (accessed October 31, 2012). All citations are to the paragraph numbers in Descartes' treatise.

9   *Passions of the Soul*, 193.

10   *Passions of the Soul*, 194.

11   *Passions of the Soul*, 194.
12   *Passions of the Soul*, 199.
13   *Passions of the Soul*, 195.
14   *Passions of the Soul*, 202.
15   *Passions of the Soul*, 153.
16   *Passions of the Soul*, 203.
17   *Passions of the Soul*, 156.
18   *Passions of the Soul*, 161.
19   See John M. Wallace, "John Dryden's Plays and the Conception of a Heroic Society," in Zagorin, *Culture and Politics from Puritanism to the Enlightenment*, 118.
20   *Passions of the Soul*, 7.
21   *Passions of the Soul*, 17.
22   Jean-Luc Marion states the contrast as follows: Thus, for Augustine, "Self-certainty thus leads self-consciousness back to the inner consciousness of God, which is found to be more essential to consciousness than itself. For the *si fallor, sum* does not aim at the ego, nor does it come to a half in the *res cogitans*, seeing as the interior *intimo meo* transports it, as a derived image, toward the original exemplar. The *si fallor, sum* remains the simply, though first, moment of a path that, in two other more rich moments (knowing one's Being and loving it), disappropriates the mind from itself by the movement of reappropriating it to its original, God. The *si fallor, sum* does not assure the mind of having its principle in itself, since it does not grant it Being in itself nor saying itself by itself (like substance). On the contrary, *si fallor sum* forbids the mind to remain in itself, exiled from its truth, in order to send it back to the infinite original. The mind is retrieved only insofar as it is exceeded." By contrast, Descartes wants to show that "by means of the certainty of Being that thought secures for what from now on becomes an ego" that the I is an immaterial substance: "What is at stake, then, is not found simply in the connection of thought and existence, however certain this connection might be. That the mind thinks, therefore that it is insofar as it thinks—this belongs to an inference that is if not banal . . . at least quite commonplace. What is peculiar to Descartes consists, as he so lucidly indicates, in interpreting the certain and necessary connection of the cogitatio and existence as establishing a substance, and moreover a substance that plays the role of first principle" (Marion, *On Descartes' Metaphysical Prism: The Constitution and Limits of Onto-theo-logy in Cartesian Thought* [Chicago: University of Chicago Press, 1999], 131–32).
23   The term "sublimation" comes from Allan Bloom's introduction to his translation of *Emile*.
24   Rousseau, *Emile, or On Education*, trans. Allan Bloom (New York: Basic Books, 1979), 233.
25   *Emile*, 234.
26   *Emile*, 264.
27   As did Diderot: "Gratitude is a burden, and one would happily shake off any burden" (quoted in Berking, *Sociology of Giving*, 21).
28   All quotations in this paragraph are from Coleman, *Anger, Gratitude, and the Enlightenment Writer*, 155–56. Coleman's chapter 5, "Rousseau's Quarrel with Gratitude," was essential to my summary of Rousseau's views on this issue.
29   Quoted in Ernst Cassirer, *The Question of Jean-Jacques Rousseau*, trans. Peter Gay, 2nd ed. (New Haven, Conn.: Yale University Press, 1989), 42.
30   *The New Heloise*, quoted in Cassirer, *Question*, 43.
31   *First Discourse on the Arts and Sciences*, quoted in Cassirer, *Question*, 45.
32   Samuel von Pufendorf, *On the Duty of Man and Citizen According to the Natural Law*, trans. Michael Silverthorne, ed. James Tully (Cambridge Texts in the History of Political Thought; Cambridge: Cambridge University Press, 1991), 64–65. Like

Locke, Pufendorf emphasizes the role of gratitude in filial relations, and argues
that the debt of grateful honor remains even when a son has grown to adulthood
and is no longer under his father's authority" (125–26).

33 Allan Bloom, introduction to *Emile*, 7.

34 Rousseau's is a misreading, a revealing and significant one. Crusoe plunders the
wrecked ship and acquires all sorts of technical devices that help him survive and
subdue the island.

35 *Emile*, 184–85.

36 Jean-Jacques Rousseau, *A Discourse upon the Origin and the Foundation of the
Inequality among Mankind*, trans. Charles Eliot (New York: Kessington, 2004),
39–40.

37 *On the Origin of Inequality*, 35. Pity plays a central role in Rousseau's educational
program of the sentiments in *Emile* as well.

38 *On the Origin of Inequality*, 49.

39 *On the Origin of Inequality*, 52.

40 *On the Origin of Inequality*.

41 See Cassirer, *Question*.

42 *Emile*, 234.

43 Jean-Jacques Rousseau, *Social Contract* (Harmondsworth: Penguin, 1968), 186.

44 Here I follow the conclusion of Coleman, *Anger, Gratitude, and the Enlightenment Writer*, 168–75.

45 Immanuel Kant, *Lectures on Ethics*, trans. Louis Infield (Indianapolis: Hackett,
1981), 219.

46 *Lectures on Ethics*, 88.

47 Quoted in Helmut Schoeck, *Envy: A Theory of Social Behavior* (Indianapolis: Liberty Press, 1987), 204.

48 I have received much help from Michael Waldstein's "Introduction" to John Paul
II, *Man and Woman He Created Them: A Theology of the Body* (Boston: Pauline,
2006), 45–63. See also the summary of Kant's views in Schoeck, *Envy*, 202–6.

49 Kant's key text on the distinction between natural "ethical" religion and potentially superstitious "ecclesiastical" religion is *Religion within the Bounds of Reason
Alone*, ed. and trans. Allen W. Wood and George Di Giovanni (1793; repr., Cambridge: Cambridge University Press, 1998). It is in essence German Pietism raised
to the level of ethical theory. On Kant, I have been aided by John Caputo, *Philosophy and Theology (Horizons in Theology)* (Nashville: Abingdon, 2006), 30–32.
Caputo explains that Kant's critiques constituted a sort of cartography, a process of
"staking off the boundaries of the various domains of knowledge, ethics, and art,
setting off their limits, and making sure everyone plays in bounds." The goal of
the "rigorous border drawing was to isolate pure and value-free knowledge, a pure
ethical command or imperative that had no content beyond its purely rational-
imperative form, and pure art, devoid of cognitive or ethical content." For Kant,
"God and religion do not have their own island, their own domain or space of play-
ing field; they must build their house of worship on someone else's property." God
does not belong to the sphere of knowledge because knowledge comes through
sciences and God doesn't appear there. Kant doesn't disbelieve in God. Rather,
he posits a God who is "a kind of common and more or less self-evident datum of
human intelligence, liberated from any particularism, any dogmatic or confessional
theology. This is a God and a theology that anyone with a head on his shoulders
could understand, which is basically the God revealed in the order of nature and
the God who supports the moral order."

50 Immanuel Kant, *Groundwork of the Metaphysics of Morals*, trans. Thomas Kingsmill
Abbott (Redford, Va.: A&D Press, 2008), 12.

51   *Groundwork*, 39.
52   Immanuel Kant, *Critique of Practical Reason*, trans. Mary Gregor (Cambridge: Cambridge University Press, 1997), 28.
53   Waldstein, "Introduction," 51 (emphasis added).
54   Immanuel Kant, *Critique of Judgment* (Cambridge: Cambridge University Press, 2000), sec. 84.
55   *Critique of Practical Reason*, 74.
56   Recent research has emphasized the importance of this later work for understanding Kant's treatment of ethics, and of gratitude in particular. See Houston Smit and Mark Timmons, "The Moral Significance of Gratitude in Kant's Ethics," *Southern Journal of Philosophy* 49, no. 4 (2011): 295–320; Patricia White, "Gratitude, Citizenship and Education," *Studies in Philosophy and Education* 18 (1999): 43–52, and the response of Mark E. Jonas, "Gratitude, Ressentiment and Citizenship Education," *Studies in Philosophy and Education* 31, no. 1 (2012): 29–46; Melissa M. Seymour, "Duties of Love and Kant's Doctrine of Obligatory Ends" (Ph.D. diss., Indiana University, 2007), esp. chap. 2. For a negative evaluation of Kant's treatment of gratitude, based on the complaint that he identifies gratitude and reciprocity and so makes it virtually impossible for the needy to show proper gratitude, see Gudrun von Tevenar, "Gratitude, Reciprocity, and Need," *American Philosophical Quarterly* 43, no. 1 (2006): 181–88.
57   Smit and Timmons, "Moral Significance," offer a clear explanation of the distinction.
58   Quoted in Smit and Timmons, "Moral Significance," 298.
59   Seymour, "Duties of Love."
60   This is especially emphasized in Seymour, "Duties of Love."
61   Quoted in Smit and Timmons, "Moral Significance," 303.
62   Quoted in Smit and Timmons, "Moral Significance," 303 n. 17.
63   Quoted in Smit and Timmons, "Moral Significance," 306.
64   Quoted in Smit and Timmons, "Moral Significance," 307.
65   Quoted in Smit and Timmons, "Moral Significance," 308.
66   Smit and Timmons, "Moral Significance," put Kant's point this way: "[W]hat one owes to one's benefactor is something that cannot be fully discharged in the sense of being extinguished—in effect ending any morally significant relationship between benefactor and beneficiary" (308).
67   Quoted in Smit and Timmons, "Moral Significance," 316.
68   Quoted in Smit and Timmons, "Moral Significance," 313.
69   Quoted in Smit and Timmons, "Moral Significance," 313 n. 27.

CHAPTER 8

1   Quoted in Michael Harbsmeier, "Gifts and Discoveries: Gift Exchange in Early Modern Narratives of Exploration and Discovery," in Algazi, Groebner, and Jussen, *Negotiating the Gift*, 406.
2   Quoted in Hyde, *The Gift*, 3.
3   David Graeber, *Debt: The First 5000 Years* (Brooklyn, N.Y.: Melville House, 2011), 108.
4   Franz Boas described the potlatch as follows: "An Indian who invites all his friends and neighbors to a great potlatch, and apparently squanders all the accumulated results of long years of labor, has two things in mind, which we cannot acknowledge as wise and worthy of praise. His first object is to pay his debts. This is done publicly and with much ceremony, as a matter of record. His second object is to invest the fruits of his labour so that the greatest benefit will accrue from them for himself as well as for his children. The recipients of gifts at this festival receive these as loans, which they utilize in their present undertakings, but after the lapse

of several years they must repay them with interest to the giver or to his heir. Thus the potlatch comes to be considered by the Indians as a means of insuring the well-being of their children if they should be left orphans still young. It is, we might say, their life insurance" (Boas, *A Franz Boas Reader: The Shaping of American Anthropology, 1883–1911* [Chicago: University of Chicago Press, 1989], 106).

5   Summary from Liebersohn, *Return of the Gift*, 99–103. As the endnotes indicate, I am heavily reliant on Liebersohn throughout this chapter.

6   Quoted in Liebersohn, *Return of the Gift*, 114.

7   Liebersohn, *Return of the Gift*, 115.

8   Quoted in Liebersohn, *Return of the Gift*, 115–16.

9   Bronislaw Malinowski, "The Primitive Economics of the Trobriand Islanders," *Economic Journal* 31 (1921): 1–16, a selection reprinted in Jerry D. Moore, *Visions of Culture: An Annotated Reader* (Lanham, Md.: Rowman Altamira, 2009), 137–51. On Malinowski's work as a whole, see Liebersohn, *Return of the Gift*, 122–38.

10   Malinowski, *Argonauts of the Western Pacific: An Account of Native Enterprise and Adventure in the Archipelagoes of Melanesian New Guinea* (1922; repr., London: Routledge, 1978), 19, 62–79.

11   Malinowski, *Argonauts*, 176–91.

12   The term is from Parry, "The Gift," 454.

13   Malinowski, *Crime and Custom in Savage Society* (Patterson, N.J.: Littlefield, Adams, 1964), 25.

14   Malinowski, *Crime and Custom*, 40.

15   Malinowski, *Crime and Custom*, 41.

16   Malinowski, *Crime and Custom*, 42.

17   Malinowski, *Crime and Custom*, 47.

18   Malinowski, *Crime and Custom*, 67.

19   Quoted in Liebersohn, *Return of the Gift*, 117.

20   Quoted in Liebersohn, *Return of the Gift*, 134–35.

21   Marcel Mauss, *The Gift: The Form and Reason for Exchange in Archaic Societies*, trans. W. D. Halls (London: Routledge, 1990), 3; cf. 79.

22   Mauss, *The Gift*, 29.

23   Mauss, *The Gift*, 38.

24   Mauss, *The Gift*, 22–23.

25   Drawing on Boas and others, Mauss describes the event: "The word potlatch essentially means 'to feed,' 'to consume.' These tribes, which are very rich, and live on the islands, or on the coast, or in the areas between the Rocky Mountains and the coast, spend the winter in a continual festival of feasts, fairs, and markets, which also constitute the solemn assembly of the tribe. The tribe is organized by hierarchical confraternities and secret societies, the latter often being confused with the former, as with the clans. Everything—clans, marriages, initiations, Shamanist séances and meetings for the worship of the great gods, the totems or the collective or individual ancestors of the clan—is woven into an inextricable network of rites, of total legal and economic services, of assignment to political ranks in the society of men, in the tribe, and in the confederations of tribes, and even internationally. Yet what is noteworthy about these tribes is the principle of rivalry and hostility that prevails in all these practices. They go as far as to fight and kill chiefs and nobles. Moreover, they even go as far as the purely sumptuary destruction of wealth that has accumulated in order to out do the rival chief as well as his associate. . . . It is essentially usurious and sumptuary. It is a struggle between nobles to establish a hierarchy amongst themselves from which their clan will benefit at a later date" (*The Gift*, 6).

26   Mauss, *The Gift*, 39. He finds a similar institution among Pacific islanders near New Guinea: "Another important kind of exchange takes on the form of exhibitions.

Such are the *sagali*, distributions of food on a grand scale, that are made on several occasions: at harvest time, at the building of the chief's hut or the new boats, or at funeral festivals. These distributions are made to groups that have performed some service for the chief of his clan: cultivation of the land, the transporting of the large tree trunks from which boats or beams are carved, and for services rendered at funerals by the members of the dead person's clan, etc. These distributions are absolutely equivalent to the Thingit potlatch. Even the themes of combat and rivalry appear" (30). The obligation to give was one of the important features of all these cultures' gift practices: "To refuse to give, to fail to invite, just as to refuse to accept, is tantamount to declaring war; it is to reject the bond of alliance and commonality. Also one gives because one is compelled to do so, because the recipient possesses some kind of right of property over anything that belongs to the donor. This ownership is expressed and conceived of as a spiritual bond" (13). As many have observed, the obligation to give and invite is evident in the numerous fairy tales and myths of the uninvited fairy or goddess who brings horrors because he or she was excluded. No Trojan War, had Eris been invited to Peleus' wedding.

27 Mauss, *The Gift*, 74.
28 Mauss, *The Gift*, 75. The potlatch "is a competition to see who is the richest and also the most madly extravagant. Everything is based upon the principles of antagonism and rivalry" (37). In the *kula* too, the aim "is to display generosity, freedom, and autonomous action, as well as greatness" (23).
29 Mauss, *The Gift*, 3.
30 Mauss, *The Gift*, 13.
31 Mauss, *The Gift*, 41.
32 Mauss, *The Gift*, 43.
33 Mauss, *The Gift*, 20, 42.
34 See the literature cited and discussed in chapter 4.
35 See the extended discussion of the responses to Mauss in Maurice Godelier, *The Enigma of the Gift* (Chicago: University of Chicago Press, 1999), 10–107.
36 Sahlins, "The Spirit of the Gift," chap. 4 of *Stone Age Economics* (Chicago: Aldine Transaction, 1974), reprinted in Alan D. Schrift, ed., *The Logic of the Gift: Toward an Ethic of Generosity* (New York: Routledge, 1997). The quotation is in Schrift, *Logic of the Gift*, 97.
37 Sahlins in Schrift, *Logic of the Gift*, 83.
38 Sahlins, *Stone Age Economics*, passim. Claude Lévi-Strauss' structuralist anthropology owed much to Mauss' work on gift, but for Lévi-Strauss the notion of a spiritual dimension to the gift was a mystification. The principle of reciprocity exists, but it is not a result of a spiritual force in the thing itself. It is a "general structural principle," and Lévi-Strauss links the pattern of gift and return to the exchanges of women in tribal societies (*Elementary Structures of Kinship* [Boston: Beacon, 1971]).
39 As we have seen earlier, this is a doubtful interpretation of liberalism.
40 Annette B. Weiner, *Inalienable Possessions: The Paradox of Keeping-While Giving* (Berkeley: University of California Press, 1992). Godelier likewise emphasizes the importance of inalienable property, finally linking it to the "sacred" (*Enigma*, passim). James Carrier charges that anthropological studies of "the gift" are an "occidentalization," a projection from Western thinkers; see Carrier, "Occidentalism: The World Turned Upside-Down," *American Ethnologist* 19, no. 2 (1992): 195–212. See also C. A. Gregory, *Gifts and Commodities* (London: Academic Press, 1982), who examines the "giftization" of Western commodities and the "commodification" of gifts in Papua New Guinea. Arjun Appadurai more generally points to the fact that things have a "social life," and cannot be simply and permanently classified as a gift, commodity, possession, tool, adornment, or whatever.

A single thing can be all of these at different moments in its social history (*The Social Life of Things: Commodities in Cultural Perspective* [Cambridge: Cambridge University Press, 1986]). Wrapping, for instance, giftizes a thing, but only in societies where that is an accepted custom.

41   Raymond Firth, *Primitive Polynesian Economy* (New York: Norton, 1965), 353: "There is a scarcity of the means available for satisfying wants, these wants are arranged on a broad scale of preferences, and on the whole choice is exercised in a rational manner in deciding how the means to hand shall be disposed of. The employment of the factors of production is governed by some recognition of the advantages of the division of labour and specialization in employments according to differential skill, and economies of scale are also secured in an elementary way in agriculture, fishing, and other co-operative work. Productive equipment and other goods are accumulated specifically to engage in further production, so that one may speak of the employment of capital. . . . [T]here is a system of property rights which regulate the relations of producers and consumers to resources and to the things produced."

42   Firth, *Primitive Polynesian Economy*, 355–61.

43   Cheal, *Gift Economy*.

44   I allude of course to Karl Polanyi's famous study, *The Great Transformation*, as Cheal, *Gift Economy*, does (5).

45   Cheal, *Gift Economy*, 15.

46   Cheal, *Gift Economy*, 16.

47   Cheal, *Gift Economy*, 19.

48   Pierre Bourdieu, *Algeria 1960: The Disenchantment of the World* (Cambridge: Cambridge University Press, 1979), 22.

49   Pierre Bourdieu, *Outline of a Theory of Practice* (Cambridge: Cambridge University Press, 1977), 60, 95.

50   See Yunxiang Yan, *The Flow of Gifts: Reciprocity and Social Networks in a Chinese Village* (Stanford: Stanford University Press, 1996), 213–14.

51   Bewate Wagner-Hasel, "Egoistic Exchange and Altruistic Gift: On the Roots of Marcel Mauss's Theory of the Gift," in Algazi, Groebner, and Jussen, *Negotiating the Gift*, 144–45. "Altruism" was a coinage of Auguste Comte (1798–1857), an "ism" derived from his motto, *vivre pour altrui*. See Comte, *System of Positive Polity* (London: Longmans, Green, 1875). From another direction, Adam Ferguson, a Scottish heir of Adam Smith and an early ethnologist, found in the primitive tribes of the American Indians some of the signs of older Republican virtue. Members of Indian tribes were selfless savages, and this was nowhere clearer than in their disdain for gifts. Ferguson cited a French explorer who observed "that the nations among whom he traveled to North America, never mentioned acts of generosity or kindness under the notion of duty." Giving ended when the gift was given and after that "the business was finished, and it passed from memory." A recipient of a gift might see it as the beginning of a friendship, or might not: there was no demand attached to the gift (quoted in Liebersohn, *Return of the Gift*, 64). Marx and Engels likewise celebrated the altruistic communism of primitive tribes. All this is but the inverted reflection of liberal order, in which reciprocity has been confined to the market to open space for "linear" gifts.

52   Mauss cites Bucher explicitly in two footnotes: n. 107 to chapter 3 (*The Gift*, 151) and n. 15 to chapter 4 (*The Gift*, 155).

53   Liebersohn, *Return of the Gift*, 48.

54   Liebersohn, *Return of the Gift*, 48.

55   Liebersohn, *Return of the Gift*, 50–51.

56   Quoted in Liebersohn, *Return of the Gift*, 56.

57   In Liebersohn's words, it is "part of the emancipation of the individual from the

personal domination that went along with traditional gift giving and the creation of a private sphere personalized as never before. The gifts for events like engagement and marriage were not a shriveled remainder of the public gifts of old; rather they embodied the emergence of a sphere of personal autonomy. Gaul wrote in a spiritual of a historically informed liberalism that appreciated the traditional importance of the gift, even as it affirmed the changing definition of the gift in modern societies" (Liebersohn, *Return of the Gift*, 56–57).

58   Liebersohn, *Return of the Gift*, 57. For a brief summary of Bucher, and of other participants in this debate, see Wagner-Hasel, "Egoistic Exchange," 156–59. Felix Somlo, for instance, described a *Geschenktausch* (gift exchange) taking place according to "clearly defined legal" rules. Karl von Amira (1848–1930) wrote a two-volume study of *The North Germanic Law of Obligations* (1882–1885), in which he noted that in premodern societies gifts were "marks of favor" that always demanded "a counter-gift." He regarded this as "a legal tenet which would have been definitively confirmed." Richard Meyer's 1898 study of the history of gift giving located the shift from reciprocal to one-sided giving in a shift in the understanding of property. Scholars of Roman law, by contrast, placed emphasis on reciprocity as a legal concept pertaining to contract. Hugo Burckhard claimed that the countergift in a contractual arrangement was the completion of the contract. Wagner-Hasel concludes that "the reciprocal nature of pre-modern gifting . . . can be presumed to have been general knowledge among legal historians, legal anthropologists, economic historians, and economic anthropologists at the beginning of the century" (Wagner-Hasel, "Egoistic Exchange," 159).

59   Patrick Geary puts forth these forceful questions: Are Mauss' constructions of gift "mental constructs derived from the European cultural tradition we seek to illuminate, but projected by the anthropologists onto other cultures? Are we really using the other to understand our own tradition, or are we deceiving ourselves with an 'other' that was really us all along? Does Mauss' sociological method provide us with a new tool for understanding medieval society, or is this tool already imbedded in the cultural tradition we seek to understand?" ("Gift Exchange and Social Science Modeling," in Algazi, Groebner, and Jussen, *Negotiating the Gift*, 129–40, 131).

60   Claude Lévi-Strauss, *Le Totemisme aujourd'hui* (Paris: Presses universitaires de France, 1962), 145, quoted in Robert Wokler, "Perfectible Apes in Decadent Cultures: Rousseau's Anthropology Revisited," *Daedalus* 107, no. 3 (1978): 107. I find Karen Sykes persuasive on this point. Sykes argues that cultural anthropology has not and cannot escape the image of the "noble savage," and that the more it attempts to do so the more ensnarled it becomes in Rousseau's legacy (or, quasi-Rousseau's legacy). See Sykes, *Arguing with Anthropology: An Introduction to Critical Theories of the Gift* (London: Routledge, 2005), chap. 2. On Rousseau's own anthropology, see Asher Horowitz, " 'Laws and Customs Thrust Us Back into Infancy': Rousseau's Historical Anthropology," *Review of Politics* 52, no. 2 (1990): 215–41. Rousseau did engage in reflections on gifts, as detailed in Jean Starobinski, "Don Fastueux et Don Pervers: Commentaire Historique d'une Reverie de Rousseau," *Annales* 41, no. 1 (1986): 7–26.

61   Jacques Godbout has done a fine job of showing the significant differences between state welfare and gift giving in *The World of the Gift*, trans. Donald Winkler (Montreal: McGill-Queen's University Press, 2000).

62   Geary, "Gift Exchange," 137–38.

63   Sahlins in Schrift, *Logic of the Gift*, 88.

64   Sahlins in Schrift, *Logic of the Gift*, 91–92.

65   Sahlins in Schrift, *Logic of the Gift*, 93. Sahlins, like Lévi-Strauss, considers this a mystification, but it is arguably at the center of Mauss' entire project. According to

Christian Arnsperger, Mauss has not actually moved past Hobbes, but still assumes "a quasi-Hobbesian vision of society, a vision of generosity as the sublimation of violence" ("Gift-Giving Practice and Noncontextual Habitus: How (Not) to Be Fooled by Mauss," in Vandevelde, *Gifts and Interests*, 72–75).

66 Again, Mauss was somewhat aware of this. He devoted a number of pages to describing similar gift practices in Roman, German, and Indo-European cultures. See *The Gift*, 47–64. The fact that he calls these "survivals" is a hint of his evolutionary assumptions about cultural development.

67 Yan, *Flow of Gifts*, 219–20.

68 George Simmel, "Faithfulness and Gratitude," in Simmel, *The Sociology of George Simmel*, ed. Kurt H. Wolff (New York: Simon & Schuster, 1950), 380.

69 "Faithfulness and Gratitude," 382. To develop his understanding of faithfulness, Simmel distinguishes between the initiation of a relationship and its continuance or endurance through time. Faithfulness seeks to preserve the relationship through time, when the affections and moods that might have initiated the relationship may have evaporated. Unlike other relational affections, faithfulness in the sense Simmel uses the word (and he recognizes alternative meanings) is not something exchanged between the parties of the relationship; it is rather the attitude that each takes toward the relationship itself. He recognizes that there are other factors that preserve a relationship (the original affections may continue, legal constraints may demand that the relationship continue, social constraints—risk of shame or embarrassment—may be a factor). Faithfulness is specifically the "affective factor" among the other factors that preserve a relationship through time. Simmel suggests that togetherness over time itself leads to the "induction" of the state of faithfulness: "mere habitual togetherness, the mere existence of a relation over a period of time, produces this induction by feeling." On the other hand, he also makes the intriguing point that faithfulness in a relationship might ultimately generate other feelings between the parties in the relationship. The "banal wisdom" that people who marry out of obligation will grow to love one another, he claims, is "quite apt": "[O]nce the existence of the relationship has found its psychological correlate, faithfulness, then faithfulness is followed, eventually, also by the feelings, affective interests, and inner bonds that properly belong to the relationship. Only, instead of appearing at the beginning, as we should 'logically' expect, they reveal themselves as its end product." Simmel sees faithfulness as a unique sociological/psychological phenomenon that incorporates the stability of external social reality into the soul. He sets up this point by distinguishing between the fluctuations of the soul and the "constantly developing life-process" and, on the other hand, the stable forms of social life. The two do not move in tandem. (Simmel describes this dualism as "tragic.") Law is by nature stable and relatively inflexible (which it must be to do what it needs to do in society), and thus cannot keep pace with the shifts and changes of actual human life. Faithfulness, however, is a bridge between these two features of society: it "has the significance that, by virtue of it, for once the personal, fluctuating inner life actually adopts the character of a fixed, stable form of relation. Or vice versa: this sociological fixity, which remains outside life's immediacy and subjective rhythm, here actually becomes the content of subjective, emotionally determined life. Irrespective of the innumerable modifications, deflections, intermixtures of concrete destinies, faithfulness bridges and reconciles that deep and essential dualism which splits off the life-form of individual internality from the life-form of sociation that is nevertheless borne by it. Faithfulness is that constitution of the soul . . . by means of which it fully incorporates into itself the stability of the super-individual form of relation and by means of which it admits to life, as the meaning and value of life, a content which, though created by the soul itself, is, in its form, nevertheless bound to contradict the rhythm or un-rhythm of life as actually lived" (382–87).

70   "Faithfulness and Gratitude," 387. As we have seen throughout this book, this is questionable, and a specifically post-Enlightenment assumption. I, for one, feel grateful to the mechanics who fix my car, despite the fact that I have also paid for the service. Simmel's gratitude-free exchange seems to rest on a distorted view of capitalist exchanges, in which, he claims "personal interaction recedes altogether into the background, while goods gain a life of their own." This may be true, and money may tempt us to ignore the personal context. But I am loyal to and grateful to my regular mechanic, not to mention the guy who keeps fixing my well pump.

71   "Faithfulness and Gratitude," 388.

72   "Faithfulness and Gratitude," 388.

73   "Faithfulness and Gratitude," 389.

74   "Faithfulness and Gratitude," 389n3.

75   "Faithfulness and Gratitude," 391.

76   Based on the findings of cultural anthropologists and historians, this too is questionable.

77   "Faithfulness and Gratitude," 393.

78   Groebner, *Liquid Assets, Dangerous Gifts*, 157. Similar criticisms have come from cultural theorists who complain that Mauss "essentializes" the gift and who emphasize that gifts have to be designated as such by various verbal and gestural cues. What is important is not the gift but the process of gifting and the strategies by which a thing is transmuted into a present. True as this is, it does seem that things become gifts in particular cultures through processes whose meanings are widely shared.

CHAPTER 9

1   See Paul F. Camenisch, "Gift and Gratitude in Ethics," *Journal of Religious Ethics* 9, no. 1 (1981): 1–34; Christopher Heath Wellman, "Gratitude as a Virtue," *Pacific Philosophical Quarterly* 80 (1999): 284–300; A. D. M. Walker, "Gratefulness and Gratitude," *Proceedings of the Aristotelian Society* n.s. 81 (1980–81): 39–55; Tevenar, "Gratitude, Reciprocity, and Need"; Fred R. Berger, "Gratitude," *Ethics* 85, no. 4 (1975): 298–309; Patrick Fitzgerald, "Gratitude and Justice," *Ethics* 109, no. 1 (1998): 119–53; Nancy S. Jecker, "Are Filial Duties Unfounded?" *American Philosophical Quarterly* 26, no. 1 (1989): 73–80; Claudia Card, "Gratitude and Obligation," *American Philosophical Quarterly* 25, no. 2 (1988): 115–27; Joseph Lombardi, "Filial Gratitude and God's Right to Command," *Journal of Religious Ethics* 19, no. 1 (1991): 93–118. Lawrence C. Becker's *Reciprocity* (Chicago: University of Chicago Press, 1990) has broader aims, but includes illuminating discussions of gratitude.

2   Terrance McConnell, *Gratitude* (Philadelphia: Temple University Press, 1993).

3   McConnell, *Gratitude*, 44–45. It should be noted that McConnell carefully examines the concepts of "voluntariness" and "intention."

4   McConnell, *Gratitude*, 56.

5   McConnell, *Gratitude*, 112.

6   McConnell, *Gratitude*, 114–47.

7   He concludes (*Gratitude*, 222) that gratitude is an inadequate basis for filial obligation.

8   Søren Kierkegaard, *18 Upbuilding Discourses* (Princeton: Princeton University Press, 1990), 94. See Rick Anthony Furtak, *Wisdom in Love: Kierkegaard and the Ancient Quest for Emotional Integrity* (Notre Dame, Ind.: University of Notre Dame Press, 2005), esp. 111–18.

9   Søren Kierkegaard, *Fear and Trembling* (Cambridge: Cambridge University Press, 2006), 12.

10   Journal entry, quoted in Furtak, *Wisdom in Love*, 116.

11   See John Llewelyn, *Margins of Religion: Between Kierkegaard and Derrida* (Bloomington: Indiana University Press, 2009), 341. Llewelyn leaves Kierkegaard far behind when he says that what interests him is "the gratitude that is not necessarily addressed to anybody one could thank, least of all a deity" (343). For Kierkegaard, such gratitude would be whistling toward the abyss. For him, gratitude is an either/or, a "God or nothing" proposition.

12   Kierkegaard, *18 Upbuilding Discourses*, 43.

13   Kierkegaard, *18 Upbuilding Discourses*, 121.

14   Friedrich Nietzsche, *Human, All Too Human*, trans. Helen Zimmern and Paul V. Conn, in *The Complete Work of Friedrich Nietzsche*, ed. Oscar Levy (Edinburgh: T.N. Foulis, 1909), 64. I have been helped throughout this section by Jonas, "Gratitude, Ressentiment." See also Laurence Lampert, *Nietzsche and Modern Times: A Study of Bacon, Descartes, and Nietzsche* (New Haven, Conn.: Yale University Press, 1993), esp. 376–87.

15   Friedrich Nietzsche, *Nietzsche contra Wagner*, trans. Thomas Common (London: H. Henry, 1896), 58.

16   Friedrich Nietzsche, *Beyond Good and Evil*, in *Basic Writings of Nietzsche*, trans. and ed. Walter Kaufmann (New York: Random House, 2000), sec. 49.

17   *Beyond Good and Evil*, sec. 260.

18   Friedrich Nietzsche, *The AntiChrist*, trans. H. L. Mencken (n.c.: The Floating Press, 2010), chap. 16.

19   Friedrich Nietzsche, *Case of Wagner*, in *Basic Writings of Nietzsche*, trans. and ed. Walter Kaufmann (New York: Random House, 2000), 646.

20   Friedrich Nietzsche, *Genealogy of Morals*, in *Basic Writings of Nietzsche*, trans. and ed. Walter Kaufmann (New York: Random House, 2000), 1.10.

21   Caputo, *Prayers and Tears*, 186.

22   Richard Polt, *Heidegger: An Introduction* (Ithaca, N.Y.: Cornell University Press, 1999), 116.

23   In what follows, I am deeply indebted to the deft outline of Heidegger's thought in Michael Inwood, *Heidegger: A Very Short Introduction* (Oxford: Oxford University Press, 2002).

24   Robert Solomon, *Continental Philosophy Since 1750: The Rise and Fall of the Self* (Oxford: Oxford University Press, 1988), 175–76.

25   Inwood, *Heidegger*, poses Heidegger's question this way: "Is the knower a pure subject wholly absorbed in the disinterested, theoretical knowledge of its subject-matter, or is it an interested human being, situated in a particular place and a particular time?" (13).

26   As Inwood, *Heidegger*, says, "Knowing is only one relation among many that we may take up to the things of the world; it is not the first relation we adopt towards them, it is taken up fairly late in one's career, and then only sporadically; nor is it the most obvious attitude to take towards, say, one's spouse or the key to one's own front door." Epistemology tends "to speak as if knowing were a uniform thing, as if electrons were known in the same way as historical events. Or if we notice that this is not so we are tempted, like Descartes, to propose an ideal form of knowledge which will guarantee unerring results about, say, the dimensions and movements of material particles. But this will not do for, say, historical events, which are thereby excluded from the realm of knowable objects" (13).

27   According to Inwood, *Heidegger*, modern knowers often operate with scientific classifications: "How do we come to divide up the world of entities in this way? The world does not naturally present itself to us carved up in readiness for the sciences. When two lovers walk hand in hand across a meadow under a starry sky, they do not see themselves and their surroundings as objects separated out for the geologist, the botanist, the meteorologist, even if they are themselves, say, geologists in their professional lives" (14).

28 Inwood, *Heidegger*, 19.

29 Inwood, *Heidegger*, 45.

30 Heidegger's conception of truth runs in the same direction. Characteristically basing his argument on an etymology (the Greek α-λήθεια), Heidegger concludes that truth is "disclosure" rather than correspondence. Truth as correspondence is not, he thinks, even coherent. If truth is correspondence, then an assertion is true if it corresponds to the facts of the case. Heidegger raises questions about both the assertion and the fact to which the assertion corresponds. For the correspondence theory to work, we have to establish the independence of the assertion from the facts. If it is not independent, then we do not actually have two entities—assertion and fact—that should correspond to one another. In many cases, the assertion is not independent of the facts: I assert that a hammer is too heavy because I need a different tool in the particular task I'm involved in. Asserting something about the hammer is not an assertion about an "idea of a hammer." Another possibility is that "words have meanings independent of the things they apply to and refer to, so that we can say that what corresponds to a fact is a meaningful sentence or a proposition? No. A word such as 'hammer' or 'culture' does not have a single determinate meaning or connotation; its meaning depends on, and varies with, the world in which it is used." Heidegger concludes, in Inwood's words, that there is "no pre-packaged portion of meaning sufficiently independent of the world and of entities within it to correspond, or fail to correspond, to the world. Words and their meanings are already world-laden." And what of the fact? For the correspondence theory to work, Heidegger says, we have to have an assertion-free access to the object to which we can compare the assertion. But Heidegger doesn't believe we ever have such access. Heidegger argues that our sensations are always sensations *as*: We hear the sounds as words, even if we don't know the language that is spoken. We never hear "mere noise," but the birds singing, or someone hammering in the distance, or an assertion that we recognize as language even if we don't understand the language being spoken. Lacking world-free assertions and language-free access to the facts, the correspondence theory cannot work. Once again, Heidegger emphasizes the embeddedness, the fact that we are always already in the world.

31 Polt, *Heidegger*, 119. Other discussions of this theme in Heidegger include Paul Gibbs, *Heidegger's Contribution to the Understanding of Work Based Studies* (New York: Springer, 2011), 135–38. I have been unable to obtain a copy of what to my knowledge is the only book-length study of this theme, Samuel IJsseling, *Heidegger: Denken et Danken, Geven en Zijn* (Antwerp: De Nederlandsche Boekhandel, 1964). The turn is in part a turn to the mystical, to Eckhardt in particular, on which see John D. Caputo, *The Mystical Element in Heidegger's Thought* (New York: Fordham University Press, 1986), 189–202.

32 Polt, *Heidegger*, 121.

33 Polt, *Heidegger*, 143. I am indebted to Polt's superb unraveling of this dense statement (143–48). The translation offered earlier is Polt's, and departs from the common English translation of Ereignis by "event."

34 Polt, *Heidegger*, 146.

35 Polt, *Heidegger*, 148.

36 Robyn Horner, *Rethinking God as Gift: Marion, Derrida, and the Limits of Phenomenology* (New York: Fordham University Press, 2001), 35.

37 This is how Roger Lundin takes Heidegger's comment: Heidegger, he says, "was fond of the seventeenth-century Pietist phrase *Denken ist Danken*, 'to think is to thank.'" Lundin expounds the point a few pages later: "Through our participation in communities of language, we *receive* our very ability to comprehend anything at all. . . . [W]ithout the gift of language—and without the traditions of practice, interpretation, and belief that are embedded in language—the isolated self would

be at a loss as to how to comprehend, let along respond to, its world" (Lundin, *The Culture of Interpretation* [Grand Rapids: Eerdmans, 1993], 132). See also William Richardson's lucid summary: "Once we see that the original German word for thought (*Gedanc*) suggests re-cord, it is not difficult to understand in what sense it also implies thanks-giving (*Danken*). Being's supreme gift to the thinker is the very Being by which he *is* a thinker: ek-sistance. Does it not warrant acknowledge-ment on man's part? Such an acknowledgement in its purity, however, is not in the first place a requiting of this gift with another gift. On the contrary, the purest form of acknowledge is simply the acceptance of the gift, sc. Assuming it, acqui-escing in it, yielding to its demands. Acceptance, then, is the most original form of thanks. Now when There-being accepts the endowment by which the thinking comes about, sc. ek-sistance, it accepts the gift of thought as such. For There-being to accept thought as thought is to do what lies within its power to accomplish thought. This is by that very fact the fulfillment of thinking. Thinking thus con-ceived in the moment of fulfillment is clearly thanks-giving" (Richardson, *Hei-degger: Through Phenomenology to Thought* [The Hague: Martinus Nijhoff, 1963], 601).

38 Hans-Georg Gadamer, *Truth and Method* (New York: Seabury Press, 1975), 444. For a careful examination of Gadamer's work, see Joel Weinsheimer, *Gadamer's Hermeneutics: A Reading of Truth and Method* (New Haven, Conn.: Yale Univer-sity Press, 1988).

39 I am using the translation of J. Glenn Gray, *What Is Called Thinking?* (San Fran-cisco: HarperCollins, 1976).

40 Heidegger, *What Is Called Thinking?* 3.

41 Heidegger, *What Is Called Thinking?* 138.

42 Heidegger, *What Is Called Thinking?* 142.

43 Heidegger, *What Is Called Thinking?* 140–41.

44 Heidegger, *What Is Called Thinking?* 4–10.

45 Heidegger, *What Is Called Thinking?* 41–44.

46 Heidegger, *What Is Called Thinking?* 141.

47 Heidegger, *What Is Called Thinking?* 144.

48 Heidegger, *What Is Called Thinking?* 142–43.

49 Heidegger, *What Is Called Thinking?* 146.

50 Steiner, *Martin Heidegger* (Chicago: University of Chicago Press, 1978), 131.

51 In his essay on the work of art, Heidegger argues that Van Gogh's painting of shoes brings the shoes into the truth of Being beyond what was true of the actual shoes. The shoes would have worn out, lost their use, and been discarded. By bringing the shoes into a work of art, Van Gogh captures what is most true about them. See Steiner, *Heidegger*, 132–34.

52 Steiner, *Heidegger*, 137–39.

53 Steiner, *Heidegger*, 139–40.

54 Heidegger, *What Is Called Thinking?* 146.

55 Rebecca Comay, "Gifts without Presents: Economies of 'Experience in Bataille and Heidegger," *Yale French Studies* 78 (1990): 89.

CHAPTER 10

1 See, for instance, the different projects of Jean Baudrillard and Georges Bataille. The former sees in Mauss the destruction of all modern linearity—of exchange, time, production, life. In the revived circle of post-Maussian civilization, the form that dominates is "extermination and death," the virtuality and "hyperreal" that follows when the modern law of value is "swamped by indeterminacy" (Baudril-lard, *Symbolic Exchange and Death*, trans. Iain Hamilton Grant [London: SAGE,

1993], 2–3). Bataille reads the history of Western economy in light of the sublime of the potlatch, luxury, excessive expenditure, which is the name of the sacred (Bataille, *The Accursed Share, Volume 1*, trans. Robert Hurley [New York: Urzone, 1989]).

2   Jacques Derrida, *Given Time, I: Counterfeit Money* (Chicago: University of Chicago Press, 1992), 24. One of the best expositions of Derrida's treatment of the gift is Caputo, *Prayers and Tears*, chap. 4. See also Horner, *Rethinking God as Gift*, chaps. 7–8.

3   Derrida, *Given Time*, 25.

4   Derrida, *Given Time*, 7.

5   Derrida, *Given Time*, 7. Milbank argues that this is completely a concession to the modern and capitalist "reduction of exchange to contract." He observes that "exchanges are not necessarily economic, and not necessarily of a legally formalized kind, acknowledging only contractual encounters. Nevertheless, exchange has been reduced to the economic and legally formalized in our capitalist society." This is an overstatement, but the point remains that Derrida has universalized what is a contingent development in Western history. Milbank suggests that what distinguishes gift and economic exchange is not the "absolute freedom and non-binding character of the gift" but instead "the surprisingness and unpredictability of gift and counter-gift, or their character in space as asymmetrical reciprocity, and their character in time as non-identical repetition" (*Being Reconciled: Ontology and Pardon* [London: Routledge, 2003] 156).

6   Derrida, *Given Time*, 13.

7   Derrida, *Given Time*, 13–14.

8   Derrida, *Given Time*, 14.

9   Derrida, *Given Time*, 23.

10 Derrida, *Given Time*, 16.

11 Derrida, *Given Time*, 17.

12 Derrida, *Given Time*, 24.

13 Derrida, *Given Time*, 27.

14 David Hart comments, "The ontological import of this line of reflection is that in the end the only gift is the radical nongift of time, the present moment, that is nothing at all but the nihilating passage of time from future to past, the dissolution of being in its manifestation of temporality: the gift is the *es gibt* of being, or the empty yielding of the *chora*, the effect of nothing, the pure giving of nothing (the present) to no one, whose delay is endlessly deferred toward that difference— that reciprocation of the gift—that can never be given, never owned, never desired. The gift is no gift: the present that is not (a) present" (*The Beauty of the Infinite: The Aesthetics of Christian Truth* [Grand Rapids: Eerdmans, 2004], 261).

15 Quoted in Caputo, *Prayers and Tears*, 165.

16 Caputo, *Prayers and Tears*, 166.

17 Caputo, *Prayers and Tears*, 167.

18 Caputo, *Prayers and Tears*, 169.

19 Derrida, "At This Very Moment in This Work Here I Am," in *Re-reading Levinas*, ed. Robert Bernasconi, trans. Ruben Berezdivin (London: Athlone, 1991), 11–49. Hans Boersma describes Levinas' project as follows: "The Western philosophical tradition, says Levinas, has had a penchant for ontological categories. The preoccupation with questions of being (ontology) has led to a tendency to understand, to grasp, and to master the exterior world. Western culture is built on attempts to analyze, scrutinize, dissect, explore, and utilize. As a result Western philosophy has encouraged a tendency toward violence. The imposition of rational categories on the exterior world has undermined all that is different or other than one's self. The alterity (otherness) of everything in the outside world gets suppressed. Our

attempts to remake the world in our own image imply an inability to accept the other as other. The philosophical tradition is focused on sameness and totality: in a totalizing fashion, we have shaped everything that we see into our own image. Sameness (le Meme) rather than alterity, totality rather than infinity, being rather than ethics lies as the basis of our modern society: 'The ontological event accomplished by philosophy consists in suppressing or transmuting the alterity of all that is Other, in universalizing the immanence of the Same (le Meme) or of Freedom in effacing the boundaries, and in expelling the violence of Being (Etre)'" (*Violence, Hospitality, and the Cross: Reappropriating the Atonement Tradition* [Grand Rapids: Baker, 2006], 28). The most flamboyant assault on Levinas is in Hart, *Beauty of the Infinite*, 79–92. According to James K. A. Smith (*Jacques Derrida: Live Theory* [London: Continuum, 2005]), Derrida's entire project can be understood in Levinasian terms: Derrida is all about introducing the other. Hellenistic philosophy must be introduced to Hebraic prophecy; philosophy to its other, literature. Deconstruction, he suggests, is "vigilance for the other," and is a "calling, a vocation, which undertakes an intense investigation of texts, structures and institutions in order to enable them to respond to the call of the other." Specifically, Derrida's notion of justice and his ethics are shaped by his insistence on alterity. Levinas' entire work, he argues, is about hospitality, and for Derrida "justice is hospitality." Derrida goes further, and suggests that metaphysics itself is hospitality, unlimited openness to the Other. For Derrida, this hospitality that is ethics, justice, and metaphysics is "infinite or it is not at all." Infinite welcome means unconditional welcome. Derrida gives a particular biblical spin to this notion. He asks whether the responsibility to welcome the stranger, which he takes as the sum of the Torah, depends on the specific revelation at Sinai, or whether there is "recognition of the Torah by peoples or the nations for whom the name, the place, the event Sinai would mean nothing." He follows Levinas in saying that there is a demand for hospitality that is prior to all revelation: "Levinas orients his interpretation toward the equivalence of three concepts—fraternity, humanity, hospitality—that determine an experience of the Torah and of the messianic times even before or outside of the Sinai, and even for the one who makes no claim 'to the title of bearer or messenger of the Torah.'" This universal and unconditional demand for hospitality becomes what Derrida calls a "structural or a prior messianicity," and this obligation is an election of the whole human race to welcome every other (13–15).

20   Miriam Bankovsky, "A Thread of Knots: Jacques Derrida's Homage to Emmanuel Levinas' Ethical Reminder," *Invisible Culture: An Electronic Journal for Visual Studies* 8 (2004): 1–19, http://www.rochester.edu/in_visible _culture/Issue_8/bankovsky.html (accessed February 26, 2013).

21   Derrida, "At This Very Moment," 12–13.

22   Bankovsky, "Thread of Knots."

23   Derrida, "At This Very Moment," 15.

24   Derrida, *Given Time*, 100.

25   Derrida, *Given Time*, 91.

26   David Hart points out that Derrida's whole argument is guided by "the altogether doctrinaire premise that goes unexamined in such reflections"—namely, "that purity of intention is what assures the gratuity of the gift, and that purity is assured by complete disinherit, defying recognition and reciprocation alike." He wonders if Derrida has "uncritically succumbed to a Kantian . . . rigorism that requires an absolute distinction of duty from desire," but suggests that if Kant is not lurking nearby it is difficulty to explain why "the thought of the gift [must] be confined to so narrow a moral definition of gratuity or selflessness, purged of desire." More fundamentally, Hart discerns in Derrida's stress on the intention of gift a notion of "the priority of a subjectivity that possesses a moral identity prior to the complex

exchanges of moral practices, of gift and gratitude." Such a self above and beyond the constituting relations of giving and reception looks a lot like the Cartesian or Idealist self that Derrida is supposed to have renounced. Finally, he wonders whether a selflessness devoid of desire is so far from hate: "Would there not be something demonic in a love without enchantment, without a desire for the other, a longing to dwell with and be recognized by the other?" (*Beauty of the Infinite*, 262).

27 Bankovsky, "Thread of Knots."
28 Derrida, *Given Time*, 30–31.
29 Derrida, *The Gift of Death*, trans. David Wills (Chicago: University of Chicago Press, 1995). On this see not only Caputo but also Smith, *Jacques Derrida*, 80–84.
30 Kierkegaard, *Fear and Trembling*.
31 Derrida, *Gift of Death*, 78.
32 Derrida, *Gift of Death*, 95.
33 See Caputo, *Prayers and Tears*, 215–17.
34 For a thorough airing of the issues, see Robyn Horner, *Jean-Luc Marion: A Theological Introduction* (Aldershot: Ashgate, 2005).
35 See Thomas A. Carlson, "Introduction" to Jean-Luc Marion, *The Idol and the Distance: Five Studies* (New York: Fordham University Press, 2001), xii.
36 Bruce Ellis Benson, *Graven Ideologies: Nietzsche, Derrida, and Marion on Modern Idolatry* (Downers Grove, Ill.: InterVarsity, 2002), 170.
37 Husserl, *The Paris Lectures*, trans. P. Koestenbaum (The Hague: Martinus Nijhoff, 1975), 8.
38 Quoted in Dominique Janicaud, *Phenomenology and the Theological Turn: The French Debate* (New York: Fordham University Press, 2000), 9.
39 Jean-Luc Marion, *Being Given: Toward a Phenomenology of Givenness* (Stanford, Calif.: Stanford University Press, 2002), 17.
40 This is Marion's rendition of Husserl, in *Being Given*, 31. It is from Husserl, *Ideas: General Introduction to Pure Phenomenology* (London: Routledge, 2012), 95.
41 Marion, *Being Given*, 31–32.
42 Marion, *Being Given*, 37.
43 Marion, *Being Given*, 42–46.
44 Marion, *Being Given*, 51–52. Or, "The painting is not visible; it makes visible. It makes visible in a gesture that remains by definition invisible—the effect, the upsurge, the advance of givenness" (52).
45 Marion, *Being Given*, 50.
46 Marion, *Being Given*, 7.
47 Marion, *Being Given*, 113–14.
48 Marion, *Being Given*, 84.
49 Risto Saarinen's *God and the Gift: An Ecumenical Theology of Giving* (Collegeville, Minn.: Liturgical Press, 2005) has been particularly useful in the following paragraphs. Marion says, "[I]n order to appear, a phenomenon must be able to give itself." Safe as this may sound, Marion has something more risky, even violent, in mind. Among the "Determinations" of givenness is the facticity of the given, which "does not consist in my being reducible to the factuality of a fact, but in exposing me to the fact, which can thus be accomplished only by weighing on me, no longer as a detached observed but as an engaged actor—or better, a critical patient into whom the fact has crashed in being visibly accomplished" (*Being Given*, 146). Phenomena bang into us, explode into our consciousness. Marion knows as well as Derrida that in French *donner* is used with *coup* as well as with *don*.
50 Practically, this is little different from Derrida's position.
51 Saarinen summarizes, "[Y]ou can describe a gift without a receiver, as in giving to

an enemy or in giving anonymously to a humanitarian association. It is also possible to describe a gift without a giver, as in the case of inheritance. There is even the possibility of gift without any giver, as in the case of Robinson Crusoe who finds a tool on the sand. The tool might not be given at all, but is just luckily lying there. And a gift can be something wholly immaterial, like giving time or giving power. For Marion, these descriptions are symptomatic of the primordial givenness of the world" (*God and the Gift*, 30).

52 The following summarizes some portions of Marion, "Sketch of a Phenomenological Concept of Gift," published in Westphal, *Postmodern Philosophy and Christian Thought*, 122–43. See also Marion, *In Excess: Studies of Saturated Phenomena* (New York: Fordham University Press, 2001), 1–29.

53 Marion, "Sketch," 132.

54 Marion, "Sketch," 133.

55 Marion, "Sketch," 133.

56 Marion, "Sketch," 139.

57 This important point is emphasized by Arnsperger, "Gift-Giving Practice," 89.

58 Marion, *Being Given*, 108.

59 Marion writes, "If . . . the economy of the gift only makes economy of the gift, the gift only becomes itself by breaking away from the economy, in order to let itself be thought through along the lines of givenness. Therefore, one must reconduct the gift away from economy and toward givenness. To reconduct is to reduce. How can we reduce the gift to givenness without falling either into tautology (Isn't the gift equivalent to givenness?) or into contradiction (Doesn't givenness necessarily imply some transcendence?). But if we must have reduction, it could only occur, even in the case of an eventual reduction to givenness, in the manner in which reduction always operates in phenomenology: by bracketing of all transcendence, whatever it might be. Reducing the gift to givenness thus signifies: thinking the gift as gift, making abstraction of the triple transcendence which affected it until now—by the bracketing of the transcendence of the giver, the transcendence of the recipient, and the transcendence of the objectivity of the object exchanged. If the epokke happens to exert itself upon the gift, it will exert itself in liberating the gift that the terms and status of object, all transcendent, of economic exchange. Thus, it will reconduct the gift to pure and simple givenness, if, at least, such a givenness may occur" (*Being Given*, 84).

60 Merold Westphal describes onto-theology this way: "Theology becomes onto-theology when Jerusalem sells its soul to Athens by buying in on the latter's project. Within Christian history, the critique of onto-theology belongs to a tradition of dehellenizing repristination. Heidegger explicitly links his critique with Luther, and thus, by implication, with a tradition that looks back to Augustine and ahead to Pascal, Kierkegaard, and Barth. He seems to confirm Jerusalem's declaration of independence from Athens when he writes, 'On the grounds of its specific positive character and the form of knowing which this determines, we can now say that theology is a fully autonomous ontic science' " ("Overcoming Onto-Theology," in John Caputo, ed., *God, the Gift and Postmodernism* [Bloomington: Indiana University Press, 1999], 157).

61 Jean-Luc Marion, *God Without Being: Hors-Texte* (Chicago: University of Chicago Press, 1995), 41.

62 Marion, *God Without Being*, 43. These two sorts of idolatry, Benson argues, are not all that different, because "it is difficult to see how, once we place God under the category of Being, God does not become 'a' being." Marion thus aspires to "think God outside of metaphysics" and "to think God without any conditions" (*Graven Ideologies*, 195).

63 Marion, *God Without Being*, xix.

64   Marion traces the rise of onto-theology, controversially, to Thomas, arguing that
      Thomas privileges ens as a description of God because of his convictions about the
      primacy of ens in human perception: "[I]f theology proceeds by the apprehension
      of concepts, as a 'science,' then for it also, the ens will be the first, and man's point
      of view normative. . . . If theology wills itself to be THEOlogical, it will submit
      all its concepts, without exception the ens, to a 'destruction' by the doctrine of
      the divine names, at the risk of having to renounce any status as a conceptual 'sci-
      ence,' in order, decidedly nonobjectivating, to praise by infinite petitions." This
      "destruction" is what Thomas refuses to do, detaching his discussion of ens from
      the discussion of divine names, leading Thomas to the position that "ens, although
      defined starting from a human conception, should be valid as the first name of
      Gxd. This claim does not easily escape the suspicion of idolatry." Thus, "it is only
      with Saint Thomas that the Gxd revealed in Jesus Christ under the name of charity
      finds himself summoned to enter the role of the divine of metaphysics, in assuming
      ens as his proper name" (*God Without Being*, 81).
65   Westphal characterizes the difference between the icon and the idol as dependent
      on the intentional gaze directed at it: "[A] given visible can function as either idol or
      icon depending on the nature of the intentional act directed toward it." It becomes
      an idol when the gaze "is satisfied or fulfilled with what it sees, when it stops,
      freezes, settles, or comes to rest at its visible object." The idolatrous gaze "admits
      no beyond" and "allows no invisible" (these last phrases are Marion's own). This
      makes the human gaze "the measure of the divine being," and ultimately the idol
      is the gazing idolater himself. Viewing a visible as an icon, however, means refusing
      to stop and rest, refusing to be satisfied or fulfilled with the visible. Iconic gazing
      seeks to "transpierce visible things." And this leads, in a Levinasian fashion, to a
      subversion of the gaze: "[T]he gaze of the invisible, in person, aims at man . . . the
      icon opens in a face that gazes at our gazes," so that "the human gaze is engulfed
      . . . does not cease, envisaged by the icon, there to watch the tide of the invisible
      come in. . . . The icon offers an abyss that the eyes of men never finish probing."
      The iconic gaze thus shattered the adequacy of our concepts. This does not entail
      an abandonment of conceptualizing: "[T]he icon also can proceed conceptually,
      provided at least that the concept renounce comprehending the incomprehensible
      to attempt to conceive it, hence also to receive it, in its own excessiveness."
66   As Benson says, "[C]onsciousness is surprised, overwhelmed and drawn up short
      by its inadequacy." Marion himself writes, "It is in fact a question of something vis-
      ible that our gaze cannot bear; this visible something is experienced as unbearable
      to the gaze because it weighs too much upon the gaze. . . . What weighs here is not
      unhappiness, nor pain nor lack, but indeed glory, joy, excess" (*Graven Ideologies*,
      192).
67   The term is Benson's (*Graven Ideologies*, 189).
68   Marion, *God Without Being*, 46.
69   Marion, *God Without Being*, 47.
70   See Benson, *Graven Ideologies*, 197.
71   Marion, *God Without Being*, 97.
72   Marion, *God Without Being*, 104.
73   Eucharist is "the test of every theological systematization" because it eludes all
      systematization. It is the final bulwark against idolatry. Historically, Eucharist has
      not played this role, since it gets absorbed into a metaphysical scheme of one sort
      or another. It has not functioned as the test or bulwark, but has been subjected
      to tests from elsewhere. As Marion puts it, "Explanation, even theological expla-
      nation, always seems to end up in a 'eucharistic physics' (. . . it matters little if
      for physics one substitutes, e.g., semiotics), that is, by attempting to reabsorb the
      Eucharistic mystery of charity in a rational conceptual system. In the case of failure,

such an effort appears either useless (if it limits itself, through theological concern, to recognizing a pure and simple 'miracle' in the succession of physical or linguistic events) or else insufficient (if it imputes its conceptual insufficiency to a mystery that it has not even approached, by an infracritical or terroristic subjectivism). But in the case of apparent success, the effort is open no less—and here the essential appears—to two other suspicions: does not one contradict oneself by seeking, in principle to reinforce credibility, to frame and then reabsorb the liturgical fact and the mystery of charity in a system, at the risk, here again, of attaining only a conceptual idol?" Eucharist is the model of gift, and as such "does not require first that one explain it, but indeed that one receive it" (*God Without Being*, 162).

74　Statistics are misleading, but it is perhaps significant that the word "gratitude" appears only three times in *Being Given*, twice in Marion's own expressions of gratitude (xi, 3) and once in a quotation from Derrida that uses the phrase "auto-recognition, self-approval, and narcissistic gratitude" (77). "Thanks" appears regularly, but never as a focus of serious examination. In *The Erotic Phenomenon* (Chicago: University of Chicago Press, 2006), "gratitude" occurs only once, in the acknowledgments (10).

75　Jean-Luc Marion, *Idol and Distance: Five Studies* (New York: Fordham University Press, 2001), 166: "The gift is received only in order to be given anew. The beneficiary, moreover, does not follow the circulation of the gift through simply altruism, as if it seemed to him decent and well intentioned, or even charitable, to share the gift with others. If the beneficiary must ensure what we call the redundancy of the gift, by putting it back into circulation as soon as it is received, this is for an otherwise radical reason: the gift cannot be received unless it is given, for otherwise it would cease to merit its name. The basin is not filled up by the cascade from above unless it ceaselessly empties itself into the basin below. Only the abandonment of that which fills it permits that the stream to come should fill it without cease."

76　Marion, *Idol and Distance*, 166.
77　Marion, *Idol and Distance*, 168.
78　Marion, *Idol and Distance*, 174.
79　Milbank, "Can a Gift Be Given?" *Modern Theology* 11, no. 1 (1995): 119–61. Milbank begins his essay with a survey of the linguistic history of the word "gift" and related words. Citing a sermon of Hugh Latimer, he complains about giffe-gaffe, the demand that receiving a gift lays an obligation to return a gift. The phrase means "give and take," and "suggests," Milbank argues, "that taking differs from giving by a single vowel." He highlights also the various ambiguities of the language of gift: Giving can slide into reception, as in the phrase "give way" or the statement that the trees "give" in a strong wind. Furthermore, "give" can be used both for a good and a bad exchange: We give a blow as well as a gift; worse, a good gift can slide into a bad (an inheritance spoils a child) and vice versa (a vicious personal attack forces us to be honest with ourselves). "Giff" in old English means "takings," and "gif" is both poison and gift; Greek and Latin, Milbank notes, contain the same ambiguity, using *dosis* to refer both to poison and medicine (119–20). Besides the linguistic ambiguities of giving/receiving, and good/bad giving, there is the ambiguity between "a subjective and value-laden usage of gift words over-against a cold, neutral and impersonal one." When we say something is simply "a given," is that because "our language is haunted by the praise of the gods or God" or "is it that nothing simply and eternally is, but always first arrives or arises, if not through space, then at least through time"? When we consider linguistic usage, it appears that " 'giving' is just as 'transcendental' a term as 'being.' " Like Derrida, Milbank plays on the English "present" (time) and "present" (gift), suggesting that "the present (thing or moment) always, despite its stasis, 'is' in

virtue of its being given from elsewhere or from the past, which is equally the arrival ahead of itself of the future" (121). He sums up this exploration: "The appearances of the English language, therefore, suggest that the gift is, first of all, inseparable from exchange (giving from giving back) and also that it is caught up in three ambiguities: to give is also to take; a good gift is also a bad gift (benefit is also corruption); and finally 'the given' is both the result of a deliberate generous donation and a brute unyielding fact or principle, alien to will or effect."

80   Milbank, "Can a Gift Be Given?" 122. Milbank considers business lunches, tips, various courtesies that "surround and support pragmatic activities which people contract into for their private benefit."

81   Milbank, "Can a Gift Be Given?" 124: Is the purest gift "a handing-over of a large bag containing bank notes to anyone in the street (anyone save one who appeared poor, since the poor are related to us via the credit of our guilt)"?

82   Milbank, "Can a Gift Be Given?" 132.

83   Milbank, "Can a Gift Be Given?" 124.

84   Milbank, "Can a Gift Be Given?" 129. Even delay and nonidentical return can be reduced, as in the work of Bourdieu, to masked contract. To Milbank, Bourdieu has assumed that economic self-interest is indistinguishable from lust for honor or religious impulses, as if all of the other motivations for giving are ultimately "really" an effort to increase one's own wealth. Bourdieu does, however, force a more precise project on Milbank: "If gifts are only given in order to render indebted, to ensure a return of honour, and if debt drives the whole system to ensure continued exact compliance with what has been laid down, marked out by the powerful, both dead and living, then there can be, we must judge, no real gift. There only can be gift if delay and non-identical repetition can be shown to be in principle irreducible to the operation of such tactics, to the ensuring of the primacy of debt, and the always identical marks of honour." Bourdieu has assumed a "liberal" idea of human behavior, but that is the issue in debate.

85   Milbank, "Can a Gift Be Given?" 132. Citing Marion, Milbank notes that "to receive the other in receiving his gift demands that the distance of the other remains in place." A gift is a gift of distance, and this militates against any effort "to possess the other and his gifts, to receive them as exactly due rewards, or as things we do not need to go on receiving." Milbank, "Can a Gift Be Given?" 145–46. Milbank traces out some contours of a biblical theology of gift, highlighting some significant features of the Levitical sacrificial system. Levitical offerings were sometimes entirely devoted to God (ascension), sometimes reserved for the priesthood (purifications) and sometimes distributed among God, priests, and people (peace offering). This implies "equal purification of all members of this society in their offering to God (and even of all peoples, universally) rather than literal 'sustaining' of a hierarchy and division of the relatively pure and impure, insider and outsider, as in most other cultures." He suggests that the point here is that the repetition of the gift is "prised away from any specific expectation or duty of return, but related instead to a heightened and infinite expectation of variegated return in acts of mercy which alone complete and legitimate a universal sacrificial offering" (148). Gifts can be given only when there is "a primary relationality," and Milbank sees this primary relationality in the biblical notion of a covenant between God and Israel. The covenant idea provides a means for bridging the gap between gift and contract. For Israel, God is not an ancestor, yet he is described in familial terms (Israel is his son), and he is alive. Since he lives, he "makes ever-new demands (as he gives ever-new gifts)" and thus "every human covenanted partner is also treated as one who needs, in himself, specific sorts of gifts." The gift is no longer a matter of "preserving the same inscriptions, but rather of sending a message appropriate to the particular recipient." The "relatively contractual" notion

of covenant "ensures that questions of justice, which is to say of appropriateness, intrude more into the sphere of gift." This is not a contamination of gift, since appropriateness is one of the conditions of a good gift. Covenant provides a way to "preserve a familial logic at the point where, otherwise, one would surrender to the formalism of contract." In a footnote, he cites Mary Douglas' point that "Levitical impurity is a fact of biology, common to all persons, and also a result of specific moral offences that anyone is liable to commit such as lying or stealing. . . . Biblical impurity is of no use in demarcating advantaged social classes or ranks" (160n79). It should be noted here that this is precisely what the Jews of Jesus' time had made it! God's mercy and goodness have no limit, and so likewise, "there is no limit to the joyful return made of Israel herself to God." The logic is transferred to alms in the sense that we give to the needy "without stint or 'counting of the cost,'" as God has given to us. And this means that "only gratitude and 'good use' are expected in return" (148–49).

86   Milbank, "Can a Gift Be Given?" 149.
87   Milbank, "Can a Gift Be Given?" 150.
88   Milbank, "Can a Gift Be Given?" 152.

CONCLUSION

1   To be sure, that is not universally held.
2   Jose Ortega y Gasset, *Revolt of the Masses* (1930; repr., New York: Norton, 1994), 36.
3   Ortega y Gasset, *Revolt of the Masses*, 39.
4   Ortega y Gasset, *Revolt of the Masses*, 120. On the other side, Joseph Amato argues that the abuses of the modern nation-state arise from the creation and then manipulation of bonds of gratitude: During the nineteenth century, "to win the loyalties of its citizens became the essential business of government. Accordingly, it had to put itself at the center of society's transactions. Government had to strive to become the primary source of justice, the final arbitrator of right, and the author of the most important gifts, which in this era are all the benefits associated with improved well-being." He cites Robert Conquest's account of Soviet praise for children who betrayed their parents, and adds, "While democratic governments cannot go to such lengths in their quest for control, they too find it essential to win their citizens' gratitude, to find a means of defining, managing, and manipulating it" (Amato, *Guilt and Gratitude*, 38–39; cf. 96–108).
5   Schumacher, *Small Is Beautiful* (San Francisco: HarperCollins, 2010), 51.
6   See, for starters, the references to gratitude in J. Matthew Bonzo and Michael R. Stevens, *Wendell Berry and the Cultivation of Life: A Reader's Guide* (Grand Rapids: Brazos, 2008).
7   Back in 1942, Ropke growled in a footnote to *The Social Crisis of Our Time* (1942; repr., Chicago: University of Chicago Press, 1950), "Everyone can probably tell from personal experience of the strikingly great proportion of the younger generation which does not know its place in the presence of its elders and assumes a studiously rude manner especially if the latter are deserving of particular respect, or even gratitude. A world that has lost its instinct for these elementary principles must be thoroughly out of joint" (28).
8   Finkielkraut, *L'Ingratitude*, esp. chap. 4.
9   Robert Raynolds, *In Praise of Gratitude* (New York: Harper, 1961), 22–26. See also Max Scheler, *Ressentiment* (Milwaukee, Wis.: Marquette University Press, 2003).
10   Thanks to my friend Rev. Richard Bledsoe for these thoughts.
11   The key text is Robert A. Emmons and Michael E. McCullough, eds., *The Psychology*

of Gratitude (Oxford: Oxford University Press, 2004). See also the extensive annotated bibliography in the appendix to that volume.

12   Sigmund Freud, "A Special Type of Choice of Object Made by Men," *Standard
      Edition* 10 (1910): 173, quoted in Peter Shabad, "Of Woman Born: Womb Envy
      and the Male Project of Self-Creation," in Wurmser and Jarass, *Jealousy and Envy*,
      78. See also Marie T. Hoffman, *Toward Mutual Recognition: Relational Psycho-
      analysis and the Christian Narrative* (London: Taylor & Francis, 2010), 151.

13   Theodore Reik, "Final Phases of Belief found in Religion and in Obsessional Neu-
      rosis," *International Journal of Psychoanalysis* 11 (1930): 258–91, 269, quoted in
      Hoffman, *Mutual Recognition*, 152.

14   Harold Bloom, *The Anxiety of Influence: A Theory of Poetry*, 2nd ed. (Oxford:
      Oxford University Press, 1997).

15   Paul Ricoeur, *Freud and Philosophy: An Essay on Interpretation* (New Haven,
      Conn.: Yale University Press, 1970), 32–37.

16   Melanie Klein, *Envy and Gratitude & Other Works, 1946–1983* (New York: Delta,
      1975), 187. See the summary in Aafke Elisabeth Komter, "Gratitude and Gift
      Exchange," in Emmons and McCullough, *Psychology of Gratitude*, 201–2.

17   Philip Watkins, "Gratitude and Subjective Well-Being," in Emmons and
      McCullough, *Psychology of Gratitude*, 167–92; Robert A. Emmons and Michael E.
      McCullough, "Counting Blessings Versus Burdens: An Experimental Investiga-
      tion of Gratitude and Subjective Well-Being in Daily Life," *Journal of Personality
      and Social Psychology* 84 (2003): 377–89.

18   Robert C. Roberts, "The Blessings of Gratitude: A Conceptual Analysis," in
      Emmons and McCullough, *Psychology of Gratitude*, 66–77. The use of the reli-
      giously charged term "blessing" is not accidental.

19   Rollin McCraty and Doc Childre, "The Grateful Heart: The Psychophysiology of
      Appreciation," in Emmons and McCullough, *Psychology of Gratitude*, 230–55.

20   See Edward J. Harpham, "Gratitude in the History of Ideas," in Emmons and
      McCullough, *Psychology of Gratitude*, 19–36. In his contribution to the volume
      ("Gratitude: Considerations from a Moral Perspective," 269), Charles Shelton
      speaks of "blending the perspectives of the humanities and psychological science"
      to arrive at a moral standard of the good life on which gratitude can be founded.

21   Michael E. McCullough and Jo-Ann Tsang, "Parent of the Virtues? The Prosocial
      Contours of Gratitude," in Emmons and McCullough, *Psychology of Gratitude*,
      125.

22   McCullough and Tsang, "Parent of the Virtues?" 128–30. See also Michael E.
      McCullough, S. D. Kilpatrick, Robert Emmons, and D. B. Larson, "Is Gratitude
      a Moral Affect?" *Psychological Bulletin* 127, no. 2 (2001): 249–66.

23   McCullough et al., "Is Gratitude a Moral Affect?" See also Ross Buck, "The Grati-
      tude of Exchange and the Gratitude of Caring: A Developmental-Interactionist
      Perspective of Moral Emotion," in Emmons and McCullough, *Psychology of Grati-
      tude*, 108–13.

24   To put it differently, they can be read as contributing to the recovery of the moral-
      ity of manners.

25   See Robert A. Emmons and Teresa T. Kneezel, "Giving Thanks: Spiritual and
      Religious Correlates of Gratitude," *Journal of Psychology and Christianity* 24, no.
      2 (2005): 140–48, 141. The authors unfortunately dress this helpful point in social
      scientific jargon. See also Michael Stein, "Gratitude and Attitude: A Note on Emo-
      tional Welfare," *Social Psychology Quarterly* 52, no. 3 (1989): 242–48.

26   McCullough and Tsang, "Parent of the Virtues?" 136.

27   Buck, "Gratitude of Exchange and Caring," 110–11.

28   Shelton, "Gratitude," 264–78. Buck, "Gratitude of Exchange and Caring," 115–
      16, examines the "dark side of gratitude."

29   Emmons and Kneezel, "Giving Thanks," 140–47; Neal Krause, "Religious Involvement, Gratitude, and Change in Depressive Symptoms over Time," *International Journal for the Psychology of Religion* 19 (2009): 155–72.

30   David Steindl-Rast, "Gratitude as Thankfulness and as Gratefulness," in Emmons and McCullough, *Psychology of Gratitude*, 282–89.

31   Barbara Fredrickson, "Gratitude, Like Other Positive Emotions, Broadens and Builds," in Emmons and McCullough, *Psychology of Gratitude*, 145–66, 150. Rather oddly, Fredrickson speaks of gratitude responding to a source such as "God, luck, fate" that "has *intentionally* acted to improve the beneficiary's well-being" (emphasis added). How luck can act, much less act intentionally, without becoming Tyche, or fate without becoming Fortuna, is not entirely clear.

32   Ronald Aronson, *Living Without God: New Directions for Atheists, Agnostics, Secularists and the Undecided* (Berkeley, Calif.: Counterpoint, 2009), 43; chapter 2 of Aronson's book is an atheist's defense of gratitude.

33   Aronson, *Living Without God*, 59–63.

34   Eisenstein, *Sacred Economics: Money, Gift & Society in an Age of Transition* (Berkeley, Calif.: Evolver Editions, 2011), 3–5.

35   Eisenstein, *Sacred Economics*, 14.

36   Revealingly, though there are entries for "religion" in his index, there is no entry for "God."

37   Eisenstein, *Sacred Economics*, 57.

38   Subtitled *Scale, Place & Community in a Global Age* (Washington, D.C.: Potomac Books, 2012).

39   David L. Schindler, *Ordered Love: Liberal Societies and the Memory of God* (Grand Rapids: Eerdmans, 2011), 168–69.

40   Schindler, *Ordered Love*, 171–73.

41   Schindler, *Ordered Love*, 177.

42   Schindler, *Ordered Love*, 177–78.

43   Schindler, *Ordered Love*, 217.

44   Godbout, "Homo Donator Versus Homo Oeconomicus," 25, 30–31; Godbout, *Ce Qui Circule entre Nous: Donner, Recevoir, Rendre* (Paris: Seuil, 2007), chap. 7.

45   Margaret Visser's paraphrase of the Japanese apologetic thanks, *doomo sumimasen* (*Gift of Thanks*, 38).

46   Thanks again to Rev. Richard Bledsoe for this suggestion.

Bibliography

Adkins, W. H. " 'Friendship' and 'Self-Sufficiency' in Homer and Aristotle." *Classical Quarterly* n.s. 13, no. 1 (1963): 30–45.

Algazi, Gadi, Valentin Groebner, and Bernhard Jussen, eds. *Negotiating the Gift: Pre-modern Figurations of Exchange.* Göttingen: Vandenhoeck & Ruprecht, 2003.

Allan, William. "Divine Justice and Cosmic Order in Early Greek Epic." *Journal of Hellenic Studies* 126 (2006): 1–35.

Alvey, James E. "Adam Smith's Higher Vision of Capitalism." *Journal of Economic Issues* 32, no. 2 (1998): 441–48.

Amato, Joseph Anthony. *Guilt and Gratitude: A Study of the Origins of Contemporary Conscience.* Westport, Conn.: Greenwood Press, 1989.

Anderson, Benedict. *Imagined Communities: Reflections on the Origin and Spread of Nationalism.* 2nd ed. New York: Verso, 2006.

Angenendt, Arnold. "*Donationes pro anima*: Gift and Countergift in the Early Medieval Liturgy." In Davis and McCormick, *Long Morning of Medieval Europe*, 131–54.

Apocrypha. Edited by Bruce Metzger. Oxford: Oxford University Press, 1965.

Appadurai, Arjun. *The Social Life of Things: Commodities in Cultural Perspective.* Cambridge: Cambridge University Press, 1986.

Aquinas, Thomas. *Summa Theologiae.* 2nd ed. Translated by the fathers of the English Dominican Province. New York: Benzinger, 1947–1948.

Aristotle. *Nicomachean Ethics.* Edited and translated by H. Rackham. Cambridge, Mass.: Harvard University Press, 1926.

―――. *Politics*. Edited and translated by H. Rackham. Cambridge, Mass.: Harvard University Press, 1932.

―――. *Rhetoric*. Edited and translated by J. H. Freese. Cambridge, Mass.: Harvard University Press, 1959.

Arnsperger, Christian. "Gift-Giving Practice and Noncontextual Habitus: How (Not) to Be Fooled by Mauss." In Vandevelde, *Gifts and Interests*, 71–92.

Aronson, Ronald. *Living Without God: New Directions for Atheists, Agnostics, Secularists and the Undecided*. Berkeley, Calif.: Counterpoint, 2009.

Augustine. *De Civitate Dei*. Edited and translated by Robert Dyson et al. Cambridge: Cambridge University Press, 1998.

Austen, Jane. *Pride and Prejudice*. 1813. Reprint, New York: Norton, 1966.

Bagby, Laurie. *Thomas Hobbes: Turning Point for Honor*. Lanham, Md.: Lexington Books, 2009.

Baker, David L. *Tight Fists or Open Hands? Wealth and Poverty in Old Testament Law*. Grand Rapids: Baker, 2009.

Bankovsky, Miriam. "A Thread of Knots: Jacques Derrida's Homage to Emmanuel Levinas' Ethical Reminder." *Invisible Culture: An Electronic Journal for Visual Studies* 8 (2004): 1–19. http://www.rochester.edu/in_visible_culture/Issue_8/bankovsky.html (accessed February 26, 2013).

Barclay, John. "Manna and the Circulation of Grace: A Study of 2 Corinthians 8:1-15." In Wagner, Rowe, and Grieb, *Word Leaps the Gap*, 409–26.

―――. *Paul and the Gift*. Grand Rapids: Eerdmans, forthcoming.

Bataille, Georges. *The Accursed Share, Volume 1*. Translated by Robert Hurley. New York: Urzone, 1989.

Battenhouse, Roy W. *Shakespearean Tragedy: Its Art and Its Christian Premises*. Bloomington: Indiana University Press, 1969.

Baudrillard, Jean. *Symbolic Exchange and Death*. Translated by Iain Hamilton Grant. London: SAGE, 1993.

Bayer, Oswald. "The Ethics of Gift." *Lutheran Quarterly* 24 (2010): 447–68.

Becker, Lawrence C. *Reciprocity*. Chicago: University of Chicago Press, 1990.

Belarmine, Robert. *De Laicis*. Translated by Kathleen Eleanor Murphy. New York: Fordham University Press, 1928.

Belfiore, Elizabeth. "Harming Friends: Problematic Reciprocity in Greek Tragedy." In Gill, Postlethwaite, and Seaford, *Reciprocity in Ancient Greece*, 139–58.

Ben-Amos, Ilana Krausman. *The Culture of Giving: Informal Support and Gift-Exchange in Early Modern England*. Cambridge: Cambridge University Press, 2008.

Benson, Bruce Ellis. *Graven Ideologies: Nietzsche, Derrida, and Marion on Modern Idolatry*. Downers Grove, Ill.: InterVarsity, 2002.

Beowulf. Translated by Seamus Heaney. New York: Farrar, Straus & Giroux, 2000.

Berger, Fred R. "Gratitude." *Ethics* 85, no. 4 (1975): 298–309.

Berking, Helmuch. *Sociology of Giving*. London: SAGE, 1999.

Bernasconi, Robert, ed. *Re-reading Levinas*. London: Athlone, 1991.

Biedelman, T. O. "Agonistic Exchange: Homeric Reciprocity and the Heritage of Simmel and Mauss." *Cultural Anthropology* 4, no. 3 (1989): 227–59.

Bijsterveld, Arnould-Jan. "The Medieval Gift." In Cohen and de Jong, *Medieval Transformations*, 123–56.

Bloom, Harold. *The Anxiety of Influence: A Theory of Poetry*. 2nd ed. Oxford: Oxford University Press, 1997.

Boas, Franz. *A Franz Boas Reader: The Shaping of American Anthropology, 1883–1911*. Chicago: University of Chicago Press, 1989.

Bobbio, Norberto. *Thomas Hobbes and the Natural Law Tradition*. Translated by Daniela Gobetti. Chicago: University of Chicago Press, 1993.

Bobertz, C. A. "Cyprian of Carthage as Patron: A Social Historical Study of the Role of Bishop in the Ancient Christian Community of North Africa." Ph.D. diss., Yale University, 1988.

Boersma, Hans. *Violence, Hospitality, and the Cross: Reappropriating the Atonement Tradition*. Grand Rapids: Baker, 2006.

Bonzo, J. Matthew, and Michael R. Stevens. *Wendell Berry and the Cultivation of Life: A Reader's Guide*. Grand Rapids: Brazos, 2008.

Boonin-Vail, David. *Thomas Hobbes and the Science of Moral Virtue*. Cambridge: Cambridge University Press, 1994.

Bouchard, Constance Brittain. *Holy Entrepreneurs: Cistercians, Knights, and Economic Exchange in Twelfth-Century Burgundy*. Ithaca, N.Y.: Cornell University Press, 1991.

Bourdieu, Pierre. *Algeria 1960: The Disenchantment of the World*. Cambridge: Cambridge University Press, 1979.

———. *Outline of a Theory of Practice*. Cambridge: Cambridge University Press, 1977.

Bowman, Alan K., Peter Garnsey, and Dominic Rathbone. *The Cambridge Ancient History, Volume XI: The High Empire, A.D. 70–192*. 2nd ed. Cambridge: Cambridge University Press, 2008.

Braund, David. "Herodotos on the Problematics of Reciprocity." In Gill, Postlethwaite, and Seaford, *Reciprocity in Ancient Greece*, 159–80.

Briones, David. "Mutual Brokers of Grace: A Study in 2 Corinthians 1:3-11." *New Testament Studies* 56, no. 4 (2010): 536–56.

Bromyard, John. *Summa Praedicantium*. Venice, 1586. Available online at archive.org (accessed February 26, 2013).

Bronwen, Neil. "Models of Gift Giving in the Preaching of Leo the Great." *Journal of Early Christian Studies* 18, no. 2 (2010): 225–39.

Brooks, Jeffrey. *Thank You, Comrade Stalin! Soviet Public Culture from Revolution to Cold War*. Princeton: Princeton University Press, 2001.

Brother Anthony of Taize. "Shakespeare's Monsters of Ingratitude." *Shakespeare Review* (Seoul) (1990): 1–10. http://hompi.sogang.ac.kr/anthony/Ingrate.htm (accessed April 10, 2013).

Brown, Elizabeth A. R. "The Tyranny of a Construct: Feudalism and Historians of Medieval Europe." *American Historical Review* 79, no. 4 (1974): 1063–88.

Brown, K. C., ed. *Hobbes Studies*. Cambridge, Mass.: Harvard University Press, 1965.

Brown, Peter. *Through the Eye of a Needle: Wealth, the Fall of Rome, and the Making of Christianity in the West, 35–550 AD*. Princeton: Princeton University Press, 2012.

Buck, Ross. "The Gratitude of Exchange and the Gratitude of Caring: A Developmental-Interactionist Perspective of Moral Emotion." In Emmons and McCullough, *Psychology of Gratitude*, 108–22.

Buckley, William F. *Gratitude*. New York: Random House, 1990.

Burke, Edmund. "Letter to a Noble Lord." www.ourcivilisation.com/smartboard/shop/burkee/tolord/index.htm (accessed February 26, 2013).

———. *Reflections on the Revolution in France*. New York: Macmillan, 1890.

Butler, Melissa A. "Early Liberal Roots of Feminism: John Locke's Attack on Patriarchy." In *Feminist Interpretations of John Locke*, edited by Nancy J. Hirschmann and Kirstie M. McClure, 91–122. University Park: Penn State University Press, 2007.

Calvin, John. *Commentaries on the Epistle of Paul the Apostle to the Hebrews*. Grand Rapids: Eerdmans, 1948.

———. *Commentary on a Harmony of the Evangelists*. Grand Rapids: Eerdmans, 1949.

———. *Institutes of the Christian Religion*. Edited by John T. McNeill. London: SCM Press, 1961.

Camenisch, Paul F. "Gift and Gratitude in Ethics." *Journal of Religious Ethics* 9, no. 1 (1981): 1–34.

Caner, Daniel. "Towards a Miraculous Economy: Christian Gifts and

Material 'Blessings' in Late Antiquity." *Journal of Early Christian Studies* 14, no. 3 (2006): 329–77.

Capellanus, Andreas. *Art of Courtly Love*. Translated by John Jay Parry. New York: Columbia University Press, 1990.

Caputo, John D., ed. *God, the Gift, and Postmodernism*. New edition. Bloomington: Indiana University Press, 1999.

———. *The Mystical Element in Heidegger's Thought*. New York: Fordham University Press, 1986.

———. *Philosophy and Theology (Horizons in Theology)*. Nashville: Abingdon, 2006.

———. *The Prayers and Tears of Jacques Derrida: Religion without Religion*. Bloomington: Indiana University Press, 1997.

Card, Claudia. "Gratitude and Obligation." *American Philosophical Quarterly* 25, no. 2 (1988): 115–27.

Carlson, Thomas A. Introduction to *The Idol and the Distance: Five Studies*, by Jean-Luc Marion. New York: Fordham University Press, 2001.

Carman, John B., and Frederick J. Streng, eds. *Spoken and Unspoken Thanks: Some Comparative Soundings*. Cambridge, Mass.: Center for the Study of World Religions, Harvard University, 1989.

Carrier, James. "Occidentalism: The World Turned Upside-Down." *American Ethnologist* 19, no. 2 (1992): 195–212.

Cartwright, Thomas. *A Confutation of the Rhemists Translation, Glosses and Annotations on the New Testament*. 1618. Reprint, New York: Da Capo, 1971.

Cassirer, Ernst. *The Question of Jean-Jacques Rousseau*. Translated by Peter Gay. 2nd ed. New Haven, Conn.: Yale University Press, 1989.

Catherine of Siena. *Letters*. Translated and edited by Vida D. Scudder. London: J. M. Dent, 1905. Available at Gutenberg.org (accessed February 26, 2013).

Cavanaugh, William. "Eucharistic Sacrifice and the Social Imagination in Early Modern Europe." *Journal of Medieval and Early Modern Studies* 31, no. 3 (2001): 585–605.

Cavell, Stanley. *Disowning Knowledge in Six Plays of Shakespeare*. Cambridge: Cambridge University Press, 1987.

Cheal, David. *The Gift Economy*. London: Routledge, 1988.

Cheyette, Fred. "Review of: Susan Reynolds, *Fiefs and Vassals: The Medieval Evidence Reinterpreted* (Oxford, 1944)." *Speculum* 71 (1996): 998–1006. www.fordham.edu/halsall/source/reynolds-2%20reviews.asp (accessed December 14, 2012).

Cicero. *De Inventione*. Edited and translated by H. M. Hubbell. Cambridge, Mass.: Harvard University Press, 1976.

―――. *De Officiis*. Edited and translated by Walter Miller. Cambridge, Mass.: Harvard University Press, 1913.

Clavero, Bartolome. *La Grace du don: Anthropologie catholique de l'economie moderne*. Paris: Albin Michel, 1996.

Cohen, E., and M. B. de Jong, eds. *Medieval Transformations: Texts, Power, & Gifts in Context*. Leiden: Brill, 2001.

Cohen, Esther. *Gift, Payment, and the Sacred in Medieval Popular Religiosity*. Wassenaar: Netherlands Institute for Advanced Study in the Humanities and Social Sciences, 1991.

Cohn, Samuel K., Jr. *Death and Property in Siena, 1205–1800: Strategies for the Afterlife*. Baltimore, Md.: Johns Hopkins University Press, 1988.

Coleman, Patrick. *Anger, Gratitude, and the Enlightenment Writer*. Oxford: Oxford University Press, 2011.

Colman, E. A. M. "The End of *Coriolanus*." *ELH* 34, no. 1 (1967): 1–20.

Comay, Rebecca. "Gifts without Presents: Economies of Experience in Bataille and Heidegger." *Yale French Studies* 78 (1990): 66–89.

Comte, Auguste. *System of Positive Polity*. London: Longmans, Green, 1875.

Coverdale, Miles. *A Spiritual and Most Precious Pearl*. 1550. Reprint, Cambridge: Cambridge University Press, 1844.

Curta, Florin. "Merovingian and Carolingian Gift-Giving." *Speculum* 81, no. 3 (2006): 671–99.

Cyprian, *Epistles*. Oxford: J.H. Parker, 1844.

Danker, Frederick W. *Benefactor: Epigraphic Study of a Graeco-Roman and New Testament Semantic Field*. St. Louis, Mo.: Clayton, 1982.

―――. "Bridging St. Paul and the Apostolic Fathers: A Study in Reciprocity." *Currents in Theology and Mission* 15, no. 1 (1988): 84–94.

Dante, Alighieri. *Convivio*. Translated by Philip Henry Wicksteed. London: J. M. Dent, 1912.

―――. *The Divine Comedy*. Translated by Anthony Esolen. New York: Modern Library, 2002.

Davies, Wendy. *Acts of Giving: Individual, Community, and Church in Tenth-Century Christian Spain*. Oxford: Oxford University Press, 2007.

―――. "When Gift Is Sale: Reciprocities and Commodities in Tenth-Century Iberia." In Davies and Fouracre, *Languages of Gift in the Early Middle Ages*, 217–37.

Davies, Wendy, and Paul Fouracre, eds. *The Languages of Gift in the Early Middle Ages*. Cambridge: Cambridge University Press, 2010.

Davis, Jennifer, and Michael McCormick, eds. *The Long Morning of Medieval*

Europe: New Directions in Early Medieval Studies. London: Ashgate, 2008.

Davis, Natalie Zemon. *The Gift in Sixteenth-Century France.* Madison: University of Wisconsin Press, 2000.

De Lorris, Guillaume and de Muen, Jean. *The Romance of the Rose.* Translated by Harry Robbins. London: E. P. Dutton, 1962.

de Lubac, Henri. *Corpus Mysticum: The Eucharist and the Church in the Middle Ages.* Notre Dame, Ind.: University of Notre Dame Press, 2007.

de Rougement, Denis. *Love in the Western World.* Rev. ed. Princeton: Princeton University Press, 1983.

Derrida, Jacques. "At This Very Moment in This Work Here I Am." In *Rereading Levinas,* edited by Robert Bernasconi, translated by Ruben Berezdivin, 11–48. London: Athlone, 1991.

———. *The Gift of Death.* Translated by David Wills. Chicago: University of Chicago Press, 1995.

———. *Given Time, I: Counterfeit Money.* Chicago: University of Chicago Press, 1992.

Descartes, René. *The Passions of the Soul.* Translated by Jonathan Bennett. http://www.earlymoderntexts.com/pdf/descpass.pdf (accessed October 31, 2012).

deSilva, David A. "Exchanging Favor for Wrath: Apostasy in Hebrews and Patron-Client Relationships." *Journal of Biblical Literature* 115, no. 1 (1996): 91–116.

———. *Honor, Patronage, Kinship & Purity: Unlocking New Testament Culture.* Downers Grove, Ill.: InterVarsity, 2000.

———. *Perseverance in Gratitude: A Socio-Rhetorical Commentary on the Epistle "to the Hebrews."* Grand Rapids: Eerdmans, 2000.

Devine, Donald J. "Adam Smith and the Problem of Justice in Capitalist Society." *Journal of Legal Studies* 6, no. 2 (1977): 399–409.

de Voragine, Jacobus. *The Golden Legend of Saint Sebastian.* Translated by Granger Ryan and Helmut Ripperger. New York: Longmans, Green, 1941. http://www.mcah.columbia.edu/medmil/pages/non-mma-pages/text_links/gl_sebastian.html (accessed December 8, 2012).

Didascalia Apostolorum. Edited and translated by R. Hugh Connolly. Oxford: Clarendon, 1929.

Dietz, Mary G. "Hobbes's Subject as Citizen." In Dietz, *Thomas Hobbes and Political Theory,* 91–119.

———, ed. *Thomas Hobbes and Political Theory.* Lawrence: University of Kansas Press, 1990.

Dio Chrysostom. *Dio Chrysostom*. Translated by J. W. Cohoon. Loeb Classical Library. Cambridge, Mass.: Harvard University Press, 1939.

Diodorus. *Library of History*. Translated by C. H. Oldfather. Cambridge, Mass.: Harvard University Press, 1989.

Dionysius of Halicarnassus. *Roman Antiquities*. In Wallace-Hadrill, *Patronage in Ancient Society*, 243–45.

Dodd, William George. *Courtly Love in Chaucer and Gower*. Boston: Ginn, 1913.

Donlan, Walter. "Duelling with Gifts in the *Iliad*: As the Audience Saw It." *Colby Quarterly* 29, no. 3 (1993): 155–72.

———. "Reciprocities in Homer." *Classical World* 75, no. 3 (1982): 137–75.

———. "The Unequal Exchange between Glaucus and Diomedes in Light of the Homeric Gift-Economy." *Phoenix* 43, no. 1 (1989): 1–15.

Drummond, Andrew. "Early Roman *Clientes*." In Wallace-Hadrill, *Patronage in Ancient Society*, 89–116.

Duby, Georges. *The Early Growth of the European Economy: Warriors and Peasants from the Seventh to the Twelfth Centuries*. Translated by Howard B. Clarke. Ithaca, N.Y.: Cornell University Press, 1974.

du Moulin, Pierre. *The Buckler of the Faith*. Newberry, 1631.

Dunn, Catherine. *The Concept of Ingratitude in Renaissance English Moral Philosophy*. Washington, D.C.: Catholic University of America Press, 1946.

Dunn, John. *Rethinking Modern Political Theory: Essays 1979–1983*. Cambridge: Cambridge University Press, 1985.

Duquoc, Christian, and Casiano Florestan, eds. *Asking and Thanking*. London: SCM Press, 1990.

Eagleton, Terence. *Shakespeare and Society: Critical Studies in Elizabethan Drama*. New York: Schocken, 1967.

———. *William Shakespeare*. Oxford: Blackwell, 1986.

Eisenstein, Charles. *Sacred Economics: Money, Gift & Society in an Age of Transition*. Berkeley, Calif.: Evolver Editions, 2011.

Elias, Norbert. *The Civilizing Process: Sociogenetic and Psychogenetic Investigations*. London: Blackwell, 2000.

Elster, Jon. "Two for One? Reciprocity in Seneca and Adam Smith." *Adam Smith Review* 6 (2012): 152–71.

Emmons, Robert A., and Teresa T. Kneezel. "Giving Thanks: Spiritual and Religious Correlates of Gratitude." *Journal of Psychology and Christianity* 24, no. 2 (2005): 140–48.

Emmons, Robert A., and Michael E. McCullough. "Counting Blessings Versus Burdens: An Experimental Investigation of Gratitude and Subjective

Well-Being in Daily Life." *Journal of Personality and Social Psychology* 84 (2003): 377–89.

———, eds. *The Psychology of Gratitude*. Oxford: Oxford University Press, 2004.

Epictetus. *Works*. Translated by Thomas Wentworth Higginson. New York: Thomas Nelson, 1890.

Figgis, J. N. *Political Thought from Gerson to Grotius, 1414–1625*. Forgotten Books, 2012. http://www.forgottenbooks.org/info/Studies_of_Polit ical_Thought_from_Gerson_to_Grotius_1414-1625_1000158717.php.

Finkielkraut, Allain. *L'Ingratitude: Conversation sur notre temps*. Montreal: Quebec Amerique, 1999.

Finley, Moses. *Economy and Society in Ancient Greece*. New York: Penguin, 1983.

———. *The World of Odysseus*. New York: Penguin, 1979.

Firth, Raymond. *Primitive Polynesian Economy*. New York: Norton, 1965.

Fitzgerald, Patrick. "Gratitude and Justice." *Ethics* 109, no. 1 (1998): 119–53.

Flaig, Egon. "Is Loyalty a Favor? Or: Why Gifts Cannot Oblige an Emperor." In Algazi, Groebner, and Jussen, *Negotiating the Gift*, 29–62.

Force, Pierre. *Self-Interest before Adam Smith: A Genealogy of Economic Science*. Cambridge: Cambridge University Press, 2003.

Forman-Barzilai, Fonna. " 'Smith on Connexion,' Culture, and Judgment." In Montes, *New Voices on Adam Smith*, 89–114.

Fowler, Harold N. "The Sources of Seneca *de Beneficiis*." *Transactions of the American Philological Association* 17 (1886): 24–33.

Fredrickson, Barbara. "Gratitude, Like Other Positive Emotions, Broadens and Builds." In Emmons and McCullough, *Psychology of Gratitude*, 145–66.

Freud, Sigmund. "A Special Type of Choice of Object Made by Men." *Standard Edition* 10 (1910): 165–75.

Frohnen, Brian P., and Kenneth L. Grasso, eds. *Rethinking Rights: Historical, Political, and Philosophical Perspectives*. Columbia: University of Missouri Press, 2009.

Furtak, Rick Anthony. *Wisdom in Love: Kierkegaard and the Ancient Quest for Emotional Integrity*. Notre Dame, Ind.: University of Notre Dame Press, 2005.

Gadamer, Hans-Georg. *Truth and Method*. New York: Seabury Press, 1975.

Galloway, Andrew. "A Fifteenth-Century Confession Sermon on 'Unkyndness' and Its Literary Parallels and Parodies." *Traditio* 49 (1994): 259–69.

————. "Layamon's Gift." *Proceedings of the MLA* 121, no. 3 (2006): 717–34.

————. "The Making of a Social Ethic in Late-Medieval England: From Gratitudo to 'Kyndnesse.'" *Journal of the History of Ideas* 55, no. 3 (1994): 365–83.

Ganshof, F. L. *Feudalism*. New York: Harper, 1964.

Garber, Marjorie. *Shakespeare After All*. New York: Anchor Books, 2005.

Geary, Patrick. "Gift Exchange and Social Science Modeling." In Algazi, Groebner, and Jussen, *Negotiating the Gift*, 129–40.

Geoffrey of Monmouth. *The History of the Kings of Britain*. Translated by Lewis Thorpe. London: Penguin, 1966.

Gerrish, Brian. *Grace and Gratitude: The Eucharistic Theology of John Calvin*. Eugene, Ore.: Wipf & Stock, 2002.

Gibbon, Edward. *Decline and Fall of the Roman Empire*. New York: Modern Library, 1932.

Gibbs, Paul. *Heidegger's Contribution to the Understanding of Work-Based Studies*. New York: Springer, 2011.

Gierke, Otto von. *Development of Political Theory*. New York: H. Fertig, 1966.

————. *Political Theories of the Middle Age*. Translated by Frederick William Maitland. Cambridge: Cambridge University Press, 1987.

Gilbert, Allan. *Dante's Conception of Justice*. New York: AMS Press, 1971.

Gill, Christopher. "Altruism or Reciprocity in Greek Ethical Philosophy?" In Gill, Postlethwaite, and Seaford, *Reciprocity in Ancient Greece*, 181–98.

Gill, Christopher, Norman Postlethwaite, and Richard Seaford, eds. *Reciprocity in Ancient Greece*. Oxford: Oxford University Press, 1998.

Glenn, Gary. "In the History of Social and Political Contract, Whatever Happened to the Sixteenth Century?" Paper presented at a panel of the Society of Catholic Social Sciences, Washington D.C., 2005.

————. "Natural Rights and Social Contract in Burke and Bellarmine." In Frohnen and Grasso, *Rethinking Rights*, 58–79.

Godbout, Jacques T. *Ce Qui Circule entre Nous: Donner, Recevoir, Rendre*. Paris: Seuil, 2007.

————. "Homo Donator Versus Homo Oeconomicus." In Vandevelde, *Gifts and Interests*, 23–46.

————. *The World of the Gift*. Translated by Donald Winkler. Montreal: McGill-Queen's University Press, 2000.

Goddard, Harold. *The Meaning of Shakespeare*. 2 vols. Chicago: University of Chicago Press, 1951.

Godelier, Maurice. *The Enigma of the Gift*. Chicago: University of Chicago Press, 1999.

Goltz, Caleb, and Joan C. Tronto. "Politics and Gratitude: Rediscovering Hobbes's Fourth Law of Nature." Unpublished paper.

Gould, John. "Give and Take in Herodotus." In Gould, *Myth, Ritual, Memory, and Exchange*, 283–303.

———. "HIKETEIA." *Journal of Hellenic Studies* 93 (1973): 74–103.

———. *Myth, Ritual, Memory, and Exchange: Essays in Greek Literature and Culture*. Oxford: Oxford University Press, 2003.

Gower, John. *Confessio amantis*. In *The English Works of John Gower*. Edited by G. C. Macauly. London: K. Paul, Tranch, Trubner, 1900.

Graeber, David. *Debt: The First 5000 Years*. Brooklyn, N.Y.: Melville House, 2011.

Granz, David. "Giving to God in the Mass: The Experience of the Offertory." In Davies and Fouracre, *Languages of Gift in the Early Middle Ages*, 18–32.

Gregory, Brad S. *The Unintended Reformation: How a Religious Revolution Secularized Society*. Cambridge, Mass.: Belknap, 2012.

Gregory, C. A. *Gifts and Commodities*. London: Academic Press, 1982.

Gregory of Tours. *History of the Franks*. Translated by Ernest Berhaut. New York: Columbia University Press, 1916.

Grierson, Philip. "Commerce in the Dark Ages: A Critique of the Evidence." *Transactions of the Royal Historical Society,* 5th ser., no. 9 (1959): 123–40.

Griffin, Miriam. "*De Beneficiis* and Roman Society." *Journal of Roman Studies* 93 (2003): 92–113.

Groebner, Valentin. "Accountancies and *Arcana*: Registering the Gift in Late Medieval Cities." In Cohen and de Jong, *Medieval Transformations*, 219–43.

———. "The City Guard's Salute: Legal and Illegal, Public and Private Gifts in the Swiss Confederation around 1500." In Algazi, Groebner, and Jussen, *Negotiating the Gift*, 247–67.

———. *Liquid Assets, Dangerous Gifts: Presents and Political at the End of the Middle Ages*. Translated by Pamela E. Selwyn. Philadelphia: University of Pennsylvania Press, 2000.

Guthrie, Harvie. *Theology as Thanksgiving: From the Psalms to the Church's Eucharist*. New York: Seabury, 1981.

Hallowell, John. *Main Currents in Modern Political Thought*. 1950. Reprint, Lanham, Md.: University Press of America, 1984.

Harbsmeier, Michael. "Gifts and Discoveries: Gift Exchange in Early Modern Narratives of Exploration and Discovery." In Algazi, Groebner, and Jussen, *Negotiating the Gift*, 381–410.

Harpham, Edward J. "Gratitude in the History of Ideas." In Emmons and McCullough, *Psychology of Gratitude*, 19–36.

Harrison, James R. *Paul's Language of Grace in Its Graeco-Roman Context.* WUNT 2, 172. Tübingen: Mohr Siebeck, 2003.

Hart, David Bentley. *The Beauty of the Infinite: The Aesthetics of Christian Truth.* Grand Rapids: Eerdmans, 2004.

———. "A Gift Exceeding Every Debt: An Eastern Orthodox Appreciation of Anselm's Cur Deus Homo." *Pro Ecclesia* 7, no. 3 (1998): 333–49.

Harwood, Britton. "Gawain and the Gift." *Proceedings of the Modern Library Association* 106, no. 3 (1991): 483–99.

Hayes, Zachary. *The Gift of Being: A Theology of Creation.* Collegeville, Minn.: Michael Glazier, 2001.

Heal, Felicity. "Food Gifts, the Household and the Politics of Exchange in Early Modern England." *Past and Present* 199 (2008): 41–70.

Heidegger, Martin. *What Is Called Thinking?* Translated by J. Glenn Gray. San Francisco: Harper/Collins, 1976.

Hendrix, Holland. "Benefactor/Patron Networks in the Urban Environment: Evidence from Thessalonica." *Semeia* 56 (1991): 39–58.

Hengel, Martin. *Judaism and Hellenism: Studies in Their Encounter in Palestine during the Early Hellenistic Period.* Eugene, Ore.: Wipf & Stock, 2003.

Herman, Gabriel. *Ritualised Friendship and the Greek City.* Cambridge: Cambridge University Press, 1987.

Herodotus. *Histories.* Edited by Robert Strassler. New York: Pantheon, 2007.

Hesiod. *Works and Days.* Translated Hugh G. Evelyn-White. Cambridge, Mass.: Harvard University Press, 1914.

Hewitt, J. W. "Gratitude and Ingratitude in the Plays of Euripides." *American Journal of Philology* 43, no. 4 (1922): 331–43.

———. "The Gratitude of the Gods." *Classical Weekly* 18, no. 19 (1925): 148–51.

———. "On the Development of the Thank-Offering among the Greeks." *Transactions and Proceedings of the American Philological Association* 43 (1912): 95–111.

———. "Some Aspects of the Treatment of Ingratitude in Greek and English Literature." *Transactions and Proceedings of the American Philological Association* 48 (1917): 37–48.

———. "The Terminology of 'Gratitude' in Greek." *Classical Philology* 22, no. 2 (1927): 142–61.

———. "The Thank-Offering and Greek Religious Thought." *Transactions and Proceedings of the American Philological Association* 45 (1914): 77–90.

Hill, Christopher. *The Century of Revolution, 1603–1714*. New York: Psychology Press, 2002.

———. *Puritanism and Revolution*. New York: Random House, 2011.

———. *The World Turned Upside Down: Radical Ideas during the English Revolution*. New York: Penguin, 1991.

Hillner, J. "Clerics, Property and Patronage: The Case of the Roman Titular Churches." *Antiquite Tardive* 14 (2006): 59–68.

Himmelfarb, Gertrude. *The Roads to Modernity: The British, French, and American Enlightenments*. New York: Knopf, 2004.

Hirschmann, Nancy J. "Gordon Schochet on Hobbes, Gratitude, and Women." Paper presented at Gladly Learn and Gladly Teach: A Conference in Honor of Gordon Schochet, Rutgers University, May 5, 2009. www.rci.rutgers.edu/~schochet/Hirschmann_Schochet-to-Me.pdf.

Hirschmann, Nancy J., and Joanne H. Wright, eds. *Feminist Interpretations of Thomas Hobbes*. University Park: Penn State University Press, 2013.

Hitch, Sarah. *King of Sacrifice: Ritual and Royal Authority in the* Iliad. Cambridge, Mass.: Center for Hellenic Studies, 2009.

Hobbes. *De Cive*. Edited by Howard Warrender. Oxford: Clarendon, 1983.

———. *Elements of Law*. Edited by Ferdinand Tonnies. Cambridge: Cambridge University Press, 1928.

———. *Leviathan*. Edited by Richard Tuck. Cambridge: Cambridge University Press, 1991.

Hoffman, Marie T. *Toward Mutual Recognition: Relational Psychoanalysis and the Christian Narrative*. London: Taylor & Francis, 2010.

Hohendahl-Zoetelief, I. M. *Manners in the Homeric Epic*. Leiden: Brill, 1980.

Holloway, Carson. "Shakespeare's *Coriolanus* and Aristotle's *Megalopsyuchos*." Unpublished paper.

Homer. *The Iliad*. Translated by Robert Fagles. New York: Penguin Books, 1990.

Hook, Brian S., and R. R. Reno. *Heroism and the Christian Life: Reclaiming Excellence*. Louisville: Westminster John Knox, 2000.

Hooker, James. "Gifts in Homer." *Bulletin of the Institute Classical Studies* 36 (1989): 79–90.

———. "Homeric φιλος." *Glotta* 65, nos. 1–2 (1987): 44–65.

Hooker, Morna. "Adam in Romans 1." *New Testament Studies* 6, no. 4 (1960): 297–306.

Hooker, Richard. *Laws of Ecclesiastical Polity*. London: J. M. Dent, 1907.

Horner, Robyn. *Jean-Luc Marion: A Theo-logical Introduction*. Aldershot: Ashgate, 2005.

314 ～ gratitude

————. *Rethinking God as Gift: Marion, Derrida, and the Limits of Phenomenology.* New York: Fordham University Press, 2001.

Horowitz, Asher. "'Laws and Customs Thrust Us Back into Infancy': Rousseau's Historical Anthropology." *Review of Politics* 52, no. 2 (1990): 215–41.

Huffman, Clifford Chalmers. *Coriolanus in Context.* Lewisburg, Pa.: Bucknell, 1971.

Hume, David. *A Treatise on Human Nature.* London: J. M. Dent, 1911.

Husserl, Edmund. *Ideas: General Introduction to Pure Phenomenology.* London: Routledge, 2012.

————. *The Paris Lectures.* Translated by P. Koestenbaum. The Hague: Martinus Nijhoff, 1975.

Hyams, Paul. "Review of: Susan Reynolds, *Fiefs and Vassals: The Medieval Evidence Reinterpreted* (Oxford, 1944)." *Journal of Interdisciplinary History* 27, no 4 (1997): 655–62. www.fordham.edu/halsall/source/reynolds-2%20reviews.asp (accessed December 14, 2012).

Hyde, Lewis. *The Gift: Imagination and the Erotic Life of Property.* New York: Vintage, 1979.

Ijsseling, Samuel. *Heidegger: Denken et Danken, Geven en Zijn.* Antwerp: De Nederlandsche Boekhandel, 1964.

Inwood, Brad. *Reading Seneca: Stoic Philosophy at Rome.* Oxford: Oxford University Press, 2005.

Inwood, Michael. *Heidegger: A Very Short Introduction.* Oxford: Oxford University Press, 2002.

Jaeger, C. Stephen. *Ennobling Love: In Search of a Lost Sensibility.* Philadelphia: University of Pennsylvania Press, 1999.

Jagendorf, Zvi. "*Coriolanus*: Body Politic and Private Parts." *Shakespeare Quarterly* 41, no. 4 (1990): 455–69.

Janicaud, Dominique. *Phenomenology and the Theological Turn: The French Debate.* New York: Fordham University Press, 2000.

Jecker, Nancy S. "Are Filial Duties Unfounded?" *American Philosophical Quarterly* 26, no. 1 (1989): 73–80.

Jewett, Robert. "The Epistolary Thanksgiving and the Integrity of Philippians." *Novum Testamentum* 12, no. 1 (1970): 40–53.

Jobert, Philippe. *La notion du donation. Convergences: 630–750.* Paris: Les Belles Lettres, 1977.

John of the Cross. *The Living Flame of Love.* Garden City, N.Y.: Image Books, 1962.

Johnson, Penelope D. *Prayer, Patronage, and Power: The Abbey of la Trinite, Vendome, 1032–1187.* New York: NYU Press, 1981.

Jonas, Mark E. "Gratitude, Ressentiment and Citizenship Education." *Studies in Philosophy and Education* 31, no. 1 (2012): 29–46.

Josephus. *Antiquities*. Translated by William Whiston. Grand Rapids: Baker, 1974.

———. *Life of Josephus*. Translated by Steve Mason. Leiden: Brill, 2001.

Joubert, Stephan. "Coming to Terms with a Neglected Aspect of Ancient Mediterranean Reciprocity: Seneca's Views on Benefit-Exchange in *De beneficiis* as the Framework for a Model of Social Exchange." In *Social Scientific Models for Interpreting the Bible: Essays by the Context Group in Honor of Bruce J. Malina*, edited by John J. Filch, 47–63. Leiden: Brill, 2001.

———. "1 Corinthians 9:24-27: An Agonistic Competition?" *Neotestamentica* 35, no. 2 (2001): 57–68.

———. *Paul as Benefactor*. WUNT 2, 124. Tübingen: Mohr Siebeck, 2000.

———. "Religious Reciprocity in 2 Corinthians 9:6-15: Generosity and Gratitude as Legitimate Responses to *Charis tou theou*." *Neotestamentica* 33, no. 1 (1999): 79–90.

Jungmann, J. A. *The Mass: An Historical, Theological, and Pastoral Survey*. Translated by Julian Fernandes and edited by Mary Ellen Evans. Collegeville, Minn.: Liturgical Press, 1976.

Jussen, Bernhard. "Religious Discourses of the Gift in the Middle Ages: Semantic Evidences (Second to Twelfth Centuries)." In Algazi, Groebner, and Jussen, *Negotiating the Gift*, 173–92.

Kant, Immanuel. *Critique of Judgment*. Cambridge: Cambridge University Press, 2000.

———. *Critique of Practical Reason*. Translated by Mary Gregor. Cambridge: Cambridge University Press, 1997.

———. *Groundwork of the Metaphysics of Morals*. Translated by Thomas Kingsmill Abbott. Redford, Va.: A&D Press, 2008.

———. *Lectures on Ethics*. Translated by Louis Infield. Indianapolis: Hackett, 1981.

———. *Religion within the Bounds of Reason Alone*. Edited and translated by Allen W. Wood and George Di Giovanni. 1793. Reprint, Cambridge: Cambridge University Press, 1998.

Kapic, Kelly. *God So Loved, He Gave: Entering the Movement of Divine Generosity*. Grand Rapids: Zondervan, 2010.

Keating, James, ed. *Spiritual and Moral Theology: Essays from a Pastoral Perspective*. Mahwah, N.J.: Paulist Press, 2000.

Kenneally, Ivan. "Thanksgiving." *New Atlantis*. http://www.thenewatlantis.com/publications/thanksgiving (accessed September 20, 2012).

Keyser, Richard. "La transformation de l'echange des dons pieux: Montier-la-Celle, Champagne, 1100–1350." *Revue Historique* 305 (2003): 793–816.

Kidd, Reggie. *Wealth and Beneficence in the Pastoral Epistles: A "Bourgeois" Form of Early Christianity?* SBL Dissertation Series 122. Atlanta: Scholars Press, 1990.

Kierkegaard, Søren. *18 Upbuilding Discourses.* Princeton: Princeton University Press, 1990.

⏤⏤⏤. *Fear and Trembling.* Cambridge: Cambridge University Press, 2006.

Kingdon, Robert. "Social Welfare in Calvin's Geneva." *American Historical Review* 76 (1971): 50–69.

Klein, Melanie. *Envy and Gratitude & Other Works, 1946–1983.* New York: Delta, 1975.

Klosko, George. "Four Arguments Against Political Obligations from Gratitude." *Public Affairs Quarterly* 5, no. 1 (1991): 33–48.

Knapp, Jeffrey. *Shakespeare's Tribe: Church, Theatre and Nation in Renaissance England.* Chicago: University of Chicago Press, 2002.

Komter, Aafke Elisabeth. "Gratitude and Gift Exchange." In Emmons and McCullough, *Psychology of Gratitude,* 195–212.

Konstan, David. "Reciprocity and Friendship." In Gill, Postlethwaite, and Seaford, *Reciprocity in Ancient Greece,* 279–301.

Krause, Neal. "Religious Involvement, Gratitude, and Change in Depressive Symptoms over Time." *International Journal for the Psychology of Religion* 19 (2009): 155–72.

Lactantius. *Works.* Translated and edited by William Fletcher. Edinburgh: T&T Clark, 1871.

Lampert, Laurence. *Nietzsche and Modern Times: A Study of Bacon, Descartes, and Nietzsche.* New Haven, Conn.: Yale University Press, 1993.

Langland, William. *Piers the Plowman.* Edited by J. F. Goodridge. Harmondsworth: Penguin, 1975.

Lavery, Gerard B. "The Adversarius in Seneca's De Beneficiis." *Mnemosyne,* 4th ser., 40, nos. 1–2 (1987): 96–107.

Leithart, Peter. *Deep Comedy: Trinity, Tragedy, and Hope in Western Literature.* Moscow, Idaho: Canon Press, 2006.

⏤⏤⏤. "The Gospel, Gregory VII, and Modern Theology." *Modern Theology* 19, no. 1 (2003): 5–28.

⏤⏤⏤. *A Son to Me: An Exposition of 1 & 2 Samuel.* Moscow, Idaho: Canon Press, 2003.

⏤⏤⏤. "Stoic Elements in Calvin's Doctrine of the Christian Life." *Westminster Theological Journal* 55, no. 1 (1993): 31–54; 55, no. 2 (1993): 191–208; 56, no. 1 (1994): 59–85.

Lemos, T. M. *Marriage Gifts and Social Change in Ancient Palestine, 1200 BCE to 200 CE.* Cambridge: Cambridge University Press, 2010.

Lévi-Strauss, Claude. *Elementary Structures of Kinship.* Boston: Beacon, 1971.

———. *Le Totemisme aujourd'hui.* Paris: Presses universitaires de France, 1962.

Lewis, C. S. *The Allegory of Love: A Study in Medieval Tradition.* Oxford: Oxford University Press, 1985.

Liebersohn, Harry. *Return of the Gift: European History of a Global Idea.* Cambridge: Cambridge University Press, 2010.

Lindsay, Dennis R. "*Todah* and Eucharist: The Celebration of the Lord's Supper as a 'Thank Offering' in the Early Church." *Restoration Quarterly* 39 (1997): 83–100.

Little, Lester K. "Monasticism and Western Society: From Marginality to the Establishment and Back." *Memoirs of the American Academy in Rome* 47 (2002): 83–94.

———. *Religious Poverty and the Profit Economy in Medieval Europe.* Ithaca, N.Y.: Cornell University Press, 1978.

Llewelyn, John. *Margins of Religion: Between Kierkegaard and Derrida.* Bloomington: Indiana University Press, 2009.

Locke, John. *Locke: Political Essays.* Edited by Mark Goldie. Cambridge Texts in the History of Political Thought. Cambridge: Cambridge University Press, 2006.

———. *Two Treatises of Civil Government, And a Letter on Toleration.* Stilwell, Kans.: Digireads, 2005.

Lombardi, Joseph. "Filial Gratitude and God's Right to Command." *Journal of Religious Ethics* 19, no. 1 (1991): 93–118.

Lucian. *On Sacrifice.* Translated by H. W. Fowler. Available at www.sacred-texts.com (accessed February 26, 2013).

———. *Works.* Edited by A. M. Harmon. New York: Macmillan, 1913–1967.

Lundin, Roger. *The Culture of Interpretation.* Grand Rapids: Eerdmans, 1993.

Lupton, Julia Reinhard. *Citizen-Saints: Shakespeare and Political Theology.* Chicago: University of Chicago Press, 2005.

Luther, Martin. *Small Catechism.* St. Louis, Mo.: Concordia, 1943.

———. *Three Treatises.* 2nd ed. Minneapolis: Fortress, 1990.

———. *Works,* Vol. 37: *Word and Sacrament.* Philadelphia: Fortress, 1961.

Machiavelli, Niccolo. *Discourses on Livy.* Translated by Christian Detmold. 4 vols. Boston: J. R. Osgood, 1882. Available at www.libertyfund.org (accessed February 26, 2013).

————. *The Prince*. Translated by W. K. Mariott. Chicago: Encyclopedia Britannica, 1952.

MacIntyre, Alasdair. *After Virtue: A Study in Moral Theory*. London: Duckworth, 1997.

MacLachlan, Bonnie. *The Age of Grace: Charis in Early Greek Poetry*. Princeton: Princeton University Press, 1993.

Macpherson, C. B. *The Political Theory of Possessive Individualism*. Oxford: Clarendon, 1962.

Maddos, Donald, and Sara Sturm-Maddox, eds. *The Medieval French Alexander*. Binghamton: State University of New York Press, 2002.

Malinowski, Bronislaw. *Argonauts of the Western Pacific: An Account of Native Enterprise and Adventure in the Archipelagoes of Melanesian New Guinea*. 1922. Reprint, London: Routledge, 1978.

————. *Crime and Custom in Savage Society*. Patterson, N.J.: Littlefield, Adams, 1964.

————. "The Primitive Economics of the Trobriand Islanders." *Economic Journal* 31 (1921): 1–16.

Malouf, David. *The Ransom*. New York: Vintage, 2011.

Malysz, Piotr J. "Exchange and Ecstasy: Luther's Eucharistic Theology in the Light of Radical Orthodoxy's Critique of Gift and Sacrifice." *Scottish Journal of Theology* 60, no. 3 (2007): 294–308.

Manning, B. L. *The People's Faith in the Time of Wyclif*. Cambridge: Cambridge University Press, 1919.

Marion, Jean-Luc. *Being Given: Toward a Phenomenology of Givenness*. Stanford, Calif.: Stanford University Press, 2002.

————. *The Erotic Phenomenon*. Chicago: University of Chicago Press, 2006.

————. *God Without Being: Hors-Texte*. Chicago: University of Chicago Press, 1995.

————. *Idol and Distance: Five Studies*. New York: Fordham University Press, 2001.

————. *In Excess: Studies of Saturated Phenomena*. New York: Fordham University Press, 2001.

————. *On Descartes' Metaphysical Prism: The Constitution and Limits of Onto-theo-logy in Cartesian Thought*. Chicago: University of Chicago Press, 1999.

————. "Sketch of a Phenomenological Concept of Gift." In Westphal, *Postmodern Philosophy and Christian Thought*, 122–43.

Marshall, John. *John Locke: Resistance, Religion and Responsibility*. Cambridge: Cambridge University Press, 1994.

Marshall, Peter. *Enmity in Corinth: Social Conventions in Paul's Relations with the Corinthians.* Tübingen: Mohr, 1987.

Martinich, A. P. *The Two Gods of Leviathan: Thomas Hobbes on Religion and Politics.* Cambridge: Cambridge University Press, 2003.

Mason, Steven, ed. *Understanding Josephus: Seven Perspectives.* Sheffield: Sheffield Academic, 1998.

Mauss, Marcel. *The Gift: The Form and Reason for Exchange in Archaic Societies.* Translated by W. D. Halls. London: Routledge, 1990.

McConnell, Terrence. *Gratitude.* Philadelphia: Temple University Press, 1993.

McCraty, Rollin, and Doc Childre. "The Grateful Heart: The Psychophysiology of Appreciation." In Emmons and McCullough, *Psychology of Gratitude,* 230–55.

McCullough, Michael E., S. D. Kilpatrick, Robert Emmons, and D. B. Larson. "Is Gratitude a Moral Affect?" *Psychological Bulletin* 127, no. 2 (2001): 249–66.

McCullough, Michael E., and Jo-Ann Tsang. "Parent of the Virtues? The Prosocial Contours of Gratitude." In Emmons and McCullough, *Psychology of Gratitude,* 123–43.

McLaughlin, Megan. *Consorting with Saints: Prayer for the Dead in Early Medieval France.* Ithaca, N.Y.: Cornell University Press, 1994.

McNeill, Desmond. "Alternative Interpretations of Aristotle on Exchange and Reciprocity." *Public Affairs Quarterly* 4, no. 1 (1990): 55–68.

Michel, Jacques. *Gratuite en droit Romain.* Brussels: University Libre de Bruxelles, 1962.

Milbank, John. *Being Reconciled: Ontology and Pardon.* London: Routledge, 2003.

———. "Can a Gift Be Given?" *Modern Theology* 11, no. 1 (1995): 119–61.

Milgrom, Jacob. *Leviticus 1–16: A New Translation, Introduction and Commentary.* New York: Doubleday, 1991.

Millar, John. *Observations Concerning the Distinction of Ranks in Society (1771).* Edinburgh: W. Blackwood, 1806.

Miller, William Ian. "Gift, Sale, Payment, Raid: Case Studies in the Negotiation and Classification of Exchange in Medieval Iceland." *Speculum* 61, no. 1 (1986): 18–50.

Millett, Paul. "Patronage and Its Avoidance in Classical Athens." In Wallace-Hadrill, *Patronage in Ancient Society,* 15–47.

———. "The Rhetoric of Reciprocity in Classical Athens." In Gill, Postlethwaite, and Seaford, *Reciprocity in Ancient Greece,* 227–54.

Missiou, Anna. "Reciprocal Generosity in the Foreign Affairs of Fifth-Century Athens and Sparta." In Gill, Postlethwaite, and Seaford, *Reciprocity in Ancient Greece,* 181–98.

Mitchell, Lynette. *Greeks Bearing Gifts: The Public Use of Private Relationships in the Greek World, 435–323 BC.* Cambridge: Cambridge University Press, 1997.

Mitchell, Mark T. *The Politics of Gratitude: Scale, Place & Community in a Global Age.* Washington, D.C.: Potomac Books, 2012.

Montes, Leonidas, ed. *New Voices on Adam Smith.* London: Taylor & Francis, 2006.

Moore, Jerry D. *Visions of Culture: An Annotated Reader.* Lanham, Md.: Rowman Altamira, 2009.

Morris, Ian. "Gift and Commodity in Archaic Greece." *Man* 21, no. 1 (1986): 1–17.

―――. "The Use and Abuse of Homer." *Classical Antiquity* 5, no. 1 (1986): 81–138.

Morrow, Glenn. "The Significance of the Doctrine of Sympathy in Hume and Adam Smith." *Philosophical Review* 32, no. 1 (1923): 60–78.

Moussy, Claude. *Gratia et sa famille.* Paris: Presses Universitaires de France, 1966.

Mueller, Melissa. "The Language of Reciprocity in Euripides' Medea." *American Journal of Philology* 122, no. 4 (2001): 471–504.

Murray, Oswyn. *Early Greece.* 2nd ed. Cambridge, Mass.: Harvard University Press, 1993.

Murtonen, A. "The Use and Meanings of the Words Lebarek and Berakah in the Old Testament." *Vetus Testamentum* 9 (1959): 158–77.

Nagy, Gregory. *The Best of the Achaeans: Concepts of the Hero in Archaic Greece.* Baltimore, Md.: Johns Hopkins University Press, 1998.

Neiman, Susan. *Evil in Modern Thought: An Alternative History of Philosophy.* Princeton: Princeton University Press, 2002.

Nelson, Benjamin. *The Idea of Usury: From Tribal Brotherhood to Universal Otherhood.* 2nd ed. Chicago: University of Chicago Press, 1969.

Nelson, Janet L. "The Settings of the Gift in the Reign of Charlemagne." In Davies and Fouracre, *Languages of Gift in the Early Middle Ages,* 116–48.

Neumann, Harry. "The Philosophy of Individualism: An Interpretation of Thucydides." *Journal of the History of Philosophy* 7, no. 3 (1969): 237–46.

Neumeyer, Peter F. "Ingratitude Is Monstrous: An Approach to Coriolanus." *College English* 26, no. 3 (1964): 192–98.

Neyrey, Jerome. "God, Benefactor and Patron: The Major Cultural Model for Interpreting the Deity in Greco-Roman Antiquity." *Journal for the Study of the New Testament* 27, no. 4 (2005): 465–92.

———. "Lost in Translation: Did It Matter if Christians 'Thanked' God or 'Gave God Glory'?" *Catholic Biblical Quarterly* 71 (2009): 1–23.

———. *Shame and Honor in Matthew*. Louisville, Ky.: Westminster John Knox, 1998.

Nietzsche, Friedrich. *The AntiChrist*. Translated by H. L. Mencken. In *The Portable Nietzsche*, edited by Walter Kaufman. New York: Penguin, 1977.

———. *Basic Writings of Nietzsche*. Translated and edited by Walter Kaufmann. New York: Random House, 2000.

———. *Human, All Too Human*. Translated by Helen Zimmern and Paul V. Conn. In *The Complete Works of Friedrich Nietzsche*, edited by Oscar Levy, vols. 6–7. Edinburgh: T. N. Foulis, 1909.

———. *Nietzsche contra Wagner*. Translated by Thomas Common. London: H. Henry, 1896.

———. *The Portable Nietzsche*. Translated and edited by Walter Kaufmann. New York: Penguin, 1977.

Nord, Walter. "Adam Smith and Contemporary Social Exchange Theory." *American Journal and Economics and Sociology* 32, no. 4 (1973): 421–36.

Norville, Deborah. *Thank You Power: Making the Science of Gratitude Work for You*. Nashville: Thomas Nelson, 2008.

Nussbaum, Martha. *The Therapy of Desire: Theory and Practice in Hellenistic Ethics*. Princeton: Princeton University Press, 2009.

Oakley, Francis. *The Medieval Experience: Foundations of Western Cultural Singularity*. Toronto: University of Toronto Press, 1988.

Oberman, Heiko. *The Harvest of Medieval Theology*. Grand Rapids: Baker, 2000.

Odonis, Geraldus. *Sententia et expositio cum quaestionibus super libros Ethicorum*. Venice, 1500.

O'Donovan, Oliver, and Joan Lockwood O'Donovan, eds. *From Irenaeus to Grotius: A Sourcebook in Christian Political Thought*. Grand Rapids: Eerdmans, 1999.

Ortega y Gasset, Jose. *Revolt of the Masses*. 1930. Reprint, New York: Norton, 1994.

Padilla, Mark. "Gifts of Humiliation: Charis and Tragic Experience in Alcestis." *American Journal of Philology* 121, no. 2 (2000): 179–211.

Pao, David W. *Thanksgiving: An Investigation of a Pauline Theme*. Downer's Grove, Ill.: InterVarsity, 2002.

Parker, Robert. "Pleasing Thighs: Reciprocity in Greek Religion." In Gill, Postlethwaite, and Seaford, *Reciprocity in Ancient Greece*, 105–26.

Parry, Jonathan. "The Gift, the Indian Gift, and the 'Indian Gift.'" *Man* 21, no. 3 (1986): 453–73.

Perkins, William. *A Golden Chain*. 1590. Reprint, Cambridge: Cambridge University Press, 1612.

Peterman, G. W. *Paul's Gift from Philippi: Conventions of Gift Exchange and Christian Giving*. Society for New Testament Studies Monograph Series 92. Cambridge: Cambridge University Press, 1997.

———. "'Thankless Thanks': The Epistolary Social Convention in Philippians 4:10-20." *Tyndale Bulletin* 42, no. 2 (1991): 261–70.

Phillips, James Emerson. *The State in Shakespeare's Greek and Roman Plays*. New York: Columbia University Press, 1940.

Philo. *Works*. Translated by Charles Duke Yonge. Peabody, Mass.: Hendrickson, 1993.

Pindar. *Odes*. Translated and edited by John Edwin Sandys. New York: Macmillan, 1915.

Plato. *Crito*. Translated by Harold North Fowler. Cambridge, Mass.: Harvard University Press, 1966.

———. *Euthyphro*. Translated by Harold North Fowler. Cambridge, Mass.: Harvard University Press, 1966.

———. *Laws*. Translated by J. B. Bury. Cambridge, Mass.: Harvard University Press, 1966.

Plutarch. *Lives*. Translated by Thomas North. Harmondsworth: Penguin, 1964.

———. *Moralia*. Translated by W. C. Helmbold. Cambridge, Mass.: Harvard University Press, 1939.

Podlecki, A. J. "Guest-Gifts and Nobodies in 'Odyssey 9.'" *Phoenix* 15, no. 3 (1961): 125–33.

Polanyi, Karl. *The Great Transformation: The Political and Economic Origins of Our Time*. 1957. Reprint, Boston: Beacon, 2001.

Polt, Richard. *Heidegger: An Introduction*. Ithaca, N.Y.: Cornell University Press, 1999.

Postlethwaite, Norman. "Akhilleus and Agamemnon: Generalized Reciprocity." In Gill, Postlethwaite, and Seaford, *Reciprocity in Ancient Greece*, 93–104.

Pufendorf, Samuel von. *On the Duty of Man and Citizen According to the Natural Law*. Translated by Michael Silverthorne. Edited by James Tully. Cambridge Texts in the History of Political Thought. Cambridge: Cambridge University Press, 1991.

Rabelais, François. *Gargantua and Pantagruel*. Translated J. M. Cohen. London: Penguin, 1963.

Rayment, Charles S. "Late Imperial Extensions of the Suit for Ingratitude." *Classical Journal* 47, no. 1 (1951): 113–14.

————. "The Suit for Ingratitude." *Classical Journal* 43, no. 7 (1948): 429–31.

Raynolds, Robert. *In Praise of Gratitude*. New York: Harper, 1961.

Reed, Jeffrey T. "Are Paul's Thanksgivings 'Epistolary'?" *Journal for the Study of the New Testament* 18, no. 61 (1996): 87–99.

Reik, Theodore. "Final Phases of Belief Found in Religion and in Obsessional Neurosis." *International Journal of Psychoanalysis* 11 (1930): 258–91.

Reuter, Timothy. "Gifts and Simony." In Algazi, Groebner, and Jussen, *Negotiating the Gift*, 157–68.

Reynolds, Susan. *Fiefs and Vassals: The Medieval Evidence Reinterpreted*. Oxford: Oxford University Press, 1996.

Rhee, Helen. *Loving the Poor, Saving the Rich: Wealth, Poverty, and Early Christian Formation*. Grand Rapids: Baker, 2012.

Richardson, William. *Heidegger: Through Phenomenology to Thought*. The Hague: Martinus Nijhoff, 1963.

Ricoeur, Paul. *Freud and Philosophy: An Essay on Interpretation*. New Haven, Conn.: Yale University Press, 1970.

Roberts, Robert C. "The Blessings of Gratitude: A Conceptual Analysis." In Emmons and McCullough, *Psychology of Gratitude*, 58–79.

Ronan, Clifford. *"Antike Roman": Power Symbology and the Roman Play in Early Modern England, 1585–1635*. Athens: University of Georgia Press, 1995.

Ropke, Wilhelm. *The Social Crisis of Our Time*. 1942. Reprint, Chicago: University of Chicago Press, 1950.

Rosenthal, Joel T. *The Purchase of Paradise: The Social Function of Aristocratic Benevolence, 1308–1485*. London: Routledge & Kegan Paul, 1972.

Rosenwein, Barbara H. *To Be the Neighbor of Saint Peter: The Social Meaning of Cluny's Property, 909–1049*. Ithaca, N.Y.: Cornell University Press, 1989.

Ross, Ian Simpson. *The Life of Adam Smith*. Oxford: Oxford University Press, 2010.

Rousseau, Jean-Jacques. *A Discourse upon the Origin and the Foundation of the Inequality among Mankind*. Translated by Charles Eliot. Whitefish, Mont.: Kessington, 2004.

————. *Emile, or On Education*. Translated by Allan Bloom. New York: Basic Books, 1979.

————. *Social Contract*. Harmondsworth: Penguin, 1968.

Rupke, Jorg. *Religion of the Romans*. Translated by Richard Gordon. Cambridge: Polity, 2007.

Saarinen, Risto. *God and the Gift: An Ecumenical Theology of Giving*. Collegeville, Minn.: Liturgical Press, 2005.

Sahlins, Marshall. *Stone Age Economics*. Chicago: Aldine Transaction, 1974.

Salisbury, Joyce. *Blood of the Martyrs: Unintended Consequences of Ancient Violence*. New York: Psychology Press, 2004.

Saller, Richard P. *Personal Patronage under the Early Empire*. Cambridge: Cambridge University Press, 1982.

———. "Status and Patronage." In *The Cambridge Ancient History, Volume XI: The High Empire, A.D. 70–192*, 2nd ed., edited by Alan K. Bowman, Peter Garnsey, and Dominic Rathbone, 817–54. Cambridge: Cambridge University Press, 2008.

Salvian. *The Writings of Salvian, the Presbyter*. Translated by Jeremiah F. O'Sullivan. Washington, D.C.: Catholic University of America Press, 2008.

Scheler, Max. *Ressentiment*. Milwaukee: Marquette University Press, 2003.

Schindler, David L. *Ordered Love: Liberal Societies and the Memory of God*. Grand Rapids: Eerdmans, 2011.

Schmitz, Kenneth L. *The Gift: Creation*. The Aquinas Lecture 1982. Milwaukee: Marquette University Press, 1982.

Schochet, Gordon J. "Thomas Hobbes on the Family and the State of Nature." *Political Science Quarterly* 82, no. 3 (1967): 427–45.

Schoeck, Helmut. *Envy: A Theory of Social Behavior*. Indianapolis: Liberty Press, 1987.

Schrift, Alan D., ed. *The Logic of the Gift: Toward an Ethic of Generosity*. New York: Routledge, 1997.

Schubert, P. *The Form and Function of the Pauline Thanksgiving*. Berlin: Alfred Topelmann, 1939.

Schumacher, E. F. *Small Is Beautiful*. San Francisco: HarperCollins, 2010.

Schwartz, Seth. *Were the Jews a Mediterranean Society? Reciprocity and Solidarity in Ancient Judaism*. Princeton: Princeton University Press, 2012.

Seaford, Richard. *Reciprocity and Ritual: Homer and Tragedy in the Developing City-State*. Oxford: Clarendon, 1994.

Seneca. *On Benefits*. Translated by Miriam Griffin and Brad Inwood. Chicago: University of Chicago Press, 2011.

Seymour, Melissa M. "Duties of Love and Kant's Doctrine of Obligatory Ends." Ph.D. diss., Indiana University, 2007.

Shabad, Peter. "Of Woman Born: Womb Envy and the Male Project of Self-Creation." In Wurmser and Jarass, *Jealousy and Envy*, 75–90.

Shakespeare, William. *The Tragedy of Coriolanus*. Edited by R. B. Parker. Oxford: Oxford University Press, 1998.

Shapin, Steven. *Never Pure.* Baltimore, Md.: Johns Hopkins University Press, 2010.

———. *The Scientific Revolution.* Chicago: University of Chicago Press, 1996.

Shapin, Steven, and Simon Schaffer. *Leviathan and the Air-Pump: Hobbes, Boyle, and the Experimental Life.* Princeton: Princeton University Press, 2011.

Shelton, Charles. "Gratitude: Considerations from a Moral Perspective." In Emmons and McCullough, *Psychology of Gratitude*, 257–81.

Shrank, Cathy. "Civility and the City in Coriolanus." *Shakespeare Quarterly* 54, no. 4 (2003): 406–23.

Silver, Allan. "Friendship and Trust as Moral Ideals: An Historical Approach." *European Journal of Sociology* 30, no. 2 (1989): 274–97.

Simmel, George. *The Sociology of George Simmel.* Edited by Kurt H. Wolff. New York: Simon & Schuster, 1950.

Simmons, A. John. *Moral Principles and Political Obligations.* Princeton: Princeton University Press, 1979.

Slatkin, Laura M. *The Power of Thetis and Selected Essays.* Washington, D.C.: Center for Hellenic Studies, 2011.

Smit, Houston, and Mark Timmons. "The Moral Significance of Gratitude in Kant's Ethics." *Southern Journal of Philosophy* 49, no. 4 (2011): 295–320.

Smith, Adam. *Theory of Moral Sentiments.* Edited by Knud Haakonssen. Cambridge: Cambridge University Press, 2002.

Smith, James K. A. *Jacques Derrida: Live Theory.* London: Continuum, 2005.

Smith, Vernon L. "The Two Faces of Adam Smith." *Southern Economic Journal* 65, no. 1 (1998): 1–19.

Soares-Prabhu, George M. "Speaking to 'Abba': Prayer as Petition and Thanksgiving in the Teaching of Jesus." In Duquoc and Florestan, *Asking and Thanking*, 31–43.

Solomon, Robert. *Continental Philosophy Since 1750: The Rise and Fall of the Self.* Oxford: Oxford University Press, 1988.

Sophocles. *Ajax.* Edited and translated by A. C. Pearson and Richard Jebb. Cambridge: Cambridge University Press, 1907.

Southern, R. W. *Scholastic Humanism and the Unification of Europe: Foundations.* London: Wiley-Blackwell, 1997.

———. *Western Society and the Church in the Middle Ages.* New York: Penguin, 1970.

Spilsbury, Paul. "God and Israel in Josephus: A Patron-Client Relationship." In Mason, *Understanding Josephus*, 172–91.

Starobinski, Jean. "Don Fastueux et Don Pervers: Commentaire Historique d'une Reverie de Rousseau." *Annales* 41, no. 1 (1986): 7–26.

Stein, Michael. "Gratitude and Attitude: A Note on Emotional Welfare." *Social Psychology Quarterly* 52, no. 3 (1989): 242–48.

Steindl-Rast, David. "Gratitude as Thankfulness and as Gratefulness." In Emmons and McCullough, *Psychology of Gratitude*, 282–89.

Steiner, George. *Martin Heidegger*. Chicago: University of Chicago Press, 1978.

Stewart, Maaja. "Ingratitude in 'Tom Jones.'" *Journal of English and Germanic Philology* 89, no. 4 (1990): 512–32.

Stewart-Sykes, A. "Ordination Rites and Patronage Systems in Third-Century Africa." *Vigiliae Christianae* 56, no. 2 (2002): 115–30.

Strauss, Leo. *The Political Philosophy of Hobbes: Its Basis and Its Genesis*. Translated by Elsa M. Sinclair. Chicago: University of Chicago Press, 1952.

Straw, C. E. "Cyprian and Matthew 5:45: The Evolution of Christian Patronage." *Studia Patristica* 18, no. 3 (1989): 329–39.

Suetonius. *The Twelve Caesars*. London: Penguin, 2007.

Sykes, Karen. *Arguing with Anthropology: An Introduction to Critical Theories of the Gift*. London: Routledge, 2005.

Tacitus. *Complete Works of Tacitus*. Translated by Alfred John Church and William Jackson Brodribb. New York: Modern Library, 1942.

Tarcov, Nathan. *Locke's Education for Liberty*. Lanham, Md.: Lexington Books, 1999.

Teresa of Avila. *The Life of the Holy Mother Teresa of Jesus*. Available at www.ccel.org (accessed February 26, 2013).

Terpstra, Marin. "Social Gifts and the Gift of Sociality: Some Thoughts on Mauss' *The Gift* and Hobbes' *Leviathan*." In Vandevelde, *Gifts and Interests*, 191–208.

Tevenar, Gudrun von. "Gratitude, Reciprocity, and Need." *American Philosophical Quarterly* 43, no. 1 (2006): 181–88.

Thieme, Adelheid L. J. "Gift Giving as a Vital Element of Salvation in *The Dream of the Rood*." *South Atlantic Review* 63, no. 2 (1998): 108–23.

Thomas, Keith. "The Social Origins of Hobbes's Political Thought." In Brown, *Hobbes Studies*, 185–236.

Thornton, Helen. *State of Nature or Eden? Thomas Hobbes and His Contemporaries on the Natural Condition of Human Beings*. Rochester, N.Y.: Boydell & Brewer, 2005.

Thucydides. *History of the Peloponnesian War.* Translated and edited by Rex Warner and M. I. Finley. Harmondsworth: Penguin, 1972.

Tierney, Brian. *The Idea of Natural Rights: Studies of Natural Rights, Natural Law, and Church Law 1150–1625.* Grand Rapids: Eerdmans, 1997.

Tilley, Charles. *Coercion, Capital and European States: AD 990–1992.* London: Wiley-Blackwell, 1992.

———, ed. *The Formation of National States in Western Europe.* Princeton: Princeton University Press, 1975.

Tonnies, Ferdinand. *Community and Society.* Translated by Charles P. Loomis. Mineola, N.Y.: Dover, 2011.

———. *Hobbes Der Mann und der Denken.* Stuttgart: Frommanns Verlag, 1912.

Trincado, Estrella. "Adam's Smith's Criticism of the Doctrine of Utility: A Theory of the Creative Present." In Montes, *New Voices on Adam Smith,* 313–27.

Tsouna, Voula. *The Ethics of Philodemus* Oxford: Oxford University Press, 2008.

Turnbull, Stephan K. "Grace and Gift in Luther and Paul." *Word and World* 24, no. 3 (2004): 305–14.

Tyndale, William. *Doctrinal Treatises and Introductions to Different Portions of the Holy Scriptures.* 1525. Reprint, Cambridge: Cambridge University Press, 1848.

———. *Parable of the Wicked Mammon.* London, 1528.

Vacek, Edward C. "Gifts, God, Generosity, Gratitude." In Keating, *Spiritual and Moral Theology,* 81–125.

Vandevelde, Antoon, ed. *Gifts and Interests.* Leuven: Peeters, 2000.

Veyne, Paul. *Bread and Circuses.* Translated by Oswyn Murray. London: Penguin, 1990.

Vickers, Brian. *Shakespeare: Coriolanus.* London: Edward Arnold, 1976.

Visser, Margaret. *The Gift of Thanks: The Roots and Rituals of Gratitude.* New York: Houghton Mifflin, 2009.

Volf, Miroslav. *Free of Charge: Giving and Forgiving in a Culture Stripped of Grace.* Grand Rapids: Zondervan, 2005.

Wagner, J. Ross, C. Kavin Rowe, and A. Katherine Grieb, eds. *The Word Leaps the Gap: Essays on Scripture and Theology in Honor of Richard B. Hays.* Grand Rapids: Eerdmans, 2008.

Wagner-Hasel, Bewate. "Egoistic Exchange and Altruistic Gift: On the Roots of Marcel Mauss's Theory of the Gift." In Algazi, Groebner, and Jussen, *Negotiating the Gift,* 141–72.

Waldstein, Michael. Introduction to *Man and Woman He Created Them: A Theology of the Body*, by John Paul II. Boston: Pauline, 2006.

Walker, A. D. M. "Gratefulness and Gratitude." *Proceedings of the Aristotelian Society* n.s. 81 (1980–81): 39–55.

———. "Obligations of Gratitude and Political Obligation." *Philosophy and Public Affairs* 18, no. 4 (1989): 359–64.

———. "Political Obligation and the Argument from Gratitude." *Philosophy and Public Affairs* 17, no. 3 (1988): 191–211.

Wallace, John M. "John Dryden's Plays and the Conception of a Heroic Society." In Zagorin, *Culture and Politics from Puritanism to the Enlightenment*, 113–34.

———. "The Senecan Context of *Coriolanus*." *Modern Philology* 90, no. 4 (1993): 465–78.

Wallace, Ronald. *Calvin, Geneva, and the Reformation*. Eugene, Ore.: Wipf & Stock, 1998.

Wallace-Hadrill, Andrew, ed. *Patronage in Ancient Society*. London: Routledge, 1989.

Walsh, Patrick. *Cicero's De Officiis*. Oxford: Oxford University Press, 2000.

Warrender, Howard. *The Political Philosophy of Hobbes: His Theory of Obligation*. Oxford: Clarendon, 1957.

Watkins, Philip. "Gratitude and Subjective Well-Being." In Emmons and McCullough, *Psychology of Gratitude*, 167–92.

Watt, W. S. "Notes on Seneca, *De Beneficiis, De Clementia*, and *Dialogi*." *Harvard Studies in Classical Philology* 96 (1994): 225–39.

Weiner, Annette B. *Inalienable Possessions: The Paradox of Keeping-While-Giving*. Berkeley: University of California Press, 1992.

Weinsheimer, Joel. *Gadamer's Hermeneutics: A Reading of Truth and Method*. New Haven, Conn.: Yale University Press, 1988.

Wellman, Christopher Heath. "Gratitude as a Virtue." *Pacific Philosophical Quarterly* 80 (1999): 284–300.

Westphal, Merold, ed. *Postmodern Philosophy and Christian Thought*. Bloomington: Indiana University Press, 1999.

White, Patricia. "Gratitude, Citizenship and Education." *Studies in Philosophy and Education* 18 (1999): 43–52.

White, Stephen D. *Custom, Kinship, and Gifts to the Saints: The Laudatio Parentum in Western France, 1050–1150*. Chapel Hill: University of North Carolina Press, 1988.

———. "Giving Fiefs and Honor: Largesse, Avarice, and the Problem of 'Feudalism' in Alexander's Testament." In Maddos and Sturm-Maddox, *Medieval French Alexander*, 127–41.

————. "The Politics of Exchange: Gifts, Fiefs, and Feudalism." In Cohen and de Jong, *Medieval Transformations*, 169–88.

————. "Review of: Susan Reynolds, *Fiefs and Vassals: The Medieval Evidence Reinterpreted* (Oxford, 1944)." *Law and History Review* 15, no. 2 (1997): 349–55.

————. "Service for Fiefs or Fiefs for Service: The Politics of Reciprocity." In Algazi, Groebner, and Jussen, *Negotiating the Gift*, 63–98.

Whitlark, Jason. "Enabling χαρις: Transformation of the Convention of Reciprocity by Philo and in Ephesians." *Perspectives in Religious Studies* 30 (2003): 325–57.

Wickham, Chris. "Compulsory Gift Exchange in Lombard Italy, 650–1150." In Davies and Fouracre, *Languages of Gift in the Early Middle Ages*, 193–216.

Widzisz, Marcel. "Timing Reciprocity in the *Iliad*." *Arethusa* 45 (2012): 153–75.

Wilken, Robert Louis. *The Christians as the Romans Saw Them*. New Haven, Conn.: Yale University Press, 2003.

Winter, Bruce W. "The Public Honouring of Christian Benefactors, Romans 13.3-4 and 1 Peter 2.14-15." *Journal for the Study of the New Testament* 34 (1988): 87–103.

Wokler, Robert. "Perfectible Apes in Decadent Cultures: Rousseau's Anthropology Revisited." *Daedalus* 107, no. 3 (1978): 107–34.

Wolin, Sheldon. *Politics and Vision*. Expanded ed. Princeton: Princeton University Press, 2004.

Wrightson, Keith. *English Society: 1580–1680*. New Brunswick, N.J.: Rutgers University Press, 2003.

Write, Thomas, ed. *The Chronicle of Pierre de Langtoft*. 2 vols. London: Longmans, 1898.

Wurmser, Leon, and Heidrun Jarass, eds. *Jealousy and Envy: New Views about Two Powerful Feelings*. London: Taylor & Francis, 2007.

Xenophon. *Cyropaedeia*. Translated by Walter Miller. Cambridge, Mass.: Harvard University Press, 1914.

————. *Memorabilia*. Translated by E. C. Marchant. Cambridge, Mass.: Harvard University Press, 1923.

————. *Oeconomicus*. Translated by H. G. Dakyns. New York: Macmillan, 1897.

Yan, Yunxiang. *The Flow of Gifts: Reciprocity and Social Networks in a Chinese Village*. Stanford, Calif.: Stanford University Press, 1996.

Zagorin, Perez, ed. *Culture and Politics from Puritanism to the Enlightenment*. Berkeley: University of California Press, 1980.

Zanker, Graham. "Beyond Reciprocity: The Akhilleus-Priam Scene in *Iliad* 24." In Christopher John Gill, et. al., eds. *Reciprocity in Ancient Greece.* Oxford: Oxford University Press, 1998.

Scripture Index

Index of Authors

Ambrose, 81–82

Anslem of Canterbury, 8, 94

Antiphon, 35

Aristotle, 6, 25, 35–38, 57–58, 62, 87,
96, 104, 117–18, 123, 143, 147, 152,
187, 199, 217; Seneca against, 48,
52, 53

Aronson, Ronald, 222–23

Augustine, 83–84, 99, 103, 148,
253n11, 276n100

Austen, Jane, 11, 143

Bellarmine, Robert, 121–22

Ben Sirach, 65–66

Berry, Wendell, 219

Biel, Gabriel, 101

Bloom, Harold, 220

Boas, Franz, 164

Bourdieu, Pierre, 172–73

Bucher, Karl, 165, 173–74

Buckley Jr., William, 2

Burke, Edmund, 11, 144–45

Calvin, John, 8, 103–5, 218, 261n19

Capellanus, Andreas, 88

Cartwright, Thomas, 104

Catherine of Siena, 95–96

Chaucer, 88

Cheal, David, 171–72

Cicero, 5, 12, 44–47, 61–62, 70,
79–80, 88–89, 94, 129–30, 138,
145, 152, 182, 217; afterlife of his *De
officiis,* 129–30, 241n15

Coverdale, Miles, 104

Dante, 89, 257n57

David (king), 63

Demosthenes, 33

Denys (Pseudo-Dionysius), 213

Derrida, Jacques, 1, 13, 196–204, 207–
10, 213–14, 218, 226, 227, 259n83

Descartes, René, 11–13, 145–48, 155,
160, 185, 205, 214, 226

Dio Chrysostom, 22, 44

Diodorus of Sicily, 22

Dionysius of Halicarnassus, 42

Douglas, Mary, 169, 296n85

Durkheim, Émile, 167, 173

Eckhardt, Meister, 8, 95, 187

Eisenstein, Charles, 222–23

Elyot, Thomas, 113–14

Emmons, Robert, 2, 220

Epictetus, 25

Euripides, 23

Firth, Raymond, 171

Gadamer, Hans-Georg, 189

Gaul, Wilhelm, 174

Geoffrey of Monmouth, 86

Gower, John, 88, 89–90

Hamann, J. G., 187

Heidegger, Martin, 1, 13, 185–93,
199–200, 203, 210–11, 218

Herodotus, 31

Hesiod, 26, 129

Hobbes, Thomas, 10, 122–29, 150,
153, 154, 174–76, 195, 218

Homer, 20–21, 22–23, 26–30, 234n49,
239n118

Hooker, Richard, 122

Horace, 154

Hume, David, 274n70

Husserl, Edmund, 205–6

Isaios, 35

Isodorus, 23

Visser, Margaret, 2

Weiner, Annette, 171
Willan, Edward, 105
William of Malmesbury, 87

Xenophon, 23, 24, 31, 41, 58, 112,
239n105

Yan, Yunxiang, 176

Subject Index

Abraham (Abram), 60, 62, 66–67,
203–4
Achilles, 20–21, 26–30
Agamemnon, 22, 27–30
alms, 7–8, 14, 68–69, 82–85, 90, 101,
104, 121, 204, 252n9, 296n85;
almsgiving and, 9, 83, 85, 91, 216
altruism, 12, 59, 68–69, 80, 105, 215,
227
aqedah, 67
Arthur, 86–87
Athens, 6–7, 14, 31–35, 37–39, 41, 48;
influence on political imagination,
33–34; 106, 109
Augustus, 54

Baudelaire, 201–2
benefaction, 41–42, 46, 58, 61, 66–67,
80–81, 131, 134, 139, 149; *beneficia*,
41; Cicero on *beneficia*, 44–47
beneficence, 45, 49, 80, 129, 140,
157–59
Beowulf, 86, 107, 218
blessing, 60–61, 63, 70, 103, 130

capitalism, 135, 144, 170, 172, 179,
195, 219; *see also* economy
charis, 19, 21, 24–28, 57, 61, 73–75,
104, 233n27, 234n49, 236n63,
250n106, 251n119

charity, 8, 57, 59, 61, 66–67, 84–85,
103, 105, 125, 133, 139; *see also*
generosity
Charlemagne, 85, 87
Christianity, 5, 6–8, 10–12, 14, 25,
57–59, 76, 81, 120, 144, 184, 214,
223, 225–29
Cimon of Athens, 32
clients: *see* patronage
Clovis, 86
consent, 10, 92, 120–22, 124, 126–28,
134, 149, 153
contemplation: *see theoria*
contract, 92, 96, 112, 118, 120–22,
125, 127–28, 132–34, 145, 149–50,
153–54, 177, 214, 284n58, 290n5,
296n84, 296n85; *see also* covenant
courtly love, 87–88
covenant, 64, 66, 101, 127–28, 216,
296n85
Crito, 6, 34, 39, 58
Cyprian, 82, 254n18

Darwin, Charles, 144
debt, 7, 14, 29, 32, 34, 39, 47, 52, 54,
61, 71, 81, 105–6, 121, 160, 197,
200, 204, 226, 228–29, 296n84; of
gratitude or obligation, 7, 10–12, 14,
21, 26–27, 30–32, 36, 42–43, 46,
48, 50–51, 57, 68, 70–71, 73–74,